JM.16

# England versus West Indies

## A History of the Tests and Other Matches

**GERRY COTTER**

## The Crowood Press

First published in 1991 by
The Crowood Press Ltd
Gipsy Lane, Swindon
Wiltshire SN2 6DQ

**British Library Cataloguing in Publication Data**

Cotter, Gerry
England versus West Indies : a history of the tests
and other matches.
1. England. Cricket. West Indian teams. Test matches with
England teams
I. Title
796.35865

ISBN   1 85223 445 8

For Laurence and Heather

**Acknowledgements**
My thanks to Don Mosey, and to John Tuck of the John
Rylands University Library of Manchester, for their help.
I am particularly grateful to Ken Kelly for providing the
photographs and, as ever, for his kindness and generosity.

Typeset by Inforum Typesetting, Portsmouth
**Printed in Great Britain by**
**Butler & Tanner Ltd, Frome**

# Contents

# Foreword

I am delighted to have been asked to contribute a foreword to this fascinating book by Gerry Cotter. A captivating study tracing the start of cricket in the West Indies and the earliest matches against English teams, and going on to give a full evaluation of the official Test Series, it is an authoritative work that will be bought by all keen followers of Test cricket. The strengths and weaknesses of the teams are assessed, the captains and leading players are portrayed, the matches are described and the whole is crafted into a gripping narrative. Ken Kelly has researched many rare and valuable photographs of the early great players, and includes a superb selection of his own action shots taken over the past fifty years capturing the power of Walcott and Weekes, the menace of the fast bowlers, the majesty of Richards. I am most pleased that the publication of this book will allow me to enjoy them again and again, and to re-live some glorious summer memories.

The popular image of the West Indies centres on endless sunshine, golden beaches, sparkling blue seas, an easy-going lifestyle – all the sort of things beloved by travel agents and their brochure writers. These bounties have always been reflected in the way cricket has been played here, especially in the way our batsmen put bowlers to the sword. How many West Indian batsmen can you think of to whom the word 'dour' might reasonably be applied? Are there any at all? All the greats from George Challenor onward have been glorious stroke-makers, every one of them blessed with the sunshine gift of revelling in their enjoyment and spontaneously communicating that enjoyment to the spectators. Such spontaneity is something that few of their English counterparts have shared; Compton, Milburn and Botham had it, but for most of the others Test cricket has been a serious business. This enviable national characteristic has stood us in good stead many times, both to get quick runs when needed and to captivate public and press, with all the attendant psychological benefits which that brings.

The way in which these islands, with their small populations, have brought forth an endless stream of world-class players is the envy of every other country, yet the explanation is simple enough. The game is deep in our blood, regarded with a fervour that England has never shown for any sport except perhaps during the 1966 World Cup; and, until recently, there have been few other sports to take the attention of our athletic youngsters. It is not sacrilegious to say that in the Caribbean the game has the status of a religion, and in view of this devotion it is hardly surprising that we have so often had the beating of England.

In reading this book I have been reminded of Ramadhin and Valentine enchanting the crowds in 1950; of the unique phenomenon of the three Ws, world-class batsmen born almost in the same place and the same time, with Frank Worrell going on to become our first regular black captain and one of the best Test leaders of all; of Kanhai the cavalier; of the thunderbolts of Wes Hall and Charlie Griffith; of Lance Gibbs and those incredibly long spinning fingers; of Clive Lloyd and a captaincy record almost beyond belief; of the mighty stroke-making of Viv Richards and Gordon Greenidge; and of the relentless army of fast bowlers from Andy Roberts onwards. West Indies' cricketing hall of fame is, quite simply, awesome in its majesty.

English fans will be acutely aware that their team's record since the Second World War is a poor one, with only four series victories and two draws in eighteen rubbers. Yet both sides have produced some memorable cricket along the way, all of which is chronicled here. In 1953–4, despite many problems, Sir Len Hutton led a noble fightback to square the series; the 1963 series was one of the best ever seen in England, with Fred Trueman's untiring efforts deserving of the highest praise; I remember well England's brave fight-back with the last three wickets in the fifth Test in 1966; John Snow's bowling in 1967–8 was a joy to watch, unlike the excruciating last over in the series when Jeff Jones had to hang on to ensure that England won. Since then it has largely been a story of English batsmen trying to stand up to West Indian bowling, with heroics from the likes of Amiss, Fletcher, Greig, Gower, Gooch, Lamb and so on, while West Indian batsmen have filled their boots at the expense of the Englishmen.

For England, Australia has traditionally been the team that you most want to beat. But ever since our marvellous tour of 1950 West Indies seem to have been a very close second and the desire for revenge has increased with the recent succession of hammerings, perhaps to put us up alongside the Aussies in the English consciousness. It would seem to me that West Indies have effectively been undisputed World Champions for a decade and a half now, and that is a remarkable length of time to stay at the top in any sport. Revenge may seem too base a motive for many; but who doesn't want to beat the World Champions? If some people feel that our emphasis on fast bowling has turned batting more into a business of courage than skill and perhaps also deprived the game of an essential element of variety by hastening the decline of the spinner, we have done no more than capitalize on our resources in the most emphatic and professional way. It is easy to criticize West Indies for our relentless fast bowling, but one should remember that envy is one of the seven deadly sins; for let no one doubt that any other country which found itself similarly supplied with top quality fast men would do the same thing. If revenge is distasteful then hypocrisy is more so.

Gerry Cotter clearly appreciates cricket for its own sake and his pleasure is apparent in the pages of this book. Read on and enjoy this celebration of the matches played between England and West Indies, and let us look forward to the coming series.

Sir Garfield Sobers
1990

# 1

# Learning to Play the Game

It is a curious thought that the drubbings which West Indian cricketers inflicted upon English cricketers during the 1970s and '80s had their origins in sugar. If the soil of the West Indian islands had been infertile and supported little agriculture there would have been few Europeans anxious to settle there since the economic rewards for doing so would have been slight. The colonists would have found small opportunity to make their fortune, so they would not have had much money for building schools for their children and bringing teachers from Britain to staff them. Without the influence of the schools in the nineteenth century, the game in the West Indies might be considerably less advanced than it now is; and as the schools were only built out of the profits of the plantations, the importance of sugar (other crops were grown too, but sugar was by some way the major one) is clear. Admittedly, cricket had arrived in the islands before the teachers did, taken there by the settlers and the soldiers, but it was mostly the teachers who developed it and inculcated the traditional values of sportsmanship, fair play and so on into their pupils.

At first the native people would have been pressed into service more or less as auxiliaries; in the hot climate they were assigned to the tiring occupations of bowling and fielding, while the white men showed them the joys of batting. As the game made its appeal to them they would have begun to learn about batting, too, so that after slavery was abolished in the 1830s the locals were able to organize their own matches and in due course form their own clubs. With the passing of the years their standards slowly improved, and before the end of the century it was clear that black men could play cricket just as well as white. The social structure meant that their opportunities for advancement were limited, of course, but there were several white clubs prepared to allow black players to join them – the gifted ones, that is.

These developments took place throughout the British-governed islands, with the largest ones – Trinidad, Barbados and Jamaica and British Guiana on the South American mainland – naturally proving the main centres. In February 1865 the first intercolonial match was played, when a team from British Guiana visited Barbados and began their cricketing history with what would prove to be their lowest score ever, 22. Since they made only 33 in their second innings, Barbados had little trouble in winning by 143 runs; but in September of the same year Barbados travelled to Guiana for a return match and this time Guiana had their revenge, just winning by two wickets. A second game had been planned but was abandoned after a boating accident on the Essequibo River in which seven people died, including two of the Guiana players. Four years later, Trinidad played their first matches against a visiting British Guiana team, and then in 1871 Guiana and Barbados played what was regarded as a decider. Barbados won convincingly by eight wickets, plunging the opposition into such gloom by doing so that it was twelve years before they played Barbados again. Many England fans at the end of the 1980s must have thought this the best solution to the West Indian problem.

During the middle years of the century the game grew steadily at school and club level throughout the colonies. Since the wickets were generally poor the ball largely dominated the bat, but the first century was scored before 1860, by one Canon E.M. Sealy at Codrington College, Barbados. The first first-class century came in 1882 when E.F. Wright made 123 for British Guiana at home to Trinidad. By the 1880s enough progress had been made for the colonies to send a joint side to tour the USA and Canada, a sure sign of self-confidence. They were captained by L.R. Fyffe of Jamaica, described by Christopher Nicole as 'a veteran whose principal value to the side was his remarkable luck with the toss', and the tour proved successful, with six of the thirteen matches (none of them first-class) won and five lost. When a year later the Americans returned the visit, they were decisively seen off.

Up to this point the main participants had been Barbados and British Guiana, with Trinidad taking part when they were able. There was no lack of interest in Jamaica, but being a thousand miles or more from the others hampered their development enormously and it would be decades before they joined in regular competition. The other three, only a day or so apart by boat, had a great advantage, and the enthusiasm was such that a triangular tournament was instituted in 1892–3; for the first fifteen years it took place more or less every other year, then became an annual event. At this point in the story we are still in the nineteenth century, however, and Barbados and British Guiana refused to allow black players to participate; since Trinidad's best bowlers were coloured, as the other two must have known, this was just a trifle unfair. It would be a long time before professionals were allowed to compete in the intercolonial tournament.

Against this background of ever-improving standards and ever-growing popularity, but in general not a great deal of method either about play or organization, the first team from England arrived early in 1895. The tour came about mainly through the hard work of Dr R.B. Anderson, an Englishman who lived for twenty-three years in Tobago and played a leading role in developing West Indian cricket. He drummed up interest in England and got some influential people such as Lord Hawke involved; Hawke had already visited Jamaica when returning from a tour to America and decided he would like to lead the team, but in the event was unable to go. Instead, the captaincy went to the Middlesex batsman Robert Slade Lucas, who had been to America with Hawke in the autumn of 1894. He played for Middlesex for much of the 1890s, for a while a regular member of a good batting side; many fine innings culminated, statistically at least, in 185 against Sussex in 1895, sharing in a partnership of 338 made at a hundred an hour. He never made it into the Test team, but did play international hockey, clearly one of those multi-gifted sportsmen which Victorian England produced as easily as the West Indies now produce fast bowlers. The party was all-amateur and nothing like first-class standard, being mostly university and good club players, although one of them, the left-arm fast bowler Hugh Bromley-Davenport, was to play four times for England in South Africa.

Seven of the matches played were first-class. The first one began on 29 January 1895 against Barbados at Kingston, and was watched by some 6,000 people; the Englishmen, having chosen to bat on a poor wicket, were quickly shot out for 48 and lost by five wickets in two days, the local hero being Clifford Goodman with 14 for 85. They followed this with a drawn 13-a-side match against United Services, but then played a remarkable return match against Barbados. On a much better wicket the home team ran up 517, easily a West Indian record, with six players scoring over sixty but none reaching ninety. In reply, Lucas's team made 303, with F.W. Bush becoming the first touring player to hit a century in the West Indies, and Goodman having 6 for 104. Under the law of the time the home captain, D. Macaulay, had to enforce the follow-on as the deficit was more than 120, which with tired bowlers could spell disaster. So it proved: Arthur Somers-Cocks, who had played for Oxford and was now teaching in Barbados, took 8 for 99, but Goodman bowled poorly, J.M. Dawson made 138, Bromley-Davenport 91 and the total of 396 set Barbados 183 to win. Matches were played to a finish, and it was the fourth afternoon when they began their innings. At 111 for 4 overnight they seemed set for victory, only to collapse for 157 next morning, leaving the

Englishmen victorious by 25 runs. Not surprisingly, the rest of the tour turned into an anticlimax.

In the other first-class matches they were beaten convincingly by Trinidad, beat Demerera (as British Guiana were then known) by ten wickets, and drew with Demerera after rain intervened. In Jamaica they easily beat an All Jamaica team and then, in the last match, lost to the same side by eight wickets. In between these games, they had had much the better of the non-first-class matches, their overall record being sixteen played, ten won and four lost. One imagines that Dr Anderson hoped the cricket would be taken fairly seriously, and perhaps it was; but the socializing was taken rather more so. The tourists were full of praise for the hospitality and had a thoroughly good time, the matches created plenty of interest and were generally well attended, and if the standard was at best no higher than county second XI it was about right for the level they encountered. All in all, the first English tour to the West Indies was a great success.

*

*P.F. Warner, born in Trinidad, returned with Lord Hawke and topped the batting.*

*A.E. Stoddart, born in South Shields, went with Arthur Priestly and topped the batting and bowling.*

One of the members of that party was Arthur Priestley, a member of MCC who was to be dismissed in his *Wisden* obituary as 'not particularly prominent in the game itself'. In the summer of 1896, after some of the other tourists had suggested another visit, he began to organize one for the following winter and heard from the four colonies that they would be delighted to receive his team. According to Priestley's version of what happened next, he then had a letter from Lord Hawke saying that British Guiana had asked him, Hawke, to send out a team, but he was thinking of going to India instead. Priestley replied that he would be happy to surrender the captaincy to Hawke, and while he had already invited eight players Hawke could choose the rest of the party himself. So far so good, the gentlemanly conduct unblemished; but then something went wrong. Hawke abandoned his India trip and began to make plans to go to the West Indies, but decided that he did not want to amalgamate with Priestley; this was fair enough, but what annoyed Priestley was the high-handed way in which he said that 'he did not desire to talk over the matter with me'. It produced a completely pointless and gloriously English piece of bad feeling on both sides, with the result that both men proceeded to organize their own tours as though the other one did not exist. Only a few years before, in 1887–8, there had been two tours to Australia at the same time, resulting in financial disaster; since these parties were both all-amateur, the money aspect was much less of a problem this time, and they did at least have the sense to keep out of each other's way.

There were some good players in the two parties. Priestley had A.E. Stoddart, who would play in sixteen Tests of which half would be as captain, S.M.J. Woods, who had played three times for Australia and three times for England, and R.C.N. Palairet, who could have gone on to great things but for a knee injury. Hawke had P.F. Warner, who would bring back the Ashes in a few years, H.D.G. Leveson-Gower, who would play in three Tests, and Bromley-Davenport from the earlier tour. The rest were rather more ordinary, leaving both groups on balance just about first-class.

Priestley's team began their tour first. They played sixteen matches of which nine were first-class, playing their first game almost immediately on arrival in Barbados and losing by an innings. Two more matches against Barbados resulted in one win apiece, then after a number of minor fixtures came the most important game so far to be played in the West Indies. On 15 February 1897 at Port-of-Spain a representative team, captained by Plum Warner's brother Aucher, opposed an English touring team for the first time, and between them they provided a game worthy of the occasion.

Priestley's team batted first and made 179, with 45 from Palairet and 38 from Stoddart the best scores. The home response centred on H.B.G. Austin, of whom we shall hear much more before long, with an unbeaten 75, and it was only the later batsmen, led by L.S. Constantine with 38, who gave them the lead, taking the score to 215. Second time around, Palairet was again top scorer with 46 out of his team's 176, the West Indian bowlers Goodman and Cumberbatch each taking nine wickets in the match. This left just 141 to win, only for four wickets to fall for 12 runs and two more by the time the total had staggered to 41. But then Constantine and A.B. Clarke came together, putting on 75 for the seventh wicket and swinging the match yet again. When Constantine went for 45 there were still 25 needed, but McAuley stayed with Clarke and the match was won by three wickets. The ball had been set rolling in dramatic fashion.

In Trinidad two games against the island team were lost. They made up for this in Jamaica, and finished with ten wins and five defeats in their sixteen games, with Stoddart top of both batting and bowling averages. In all matches he scored over 1,000 runs, made six centuries and took over 100 wickets at under eight apiece; it made a sharp contrast with his captain who averaged just five with the bat and bowled three unrewarded overs.

**Combined West Indian XI v. Mr A. Priestley's XI**
*Port-of-Spain, Trinidad 15, 16, 17 February 1897*
Toss: Priestley's XI

**Mr Priestley's XI**

| | | | | |
|---|---|--:|---|--:|
| R.C.N Palairet | lbw. b. Goodman | 45 | c. & b. Cumberbatch | 46 |
| H.T. Stanley | c. Constantine b. Goodman | 8 | c. Warner b. Goodman | 10 |
| A.E. Stoddart | c. Cumberland b. McAuley | 38 | c. D'Ade b. Goodman | 6 |
| R. Leigh-Barratt | b. Goodman | 13 | b. Cumberbatch | 33 |
| S.M.J. Woods | c. Goodman b. Cumberbatch | 19 | b. McAuley | 26 |
| J. Leigh | b. Cumberbatch | 26 | b. Cumberbatch | 14 |
| G.A. Beldam | c. D'Ade b. Cumberbatch | 7 | c. Austin b. Cumberbatch | 5 |
| F.W. Bush | c. Smith b. Cumberbatch | 17 | c. Cumberbatch b. Goodman | 5 |
| A. Priestley | st. Constantine b. Goodman | 1 | b. Cumberbatch | 3 |
| W. Williams | c. & b. Goodman | 1 | b. Goodman | 9 |
| R.P. Lewis | not out | 0 | not out | 0 |
| Extras | b. 1, l.b. 3 | 4 | b. 19 | 19 |
| **Total** | | **179** | | **176** |

| Bowling | O | M | R | W | O | M | R | W |
|---|--:|--:|--:|--:|--:|--:|--:|--:|
| Goodman | 30 | 7 | 72 | 5 | 30 | 11 | 53 | 4 |
| Cumberbatch | 28 | 9 | 66 | 4 | 32 | 11 | 67 | 5 |
| Austin | 5 | 0 | 22 | 0 | | | | |
| McAuley | 4 | 1 | 15 | 1 | 14 | 6 | 26 | 1 |
| Sproston | | | | | 3 | 0 | 11 | 0 |

**Combined West Indian XI**

| | | | | | |
|---|---|---|---|---|---|
| M. Smith | b. Bush | 2 | c. Leigh b. Stoddart | 0 |
| L.S. D'Ade | b. Stoddart | 3 | c. Lewis b. Stoddart | 1 |
| S.W. Sproston | c. Stanley b. Stoddart | 14 | c. Palairet b Stoddart | 24 |
| H.B.G. Austin | not out | 75 | c. Palairet b. Stoddart | 3 |
| A.B. Clarke | c. Beldam b. Williams | 15 | not out | 35 |
| O. Weber | b. Williams | 3 | b. Stoddart | 4 |
| R.S.A. Warner | b. Stoddart | 21 | lbw. b. Woods | 0 |
| L.S. Constantine | c. Stoddart b. Williams | 38 | c. & b. Woods | 45 |
| D. McAuley | lbw. b. Woods | 1 | not out | 15 |
| C.E. Goodman | b. Williams | 14 | | |
| A. Cumberbatch | c. Palairet b. Stoddart | 20 | | |
| Extras | b. 3, l.b. 5, w. 1 | 9 | b. 15 | 15 |
| **Total** | | 215 | (seven wickets) | 142 |

| Bowling | O | M | R | W | O | M | R | W |
|---|---|---|---|---|---|---|---|---|
| Stoddart | 29 | 9 | 74 | 4 | 29.2 | 15 | 49 | 5 |
| Bush | 12 | 2 | 24 | 1 | 4 | 1 | 11 | 0 |
| Woods | 10 | 2 | 29 | 1 | 26 | 9 | 49 | 2 |
| Williams | 15 | 3 | 53 | 4 | 5 | 1 | 8 | 0 |
| Leigh-Barratt | 13 | 4 | 26 | 0 | 5 | 1 | 10 | 0 |

Combined West Indian XI won by three wickets.

Trinidad clearly had a good team at this time for they also beat Hawke's team twice in their opening first-class fixtures, which meant that all three touring parties thus far had lost their initial first-class game, no doubt because of unfamiliarity with the light and the hardness of the wickets. These were, though, the only defeats of Hawke's tour; they played five more first-class games – one win against Barbados, two against British Guiana and a draw against each – and fourteen in all, finishing with nine wins. Their hero was Warner, who began the tour in the land of his birth, Trinidad, with 119 in a minor match, and went on to make three more hundreds and almost 1,000 runs in all.

The opinion of the time seems to have been that having two touring parties was not a good thing, yet the matches were fairly well attended and each played their part in helping the development of the game in the Caribbean. Those who had toured twice said that standards had improved even in two years, and it was clear that there were many players of English first-class ability. The enthusiasm was such that it was inevitable that before very long they should be invited to send a team to England.

*

It was Lord Hawke, the great organizer of the period, a kind of caped crusader who did much for cricket in the developing countries, who in the summer of 1899 invited the West Indians to send a team to England the following year. When they chose their team early in 1900 they did it on the quota system, Barbados and Trinidad each supplying four players, Guiana three, Jamaica two and St Vincent and Grenada one each. It was an early instance of the jealousy among the colonies bedevilling the cricket, for the party would undoubtedly have been stronger with an extra player from Barbados and Trinidad at the expense of the Jamaicans or the Grenadian. There was no colour bar in operation, but because of the quota system no place was found for Cumberbatch, the black Trinidadian bowler who had been rated by the English tourists as the best they encountered. Clifford Goodman, who had been the outstanding bowler of the previous decade with his high-class fast-medium deliveries, had ended his career before the age of thirty so he, who would certainly have troubled the top English batsmen, was not amongst the party though his brother Percy, rated the best of the West Indian batsmen, made the trip. The party also lacked the services of Harold Austin, for a reason that places this tour firmly in its historical niche: he was in South Africa, not selling his soul for krugerrands but fighting the Boers.

The captain was Aucher Warner, who had led the Combined XI well against Priestley's team. He was a very capable batsman, but at 41 – he was fourteen years senior to his brother – was rather old for the rigours of a cricket tour and made only one score above fifty in the seven matches he played. He then went down with malarial fever and missed the second half of the tour, the captaincy being taken over by Stanley Sproston of British Guiana who, according to P.F. Warner in *Wisden*, 'acquitted himself right well'. MCC ruled, incidentally, that none of the matches should be counted as first class. The English view of the tour was encapsulated in a cartoon that appeared in the *Star* showing a huge W.G., bat in hand, surrounded by six small black men, all shedding tears and saying, 'We have come to learn, sah!' Why the tears, one wonders.

Since the players were totally unaccustomed to English conditions, the tour began disastrously. In the first match, W.G. Grace's London County beat them by an innings and 198 runs; Worcestershire beat them by 215 runs and Warwickshire by an innings and 111 runs. When they came to play their first match at Lord's against Gentlemen of MCC, morale, obviously, was low. They were not helped by the fact that Warner proved incapable of winning the toss, and after the first day had been lost to rain, MCC, who included Grace, Stoddart and Lord Harris in their number, ran up 379 thanks to a century from A.F. Somerset at number seven, a player who would later make three tours to the Caribbean. MCC's bowling was hardly strong, but the visiting batsmen found the pitch difficult and only

Learmond got to fifty. 190 all out saw them following on and in big trouble at 132 for 8 until Constantine and Burton rescued the innings; Constantine recorded the first century by a West Indian in England, making 113 in ninety minutes and, with 64 not out from Burton, the total reached 295. MCC were left with two hours in which to score 107 and soon tumbled to four for 36, but Mordaunt and Page saw them home for a five-wicket win with a few minutes to spare.

That Lebrun Constantine should have had the honour of the first West Indian century in England is appropriate in view of what his son went on to achieve. Known as 'Cons', and in due course 'Old Cons', he was a batsman who already had some good scores to his name against the English touring teams and had shown qualities as a fielder that his son was to take to unprecedented heights. In all matches on this tour he scored 610 runs at 30, and six years later he made 1,025 runs at 29. Yet he almost did not make it; not being a professional his passage was not paid for him, and as he could not afford the fare himself he had not joined the ship, despite being chosen. When he was found standing in the street after the ship had left a public subscription was organized immediately, a launch was chartered and he was deposited on the ship before it reached the open sea; a remarkable little tale that says much about the lack of official organization and the importance of cricket to the people. In Trinidad he was an overseer on an estate, a fairly good position for a black man in those days, and he was very much his own man; on one occasion years later, for instance, there was a dispute about an umpire and he withdrew his team from the game rather than play under an umpire he did not want. Cricket was of enormous importance to him and he played it for many, many years, always in a dignified and sporting manner, becoming something of a revered patrician figure in Trinidad. It gave him the chance, rare for a black man at the time, of being the equal of anyone.

In the next game they at last recorded a win, even if it was only against Minor Counties. The jubilation died against Gloucestershire when Jessop hammered 157 in an hour, and an interesting little incident occurred when Woods asked his captain if he could take his boots off as he could only bowl properly without them. Warner refused and poor Woods had to soldier on. At Leicester the team was joined by Plum Warner, qualified by birth to play for them. He opened the innings and made 113, putting on 238 for the first wicket with Ollivierre, who scored 159, and setting the foundation for victory by an innings. Three defeats – one of them an abject one by Wiltshire – and two draws followed, but then at last the team began to get its act together. Hampshire were beaten by 88 runs and, the highlight of the tour, Surrey by an innings. Surrey were some way from full strength but were the reigning champions at the time and fielded by no means a poor side, so it was a notable victory. Two more draws and the tour was rounded off with an innings win over Norfolk, who were bowled out for 32 as Burton took eight wickets for nine runs.

So seventeen matches yielded five wins and eight defeats, which was regarded as a very creditable performance even allowing that 'they were treated with extreme consideration by the counties', as *Wisden* put it. The leading batsman was Charlie Ollivierre of St Vincent, who stayed behind to qualify for Derbyshire, just ahead of Constantine in the averages, while the two professional bowlers, Woods of Trinidad and Burton of British Guiana dominated the attack with 72 and 78 wickets respectively, far more than anyone else.

One wonders what the English public made of the fact that three of the four best cricketers of the party were coloured. Probably very little, since the English public had shown themselves singularly uninterested in the tourists, and gate receipts proved very disappointing. Plum Warner, in his review of the tour, said that the weakest aspects were the lack of a reliable wicket-keeper and the running between the wickets which in the early games was the worst he had ever seen. The summary in the *Sun* was that

They field fairly well, but their bowling is weak and their batting crude and possessing little style. None of them seem to have any idea of forward play, and there is little variety in their strokes. Few of them score freely on the off-side, but one and all are good at the old-fashioned leg stroke and time the ball admirably.

The one thing which no one could fault was their sportsmanship, for they had been educated by teachers who would have placed even more emphasis on that than their counterparts in England. All in all, apart from the poor crowds, there was plenty to encourage them; and, if the patronizing 'We have come to learn, sah!' of the *Star*'s cartoonist stuck in their gullets as it now does in ours, they undoubtedly *had* learned a good deal.

# 2

# Arcadian Days

For all that Jamaica was isolated from the 'big three' the game was very popular there, though it was clear that the lack of intercolonial competition kept the standard low. A picture of the game there appeared in *Cricket* magazine in February 1902 from one C.P. Hurditch, the editor of the *American Cricketer*:

Teams from every part of the island of Jamaica indulge in friendly games with each other and neighbouring towns; every parish has its eleven, and visits are duly exchanged in the course of the year. One thinks nothing of riding overnight seventy-five miles or so in a buggy to participate in a game, and the man who scores the century is known all over the country in no time. Blacks and whites alike are equal on the field, and even the inmates of the asylum have their matches. . . . On the first of January every year a spectacular match is held, and the players don all sorts of fancy costumes. Admission is charged and large numbers attend, the Governor and suite rarely failing to put in an appearance. . . . The costumes are most original and each one tries to outdo the other in grotesqueness, while the antics of the players cause howls of laughter all around the ground. Uncle Sam never fails to be represented, while Columbia may often be seen promenading arm in arm with Britannia. These matches realize quite a respectable sum of money, which goes to beautifying the club's pavilion, or swelling the fund for entertaining visitors at the smoking concerts, which are often held out on the green sward. . . . The Kingston Cricket Club is by far the oldest and most important. Very up-to-date in all its transactions, it now has over 450 members on its club list, and the ground at Sabina Park is one of the best in the island. The financial end of the club is in a very flourishing condition, and year after year they show a balance on the right side of the ledger.

It was an age of innocence, of course, at least in the cricketing sense. With the other colonies losing theirs all the time as the game was taken ever more seriously, it is a matter of opinion whether the Jamaicans were unfortunate to be left behind or fortunate to be able to continue to enjoy their Arcadia.

Hurditch's article was published to coincide with another all-amateur tour of the West Indies in 1901–2. The party was selected by H.D.G. Leveson-Gower, but when he was not able to make the trip the captaincy fell to Richard Bennett, a batsman who played a number of times for Hampshire around this period. There were some useful cricketers in the party, including B.J.T. Bosanquet, F.L. Fane and E.R. Wilson who would all play for England. They played nineteen games of which thirteen were first-class, winning thirteen and losing five. After losing to and then defeating Barbados, they played a Combined West Indies team. Burton and Woods, the bowlers who had done so well in England, showed their skill yet again, Burton taking 7 for 54 as Bennett's team were put out for 147. Austin, back from the Boer War, top-scored for his team with 68 as they reached 236, but then came disaster for the Englishmen on a rain-affected pitch: Woods took 7 for 38, Austin, who played as a stop-gap wicket-keeper, took eight victims in the match, and an all-out total of 85 gave West Indies victory by an innings and four runs. So Bennett and his men went to Jamaica and thrashed the poor locals several times.

In Trinidad they twice beat the home team, then the intercolonial champions, before playing another representative match. According to *Cricket* magazine, it was played on 'another bad pitch, which it would seem impossible to help in Trinidad, where the mole cricket reigns supreme'. West Indies, winning the toss, had the best of the conditions, and with Constantine, promoted to open, making 84 and Weber 59 they just reached 200. In the Trinidad matches they had encountered a young slow left-arm bowler named Sydney Smith who had taken a hatful of wickets; on a helpful pitch he now annihilated them. His first innings figures were 9 for 34 as the Englishmen collapsed for 71; West Indies batted again and struggled to 79, and then Smith again did the business. Seven for 51 saw Bennett's team all out for 97, the victory margin being 111 runs.

Cricket being the perverse game that it is, in British Guiana they twice lost to the colony team, reckoned the weakest of the 'big three', but in between times played another representative game and won it by a street. This time the bowling honours went to E.R. Wilson with 7 for 46 as West Indies were skittled out for 92 before the Englishmen piled up 455; Dowson made a century and Bosanquet, who would top the averages, Whatman and Dillon all scored well. If this supremacy was not enough, they then rubbed it in completely, Wilson taking 7 for 16 as the home team crumbled for 33, leaving Bennett and his merry men winners by an innings and 330 runs.

Once again, a good time was had by all. Touring in places such as Australia, New Zealand and South Africa at this time could be gruelling since there were long overland journeys involved; but as long as you were a good sailor a trip to the West Indies seems to have been altogether less taxing. One gets the impression that tour organizers did not have much trouble in filling the places.

*

So far, not one English professional had toured the West Indies, slightly surprising since they had figured far more prominently in the early tours to other countries than had the amateurs. The first two to do so were George Thompson of Northamptonshire and Ernie Hayes of Surrey, both all-rounders, with Thompson primarily a bowler and Hayes a batsman, and both were to have a very successful tour. This 1904–5 team was led by Lord Brackley and was the strongest to visit the Caribbean so far; apart from some good county players, there was the Hampshire batsman Major E.G. Wynyard and the lob bowler George Simpson-Hayward, both of whom, as well as the two professionals, played a few games for England. Twenty games were played in all, ten first class and ten not; six of the first-class games were won and three lost, with eleven won and three lost overall.

They achieved something which none of their predecessors had done by salvaging a draw out of the opening game, though, as they had only four wickets left and were way adrift, they obviously had as many problems with the unfamiliar conditions as everyone else. By the time they played the first game against the West Indies XI, they had beaten Jamaica and Barbados convincingly, getting their eye in for a walloping of a West Indies team that lacked some of its best players. Wynyard, who was nearly forty-four, made a century, and with 78 from Ebden and 67 from Simpson-Hayward, the total reached 353. Thompson and Simpson-Hayward then routed them for 107, and second time round disposed of them for 229 to win by an innings and 17 runs. The highlight of this was a fine knock of 83 by Harold Austin, but Thompson still finished with figures of 11 for 101 on a good wicket; his fast-medium bowling was probably the best the West Indians had so far met, and, lacking their top bowlers, West Indies were never in with a chance.

Barbados avenged their earlier defeat, but British Guiana were seen off and the minor matches produced no upsets; in little St Vincent the home team had the better of two draws, but the Englishmen were not at all happy about the umpiring. For those who keep a record of such matters, this was the first time that dodgy West Indian umpiring was mentioned in *Wisden*; what the oracle does not record is that some of the Englishmen – the amateurs, inevitably – made themselves less than popular by their haughty attitude. The tour finished in Trinidad with a second representative match sandwiched between two against the colony. The first proved a great triumph for Cumberbatch, he who had not been taken to England in 1900, as he took 13 for 57 to give his team a good victory, and he did well again in the final match as Trinidad recorded their second win. In between times, the match against the West Indies XI at St Clair produced enormous excitement.

With Wynyard absent with a leg injury and the likes of Constantine, Cumberbatch, Burton and Sydney Smith playing for West Indies, the sides were much more balanced. Brackley won the toss and Hayes and Thompson made a decent start, but then wickets tumbled and it was the captain himself and Hesketh-Prichard, the number ten, who saw the total to 181. The West Indian innings then took a similar course, with a useful knock from Constantine to start with but not much else till their number ten, Morrison, top-scored with 40 to take the total to 170. When the Englishmen batted again it was the middle order that saw them to 147, with an unbeaten 49 from Somerset the best effort. This left West Indies with 159 to win and Constantine set them going with 56; but wickets drifted away until just three were left with 15 more to get. One does not associate exciting finishes in the West Indies with the 'breathless hush' of the English public school, and no doubt the clamour was considerable; but whether noisy or quiet, tension is tension, and two batsmen showed they were suffering from it by running themselves out. This left Hinds and Cumberbatch to get 14 and they played well for nine of them – only for Thompson and Hayes to combine for one final crucial moment. Thompson found the edge of Hinds' bat, Hayes at slip did his stuff and the Englishmen had won by four runs. Pulsating stuff.

There was no doubt that the standard of West Indian cricket was improving. Brackley's team was a pretty good one and yet had been beaten convincingly by Trinidad twice and Barbados once, and the Combined XI had come so close. Certainly at this time they were in advance of New Zealand and India, the two countries which a quarter of a century later would follow them into the Test arena. Already there were several professionals playing, whereas New Zealand, for instance, remained strictly amateur until quite recently and, in terms of cricketing development, paid the price. There were various factors in this: the climate gave them the advantage of being able to play and practise for much of the year; there were wealthy people prepared to spend money to improve conditions, facilities and so on; there was a well-organized network of clubs; travel among the 'big three' colonies and the smaller islands of St Lucia, St Vincent and Grenada was fairly easy; and the schoolteachers were as involved as ever in coaching the youngsters and helping the game develop. Perhaps most important of all was, quite simply, the sheer enthusiasm of both white and coloured populations, something which has just grown and grown. Cricket in England has had to contend with other major sports, while in New Zealand it suffered badly from the great popularity of rugby. In the West Indies it has always been far and away the paramount sport, and it is hardly surprising that they have been so good at it for so long.

*

The following year, 1906, saw the second West Indian tour of England. Their progress was acknowledged by making the county matches first class, but when they lost their first seven first-class games, and two out of four minor ones as well, the authorities must have regretted it. In the event, the last six first-class matches yielded three wins and two draws as they belatedly got their act together, but it was clear that the programme had been too ambitious. Since this had been the problem six years earlier, it was a pity the lesson had not been learned.

Harold Austin was appointed captain and certainly had some good players under him, but he also had some very ordinary ones, especially the Jamaicans, while Burton, so successful before, was now past his best and did next to nothing. In short, it was not a very well selected party, and their poor showing at first meant that the public soon lost interest so that, like the previous visit, it was a failure financially. The outstanding player was Sydney Smith who, in all matches – thirteen first-class and seven minor – did the double and topped both batting and bowling averages, although he was relatively less successful in the first-class games alone. In the first-class games Percy Goodman and Constantine, both touring for the second time, respectively headed the batting averages and scored most runs, while the bowling averages were topped by Richard Ollivierre, the brother of Charlie who had stayed behind after the previous tour to qualify for Derbyshire. English fans also got a first taste of the exciting new talent of George Challenor, soon to show himself as the first truly great West Indian batsman. There were some fine players here; the problem was that there were too many passengers.

That anyone other than H.B.G. Austin should captain the team would never have been considered. He was a very important man in the Caribbean, the son of a Bishop of the West Indies, a wealthy businessman, and in due course would become Senior Member for Bridgetown in the House of Representatives of Barbados, chairman of the Barbados Board of Education, President of the Chamber of Commerce of Barbados, and so on. He was also a fine batsman and a fine administrator, who for many years worked untiringly to build West Indian cricket into a unified whole. So much so that he is often referred to as the father or godfather of West

Indian cricket, and was revered by the players under him in a way that we can probably no longer understand; Learie Constantine, for instance, ranked him along with his father and Jack Hobbs in his 'cricket trinity'. As a player, his career just went on and on; he was still a good enough batsman on the 1923 tour, when in his mid-forties, to finish fourth in the party's averages, and against the MCC tourists of 1925–6 he was still performing well. Inevitably, he became the first president of the West Indies Cricket Board of Control and was knighted. Without him there is no doubt that cricket in the Caribbean would have taken much longer than it did to get itself together.

As defeat followed defeat, the counties, as before, fielded under-strength teams in order not to overwhelm them. They did notch up wins against Minor Counties and South Wales in non-first-class games, but by the time they played MCC and Ground their morale must have been low. Challenor marked his first visit to headquarters with 59 and Cumberbatch (not the same one who had played before the turn of the century) at number nine chimed in with the same score, undefeated, but there was little other support and they were all out for 240. The MCC team was a curious one in that three of the four bowlers batted in the first six, so that after Plum Warner had made 87 and most of the others had failed it was two supposed tail-enders, Veal and Weigall, who took the total past the visitors' score to 269. Thus far, as *Wisden* said, it 'held out promise of a capital struggle'; instead of which Bert Vogler, the South African leg break and googly merchant, took 9 for 44, shot them out for 115, and MCC cruised to a six-wicket win.

By the time West Indies played an England XI in Blackpool shortly afterwards they had at last clocked up a first-class victory, beating the might of Scotland by four wickets. The England XI was hardly a world-beater, but had the likes of Lilley, Quaife, Kinneir and Hargreave in it, all fine players. West Indies batted first and, as so often, it was Constantine who top-scored with 54, Cumberbatch again doing well down the order to help the total to 201. It was not much of a score, but when Ollivierre and Smith set about the English batsmen it began to look worthwhile, and 138 all out gave the visitors a lead of 63. Then it was Hargreave's turn: once again, only Constantine stood firm for another fifty as wickets slipped away, Hargreave taking 7 for 49 to dismiss West Indies for 158. The target was 222, but only an hour's play was possible on the third day because of rain. By then the England XI had reached 129 for 4 and, with 93 still to get, anything could have happened. It seems to have done wonders for the visitors' confidence, for after winning a minor match they thrashed Yorkshire – admittedly some way below full strength – by 262 runs, bowling them out in the first innings for 50. The last first-class game also saw another good win, this time over Northamptonshire.

Sydney Smith took 12 for 99 in this last game, rounding off such a successful tour that he became the second West Indian to elect to remain in England to qualify for a county, in this case Northants. His arrival in 1909 saw an immediate surge in the county's fortunes and he played with great success up to 1914, doing the double three times and captaining them in the last two seasons. They had been a first-class county for only four years before he joined them and he became their first batsman to reach 1,000 runs in a season; as a slow left-arm bowler of immaculate length he also twice did the hat-trick for them, one of these being four wickets in four balls. He played for the Gentlemen several times, toured West Indies with two MCC teams, and in 1915 was one of *Wisden*'s five cricketers of the year. After the war, he moved to New Zealand and played a few times for the national team before they gained Test status. Obviously his departure was a serious loss to Trinidad and West Indies cricket, and some of his countrymen had strong words to say about English 'poaching'. West Indies could certainly have done with him during the two MCC tours before the war when results in the representative games kept going against them, especially as he did rather well for the opposition.

The 1906 tour indicated that West Indies had not made as much progress as had been hoped, and they were still not a match for a full-strength English county side. In a way, the tour was less successful than the first, in that more was expected of them but was barely achieved; yet it was clear, too, that they were learning all the time and were capable of producing outstanding players, which was more than some countries could claim. That, after all, was the *sine qua non* for advancing their cricket.

*

There had been eight tours under the MCC banner to various parts of the world before one went to the West Indies in 1910–11. Even then it nearly did not go – there was a dispute between the shipping company and the government which almost led to its being abandoned. Remarkably, there were only eleven players in the party after three had to withdraw, eight amateurs and three professionals, and it looked such a weak one that the whole enterprise hardly seemed worth while. The press were dismissive before they went, and the following year *Wisden* accorded the tour only a couple of pages. The leader of the band was Arthur Somerset, then aged 45, who had in his time been a good all-rounder, even to the extent of keeping wicket as well as bowling fast and batting. Like so many of the amateur tourists before the First World War, he played the first-class game only sporadically, though he captained the Gentlemen of Sussex for twenty years. Another of these Victorian sportsmen of many parts, he had been a fine rugby forward and a good heavyweight boxer in his day; and his day was not finished yet, for he would be leading another team to the Caribbean in two years' time.

It was a curious tour in that their only victories, apart from one in British Guiana and one in the only minor match played, were against the West Indies in the so-called 'Test' matches, although the standard of most of the players who participated was a mile from Test level. The opening games in Barbados were both lost by an innings, but the problem which then faced West Indies was that quarantine restrictions against Trinidad meant they could send no players for the representative match. The team that turned out was thus almost entirely composed of Barbadians, yet somehow they did not seem to take the game too seriously. West Indies batted first and were given a good start by George Challenor and his brother; the middle order collapsed, though, and the final total made 271. In reply, Holloway made 71, Young 49, Sydney Smith scored well against his former colleagues and MCC took a small lead with 288. Then the match swung towards MCC as the batsmen got themselves out, a total of 165 setting the visitors a modest target of 149. There were some early alarms, but an unbeaten 54 from Smith saw MCC home by five wickets. One wonders how he really felt about it.

They went on to British Guiana and a win against the colony team before the second 'Test'. The West Indies team contained some unfamiliar names, and, with Hearne and Smith bowling well on a good wicket, they were all out for 172. MCC subsided to 92 for 6 before they ran up 301 with Smith again in the action, his 59 being bettered only by Young's 73 at number nine. At least West Indies then made a fight of it, Bayley and Layne both scoring 59 to help the total to 272, setting a target of 144; the wicket was still playing well, though, and MCC got home with four wickets intact.

The plan had been for a second match against British Guiana but it was felt that another representative game would be more interesting so 'A West Indian XI', rather than 'West Indies', was hastily convened. There was fun before the start when two Barbadians dropped out because they objected to the omission of another Barbados player, so two Guianans were drafted in. To remind us that the First World War still lay in the future, *Cricket* magazine states, with wonderful self-conceit, that 'the incident was an unfortunate one, especially as it occurred during the visit of an English team'. The West Indians again batted first, but after a good start, with 66 from Hunter, the innings fell away and closed at 203, Hearne taking another six-wicket haul. MCC also made a good start only to lose a crop of wickets, and the eighth one fell at 180; but with Gaussen being dropped four times in his 77 and the captain making 60, the total reached 332. This highlighted a long-standing West Indian problem which had let them down often, especially in England – their fielding in general and catching in particular were just not good enough. On this occasion it almost certainly cost them the match, for in the second innings they ran up 224, with Hunter again top-scoring, leaving MCC just 96 to win; in the event, time ran out with the score on 72, but as five wickets had gone the dropped catches became doubly important.

Trinidad thumped MCC twice and they then became the first touring team to fail to beat Jamaica, drawing twice and bringing the tour to the most exciting of conclusions with the first tie in West Indian cricket. It made a fitting end to what, with weak teams and perverse results, was an odd tour all round. Beyond the need to improve their fielding, West Indies cannot have learned much from it. Yet in these formative years for countries such as West Indies and New Zealand, it was always a problem for MCC to know how strong to make their team. Naturally they did not want to lose but neither did they want to annihilate the opposition as a strong team could easily have done; furthermore, with finance always a factor, the spectators would want to see, and would pay to see, good English players rather than ordinary ones, but the good English players would simply be too strong for the locals. All in all it was a tricky business, especially as many players would not be available to tour. Sometimes, as now, they just got it wrong.

*

They got things only slightly better two years later in 1912–13, when Somerset again led the party and *Wisden* again gave them scant attention. Failing to find anything constructive to say, *Wisden* resorted to 'Albert Relf was disappointing as a bowler, and W.C. Smith bowled to no purpose'. No mention was made of the fact that Relf was first and Smith third in the batting averages, but they were only professionals, after all. In terms of playing to no purpose, the same person finished bottom of both batting and bowling averages – but since he was the captain's son, and had four Christian names, his fallibility went unremarked. Overall, the party was a little stronger than before, but not a great deal.

As usual, Barbados wiped the floor with them, winning each match by an innings with Challenor scoring a century in each. Then, as before, MCC came good in the first 'Test'. Somerset won the toss and chose to field, whereupon Humphreys, the other professional in the party, proved the decision a good one and took 7 for 75 as West Indies were all out for 167. By the close, MCC had the hundred up for just one wicket and next day they capitalized, Whittington, Burton and, almost inevitably, Sydney Smith scoring well and taking the total to 324. Second time around, West Indies fared just as badly, only R.L. Challenor, George's brother, living up to the family name with 77 and everyone else failing. 171 all out left MCC just 15 to get – and they lost three wickets in doing so.

They then beat Trinidad and drew with them before the second 'Test' in Port-of-Spain. MCC made a reasonable start when they batted, but then suddenly the wickets clattered, mostly to Ollivierre – 115 for 8 and dire trouble. They were rescued mainly by Doll, who made 52, and the total crept to 202. When West Indies batted, Ince and Cumberbatch dominated poor bowling and fielding to make 138 for the first wicket, but not without incident: Ince had made 68 when his wicket was hit by Relf without the bails falling, and Cumberbatch was bowled when he deliberately made no attempt to play the ball as leaves were blowing across the field. He was given out by the umpire, but when he appealed to Somerset he, as befitted a Gentleman of Sussex, allowed him to continue. Four middle-order batsmen passed thirty while the left-handed Ince just pressed on, playing the longest innings ever against an English team in the Caribbean and finally going for 167. The total made 399, whereupon MCC lost wicket after wicket; 9 were down for 102 when Somerset joined Burton with nearly two hours left, yet they scored 89 at a run a minute (this was cricket's Golden Age, don't forget) before the captain fell with just twenty minutes left, leaving West Indies victorious by an innings and six runs.

The tour finished with three matches in British Guiana, with the decider in the 'Test' series coming between two defeats of the colony team. On a good Bourda wicket West Indies were soon heading for a big score as the first four batsmen did well, especially Rogers who remained unbeaten on 69. Unfortunately, while Rogers was doing his stuff his colleagues were returning to the pavilion in rapid order, and were all out for 219. When MCC batted, 'Punter' Humphreys gave four chances in his first eight runs; but none of them was taken and he clocked up exactly a hundred to round off an excellent tour in which he would score most runs, take most wickets, top the bowling averages and finish second in the batting averages. With Whittington making 54 and good scores all down the order – and

53 extras – the total reached 441. George John of Trinidad took six wickets but, with little spin to vary the attack, the Englishmen found few problems. To think that an English team ever scored over 400 against a pace-bowling West Indian attack!

West Indies' second innings centred on Moulder, who carried his bat for 104. With Hunter he put on 84 for the first wicket and with Ollivierre 83 for the sixth, but the rest, as Hamlet might have said, is better left to silence: 264 all out left MCC just 43 to get and they lost no wicket in making it. Fittingly, perhaps, Sydney Smith, in his last representative game in the Caribbean, was in at the death. With MCC thus taking the rubber 2-1, West Indian journalists started writing about 'the Ashes going home'.

Eighteen months later the Great War had begun, W.G. Grace had made his muddle-headed pronouncement that cricketers ought to come to the help of their country without delay in its hour of need, and the game had shut up shop for the duration – thereby depriving everyone of an escape valve from the rigours of war. It was five years before first-class cricket resumed in England, six in the West Indies.

# 3

# Disappointment

When the world emerged from the dark tunnel of war it steadily became clear that English cricket had suffered grievously. Only a small number of top players had actually been killed, but injuries and illness had ended the careers of plenty more, and many of those who returned to the cricket fields seemed debilitated by their experiences. They duly lost heavily to Australia in the first two Test series at the beginning of the 1920s, since the Australians had not only contributed greatly to the fighting but appeared to have used the war for the express purpose of producing top-class cricketers. The difference between the two countries could hardly have been more marked, as eight consecutive Test wins showed. West Indies' experience was rather closer to Australia's than England's, with most of their best players of the pre-war years still on the scene and some fine young ones emerging as well. They would repeat the trick, as would Australia, a quarter of a century later.

1923 was the first big year after the war for the West Indians, as their tour of England would give them the opportunity to show that they were approaching Test class; had the war never happened they would almost certainly have been ready for the step up by now. Harold Austin, now well into his forties, was the captain and once again he was hampered by the quota system. Effectively this meant that he had to leave one of his best bowlers behind, since from Barbados Challenor, Tarilton and Ince were certainties while he then had to choose between Herman Griffith and the unknown young George Francis, who had impressed him very much in practice. Francis was to prove Austin's judgement correct and have an outstanding tour, but it was hard on Griffith, a top-class bowler. The team also included a 21-year-old from Trinidad named Learie Constantine, another of the captain's inspired choices. Austin, without a doubt, was one of the great judges of an up-and-coming cricketer.

The party was really quite a useful one, but they were very unlucky with what *Wisden* called 'our quaint climate'. May and early June were 'bleak and bitter' and not surprisingly in these conditions they lost three of the first five matches, although they beat Sussex in their second outing. The third match was against MCC and was ruined by the weather, with play only possible on a day and a bit. It was hardly a strong MCC team but the cold handicapped almost everyone; Randall Johnson scored a century for MCC out of a total of 228, and West Indies had struggled to 121 for 8 when the quaint climate called a halt. This was meant to be one of the show-pieces of the summer that would fire the public's imagination and get them clamouring to see the tourists, but it did not quite work out.

Wins against Oxford University and Essex got them going, and over the next few weeks they won several minor matches, had some honourable draws against the counties and lost to Lancashire. Warwickshire were convincingly beaten, then after another draw came the best performance of the tour. On the excellent Oval pitch, Surrey, then in one of their strong periods, were shot out for 87, and, although they recovered in the second innings, splendid batting by Challenor and 10 for 76 from Francis saw West Indies home by ten wickets. That *did* get the public going and, although they lost to Glamorgan, they came up with a fine win over Somerset.

As a result of the Surrey game they were invited to take part in the Scarborough Festival, where H.D.G. Leveson-Gower confronted them with a team that was not far short of a full Test side. It was the last game of the tour and the West Indians clearly saw it as their chance to impress at a high level – only for their batting to let them down. 110 all out seemed dismal, but Francis and John bowled well and only 97 from Ernest Tyldesley allowed the home team to reach 218. Then once again the batsmen failed, and 135 all out left the home team needing just 28 to win. That final innings was quite astonishing. Hobbs went lbw for 2, Stevens was caught for 6, and Tyldesley fell with the score on 14. Still no problem – until Rhodes, Chapman and Mann left with just 19 on the board. Francis had four wickets, John two and two catches. The miracle was not quite to be as Douglas survived a confident lbw appeal before, with Fender, seeing his team home by just four wickets; but such a demonstration of fighting spirit did West Indies no harm in pressing their claims for Test status.

Francis and John formed West Indies' first pair of top fast bowlers, and they were every bit as fast and fearsome as the recent pace merchants have been. George John of Trinidad was the older, born around 1885 although no one seemed to know for sure, and, as depicted by C.L.R. James in *Beyond a Boundary*, was a fascinating character. About five feet ten (1.8 metres) and powerfully built, his main weapon was sheer pace and he had the traditional fast bowler's hatred of the batsman; 'John was not hostile, he was hostility itself,' wrote James. His captain never took him off, he took himself off when he was ready, and if two batsmen put together a stand he would just bowl until he had broken it, apparently indefatigable. Very much a man of his people, he was fiercely independent, had a total belief in his own ability, and anyone who crossed him did so at their peril; James's stories about him make enthralling reading. He was unfortunate that his best years coincided with the First World War and by 1923 he was past his best, so that he was not played in as many games as he felt he should have been. Still, in ten matches he took 49 first-class wickets at under 20 and left a lasting impression. He became head groundsman at the Queen's Park Oval and ruled the place like a dictator.

George Francis, having been taken on the tour just through impressing Austin at practice, began it by taking 10 for 83 against Sussex and did not look back. Eighty-two first-class wickets at 15 announced the arrival of an uncomplicated bowler who simply aimed at the stumps and got most of his wickets through sheer pace. Like John, Challenor and various others, Test status came a little too late for him; he did play in ten Tests – for the last one in 1933 he was summoned from Radcliffe in the Bolton League – but without recapturing the form of this tour, and took only 23 wickets at

*George Francis bowled the first ball by a West Indian in Test cricket.*

33, though he did play an important role in West Indies' first ever win over England. Against the fairly strong English tourists of 1925–6, he turned in some excellent figures for Barbados, but since his record in representative matches is fairly ordinary it is not easy to assess his position in the pantheon. Perhaps he was not one of the greats, but, like so many of the players of various nationalities around this period, he leaves one with the impression that in a later, more confident, era he could well have been.

The outstanding success of the tour was George Challenor, with 1,556 runs in twenty first-class matches at an average of nearly 52, with six centuries. He finished behind only Hendren and Mead in the national averages and was clearly one of the finest batsmen in the world. Of medium height and strongly built, he was principally an off-side player though with great power in the pull and on-drive too. He had a wonderful gift of timing, superb footwork and a sound defence, and took the standard of West Indian batsmanship to levels undreamed of. Most of the great West Indians have been black, but while Challenor was white he batted in a style that has come to be recognized as essentially Caribbean – always looking to attack, always trying to dominate the bowlers, and with a kind of joyfulness about it that is simply different from most Englishmen.

He made his debut for Barbados in the 1905–6 intercolonial tournament and showed enough promise to be included in the 1906 tour, aged only 18. Batting in the Lord's nets one day he was watched by W.G. Grace, who asked who he was. 'Take note of him,' the great man is reported to have said. 'You will hear of him one day.' In the event, he had a satisfactory tour without being outstanding, and then in the years before and after the war proved the doctor right by making some prodigious scores for his colony. Barbados had some outstanding batsmen at this time, with the likes of Tarilton, Ince and C.A. Browne; Tarilton was perhaps more reliable, but Challenor was the stylist whom everyone wanted to see and so achieved the greater popularity and immortality. Crowds do tend, after all, to like batsmen who try to hit sixes in the first over, as Challenor often did.

In 1923 he was at his peak; his misfortune was that West Indies did not enter the Test arena until 1928, for his fortieth birthday fell during the first series and by then he was in decline – six innings produced just 101 runs. All this means is that, of all great players, Challenor's Test record is less relevant than most; his significance in terms of West Indian batmanship, though, is enormous. Not only did he set new standards of sparkling stroke-play, but he had a great influence on the young Derek Sealy who, in turn, as a schoolmaster, influenced Frank Worrell. As Worrell is *the*

*George Challenor, the man who set the standard for all the top-class West Indian stroke-makers who followed.*

central figure in West Indian cricket, Challenor's importance is clear. As C.L.R. James put it: 'The history of West Indies maturity is unintelligible unless it begins with the batting of George Challenor.'

\*

MCC had intended to send a team to the Caribbean in 1924–5 and had appointed Captain Robert Fowler to lead it, but it was called off. It was rearranged for the following winter but by that time Fowler had died, aged only 34, and the captaincy went to the Honourable Freddie Calthorpe. The epitome of the cavalier amateur, Calthorpe was no mean all-round cricketer. An attractive batsman who played his shots with style and flair, he was also a medium-pace bowler with a strange corkscrew run – a statement which, taken literally, conjures up the most ludicrous picture – who took many wickets with the swerve he was able to give the ball. He played for Cambridge before and after the war, and would have captained them in 1919 had the letter of invitation not gone astray. That same year he joined Warwickshire, took over the captaincy the following season, marked the appointment by doing the double, and led them till 1929. Almost 12,600 runs at 24 and 782 wickets at just under 30 indicate a good solid performer, and, if he was not in the very front rank as a player, he had one great attribute to compensate: he believed cricket – and life – was about enjoyment, and he gave much pleasure to many people. His only Tests came on the next MCC tour of West Indies, when he led England in their first Tests there. He died aged only 43 but left two legacies to the game: he helped to start the Folkestone Cricket Festival (Plum Warner wrote that he *was* the Folkestone Cricket Festival) and founded the Cricketers' Golf Society. He was a highly popular man, and his early death was greatly mourned.

The team which Calthorpe led in 1925–6 was by a long way the strongest to visit the Caribbean thus far. It contained eight professionals including the young Walter Hammond and the likes of Percy Holmes, Fred Root, Ewart Astill, Roy Kilner and 'Tiger' Smith, and was rated as strong county standard, although one oddity was that George Collins of Kent was the only fast bowler. In the event, the weather spoiled several games, so that of the twelve first-class matches nine were drawn, with MCC winning two of the others. Three 'Test' matches were arranged, with Austin once again in charge of the home team.

They soon found how good Barbados were as they were thumped by an innings after losing the toss on a drying pitch. When the first 'Test' began a couple of days later the pitch had improved considerably and, having won the toss this time, they put it to good advantage. In the match before, Francis had taken 9 for 56; now it was 1 for 94 as MCC rattled up 597 for 8 declared. Hammond led the dance with 238 not out, Jameson fell two short of his century, and Smith, Astill and Holmes all made over sixty – whereupon, after a start of 96 from Challenor and Tarilton, the West Indies disintegrated and were all out for 147. Following on, two men fell quickly, and on the final day four more were back in the pavilion with just 21 on the board. At that point, the rain that had been interrupting play came down in torrents and that was that. Oddly enough, in the return against Barbados it was only time that saved MCC from an innings defeat, the ninth-wicket pair just holding on for a draw after following on.

After drawing twice with Trinidad, the second 'Test' at Port-of-Spain proved an excellent game. West Indies began with 275, C.R. Browne making 74 in under an hour and Dewhurst 55, MCC replying with 319 –

79 from Watson, 65 from Holmes and 32 from Kilner at number ten. Second time around, most of the home batsmen got a few then got out, and it was 75 from Wiles and 69 from the captain (still a fine batsman despite the years, good enough for 114 runs in the match) who took the total to 281. This left MCC to make 238 in less than even time and, after a slowish start, they had 149 to get in the final session when the batsmen began to lay about themselves. The top order all did well and the target was reached with a few minutes to spare and five wickets in hand. The only pity was that a disproportionate amount of the excitement on the tour was concentrated in one match.

The third 'Test' in Georgetown saw something of a reversal of the first. Challenor and Dewhurst led off with 127 for the first wicket, Wilton St Hill chipped in with 72, and C.R. Browne and Wight put on 173 for the seventh wicket, with the former making an unbeaten century despite being hit on the head. Faced with 462, MCC never looked like avoiding the follow-on; Watson and Holmes made fifties, but the innings closed at 264. At the second attempt they did no better, and only a stand of 71 for the eighth wicket between Astill and Tennyson saved the innings defeat. After Astill went, Kilner stayed with Tennyson until the rain came to save them; on 243 for 8 they were just 45 ahead, a bit better than West Indies had been in the first match but still likely to have lost without the rain. At least the Caribbean weather gods showed themselves to have a sense of justice.

They achieved their other win in Jamaica and so were able to return home in credit. More importantly, the *Wisden* oracle was able to pronounce that 'the team met with such powerful opposition on almost every occasion that the tour afforded further evidence of the rapid progress of the game in the West Indies'. Before those words appeared in print, MCC had decided that the time had come to admit West Indies into the Test-playing ranks and had sent out one of their committee members, R.H. Mallett, to help them set up a regional body to co-ordinate matters. Mallett was a familiar figure to the West Indians as he had managed their tours in 1906 and 1923, would do so again in 1928 and also take the team to Australia in 1930–1. Under his guidance, the West Indies Cricket Board of Control was set up on 22 January 1927; the big moment was drawing near.

*

When the moment arrived they found it all went horribly wrong. With their Test debut scheduled for Lord's the following June, they organized three trial games in Barbados at the end of 1927 and beginning of 1928 and from these produced a party that seemed quite a strong one, except that it lacked a top-class wicket-keeper. The problem they encountered is easy to state but harder to explain; they had, for the most part, a collective loss of form, won only five of the thirty first-class matches, lost each of the three Tests by an innings, and generally wished they had stayed at home. Constantine was the major exception to this, scoring nearly 1,400 runs and taking 107 wickets but, like the others, he failed drastically in the Tests.

After all he had accomplished it was sad that Harold Austin was too old to make the tour. His successor as captain was Karl Nunes of Jamaica, his vice-captain in 1923, a left-hander with a good range of strokes. Usually he opened, although in the Tests he did not as he was also the main wicket-keeper and had enough responsibility as it was. He had been educated at Dulwich College, had been one of the founder members of the Jamaican Board of Control in 1926 and, aside from his playing ability, generally had the necessary background for the office of captain – an important consideration in the West Indies for a long time still to come. It hardly needs to be stated that he was white, for the idea of a black man leading them was inconceivable. Years later in 1945 he became president of the WICBC for seven years and, in 1951, was awarded the CBE for public services. If these three Tests were disappointing for him, he had one more when he showed what he was made of, leading the team at the end of the next series and going out in some style.

Six others had toured before, but only Constantine did better this time. Four of the batsmen passed 1,000 runs but in a good summer with plenty of runs the highest average, Hoad's, was only 36 and some of them disappointed badly; Wilton St Hill, in particular, rated second only to Challenor back home, had a disastrous time. Four bowlers took fifty or more wickets, but Francis lacked the penetration of before and they were all let down by poor catching. Wicket-keeping was a great problem, since neither Nunes nor his vice-captain, C.V. Wight, who was also deputy keeper, was a specialist with the gloves. By contrast, the ground fielding was outstanding, Constantine confirming the earlier impression that he was one of the greatest cover fielders of all, but *Wisden* complained that with many of the players good fielding was then negated by a poor return to the wicket so that run-out chances were missed. For *Wisden* the overall performance was 'extremely disappointing'.

At least they made a better start than in the past. After a few minor games they just beat Derbyshire, then drew three before the MCC game. This proved a wash-out, with only one and a half hours play on the first day and none thereafter, which was sad as the MCC team was a strong one without being excessively so, and the teams looked evenly matched. Cambridge were then beaten, and only in the seventh first-class match did they at last lose – to Ireland. They came back with a good win over Middlesex in which Constantine produced a superb all-round performance, then prepared for the first Test by losing to Minor Counties after making them follow on. A drawn two-day game against the Civil Service was their last preparation for the high peak of their careers.

The England selectors put virtually a full-strength team out for the Tests, with only Hobbs missing from the first through injury. The captain was Percy Chapman, the young man who two years before had gained himself a degree of immortality by being made captain for the final Test against Australia and regaining the Ashes in one of the most famous of

*Percy Chapman led England in the first Test series against West Indies. Just behind him is 'Patsy' Hendren, who had a prolific tour in 1929–30.*

victories. Chapman was one of the great cavalier batsmen, a left-hander whose main aim was to enjoy his cricket and give the crowd plenty of entertainment by attacking the bowling at any opportunity. He was also one of the finest of close fielders, with huge hands and lightning reflexes that allowed him to dominate many batsmen simply by his presence in the gully. He came to the captaincy at a time when a good team was taking shape and for a few years led them successfully, with a 4–1 beating of Australia in 1928–9 the peak of his career. He was a very sociable character with a cheerful approach to life to which the players readily responded, and, if he was not one of the great tactical maestri, this did give him an uncanny ability to inspire his men to great deeds.

Saturday, 23 June 1928 was the historic day when West Indies first took up the field in a Test match, Lord's of course being the venue. Chapman won the toss and batted, the first ball was bowled by George Francis and the first wicket was taken by Constantine when he had Hallows caught by Griffith for 26. The same bowler almost got Ernest Tyldesley straight away with a slower ball, but the luck was with England and soon the runs were flowing. Tyldesley and Hammond put on 77 in less than fifty minutes, Jardine on debut made a quick 22, and then Tyldesley and Chapman scored 96 in sixty-five minutes for the fifth wicket. When Tyldesley eventually left he had 122 to his name in his first Lord's Test. Happily the West Indies did not go to pieces under this onslaught but continued to bowl solidly, took three more wickets and polished things off next morning for a total of 401. Thus far they had given a creditable account of themselves, Constantine taking four wickets and Francis, Griffith and Small two apiece. Tyldesley was dropped on 73, but overall their fielding had been good.

Challenor, naturally, took the honour of receiving the first ball and, in partnership with 'Freddie' Martin, made a solid, rather cautious start. A quarter of an hour after lunch they were 86 without loss; hardly more than two hours later they were all out for 177. Martin, Challenor and Fernandes fell in successive overs, St Hill and Roach soon followed, and only Nunes stayed for any time as he made 37. Francis at the death made an unbeaten 19 but there was little else to offer and they were soon following on – and losing wickets: six more clattered that evening, and they finished the day with only 44 on the board. Next morning the tail redeemed things a little, with 52 from Small and 44 from Browne taking the total to 166, leaving England winners by an innings and 58 runs.

The tourists responded by thumping Northants by an innings in two days, though before the second Test they had lost to Yorkshire and

Warwickshire. The last game before the Test was a run-spree at Worcester, with both teams making over 400, just what the West Indies batsmen needed, although the bowlers managed only two wickets. The pity was that when they assembled at Old Trafford they could not reproduce the same form.

Nunes won the toss and batted, and again the innings began soundly. Roach made 50, and after Challenor had gone he and Martin took the score to 100 for 1 before the problems began. Three wickets went for thirteen runs and the innings was doomed; Browne and Scott dragged the score to 206, but when Hobbs and Sutcliffe posted their tenth century opening partnership it looked very inadequate. Hammond and Jardine piled on the runs with 120 for the fourth wicket, although Jardine was given not out when he trod on a stump on 26, and Tate and White then took the game ever more England's way. West Indies bowled well enough, but four dropped catches allowed England to reach 351. There was enough time on the second day to decide the match; Challenor and Roach went without scoring, and though Martin and St Hill took the score to 55, four wickets had gone by the close. Needing another 74 to avoid an innings defeat, the last six went for 44 runs in fifty minutes next morning, Freeman finishing with 5 for 41 to have match figures of 10 for 93. This time it was an innings and 30 runs.

They followed this defeat with one against Wales where a gentleman named S.F. Barnes, then aged 55, took 12 for 118. After a series of draws came the final Test at the Oval, and it took a course depressingly similar to the previous one. With the pitch good and the weather fine it was a good toss to win, and Nunes obliged. So too did Challenor and Roach, with an opening stand of 91. Yet three wickets fell before lunch, six were down for 177, and, although Constantine and Wight put on 54 in half an hour, the total made only 238, with Chapman holding four catches. In reply, Hobbs and Sutcliffe produced their regulation century opening stand with 155, and on the second day Hobbs and Ernest Tyldesley put on 129 in under two hours, Hobbs finally going for 159, his last Test century in England. With the score on 284 for 2, five batsmen went for just 49 runs, all of them to Griffith. It was the last three wickets that swung the match, Tate, Larwood and Freeman putting on 105 in an hour to take the total to 438. Faced with a deficit of exactly 200 with well over a day left, only Martin showed much defensive grit; four were down for 61 at the close and the other six lasted just seventy-five minutes next morning. It was an innings and 71 runs this time.

The high spot of the closing stages of the tour was a good win over a strong Kent side, while at Folkestone they lost to a powerful England XI by just four wickets after Woolley scored 151 in the second innings. By the end they had played thirty first-class matches, losing twelve and winning just five. 'Whatever the future may have in store,' stated *Wisden*, 'the time is certainly not yet when the West Indies can hope to challenge England with a reasonable hope of success.' At least financially all was well, for the Tests had been well attended and there was a profit of £2,000. Just for the record, a day at the Oval Test would have cost you two shillings, which even then must have been pretty good value.

Top of the bowling averages for the Tests was Herman Griffith, who had been so unlucky not to make the 1923 tour. A short man but a very strong one, he was a medium-fast, or sometimes genuinely fast, bowler with a fine out-swinger that brought him many slip catches and, no doubt, given the quality of some of the slip fielders, many frustrations. Quite indefatigable, he had the reputation of hating being hit, and did his best to make sure he was not. He was something of a late developer, for by the time of this tour he was thirty-four and, as he came on the scene only in 1921–2, he had quite likely lost his best years to the war. Not being as fast as Francis or Constantine, he was used more as a stock bowler on this

*Herman Griffith – unlucky to be left behind in 1923, and made English batsmen pay for it later.*

tour, but still, at the Oval, became the first West Indian to take six wickets in a Test innings; and 11 wickets at under 23 for the series looked much better than anyone else's figures. He went on to play in thirteen Tests and take 44 wickets at 28, including fairly successful series against England in 1929–30 and Australia a year later; when he got Bradman for 4 and 0, he amused himself by referring to him as his 'rabbit'. He was almost forty when he made his last tour in 1933 and not surprisingly he was pretty ordinary by then; sad, really, for he was a very forthright character renowned for saying exactly what he thought of anyone and anything, and his relative toothlessness must have been hard to take. As with several of the West Indians around this period, especially the bowlers, there is a strong feeling that in a later era he would have been highly successful.

In one respect, though, the tour was to have far-reaching implications. Learie Constantine's brilliance, especially during the Middlesex game in which he should not have been playing after tearing a muscle, led to Nelson in the Lancashire League inviting him to join them as professional the following year. He did so and played for them until 1937, helping them win the championship seven times out of nine, proving such a draw that gate receipts broke all records, transforming their bank account from the red substantially into the black, and turning in quite remarkable all-round performances for season after season. In terms of West Indian cricket this was an important departure as he was to blaze a trail which many of his countrymen would follow; rather more surprisingly, it also played its part in West Indian political independence.

Constantine was born in Trinidad in 1902, his father, as we have seen, being a fine batsman and fielder and his uncle, Victor Pascall, a slow left-armer who toured England in 1923. When he was six or seven his father set up his own matting wicket and had the whole family, including Learie's mother and sister, playing on it at every opportunity. Old Cons did not believe in coaching, but he did believe that the best way to learn something is to do it and he knew that endless practice for his son at this age would find its rewards later. Constantine wrote: 'If I have made any reputation in fielding and catching in big cricket, it is because of uncountable knuckly raps on the head, back in those childish days under the palms; every time I missed or dropped anything there was a rap; and to this day I know nothing like raps for teaching the tense concentration that is the one and only hallmark of a fine fielder.'

He made his debut for Trinidad in the 1921 intercolonial competition, and did enough then and the following year to convince Austin to take him to England in 1923. With bat and ball he proved sound if unexceptional, but immediately showed that he was something very special as a cover fielder, with electrifying speed and a deadly return the like of which no one could ever remember seeing. In later years, as he turned himself into one of the great all-rounders, it was this astonishing ability in the field that seemed most to impress the spectators, for when not patrolling the covers he was a superb slip and short leg fielder who took many blinding catches. He took them apparently spontaneously in what C.L.R. James called 'an explosion of hand and eye and energy', with an ability to anticipate that bordered on the paranormal; but, in fact, many of them were carefully plotted for by a man with an acute brain, who would place himself close to the bat and rely on the bowler to follow his instructions carefully. Years later, players such as Colin Bland and Clive Lloyd would challenge Constantine's supremacy as a cover fielder, but informed opinion has it that for all-round fielding ability he has never been surpassed.

If one word more than any other has been applied to Constantine's cricket, and especially his batting, it must be spontaneous. To say he was unorthodox as a batsman hardly begins to state the case; broad of shoulder and long in the arm, he invented shots which no one had thought of, always ready to improvise at any opportunity. James, for example, describes a ball from Hammond during the 1926 tour which Constantine saw breaking into him, whereupon he doubled himself almost in two to give himself space and cut the ball to the left of point for four. At Lord's he once hit Maurice Allom over his own shoulder for a six nearly into the press box, and struck Gubby Allen over cover for a six way up into the Grand Stand. In a league match he twice glanced Ted McDonald from outside the off stump to long leg for four. So it went on, runs, when they came, always doing so quickly. The crowd loved it, of course, and he became an enormous attrraction, with a drawing power that was scarcely equalled even in those days of Hobbs, Hammond, Bradman, Larwood, Woolley and other immortals. Inevitably, with such an approach failure was not uncommon, and his first-class average was a rather modest 24, with 197 visits to the crease yielding just five centuries, three of them in 1928; but if the quantity was not great, the quality was certainly there. In Tests he had his moments but overall was a little disappointing, making 635 runs in eighteen games at an average of 19; his top score was 90 in the 1934–5 series, and in his last Test innings at the Oval in 1939 he scored a glorious 79. One wonders what he might have accomplished in one-day cricket.

Scarcely more than average height, as a bowler he was distinctly quick off a fairly short run, with a high action and smooth delivery. As the years went by he became ever more subtle, varying his pace skilfully, and in

*Learie Constantine found the Lancashire climate rather wetter and colder than he would have liked and the thick overcoat had frequent use. On the field his all-action play kept him warm.*

1939 bowling slow-medium with such effectiveness that he took over a hundred wickets on the tour. His career tally was 439 wickets at 20, of which 58 came in Tests at 30 each, his best Test return coming in his last game when he took five English wickets for 75.

If southerners thought it a pity that his first-class cricket in England was confined to West Indies tours, the people of Lancashire were undoubtedly the beneficiaries. Year after year he scored hundreds of runs and took the best part of a hundred wickets, and in 1933 would surely have done the double, something never before achieved, but for missing two games to play for his country. Yet for all the merriness that accompanied his batting he was always very aware that he was the professional, the man who was paid to perform well. Playing for the West Indies he could be his exuberant Caribbean self, but in league cricket he had to be more disciplined, more responsible. Because his skills made him the prime target of the best bowlers, he had to develop his batting to counter them, had to work out how to minimize the risks and still score runs. With his intelligence and his adaptability this challenge was met, so that James could write that, 'by 1932, when I first saw the league, he was no longer a Test cricketer who played in the league. He was a league cricketer who played in Tests. It was after he became a finished league player that he found his finest form in Tests and big cricket'.

There was just one irony: he had gone to England determined to do well so that he would be offered a league contract, and he had done that because the opportunities open to him, as a black man, in Trinidad were so limited. National hero he might be, but working as a solicitor's clerk, and living on that level of income, had little appeal. As always, it was the racial question. 'Had his skin been white, like George Challenor's', wrote James, 'or even light, he would have been able to choose a life at home.'

To most 'southron folk', as Francis Thompson called them, league cricket is simply a closed book. To many northerners it is an integral part of community life, and Constantine's effect on it was like nothing that had gone before. Wherever he played the crowds turned up to see him, helping the clubs to a financial security that had been ebbing steadily away. By showing what one highly gifted player could do, he made the clubs hungry to sign more from overseas, and over the years many, many up-and-coming players were able to find employment in league cricket, develop their game, draw the crowds and give pleasure to thousands – and still do, in substantial numbers, earning in a few months what would take them years at home. Constantine's achievement was to set the pace, in James' words, 'to create the strategy, the style, the temper and the tone of league cricket'. Fate sent along the right man at the right time, and he fulfilled his destiny.

There was more to his destiny than that, though, for he had a vital role to play off the field. He and his wife were virtually the only coloured people in Nelson, and at first there was a degree of prejudice against them. That disappeared not just because of deeds on the field, but because the people came to respect them and like them for their friendliness and modesty, their quiet dignity and humour, their patience and their devout Catholicism. They made many friends and after two or three years were accepted by all, so much so that when they eventually left just about the whole town begged them to stay; and years later in 1963 he was made a Freeman of the Borough of Nelson. In terms of paving the way for future coloured professionals this relationship was crucial.

His acceptance also meant that he was able to work toward what he saw as the most important goal of all, the political independence of the West Indies. James joined him in Nelson and together they taught people about life in the Caribbean, giving lectures, writing pamphlets and making broadcasts to argue that people there were westernized and quite capable of governing themselves. Few Lancashire folk knew much about the West Indies, but the interest they aroused was enormous and their audience became more and more a national one. It was a potent combination, Constantine the famous sportsman who was also a highly intelligent man, and James the intellectual who could write and speak supremely well, both of them passionate about their cause. James published *The Case for West Indian Self-Government*, and steadily the movement grew. It took decades to achieve but, as for a long time they were the only campaigners in Britain, their activities were to do much for their fellow-countrymen.

On the outbreak of war, Constantine chose to stay in England and play his part. From 1942 to 1947 he was a Welfare Officer in the Ministry of Labour and National Service, responsible in particular for West Indian workers, and was awarded the MBE for his efforts. He also received an illuminated scroll from the men he worked with which gave him enormous pleasure. His main ambition, though, was to become a lawyer and finally, in 1954, after something of a struggle as he had been away from studying for so long, he passed his Bar Finals and was called to the Middle Temple. Not long afterwards he returned to Trinidad as he wanted to work among his people, was elected to the first Legislature and became Minister of Works and Transport. In 1961 he decided not to stand for re-election, but was then appointed High Commissioner for Trinidad and Tobago in London, and was knighted. His public service continued: he became a member of the Race Relations Board, a member of the Sports Council, Rector of St Andrews University and a governor of the BBC. In 1969 he was made a life peer, becoming Baron Constantine of Maraval in Trinidad and Tobago and of Nelson in the County Palatine of Lancaster. Two years later he died, and Trinidad posthumously awarded him the country's highest honour, the Trinity Cross.

Achievement in cricket tends to be measured principally in terms of success in the Test arena, and by this yardstick Learie Constantine was fairly ordinary. Nothing could demonstrate more clearly the limitations of the yardstick.

| 1928 | Lord's | E 401; | WI 177, 166 | E inns 58 runs |
| | Old Trafford | WI 206, 115; | E 351 | E inns 30 runs |
| | Oval | WI 238, 129; | E 438 | E inns 71 runs |

**1928 Test Series**

**England**

| Batting | Innings | NO | HS | Runs | Average |
|---|---|---|---|---|---|
| J.B. Hobbs | 2 | 0 | 159 | 212 | 106.00 |
| G.E. Tyldesley | 3 | 0 | 122 | 198 | 66.00 |
| H. Sutcliffe | 3 | 0 | 63 | 165 | 55.00 |
| D.R. Jardine | 2 | 0 | 83 | 105 | 52.50 |
| W.R. Hammond | 3 | 0 | 63 | 111 | 37.00 |

| Bowling | Overs | M | Runs | W | Average |
|---|---|---|---|---|---|
| A.P. Freeman | 140 | 50 | 302 | 22 | 13.72 |
| V.W.C. Jupp | 56 | 18 | 142 | 9 | 15.77 |
| J.C. White | 27.3 | 10 | 53 | 3 | 17.66 |
| M.W. Tate | 127 | 43 | 246 | 13 | 18.92 |
| H. Larwood | 50 | 13 | 114 | 6 | 19.00 |

**West Indies**

| Batting | Innings | NO | HS | Runs | Average |
|---|---|---|---|---|---|
| F.R. Martin | 6 | 0 | 44 | 175 | 29.16 |
| O.C. Scott | 4 | 1 | 35 | 74 | 24.66 |
| C.A. Roach | 6 | 0 | 53 | 131 | 21.83 |
| C.R. Browne | 4 | 0 | 44 | 84 | 21.00 |
| G. Challenor | 6 | 0 | 46 | 101 | 16.83 |

| Bowling | Overs | M | Runs | W | Average |
|---|---|---|---|---|---|
| H.C. Griffith | 79.5 | 20 | 250 | 11 | 22.72 |
| G.N. Francis | 75 | 12 | 252 | 6 | 42.00 |
| O.C. Scott | 23.2 | 1 | 103 | 2 | 51.50 |
| L.N. Constantine | 71.4 | 19 | 262 | 5 | 52.40 |
| J.A. Small | 30 | 3 | 106 | 2 | 53.00 |

Wicket-keepers: H. Smith (E) 1 dismissal   H. Elliott (E) 2 dismissals   G. Duckworth (E) 2 dismissals   R.K. Nunes (WI) 1 dismissal

# 4

# The Ball Begins to Roll

The winter of 1929–30 saw two England teams in action in different parts of the globe, only the second time this had happened. While one went to the Caribbean, the other initiated New Zealand into the joys of Test cricket, and though there were some famous names on both tours neither one bore much resemblance to a team for Australia. Eighteen months earlier, the West Indians had failed to convince anyone that they were ready to do Test battle, and the party chosen by the England selectors reflected this. Hendren and Sandham were prime batsmen but were around forty, George Gunn and Rhodes were fifty and fifty-two, while Calthorpe, who was again captain, had no Test experience. At the other end of the scale, Ames and Voce were beginning their Test careers, while the likes of Stevens, Haig and Astill were all powerful performers. MCC must have rated the party quite strong enough to see off the Test infants.

As usual, the tour began in Barbados, but not as usual the tourists did not lose. Both matches were drawn, with MCC making over 500 in each. The first was notable for being Challenor's last game for the colony (he scored 51), for a century by a 17-year-old named Derek Sealy, and for an unbeaten double century by Hendren that set him off on an orgy of run-making that would see him average over 100 for both first-class and Test matches. The first Test match in the Caribbean then began at the Kensington Oval, Bridgetown on 11 January 1930, one day after the first in New Zealand. Interestingly, the New Zealand games were of three days while the West Indian ones were of five, although the hours of play were shorter in the Caribbean. With New Zealand losing in two days, it was soon clear which set of colonial cousins was the stronger.

Yet if New Zealand did not have the class players that West Indies did, at least they did not have the problem of internal politics and internal jealousies that beset West Indian cricket for decades. The WICBC was still finding its feet and not yet responsible for Test selection, which was done through each local authority; the result was that a different captain was appointed for each Test, the man in question coming, of course, from where the Test was played. In Barbados it was Teddy Hoad, in Trinidad

Nelson Betancourt, in British Guiana Maurice Fernandes and in Jamaica Karl Nunes; for the first three it was their only game in charge, for Betancourt, indeed, his only Test. The selection policy, and the fact that several men had to miss games because they could not get time off work, meant that twenty-eight players appeared in the four Tests. Even in the depths of 1988 England did not match that.

Hoad won the toss and batted on a beautiful pitch, and he and Roach put on 90 for the first wicket, which was 85 more than New Zealand had managed for theirs the day before. Roach went on to become the first West Indian Test century-maker with 122 (it was also his first in first-class cricket), de Caires made 80, and Derek Sealy, at 17 years 122 days the youngest ever Test player at the time, contributed a very composed 58; 369 all out. England's innings was opened by Gunn and Sandham, Gunn's last Test appearance having come in the 1911–12 series in Australia, 17 years and 316 days before – not only the record interval between Test appearances, but over six months before Sealy was born. Sandham notched up 152, Hendren got 80 and several others got thirties and forties, taking England to 467 all out. On such a good pitch there was little chance of any collapse, and the score passed 300 before the third wicket went down. Roach and de Caires made seventies, but the main honours went to a young man named George Headley who made a glorious 176. He was 20 years 230 days old, and no West Indian has since scored a century at a younger age. The rest of the wickets fell quite rapidly for 384 all out, Stevens taking ten in the match, but by then England had only 165 minutes to score 287 runs and made no attempt at it, finishing on 167 for 3.

In Trinidad, the two games against the colony finished one apiece. In the Test Calthorpe won the toss, only to see three wickets go down for twelve before Hendren, supported by O'Connor and Ames, pulled the score round to 208 all out. It was this innings that gave the game one of its now standard pieces of terminology. Ellis Achong was a Trinidadian of Chinese descent, a left-arm wrist-spinner. When Hendren had made 77 he failed to pick Achong's 'wrong 'un' and was bowled; returning to the dressing-room he slumped down on his seat and exclaimed, 'Bowled by a bloody Chinaman!' The left-arm wrist-spinner's ball which turns in from the off now had a name which it has never lost. When West Indies batted it seemed for some time that they would not do much better, with only 58 from Hunte providing much substance. Then along came Constantine with a quick fifty, put on 71 for the eighth wicket with Betancourt, and gave his team a lead by helping them to 354. Three England wickets then went down for 52 before Hendren and Ames put together the decisive

*Patsy Hendren – four
double centuries on the
1929–39 tour.*

*Les Ames, the wicket-
keeper who made three
Test centuries against West
Indies.*

partnership of 237, helped by an injury to Achong; Ames became the first wicket-keeper to score a century for England, and when Calthorpe declared on 425 for 8, Hendren was unbeaten on 205. The rest of the game belonged mainly to Voce. After his 199 runs in the first Test, Roach recorded a pair and, though most of his team-mates got a few runs, none got very many as Voce finished with 7 for 70. 212 all out left England winners by 167 runs.

MCC prepared for the third Test in Georgetown with two innings victories over British Guiana, but then found their form evaporating in the Test. When West Indies batted first, a string of catches went down to allow Roach and Hunte to make 144 for the first wicket, and after Headley joined Roach the score had risen to 336 before they took the second. Headley finished on 114 and Roach became their first double centurion with 209, the total eventually climbing to 471. England's response was to collapse. Hendren and Ames put on 70 for the fourth wicket, but with everyone else failing they were all out for 145. Since this had occupied barely more than sixty overs, the bowlers could hardly have been exhausted, yet Fernandes chose to bat again. This gave Headley, with 112, the opportunity to become the first West Indian to score a century in each innings of a Test, and although the innings began slowly Browne later threw the bat for 70 not out and they were all out for 290. Setting out to save the game, Sandham went immediately; Gunn and Wyatt defended for a while, but it was the middle order that failed, only Hendren standing firm for 123. With eight wickets down, the game seemed to be in the home team's grasp, only for Calthorpe to make a spirited 49 not out and almost save the day. In the end, the last wicket fell with just a quarter of an hour left, Hendren being given out to a dubious lbw decision. Constantine took 5 for 85 as England's total of 327 gave West Indies their first victory by the crushing margin of 289 runs. The celebrations were in the best Caribbean tradition.

Clifford Roach's batting was rated second only to George Headley's at the time, yet he is now forgotten outside the Caribbean. Usually an opener, he was a powerful stroke-maker all round the wicket in the best West Indian tradition, although he failed rather too often for an opening batsman: twice in his sixteen Tests – the first sixteen West Indies played – he recorded a pair. When the runs came, though, he was a joy to watch, and 437 of them came in this series at an average of 58. This was certainly his peak, for his full Test record is a rather more modest 952 at 30, with two hundreds, but contributing a double century to your country's first Test win is not something that many people can boast about. A Trinidadian, he was famed as being almost as good a cover fielder as Constantine, so that playing against the two of them together must have made life frustrating for batsmen who favoured the off side. He toured England in 1928 and 1933 and had a similar record each time, 1,200 odd runs at around 26, one achievement on the second tour being 180 against Surrey at more than a run a minute, with a century before lunch on the first day. Not too many people can boast about doing that, either.

With the series level going into the final match, it was decided that that game would be played to a finish, and the Jamaican ground staff were instructed to prepare a pitch that would last. They came up with one that would have suited Methusaleh. Calthorpe won the toss and cannot have debated long about what to do, especially as Constantine and Francis were missing. England began with 173 for the first wicket from Sandham and Gunn, with 85 from the latter; 58 from Wyatt took it to 321 when the second wicket fell; 61 from Hendren meant 418 when the third went down. This was small beer, though, as Ames joined Sandham and they put on another 249 for the fourth, with Ames making 149. O'Connor made 51, Haig 28, Astill 39 and even Voce at number eleven chipped in 20. Sandham's contribution to all this, in what was to be his final Test, was 325, the first ever Test triple century; it took him ten hours and included a seven, a five and twenty-seven fours. The total of 849 was at the time the highest ever Test innings.

West Indies made a reasonable start, only for the wickets to slip away. No one could improve upon Nunes's 66, and when the last wicket fell at 286 England had a lead of 563. And then came one of the most remarkable decisions in cricket history: despite warnings that the weather, which had been glorious all through the tour, was about to break, Calthorpe chose not to enforce the follow-on. He batted again and declared only on the sixth morning when nine wickets had fallen for 272, leaving West Indies either to score 816 or to survive until the rain came. Calthorpe's decision meant that 'Tommy' Scott, having taken 5 for 266 in the first innings, finished the match with 9 for 374, the most runs ever conceded in a Test – a record he still holds. For Headley the record was rather more attractive, as he became the only man to score four Test centuries before the age of 21 and the youngest to score a Test double century. With Nunes making 92, Headley battled for six and a half hours for 223, and by the time he was out the rain clouds were gathering over the Blue Mountains. When the rain came, West Indies were on 408 for 5, and after two days of watching it fall England had to get their ship home to be in time for the start of the new season.

At seven days it was the longest Test thus far played and had produced the highest aggregate, 1,815 runs. It was also Wilfred Rhodes's last Test, and he set two records which will surely remain for ever: his Test career spanned 31 years 315 days, and at 52 years 165 days he is the oldest Test player. His match bowling figures make interesting reading for a 52 year old: 44.5 overs, 25 maidens, 39 runs, 2 wickets. To say 'they don't make 'em like that any more' hardly begins to state the case. Fortunately, they do not often make decisions like Calthorpe's any more, either.

George Headley was, arguably, the most completely natural genius of all the great batsmen, whose only tuition had been to spend many hours watching top batsmen in action; when Ernest Tyldesley, for instance, went to Jamaica with Lionel Tennyson's team early in 1927, Headley was seventeen and crazy about cricket, and he acknowledged that he learned a great deal just by watching Tyldesley amass his runs. With a perfectly sound defence when it was needed, he would attack the bowling at any opportunity, often, especially in his young days, going down the pitch to hit the bowler back over his head. Like other top players of his era, he could never understand how or why the game should have become so defensive by the 1960s, with batsmen apparently willing to surrender the initiative and then feeling pleased at scoring twenty-five an hour. Perhaps those batsmen would reply that we cannot all be geniuses, and have to make do with performing as well as we can.

He was essentially a back-foot player, maybe the most accomplished back-foot player ever, with perfect balance, speed of footwork that was quite dazzling, and always so much time that often the ball would be played at the latest possible moment. All the strokes were there, of course, the driving being especially fearsome and the cutting especially glorious. At first he had a preference for the offside and gained a reputation for being almost invincible there. So much so that when he went on the first West Indian tour of Australia in 1930–1 the bowlers soon realized that their only chance of getting him was to concentrate on the leg stump, and for a few matches his scores declined badly. Like all the best geniuses he won through, working hard and rapidly turning himself into as fine an on-side player as off-side. The Australians were mightily impressed, Clarrie Grimmett rating him as good an on-side player as any he had bowled to. It was the Australians who called him the black Bradman; the West Indians, unoriginally but justifiably, responded by calling Bradman the white Headley. There were just nine months between them, in fact, with Headley the junior, and they were both of similar compact build. In the Test averages Headley, on 60.83, ranks behind only Bradman and Pollock, but there is no doubt that his figure would have been higher had he not had to carry his team's batting to such a large extent for most of his career. Bradman had the luxury of knowing that if he failed there were the likes of Woodfull, Ponsford, McCabe, Brown and Kippax to score a hundred or two, and if Headley had enjoyed such a cushion he must have done even better than he did. He was also ill served by being brought back for one last Test in 1953–4 when he was way past it, and his average suffered accordingly.

That first Test series produced 703 runs at almost 88, and by the end of his career he had played in 22 games and scored 2,190 runs, with ten hundreds. His career average is a remarkable 69.86, behind only Bradman and Merchant, with 9,921 runs including 33 centuries. In no Test series did he fail, averaging 55, 97 and 66 in his pre-war rubbers against England and 37 in Australia for a team that was quite outclassed. His highest score was 270 not out on his home pitch in Kingston in 1934–5, a performance that won the deciding match for his team to give them their first series victory. In 1939, he became the first batsman to score a century in each innings of a Lord's Test. After the war he played in three Tests but, hampered by injury and the passing years, failed in all of them. In the first of these, though, against England at Barbados in 1947–8, he was the first black man to captain West Indies, only to have to withdraw from the rest of the series with back problems.

The story of his entry to first-class cricket sounds as though it were written by Thomas Hardy in a good mood. He was born in Panama in 1909 of Jamaican parents, and because the language of Panama is Spanish and his parents wanted him to learn English he was sent to Jamaica as a ten year old. He fell in love with cricket, played it at any opportunity, and as he grew older the authorities began to take notice of him. It was decided, though, that he would go to the USA to study dentistry, and actually had his ticket to do so, when there was a delay in receiving his passport. While awaiting the passport early in 1928, Lionel Tennyson's team arrived for their second visit in two years and Headley was given a game by the Jamaicans. He made 71, was played in the second match and made 211. He did not need much persuading to stay in Jamaica and play cricket, and, although Jamaica was still isolated from the other islands, from this time on they began to exchange visits more readily. The fact that the other islands wanted to see Headley may just have had something to do with that.

If he were not already a complete batsman when he went to England in 1933, there remained just one more hurdle to conquer: batting well on wet wickets. It has usually been said that if Bradman had any sort of failing it was an uncertainty on wet wickets, but Headley soon proved himself quite at home on them. C.L.R. James wrote that he simply loved to bat on them since he felt the batsman was compelled to attack: 'If the bowler pitched up, you had to drive; if he pitched short, you had to hook.' It sounds so simple; how could so many people have had such trouble? It must be nice to be a genius. For all his aggressive stroke-play, though, Headley was never one to get excited and allow himself to be carried away; bowlers were put to the sword calmly and unflappably, in the finest tradition of chivalry.

Headley's achievement, apart from carrying his country's batting for a decade, was to continue the tradition of West Indian stroke-playing batsmanship just as Challenor was ending his career and to take it to heights hitherto unknown. It was in the 1930s that Test cricket developed into a win-at-all-costs business with the accent on defence, and Headley's attacking play enlivened it greatly, taking it back to the best days of the Golden Age. By adding modern technique, as learned from watching Ernest Tyldesley and others, to his natural Caribbean exuberance and brilliance and assurance, he became a source of inspiration to youngsters as he perpetuated the stroke-playing tradition which others, such as the three Ws, would take ever onward. West Indies have produced a steady line of absolutely top-class batsmen culminating at present in the mighty Viv Richards, but there will be no shortage of informed followers who have watched them all and will be only too eager to insist that none has approached Headley for all-round batting quality. It is difficult to think of a greater accolade than that.

\*

1933 had a rather uncomfortable resemblance to 1928 for the West Indians. The sun shone beautifully to give conditions that should have suited them, but somehow, with the exception of Headley and Martindale and two or three other reasonable performances, they failed badly. Of thirty first-class matches they won only five and lost nine, including two of the three Tests by an innings. They were unlucky to lose 'Freddie' Martin after only six games when he trod on a ball and had to miss the rest of the tour, for he had begun well with both bat and ball, and this meant that they now had only one spinner, Achong, in the party. Martindale apart, the bowlers had a thin time of it, while the batsmen had great trouble with the top English spinners as they had never encountered anyone of such class before. Seven of them managed over 1,000 runs for the tour but, apart from Headley, who made 2,320 runs at 66 and was duly named as one of *Wisden*'s cricketers of the year, and Ben Sealey, who averaged just under 40, the rest barely scored at 30 an innings. In a fine summer it was simply not good enough. They had hoped that Constantine would be released by Nelson to play in several games but in the event he appeared in just five, one of them the Old Trafford Test.

Since the countries had last met, West Indies had played a series in Australia and lost it 4–1. England, by contrast, were fresh from playing a series in Australia which they won 4-1. Whether they would have done so had they not employed some rather questionable tactics we shall never know, but Douglas Jardine's fast leg-theory or 'bodyline' attack undoubtedly made him the most unpopular man ever to visit Australia. As he was still in charge of England for the first two Tests, the Australians must have been delighted to hear that the West Indians dished out the same medicine to him – and less delighted when told that he coped with it admirably. For he was a very fine batsman, as a Test average of 48 shows; surprisingly, in twenty-two games he scored just one century, and the lovely irony of that was that it was the only time he came up against an attack bowling 'bodyline'.

His leadership seemed to vary between the shrewd and imaginative and the leaden and stolid, depending partly on his mood and partly on the opinion of the observer. As a captain he inspired total loyalty in some and intense dislike in others, for he pursued victory with a single-mindedness which even today many would find disturbing. His reputation for unyieldingness and joylessness can scarcely have endeared him to the West Indians, whose experience of England captains thus far had been of Chapman and Calthorpe, both as far from Jardine in their approach to cricket as humanly possible.

If Jardine has gone down as not always playing the game in the best sporting traditions, the reverse is true of his opposite number. George or 'Jackie' Grant from Trinidad was a Cambridge blue who was a very capable middle-order batsman and an outstanding gully fielder. He led West Indies in all twelve of his Tests, beginning in Australia and ending with a splendid finale in Kingston in 1934–5. If his overall record of 413 runs at under 26 is ordinary, he still had some good days, beginning with over 120 runs in his first Test without being out. After this 1933 tour, *Wisden* praised him for his enthusiasm, the astute way he handled his bowling and placed his fields, and for the fine example he set by his close fielding and plucky batting, although he did little in the Tests. 'No matter how gloomy the outlook, he never allowed it to depress his spirit. . . .

Above all, Grant himself played the game, and insisted on those under him doing so, in the most sporting spirit.' Thus spake *Wisden*, and if it sounds old-fashioned now, then perhaps the loss lies with the modern world.

After several minor games the opening first-class match was a heavy defeat by Northants. They did manage a couple of wins and then encountered a fairly strong MCC team at Lord's. This was just about the high spot of the tour. West Indies batted first and were mainly indebted to Headley, with 129, for the score reaching 309. Martindale and Constantine sent back half the home team for 70 before Chapman and Valentine put together some runs, and after Chapman fell for 97 the total struggled to 246. Seeking to press home the advantage, most of the West Indians then got a few, with Constantine notching 51 at two a minute, and the total of 268 left MCC to get 332 to win. They never looked like getting anywhere near it as only Hendren reached 50 and seven of them did not get past single figures. 179 all out gave West Indies a win by 152 runs, and when they followed that by beating Hampshire they had won four matches on the trot. It proved to be a case of peaking early and then going off the boil.

**MCC v. West Indies**
*Lords 20, 22, 23 May 1933*

**West Indies**

| | | | | |
|---|---|---|---|---|
| E.L.G Hoad | b. Allom | 5 | c. Valentine b. Brown | 19 |
| C.A. Roach | b. Bowes | 41 | lbw. b. Bowes | 14 |
| G.A. Headley | c. Franklin b. Allom | 129 | c. Franklin b. Allom | 20 |
| C. de L. Inniss | b. Allom | 42 | b. White | 1 |
| G.C. Grant | b. Bowes | 0 | c. Hulme b. Brown | 30 |
| O.C. Da Costa | b. Allom | 13 | b. White | 21 |
| L.N. Constantine | c. Hendren b. Brown | 11 | b. Bowes | 51 |
| I. Barrow | b. Bowes | 11 | c. Franklin b. Bowes | 27 |
| C.A. Merry | lbw. b. Allom | 5 | c. Allom b. White | 47 |
| E.A. Martindale | b. Bowes | 19 | c. Brown b. White | 11 |
| E.E. Achong | not out | 4 | not out | 0 |
| Extras | b. 12, l.b. 10, w. 7 | 29 | b. 22, l.b. 3, w. 2 | 27 |
| **Total** | | 309 | | 268 |

| Bowling | O | M | R | W | O | M | R | W |
|---|---|---|---|---|---|---|---|---|
| Bowes | 26.2 | 6 | 72 | 5 | 25 | 7 | 69 | 3 |
| Allom | 23 | 0 | 85 | 5 | 20 | 3 | 56 | 1 |
| White | 29 | 12 | 45 | 0 | 29.1 | 9 | 77 | 4 |
| Brown | 14 | 3 | 57 | 1 | 11 | 2 | 39 | 2 |
| Hearne | 10 | 1 | 21 | 0 | | | | |

MCC

| | | | | | |
|---|---|---|---|---|---|
| J.W. Hearne | c. Barrow b. Constantine | 12 | c. Merry b. Martindale | 9 |
| J. Hulme | c. Barrow b. Constantine | 14 | c. Roach b. Achong | 30 |
| W.B. Franklin | b. Martindale | 5 | c. Barrow b. Da Costa | 1 |
| E.H. Hendren | c. Roach b. Constantine | 6 | b. Achong | 61 |
| D.R. Jardine | c. Roach b. Constantine | 7 | c. Barrow b Da Costa | 44 |
| B.H. Valentine | lbw. b. Headley | 60 | c. Barrow b. Achong | 3 |
| A.P.F. Chapman | c. Headley b. Constantine | 97 | c. sub b. Achong | 9 |
| F.R. Brown | c. Da Costa b. Martindale | 18 | c. Martindale b. Da Costa | 0 |
| J.C. White | c. Da Costa b. Martindale | 10 | c. Grant b. Achong | 0 |
| M.J.C. Allom | b. Martindale | 2 | not out | 13 |
| W.E. Bowes | not out | 0 | run out | 0 |
| Extras | b. 6, l.b. 8, n.b. 1 | 15 | b. 3, l.b. 6 | 9 |
| Total | | 246 | | 179 |

| Bowling | O | M | R | W | O | M | R | W |
|---|---|---|---|---|---|---|---|---|
| Martindale | 20.5 | 3 | 70 | 5 | 10 | 2 | 26 | 1 |
| Constantine | 22 | 2 | 88 | 4 | 10 | 3 | 27 | 0 |
| Merry | 3 | 0 | 11 | 0 | 7 | 0 | 25 | 0 |
| Da Costa | 8 | 0 | 32 | 0 | 18.3 | 3 | 38 | 3 |
| Achong | 4 | 0 | 18 | 0 | 22 | 6 | 49 | 5 |
| Grant | | | | | 1 | 0 | 2 | 0 |
| Hoad | | | | | 1 | 0 | 3 | 0 |

West Indies won by 152 runs

For the first Test at Lord's, Nelson refused to release Constantine and so Francis, playing for Radcliffe, was drafted in for one more Test, and probably wished he had not been. Most of the first day was lost to rain, and on the second England seemed to be struggling at 194 for 7, with only a debut fifty from Walters of any substance. It was Ames who, as usual, came to the rescue with 83, taking the total to 295. In the last session, with Headley troubled by an ankle injury, West Indies collapsed to 51 for 6; next morning they were all out for 97, Robins taking 6 for 32. Following on, Roach went first ball to complete a pair and only Headley, Hoad ('without disclosing many scoring strokes', said the oracle) and Grant put up much resistance. By four o'clock it was all over, a total of 172 giving England a win by an innings and 27 runs.

At Old Trafford, West Indies finally got their batting together in a Test in England. Headley, naturally, was the chief architect with a fine 169, and his principal assistant was the wicket-keeper, Ivan Barrow, with 105, as they put on 200 for the second wicket. Batting into the second morning they were all out for 375; and when England batted, Martindale and Constantine bowled fast leg-theory, the first time an English Test crowd had been treated to this form of entertainment. 'Most of those who were watching it for the first time,' said *Wisden*, 'must have come to the conclusion that, while strictly within the law, it was not nice.' Hammond had his chin cut open before succumbing to the trap, but this was Jardine's finest hour. The sixth wicket fell at 234, but he and Robins put on 140 in two hours, with 127 to the captain, before the last three wickets went at the same score, and, with Macaulay unable to bat, England finished just one run behind West Indies. When the tourists batted again, Clark had to bowl bodyline, of course, but Roach made 64 to stave off any quick collapse. As wickets began to tumble there was an outside chance of an England victory, but Constantine hammered a quick sixty and the match was drawn. James Langridge, on debut, took 7 for 56 as West Indies were all out for 225, to complete his season's double with a week of July still left.

West Indies recorded their other first-class win shortly before the third Test at the Oval, but it scarcely inspired them. They did reduce England to 68 for 4 at one stage, but with a century from Bakewell and then the lower middle order doing well – not surprisingly, with Charlie Barnett at number eight – the score reached 312. The West Indian bowling and fielding had been capable enough, but it was the batsmen who now let them down; Sealey's 29 was the highest score by some way, and although the conditions were gloomy a total of 100 was poor stuff. Following on, Roach produced a quick fifty but most of the others just got into double figures then got out, as C.S. 'Father' Marriott took the second-best Test debut figures for England of 11 for 96 with his leg-breaks and googlies. Being almost 38 at the time, it proved his only Test but, by helping to dismiss West Indies for 195, he saw his team to victory by an innings and 17 runs. The last two wickets fell on the third morning, just a few minutes before the heavens opened.

For *Wisden*, West Indies 'did not convey the impression of being fitted temperamentally for matches of such an important nature'. Yet when they followed on here Roach was praised for scoring the bulk of a first-wicket stand of 77 in just forty minutes, while 'the rest of the cricket was rather dull, nearly everyone playing a sedate game'. Nowadays anyone playing a 'sedate game' would be praised for trying to hold out and save the match, and anyone throwing the bat instead of defending would be criticized. It shows how expectations concerning Test cricket have changed.

So for another tour too many players had failed to produce their home form in unfamiliar conditions, and the result was disappointment. Without Headley the batting would have been a disaster and the same was true of the bowling without Martindale. Manny Martindale played in only ten Tests but he was one of the finest players of these early years, just 5 feet 8½ inches (1.7 metres) but a fast bowler of enormous pace. He had only recently established himself with Barbados, but with 103 wickets at just

*By the 1930s 'Manny' Martindale already had a tradition of West Indian fast bowling to maintain, and did so fearsomely.*

under 21 for the tour – including three eight-wicket hauls in an innings – English batsmen were not sorry to see him boarding the boat at the end. One irony relating to his bodyline bowling at Manchester was that he was similar in both physique and style to Harold Larwood, the number one practitioner of the art form, with a long run culminating in a splendid action that saw the ball delivered with great precision and great speed. He had a particularly dangerous inswinger that got him many wickets. In these three Tests he had fourteen wickets at just under 18 each, and then reached his peak in the next series when he took nineteen wickets at only 12 apiece, forming with Constantine and Hylton a trio that was rated by some as the best in the world for a short time. By the 1939 tour he was past his best and had a rough time of it, ending his Test career with 37 wickets at 21 each. He followed Constantine to Lancashire where he played for Burnley for several years, later returning to Barbados to be a coach. If he is not quite up with Headley and Constantine in the ranks of the gods, he has an honoured position in the top echelon of the mortals.

*

At the end of 1934, MCC returned to the Caribbean with a weak team that showed plainly what they thought of the state of West Indian cricket. Their arrogance was duly rewarded. It was a considerably different team from the one that had taken on Australia the previous summer, the bowling being appreciably weaker. When the batsmen largely failed as well, with none averaging thirty in the Tests, the proverbial writing was on the wall. The captain was Bob Wyatt, and he came in for criticism especially in the second Test. Fate seemed to deal rather unkindly with Wyatt, for although he was a very fine batsman who scored over 39,000 runs at an average of 40, with no less than 85 centuries, his Test average was under 32 and his record as England captain was a poor one, with three wins and five defeats in sixteen games in charge. He also had an unfortunate habit of losing the Ashes in the last game of a series. He led Warwickshire for much of the 1930s and Worcestershire for a few years after the war, and was a great believer in analysing the opposition's strengths and weaknesses and working out a masterplan to beat them, usually giving bowlers plenty of instructions. Yet somehow he seemed to lack that certain something that makes for a successful captain; the luck rarely seemed to go with him and he was also very injury prone, but there is always the feeling with Wyatt that a man who was such a good player – he was a more than useful medium-pace swing bowler as well, good enough to take over 900 wickets – and who studied the game so closely, should have had a better record as captain than he did.

After a very rough sea crossing they arrived in anything but shipshape condition, and soon found themselves up against the might of Barbados. They managed two draws, with Hammond scoring a massive double century in the second, thereby making over a third of his runs for the tour in one innings. Come the first Test and they found that West Indies had learned from their previous mistakes and become altogether more unified; Jackie Grant had been appointed captain for the series, and they were determined to keep as settled a team as possible. In the event, Grant and six others played in all four Tests and two more played in three. They were learning.

The Barbados Test proved to be one of the oddest ever played. On a rain-affected wicket, Wyatt won the toss and put West Indies in and Farnes took four quick wickets. Only Headley could make anything of the pitch and notched up 44 before he was run out. With the spinners Hollies and Paine going through the rest, West Indies were all out for 102, only for the England innings to go the same way, with Hammond playing Headley's role for 43. When they were 81 for 7 Wyatt declared in the hope that West Indies would have the worst of the pitch and that it would later improve. Grant reversed his batting order and promptly lost three wickets for four runs, but they eventually struggled to 51 for 6 – Big Jim Smith had 5 for 16 – before Grant declared, setting England a target of 73 on a pitch drying under a bright sun and strong breeze. Wyatt duly reversed *his* batting order, but six wickets had gone down for 48 – 5 for 22 to Martindale – before he and Hammond came together. Thereafter it was Hammond's match, and he finished it with a six off Martindale for a four-wicket win.

In Trinidad Wyatt again won the toss and chose to field, and this time it backfired. The wicket proved more placid than anticipated, and with Farnes out injured the English attack was fairly ordinary. Derek Sealy made 92 and then Constantine hammered 90, taking the score to 302 all out. When England batted they were reduced to 23 for 5 before the rot was stopped by Hendren and Iddon and 168 was reached before the seventh wicket fell. Then came Errol Holmes' big moment, with 85 not out before the innings closed at 258. West Indies' second innings proved surprisingly quiet, with Headley making a subdued 93, and only Constantine and Rolph Grant, the captain's brother, throwing the bat. Grant declared at 280 for 6 at lunchtime on the fourth and final day, only for Wyatt to reverse his batting order once again. He was probably the only person who understood why, but his theory was along the lines of 'England can't win, but West Indies might if they dismiss the top batsmen with the new ball'. In the event they dismissed everyone, although it is worth noting that Constantine was warned by the umpire for overdoing the short stuff. Leyland and Holmes came together as the last pair and defended for a while, only for Constantine to have Leyland lbw with the penultimate ball of the last over. It may have been that the umpire was a little over-zealous in his decision, for as he left the wicket Leyland is supposed to have said to Grant, 'And you a Cambridge man'. All out 107 gave West Indies a win by 217 runs, and Wyatt was not the most popular man back in England.

Each of the four Tests was preceded by two games against the colony team, and in British Guiana they recorded their only win, all the others being drawn. After the excitement of the first two Tests, the Georgetown game was an uninspiring affair. Wyatt actually chose to bat this time, but apart from Smith, who hit 25 in ten minutes, everyone was subdued and the score meandered to 226 all out as the lower order drifted away. West Indies were no better, only Headley showing much life over his fifty. They had plenty of trouble with Hollies, and he finished with 7 for 50 in their

*Bob Wyatt's captaincy on the 1934–5 tour came in for criticism, and a broken jaw didn't make life any easier for him.*

total of 184 as the lower order likewise lost their way. When England batted again they lost four wickets for 60 but Wyatt and Hendren took them to 160 for 6 before Wyatt declared, setting West Indies 203 to win in under two hours. It was 104 for 5 at the close as the game petered out.

The Jamaica Test proved a very different business. Grant at last won the toss and then watched contentedly as Headley showed his greatness. With Sealy he put on 202 for the third wicket and with Rolph Grant 147 for the seventh; at the declaration they were 535 for 7, and Headley was unbeaten on 270, scored in only a little over eight hours and containing just one chance. There cannot have been many innings that *Wisden* has described as 'truly wonderful', and it is pleasant to let the imagination conjure up a picture of this dazzling little batsman stroking the ball all over the field. English woes continued when they batted; Wyatt had his jaw fractured by a ball from Martindale when he had scored only one, and then four wickets fell for 26. Ames led a recovery with a fine century, helped first by

Hendren and then Iddon, but they were all out for 271. When England followed on they were soon losing wickets, but West Indies then lost their captain as he sprained an ankle and had to go off. Somewhat surprisingly, the captaincy was handed to Constantine – he was certainly the senior player, but his skin was the wrong colour to be able to lead a national cricket team – and he celebrated by getting Ames' wicket just as he was beginning to dig in. The rest crumbled away and soon after lunch on the last day they were all out for 103, leaving West Indies winners by the emphatic margin of an innings and 161 runs and so notching up their first series victory. The Jamaican crowd, unaccustomed to success, made the most of it. Jackie Grant's captaincy came in for much praise; he was not yet 28 and seemed to have a good cricketing future ahead, but he chose instead to do missionary work in Africa. He stayed there for forty years.

| 1929–30 | Bridgetown | WI 369, 384; | E 467, 167–3 | Drawn |
| | Port-of-Spain | E 208, 425–8d; | WI 254, 212 | E 167 runs |
| | Georgetown | WI 471, 290; | E 145, 327 | WI 289 runs |
| | Kingston | E 849, 272–9d; | WI 286, 408–5 | Drawn |
| 1933 | Lord's | E 296; | WI 97, 172 | E inns 27 runs |
| | Old Trafford | WI 375, 225; | E 374 | Drawn |
| | Oval | E 312; | WI 100, 195 | E inns 17 runs |
| 1934–5 | Bridgetown | WI 102, 51–6d; | E 81–7d, 75–6 | E 4 wkts |
| | Port-of-Spain | WI 302, 280–6d; | E 258, 107 | WI 217 runs |
| | Georgetown | E 226, 160–6d; | WI 184, 104–5 | Drawn |
| | Kingston | WI 535–7d; | E 271, 103 | WI inns 161 runs |

**1929–30 Test Series**

**England**

| Batting | Innings | NO | HS | Runs | Average |
|---|---|---|---|---|---|
| E.H. Hendren | 8 | 2 | 205* | 693 | 115.50 |
| A Sandham | 8 | 0 | 325 | 592 | 74.00 |
| L.E.G. Ames | 8 | 1 | 149 | 417 | 59.57 |
| G. Gunn | 8 | 0 | 85 | 276 | 34.50 |
| J. O'Connor | 5 | 0 | 51 | 142 | 28.40 |

| Bowling | Overs | M | Runs | W | Average |
|---|---|---|---|---|---|
| L.F. Townsend | 23.3 | 8 | 73 | 4 | 18.25 |
| G.T.S. Stevens | 68.4 | 9 | 241 | 11 | 21.91 |
| R.E.S. Wyatt | 37.3 | 7 | 125 | 4 | 31.25 |
| N.E. Haig | 148 | 50 | 360 | 11 | 32.73 |
| W. Voce | 188.2 | 35 | 584 | 17 | 34.35 |

### West Indies

| Batting | Innings | NO | HS | Runs | Average |
|---|---|---|---|---|---|
| G.A. Headley | 8 | 0 | 223 | 703 | 87.88 |
| R.K. Nunes | 2 | 0 | 92 | 158 | 79.00 |
| C.A. Roach | 8 | 0 | 209 | 467 | 58.38 |
| L.A. Walcott | 2 | 1 | 24 | 40 | 40.00 |
| F.I. de Caires | 6 | 0 | 80 | 232 | 38.67 |

| Bowling | Overs | M | Runs | W | Average |
|---|---|---|---|---|---|
| G.N. Francis | 47.5 | 16 | 109 | 6 | 18.17 |
| L.N. Constantine | 163.4 | 42 | 497 | 18 | 27.61 |
| H.C. Griffith | 190.1 | 38 | 508 | 16 | 31.75 |
| E.E. Achong | 24 | 3 | 76 | 2 | 38.00 |
| C.R. Browne | 93 | 31 | 163 | 4 | 40.75 |

Wicket-keepers: E.A.C. Hunte (WI) 5 dismissals   I. Barrow (WI) 3 dismissals   L.E.G. Ames (E) 12 dismissals

In the first match J.E.D. Sealy became the youngest Test player and is still the youngest to represent West Indies; C.A. Roach became the first West Indian to score a Test century and G.A. Headley became, and remains, the youngest to do so. In the third match, West Indies' first Test victory, Roach became their first to score a double century and Headley their first to score a century in each innings. The fourth match set records for the longest match (7 days), the highest total (England's 849), the highest individual score (A. Sandham's 325, the first treble century in Tests) and the highest individual match aggregate (Sandham's 375). O.C. Scott's figures of 9 for 374 are still the most runs conceded in a Test. Headley became, and remains, the only batsman to score four Test centuries before the age of 21. W. Rhodes finished the world's longest Test career and remains the oldest Test cricketer.

## 1933 Test Series

### England

| Batting | Innings | NO | HS | Runs | Average |
|---|---|---|---|---|---|
| A.H. Bakewell | 1 | 0 | 107 | 107 | 107.00 |
| L.E.G. Ames | 3 | 1 | 83* | 167 | 83.50 |
| D.R. Jardine | 2 | 0 | 127 | 148 | 74.00 |
| C.J. Barnett | 1 | 0 | 52 | 52 | 52.00 |
| M.S. Nichols | 1 | 0 | 49 | 49 | 49.00 |

| Bowling | Overs | M | Runs | W | Average |
|---|---|---|---|---|---|
| C.S. Marriott | 41.1 | 8 | 96 | 11 | 8.72 |
| James Langridge | 33 | 6 | 102 | 7 | 14.57 |
| G.O.B. Allen | 24 | 8 | 46 | 3 | 15.33 |
| R.W.V. Robins | 63.4 | 5 | 220 | 11 | 20.00 |
| E.W. Clark | 84 | 22 | 233 | 11 | 21.18 |

### West Indies

| Batting | Innings | NO | HS | Runs | Average |
|---|---|---|---|---|---|
| G.A. Headley | 6 | 1 | 169* | 277 | 55.40 |
| L.N. Constantine | 2 | 0 | 64 | 95 | 47.50 |
| I. Barrow | 6 | 0 | 105 | 143 | 23.83 |
| C.A. Roach | 6 | 0 | 64 | 141 | 23.50 |
| B.J. Sealey | 2 | 0 | 29 | 41 | 20.50 |

| Bowling | Overs | M | Runs | W | Average |
|---|---|---|---|---|---|
| B.J. Sealey | 5 | 1 | 10 | 1 | 10.00 |
| E.A. Martindale | 72.3 | 9 | 251 | 14 | 17.92 |
| H.C. Griffith | 40 | 11 | 92 | 3 | 30.66 |
| E.E. Achong | 95 | 21 | 237 | 5 | 47.40 |
| L.N. Constantine | 25 | 5 | 55 | 1 | 55.00 |

Wicket-keepers:   L.E.G. Ames (E) 11 dismissals   I. Barrow (WI) 6 dismissals

In the third match C.S. Marriott, in his only Test, took 11 for 96 for the second-best debut figures for England.

## 1934–5 Test Series

### England

| Batting | Innings | NO | HS | Runs | Average |
|---|---|---|---|---|---|
| E.H. Hendren | 8 | 1 | 41 | 202 | 28.85 |
| J. Iddon | 6 | 1 | 73 | 141 | 28.20 |
| L.E.G. Ames | 7 | 1 | 126 | 164 | 27.33 |
| W.R. Hammond | 8 | 1 | 47 | 175 | 25.00 |
| R.E.S. Wyatt | 7 | 2 | 71 | 124 | 24.80 |

| Bowling | Overs | M | Runs | W | Average |
|---|---|---|---|---|---|
| W.E. Hollies | 93 | 24 | 217 | 10 | 21.70 |
| R.E.S. Wyatt | 44 | 17 | 88 | 4 | 22.00 |
| K. Farnes | 48 | 10 | 134 | 6 | 22.33 |
| G.A.E. Payne | 174 | 43 | 467 | 17 | 27.47 |
| C.I.J. Smith | 119 | 30 | 329 | 11 | 29.90 |

### West Indies

| Batting | Innings | NO | HS | Runs | Average |
|---|---|---|---|---|---|
| G.A. Headley | 6 | 1 | 270* | 485 | 97.00 |
| J.E.D. Sealy | 6 | 0 | 92 | 270 | 45.00 |
| L.N. Constantine | 5 | 0 | 90 | 169 | 33.80 |
| R.S. Grant | 6 | 1 | 77 | 122 | 24.40 |
| C.M. Christiani | 7 | 2 | 32* | 98 | 19.60 |

| Bowling | Overs | M | Runs | W | Average |
|---|---|---|---|---|---|
| E.A. Martindale | 100.3 | 23 | 239 | 19 | 12.57 |
| L.N. Constantine | 109.1 | 36 | 197 | 15 | 13.13 |
| J.E.D. Sealy | 19 | 4 | 41 | 3 | 13.66 |
| L.G. Hylton | 97 | 23 | 251 | 13 | 19.30 |
| R.S. Grant | 120 | 27 | 245 | 9 | 27.22 |

Wicket-keepers:   C.M. Christiani (WI) 7 dismissals   L.E.G. Ames (E) 5 dismissals

In the fourth match G.A. Headley's 270* was the highest against England until 1973–4. West Indies won their first rubber in their fifth series.

# 5

# Coming of Age to the Sound of Calypsos

By the time his team played another Test match Jackie Grant had been in Africa for some time. It was 1939 before they did so and, although they lost the Test series, they showed that they were maintaining their improvement. They were led by Rolph Grant, and he proved himself as good a captain as his brother. He was a splendid all-round sportsman, a Cambridge blue at cricket and soccer and half-blue at boxing, who played in goal for England's amateur football team and became heavyweight boxing champion of Trinidad. He was a good, if not outstanding, forcing batsman, a useful off-spinner and a superb fielder, especially at short leg; in seven Tests he took thirteen catches, and *Wisden* even dared to compare him to Constantine. As a captain he was in the same mould as his brother, a typical Oxbridge amateur for whom sportsmanship was paramount. He had an excellent rapport with his players and the tour was a happy one, apart from the gathering clouds of war that brought it to an early end.

English cricket had on the whole been pretty strong during the 1930s (although their only Ashes success had come when Jardine took the law into his own, or rather Larwood's, hands), and one reason for this had been the all-round skills of Walter Hammond, most majestic of batsmen, superb slip fielder and more than useful medium-pace support bowler. He had turned amateur before the 1938 season in the hope of being offered the England captaincy, and duly led the team against Australia; the Ashes were not regained but his leadership was described by *Wisden* as sagacious and inspiring, and he went on to lead England to a series victory in South Africa. After the war he would have one more rubber in Australia and there, beset by fibrositis and various personal problems, his leadership was a disaster, a magnificent career petering out into a sad ending. For now, though, he was in charge against the West Indians, and after their beating in the Caribbean a few years earlier the England selectors made sure that the team was a fairly strong one. The Test series, incidentally, was the only one in which eight-ball overs have been used in England.

This time the tourists did not make an auspicious start, not recording their first win until the sixth game. The MCC game was washed out without West Indies batting but, as the home team had reached 435 for 7, perhaps they were not too sorry to see the rain. By the time of the Lord's Test they had put a few victories together and their confidence was growing, though the batting still relied too heavily on Headley. One exception was the 18-year-old Jeffrey Stollmeyer, who made 59 in his first Test innings, but once he had gone Headley had little support. Playing carefully, with a north wind to make life difficult, it took him over four hours to make 106, clear evidence of how seriously he took his responsibility; 277 all out after being 226 for 3. On the second day, in much better weather, England ran away with it, Hutton and Compton – both dropped early on, Compton off two successive balls – the young heroes as they scored 248 in 140 minutes, with Hutton falling just four short of a double century and Compton making 120. Hammond declared at the overnight score of 404 for 5 (these were still three-day Tests) and once again it was all down to Headley. He had some support from Grant and Sealy but wickets fell steadily; after three hours fifty minutes Headley was out for 107, having become the first man to score a century in each innings of a Lord's Test. All in vain: when the innings closed for 225, England had 110 minutes to score 99 and they got them in 75 minutes for the loss of two wickets.

At Old Trafford, as had happened once or twice before, a lot of time was lost to rain and the game was played in gloomy conditions. Only a few minutes' play was possible on the first day, and on the second England, having been put in, were indebted to Hardstaff's 76 for reaching 164 for 7 declared. Only Grant and Headley did anything in reply; on a wet pitch Bowes celebrated his birthday by taking 6 for 33, and they were all out for 133. With only four and a half hours left Hutton and Fagg then played cautiously, allowing the bowlers to get on top. As a result, six wickets went down for 128 before Hammond declared, leaving West Indies with the task of scoring 160 in 70 minutes. It was 43 for 4 at the end, one highlight being that Hammond became the first non-wicket-keeper to take a hundred Test catches. His victim, perhaps appropriately, was Headley.

The Oval saw 1,216 runs scored while only 23 wickets fell, and against a rather mediocre attack West Indies did well. England batted first and after Keeton was out immediately, Hutton and 'Buddy' Oldfield, on debut, put on 131 for the second wicket. Hammond and Compton could not really get going, but Hardstaff and Nichols put on 89 in 65 minutes before Constantine threw down Nichols' wicket from cover – having just bowled

*Walter Hammond and wicket-keeper Arthur Wood look on as the incomparable George Headley demonstrates Caribbean batsmanship of the highest class during the 1939 tour to England.*

the ball. The tail duly collapsed and Hardstaff missed his century by six runs; all out 352, with 5 for 75 to Constantine. On the second day England bowled and fielded poorly, and it took one of Hutton's three Test wickets to break a second-wicket stand of 113 between Stollmeyer and Headley. This brought in Vic Stollmeyer, who had missed the first two Tests because of tonsillitis, and in what proved his only Test innings he ran out Headley and then made 96. When he was joined by Kenneth Weekes – 'Bam Bam' to his friends – they hammered 163 in 100 minutes, and Weekes went on to 137, his only Test century. Constantine rounded things off by hammering 79 and was last out with the total on 498. Only an England collapse could have produced a result but this was not to occur. Hutton and Hammond proceeded to set a new world Test record for the third wicket, putting on 264 in three hours, with 138 to Hammond and Hutton 165 not out. Hammond declared on 366 for 3 and there Test cricket ended for seven years.

It was also the last match of the tour as the rest were abandoned because of the coming conflict. It left West Indies in credit both in results and finances, twenty-five first-class games yielding eight wins to six defeats and their share of the receipts amounting to £4,684. Headley and Constantine were very much the heroes, with Headley topping the national averages and Constantine named as one of the cricketers of the year. The Test series may have been lost but it was clear that there were some good players coming through: the leg-break bowler Bertie Clarke had had a good tour with 87 wickets and the Stollmeyer brothers looked class batsmen. And back in Barbados, could the world but have known it, there were three young men still at school, their surnames all beginning with the same letter, who would make quite a name for themselves when the world returned to normal.

*

West Indies were the last country to resume Test matches after the war, not taking the field until January 1948. When they did so it was against one of the most unprepossessing teams England have ever put out. The squad which MCC sent out under the leadership of the 45-year-old 'Gubby' Allen lacked most of the top players of the time such as Compton, Edrich, Washbrook, Bedser, Wright and Yardley, and Hutton only joined it half-way through when Allen cabled for help because they had a string of injuries. Even allowing that most of these players had not been available to tour, the selectors were nonetheless guilty of underestimating the opposition, and they came a spectacular cropper; for the first time ever an MCC team returned home from an overseas tour without a single victory to their name. Admittedly, they were very unfortunate with illness and injury, but they were comprehensively outplayed in the Tests.

Viewed from this distance, English cricket in the years immediately after the Second World War has a slight feeling of unreality about it. The endless sunshine of 1947 saw Compton and Edrich achieve batting feats that had never been dreamed of; another wonderful summer in 1949 saw the New Zealanders Sutcliffe and Donnelly winning matches by scoring at a quite preposterous speed; against South Africa in 1948–9 England won the first Test with a leg-bye off the final ball and the fifth Test with just one minute left; in two series against Australia, England were so thoroughly outplayed that it was embarrassing; and the 1947–8 tour to the West Indies has every indication of having been a shambles.

The England captain, Norman Yardley, was not able to tour and was replaced by G.O. Allen, a man of 45 who had played just two innings in the Championship in the preceding season; Allen was then given a squad of whom seven had no Test experience at all and three more had played in only one match. And they travelled out on an unballasted banana boat which was delayed for three days by bad weather so that by the time they arrived the first game was almost upon them. Once there, things got steadily worse as one player after another succumbed to illness and injury – beginning with Allen who pulled a calf muscle while skipping on the boat and had to miss the first three games including the opening Test – so that when Hutton arrived it was just in time to prevent them from having to take the field with only ten fit men.

There was no excuse for sending such an inexperienced team, since if the selectors had done their homework they would have known that West Indian intercolonial cricket had in recent years produced some outstanding young batsmen. They all played for Barbados and their surnames all began with W. Worrell, Weekes and Walcott were about to make their entry into world cricket.

They did so against a background that had changed considerably from pre-war days. Jamaica had become self-governing in 1944 and now had a highly developed trade union movement, as did Barbados and Trinidad, and all adults in these countries now had the vote. The class structures and strictures were still strong, especially in Barbados, but not as rigid as they had been. It took a lot of negotiating, mostly by Noel Nethersole, the deputy leader of Jamaica's People's National Party, but in the first Test after the war that which had been unthinkable before the war came to pass – a black man was appointed captain of West Indies.

George Headley, of course, was the man in question, but the arrangement that was reached was one that to the outsider seems a remarkable compromise, for he was still by no means the automatic choice. Headley was appointed for the first Test in Barbados and the last in Jamaica, Jeffrey Stollmeyer for the second match in Trinidad, and John Goddard, captain of Barbados, for the third at Georgetown. In the event it was all to go wrong for Headley. He was now 38 and no longer the batsman he had been. After scoring 29 in the first innings he strained his back and had to bat last in the second innings, which he declared when he was 7 not out; the injury then proved serious enough for him to miss the rest of the series. Having steered his team to a dominant position, he was robbed of the chance of victory when much of the last day was lost to rain.

In the absence of Allen, England were led in the first Test by Ken Cranston, the Lancashire dentist who played first-class cricket only in 1947 and 1948 but who would have had a notable career had he not preferred to return to dentistry. He captained his county in both years, taking them to third and fifth in the table, scored over 3,000 runs, took 178 wickets, played in eight Tests and deputized as captain on this one occasion, earning praise from Wisden for his handling of limited bowling resources. He lost the toss, though, and Stollmeyer and Gomez took the score to 244 for 3 by the end of the first day. Of the five English debutants in the match only one would go on to greatness, and he presaged things to come on the second morning. Overnight rain helped Jim Laker transform 1 for 78 to 7 for 103 in the space of nine overs, and West Indies were all out for 296.

In reply, Robertson made 80 and Hardstaff fell two short of a century, but there was little else on offer and England were all out for 253. Another debutant, Robert Christiani, then almost had his moment of glory in the home team's second innings, only to fall lbw to Cranston for 99 – and, it is said, to cry bitterly when he returned to the dressing room. The fireworks, though, came from 'Foffie' Williams, who was in the team only because Worrell had withdrawn through food poisoning. The first four balls he received were from Laker and were despatched for two sixes and two fours; the next two, from Ikin, also went for four, an unprecedented start to a Test innings. His fifty came in thirty minutes, a feat only twice surpassed in Tests, and he finished with 72 in just over an hour. Headley declared at 351 for 9; England were left to get 395 to win. Two wickets fell for 60 by the close of the fourth day, and two more went down on the last morning; but after just over an hour, with the score at 86 for 4 and things looking grim for England, a rainstorm flooded the ground and washed out play completely. Poor Headley.

The second Test in Port-of-Spain contained some remarkable feats. Allen returned to lead England, but the home team's captaincy arrangements were further confused when Stollmeyer was injured. One might have expected Goddard, who had been named for the next Test, to take over for this one as well, but no; Gerry Gomez was given his only game in charge. An all-rounder who was a great stalwart of the team in the years after the war, he had made his debut in 1939 and would go on to play in 29 Tests, scoring over 1,200 runs at 30, taking 58 wickets at 27 with his fast-medium swing bowling, and holding some superb close catches. A year earlier, for Trinidad against British Guiana, he and Stollmeyer put on 434 for the third wicket, still the West Indian record for that wicket, and a year later he was one of four West Indian centurions in their first ever Test against India, his only Test century. His best series came in Australia in 1951–2 when so many of his team-mates performed poorly, heading the batting averages and taking 18 cheap wickets including 10 for 113 in the last Test. After he retired he became a radio commentator, was manager on the great 1960–1 tour of Australia, and put in many years' service on the WICBC.

England's injury problems were such that they had only one fit opener, and Allen was alleged to have decided that the replacement would be the first man who walked through the dressing-room door after pre-match practice. Billy Griffith, the reserve wicket-keeper, duly found himself opening with Robertson after Allen had won the toss, only to run out his partner with just five on the board. Wickets fell periodically throughout the day and at the close England were 230 for 6 – but Griffith was still there, having become the only England batsman to score his maiden first-class century in his first Test innings. 'Like a true cricketer,' says the oracle in expansive mood, 'the Sussex amateur never allowed the responsibility to worry him. . . . One cannot praise Griffith too highly for this stupendous effort.'

His 140, and 55 from Laker at number nine, helped England to 362, whereupon Carew and Ganteaume, the West Indies openers, both scored centuries too. Carew had played one previous Test thirteen years earlier but had fallen first ball in his only innings, while Ganteaume was playing in what proved to be his *only* Test innings. 'Wearing a chocolate-coloured felt hat and chewing gum the whole time', Carew gave an exciting display that took him to his hundred just before the close, with his partner having just passed fifty. He went for 107, after which Weekes and then Worrell joined Ganteaume. His century came up in four and a half hours which, while slow, is hardly desperately so in the context of a five-day Test. A note was sent out by Gomez telling both batsmen to get on with it as they were behind the clock, whereupon Ganteaume promptly holed out for 112. Worrell, also in his first Test innings, fell just three short of his century, and, with Gomez himself scoring a sprightly 62, West Indies finished on 497. Robertson, in his third game, then became the fourth

*Andy Ganteaume, possessor of one of the oddest Test records of all – a century and then dropped.*

player to make his maiden Test century, scoring 133 out of 275 in a dogged effort to save the match, with most of the support coming from the lower order. He was successful in that West Indies needed 141 in just 57 minutes, which of course they did not reach; but had it not been for the loss earlier of two hours to rain they undoubtedly would have done.

Of those four maiden centurions, Ganteaume did not play again, Griffith played twice more for 13 runs, and Carew played twice more for 45 runs; Robertson had eight more Tests and did manage one more hundred. Worrell, who just missed out, went on to greater things. Ganteaume, writing years later, attributed his subsequent omission to the fact that he was not an Establishment man; whatever the reason, his is certainly one of the strangest of Test records.

Having been twice thwarted by the rain, West Indies were helped by it at Georgetown. Early on they were 48 for 3, but fifty from Christiani and a hundred from Worrell took them to 284 for 5 before rain intervened. No play was possible till after lunch on the second day, when they lost three more wickets for just 13; but Goddard, realizing the pitch would take spin, declared on 297 and took his only five-wicket Test haul with his slow-medium off-breaks to help put England out for 111, after having been 59 for 0. Following on, they found that the pitch had eased somewhat, and were able to bat through the third day and into the fourth for 263; but the 78 that this left the West Indies to make, in the best part of two days, presented them with few problems. A seven-wicket win meant that justice had at last been done.

Headley's injury meant that Goddard, whose captaincy at Georgetown had been widely praised, kept the leadership in Jamaica. After Robertson and Hutton had put on 129 for the first wicket, the other batsmen could manage only 98 between them, to which West Indies replied with no less than 490. Everton Weekes, who had not done himself justice so far, was missed by Evans very early on and went on to 141 – the first of a record run of five centuries in consecutive Test innings. He was in the team only because of the injury to Headley and was summoned so late that he did not take the field till the first afternoon, and when he did so he got some stick from the crowd who thought that Holt, their local hero, should have played. With Rickard, Walcott and Ferguson all scoring quickly, England were left with an enormous task to save the game. The top order did their best, with Place making his only Test century. They were 263 behind when they began, and by lunch on the last day they were 49 ahead with six wickets left. An hour or so later they were all out for just 24 more runs, and Hines Johnson, a 37-year-old Jamaican fast bowler making his debut, had match figures of 10 for 96. Goddard and Stollmeyer polished off the 74 needed in only 34 minutes.

Later in the year Goddard was rewarded with the captaincy on the tour of India, the first series between the two countries; the Indians had asked that Headley be included and he duly was, but he was not offered the captaincy. He was by far the most experienced player and had proved with Jamaica that he was an excellent captain; but he was black.

'Gubby' Allen was at least able to claim the distinction of being the second oldest Test captain after W.G. Grace, although there was little else in the tour for him to enthuse about. Having missed the first Test he pulled muscles again near the end of the second match and early in the third, thereby weakening an attack that was already desperately thin. It was a sad end to a fine playing career that could have been quite outstanding had he been able to give more time to the game; he was a genuine all-rounder, a fast bowler with a classical action, a brave and determined batsman and a fine close fielder. He had been on Jardine's tour to Australia and taken 21 wickets in the Tests without resorting to bodyline; he then led England at home to India in 1936 (winning 2–0) and in Australia in 1936–7, losing the series 3–2 when the luck turned against him, after having won the first two games when the luck had been with him. Yet if his Test career ended sadly, he still had decades of close association with the game ahead of him, becoming a selector, Chairman of Selectors, and president and treasurer of MCC. When he was finally knighted the only surprise was that it had been so long in coming.

*

For John Goddard it was the beginning of four years in charge of the Test team. Against India he won all five tosses and took the rubber 1–0, but in 1951–2 he went down 4–1 in Australia, although two defeats were very close; he also beat New Zealand 1–0 in two Tests at the end of the Australian tour. The apex of his career, though, was undoubtedly the 1950 tour of England when, as has often been said, West Indian cricket 'came of age'.

He was an all-rounder who, if hardly out of the top drawer, put in plenty of useful Test performances. In 27 Tests he finished with an average of 30 thanks to a high proportion of undefeated innings, and took 33 wickets at just under 32 with his medium-pace or off-break bowling. Perhaps his batting, which was left-handed, never really fulfilled the promise of the young man who had scored 218 not out for Barbados against Trinidad in 1943–4, sharing an unbroken stand of 502 with Frank Worrell for the fourth wicket, but it never lacked in determination and could be very attractive. As a fielder he was outstanding and quite fearless, excelling at silly mid-off where he took some memorable catches. As a captain he had his share of peaks and troughs; as the winning captain in an especially memorable series in 1950 he has an honoured place in cricket history, and he certainly led the team ably and thoughtfully and got the very most out of them. Obviously, he was lucky that the batsmen were all in form and Ramadhin and Valentine emerged from nowhere to go down in legend and song, but he made the most of his fortune. According to C.L.R. James, he 'let his batsmen and his bowlers have their heads', and it is difficult to quarrel with this as a strategy in the circumstances. Not least to his credit was the fact that he had been in favour of including the young spinners in the party.

England were led in the first three Tests by Norman Yardley, the Yorkshireman who had taken such a pasting from Bradman's Australians two

*Norman Yardley led England in 1950, only to find two young spinners haunting his dreams.*

years earlier. An all-rounder who played in 20 Tests, his record is not an especially distinguished one but he was never one to be much bothered about averages; more importantly, he was a useful performer at a time when English cricket was getting itself together again after the war. He was seen as probably the best tactician among the county captains, particularly good at weighing up the risks involved in a move and always ready to take a chance if it seemed reasonable. Yet in fourteen matches as captain he had the ill-luck twice to come up against a world-class pair of bowlers. At least in 1948 he knew in advance about Miller and Lindwall, but when Ramadhin and Valentine popped up from nowhere he must have wondered whom he had offended. Throughout his reverses, though, he remained cheerful and courteous, always very popular with his players for his friendliness, and it is pleasing to think that he did at least have one successful series, at home to South Africa in the legendary summer of 1947.

From early in the tour it was clear that the West Indian batsmen were in form. Before the first Test Rae, Worrell and Christiani had all made centuries, Weekes had followed 232 against Surrey with 304 not out at Cambridge, and some substantial scores had been piled up: 537 for 5 at the Oval, 730 for 3 at Fenner's, 454 for 7 against Lancashire. Just as ominously, Ramadhin and Valentine had begun to cause problems. Come the Test, though, and the batsmen were altogether less happy.

The problem was the Old Trafford pitch. It had been badly underprepared and took spin almost from the start, so that batting on the dry, dusty surface was hard work throughout. Only one specialist fast bowler, Hines Johnson, played in the match, and he bowled just ten overs; England's two pacemen, Bailey and Edrich, had only 18 overs between them. Yardley won the toss and batted, only to see his team subside to 88 for 5 by lunch, with Valentine marking his first session in Test cricket by taking all the wickets for 34 runs. The crucial partnership of the match then followed, however: Evans joined Bailey and they put on 161, Evans making his maiden Test century. Valentine became the only bowler to take the first eight wickets to fall in his first Test innings, but England still reached 312, clearly a good score on that pitch.

By this time, even slow balls on a length were jumping like firecrackers, one from Eric Hollies even bouncing over both batsman and wicketkeeper. Another left-arm spinner making his debut, Bob Berry of Lancashire, enjoyed the conditions, taking 5 for 63, and only Weekes could reach fifty as West Indies were all out for 215. England's second innings centred on Bill Edrich's 71, and when they were all out for 288 West Indies were faced with a deficit of 385 and well over two days to survive. Only Stollmeyer, with an elegant 78, put up much resistance, and England were left with a 202-run victory. Ramadhin and Valentine took 15 wickets between them, but their lack of experience meant that they were not able to exploit the surface as well as they would have done later. The visitors made their feelings about the pitch very clear, and went to Lord's resolved to show that if the groundsman gave them a decent stage they were one of the best sides in the world.

They tuned up for the match by hammering Nottinghamshire and Sussex by an innings, Rae and Stollmeyer putting on 355 for the first wicket in the latter match. A capacity crowd saw Goddard win the toss and bat, saw Wardle take a wicket with his first ball in a Test in England – and saw Worrell play one of those innings which, for sheer quality, enters the folklore of the game. A delicate late cut had even the English players applauding, and he followed it with a dazzling array of strokes. The fact that most of the really memorable innings are higher than the 52 he made

*The secret of Eric Hollies' accuracy – a wicket in the garden of his Staffordshire home where he practised endlessly. With 550 more wickets than runs in his entire career perhaps some batting practice would have come in useful, but the neighbours would probably have complained.*

shows just how good it was. At the other end Rae was building up a patient century, and when Weekes replaced Worrell and served up more entertainment, the score reached 233 for 2. It was a memorable day for Roly Jenkins too, however, as he took his one Test five-wicket haul to put them all out for 326.

In reply, Hutton and Washbrook made a sound start with 62 – and then one moment transformed the game. Hutton went down the wicket to Valentine, the ball spun prodigiously, and he was stumped. Thereafter, eight more went down for just 60, before Wardle threw the bat to take the total to 151. It was a painful business, drawn out for 106.4 overs; Ramadhin and Valentine bowled 88 of them and sent down no fewer than 55 maidens, taking nine wickets. The match was clearly there for the taking, but for a while the second innings looked stodgy; only when Weekes cut loose did it gain momentum, but Walcott then ran him out for 63 by calling for a non-existent single. English joy must have been tempered by apprehension at what Walcott would do to make up for his error, and sure enough he made mincemeat of the bowlers for an unbeaten 168. A stand of 211 for the sixth wicket with Gomez allowed Goddard to declare on 425 for 6; the lead was exactly 600.

Neither Hutton nor Edrich stayed long, and only Parkhouse, with 48, gave Washbrook any real support. The Lancashire opener reached his century on the final morning, not without problems against the young spinners, but as each wicket fell and it was obvious there would be no escape, the West Indian fans grew ever more ecstatic. Then minutes after lunch Worrell had Wardle lbw and it was all over – West Indies had won their first Test in England by the rather comprehensive margin of 326 runs. Nowadays the spectators are obliged to surge on at the end of a big game, chanting inanely, alcoholically and obscenely; but in far-away 1950 they did it rather more spontaneously, and made up calypsos about their heroes. Ramadhin and Valentine, with 18 wickets between them, became quickly immortalized, and the celebrations as the fans danced in front of the pavilion singing their songs have passed into the legend of the game. Denys Rowbotham in the *Guardian*, describing the scenes, concluded: 'Imagination boggles at what may be happening in the West Indies.'

It was an important moment in the history of the game. For a while Test cricket would be played, by one team at least, in a spirit of enjoyment that had hardly been seen for decades. Three great batsmen, two remarkable young spinners and a fine supporting cast would produce pulsating entertainment of a kind to warm the memories, in old age, of those lucky enough to see them. Calypso cricket had arrived.

Before the next Test they produced yet more big scores, with Worrell and Weekes both making unbeaten double centuries against Leicestershire. By the time of the Trent Bridge Test they were confident, and in form, in a way that no West Indies team had ever been. England, by contrast, were rattled by the ease of their defeat and made five changes, one of them enforced by Hutton's illness. Yardley won the toss well enough, but no doubt wished he had not; the wicket was green, and when he decided to bat his worst fears were realized – 4 for 25 in next to no time. The rest of the batsmen all managed to get in before getting out, though, and the score struggled to 223. By now the early life had gone out of the pitch and the West Indian openers were able to put on 77 before they were separated just before the end of the first day. The second day saw one of the greatest feasts of batsmanship that even the West Indies have ever produced.

After Christiani and Rae had gone, Worrell and Weekes came together; by the close their partnership was worth 241 and the score was 479 for 3. It was one of those days on which grown men might have wept at the beauty of it all, the effortlessness, the grace, the irresistibleness, the inevitableness. Whatever the bowlers tried, they had an answer; as soon as Yardley plugged one gap they opened another, and ran the fielders steadily ragged. Worrell, scoring faster than his partner, reached first one century and then two; Weekes, when the new ball was taken towards the end, smashed the first three deliveries with it to the boundary to move from 90 to 102. It was, simply, one of those days.

Worrell went next morning for 261, his highest Test score. Together they had scored 283 runs in 210 minutes, and though the rest of the innings subsided a total of 558 gave them a useful little lead of 335. To their credit England did then make a game of it, as Simpson, with 94, and Washbrook, 102, put on 212 for the first wicket. Parkhouse and Dewes carried on and each made sixties, and at one point the score was 326 for 2; but after they had gone, only Evans, with another sixty, made any runs, and the innings closed at 436. Just 102 was wanted to win with plenty of time, and Rae and Stollmeyer needed no assistance in getting there. The streets of Nottingham echoed to the unwonted sound of calypso rhythms.

Selectors, being human, never seem to learn that responding to defeat by making wholesale changes in the team rarely has the desired effect. It certainly did not here. Only three England players survived till the final Test at the Oval, although some of the changes were forced upon them. Not least of these was the captain, for as Freddie Brown had been appointed to take the team to Australia in the winter he replaced Yardley. An

*Fred Gardner of Warwickshire watches the ball disappear from the
mighty bat of Clyde Walcott during the 1950 tour.*

The three Ws. Charlie Grove of Warwickshire beats wicket-keeper
Walcott, Weekes (on as substitute) and Worrell in the 1950 tour match at
Edgbaston.

all-rounder who, like Allen, could have been a top-class player had he
been able to give more time to the game during his prime years, he came
late to captaincy and transformed Northamptonshire after years in the
doldrums. In Australia, with little luck going his way, he was to lose the
series 4–1, but as one of the most cheerful of all cricketers, he helped make
it as good natured an Ashes series as there has been. He had led England
twice the previous year against New Zealand, and was to have a successful
series against South Africa in 1951 – but his present problem was that he
was in charge of a totally outclassed team.

He lost the toss as well, consigning his team to some hard labour as
West Indies notched up another big score. Rae produced another century,
but once again the honours belonged to Worrell. 138 this time, all of them
crafted by a master batsman at his peak, and all the more brilliant since he
retired at 116 feeling unwell. With 74 from Gomez and 58 not out by the
captain, the innings closed at 503. England's reply belonged almost entirely to Hutton. Partner after partner came and went, but in all they
stayed just long enough to allow him to score England's first double

century in a home Test against West Indies. He is still the only Englishman to carry his bat through a completed innings against West Indies, and was to repeat the feat in Australia the following February to become the only Englishman to achieve it twice. It was a superb effort, but it did not stop England from having to follow on since they reached only 344. During the latter part, rain had made the pitch difficult so that following on meant almost certain defeat. When Hutton went for just 2 the batting had no anchor; all out for 103 and defeat by an innings and 56 runs. It could have been worse for England – there could have been five Tests instead of four.

Alf Valentine took 10 for 160 in the match to finish the series with 33 wickets at 20 apiece; Sonny Ramadhin had 26 wickets at 23. Like all the best double acts their names are inextricably linked, and the way in which, young and inexperienced, they rose from nowhere to secure a great triumph gave cricket one of its most romantic story-book tales. Throughout the game's history slow bowlers have traditionally taken years to perfect their craft and reach their peak, yet Ramadhin, from Trinidad, was 21 when the tour began and the Jamaican Valentine a year younger; both had just two first-class games to their name when they were chosen. The odds against two such talents – complementary talents at that – emerging simultaneously must be astronomical.

Ramadhin was the right-hander who could bowl off-spin, leg-spin and straight balls with no discernible change of action; Clyde Walcott, the wicket-keeper in 1950, confirmed that he could never tell which way the ball would go. At first he had trouble with his length against left-handers, but once he had worked them out his length rarely wavered to anyone, and variations in pace and flight brought him many victims. Just 5 feet 4 inches (1.6 metres) tall, sleeves buttoned at the wrist and cap on head, he had an energetic little run-up which culminated in a windmilling of the delivery arm, leg-break as well as off-break spun with the fingers rather than the wrist. On the tour as a whole he took 135 wickets at under 15, and if he never touched such heights again he still had some very fine days ahead of him, New Zealand in particular providing him with agreeable opposition. When England went to the Caribbean in 1953–4 he was the leading home wicket-taker in the Tests by a street with 23, none of his colleagues even getting into double figures.

It was in his third series against England, in 1957, that it was all to go wrong. In the first innings of the opening Test he took 7 for 49 – his best Test figures – and another few weeks of misery seemed in prospect for the England batsmen; and then suddenly his threat evaporated as Colin Cowdrey countered his spin by thrusting his pad repeatedly down the pitch, he

*Sonny Ramadhin (above) and Alf Valentine – instant legends in 1950. In a later era the calypso about them would probably have topped the pop charts.*

and May having decided that the best way to play him was to treat every ball as an off-spinner. As appeal after appeal was turned down, Ramadhin became more and more puzzled and frustrated and, by the time the fourth wicket had realized 411 he was effectively finished as a mystery bowler. Like bodyline a quarter of a century earlier, the batsmen's tactics were within the law of the game if not in its best spirit, and the lbw law was changed largely as a result of this innings. For Ramadhin, though, it was the beginning of the end; on the tour he took 119 wickets at under 14, but the other four Tests produced only five wickets. Before May and Cowdrey came together he had taken 122 wickets and was in his 29th match; after it finished he played in a further 14, and took just 36 more wickets. Those 158 wickets cost under 29 runs apiece, but it is hard not to wonder what he might have achieved had that one partnership not thwarted him. After playing league cricket in England, he settled in Lancashire as a publican in the mid-1960s, and has stayed there ever since.

His sidekick Valentine, taller, bespectacled and smiling, ranks as one of the best left-arm spinners since the war. After a rather flat-footed run up the ball was given a lot of spin, which did his index finger no good at all and necessitated regular treatment with surgical spirit. By the same token, though, the resultant curve of the ball did the batsman no good at all, especially as his accuracy was legendary. At first there was little variation, barely a hint of the subtleties that were to come; but shortly before the first Test he took 13 for 67 against Lancashire and the break-through was made. Becoming the first man to take eight wickets in an innings on Test debut meant that he had a lot to live up to and, like Ramadhin, he never touched the heights of this rubber again. He had good series against Australia and India during the next couple of years, and reached 100 wickets in the very quick time of 3 years 263 days but after that the wickets became ever more difficult to find. Against England in 1953–4 he took only seven expensive ones, and on the 1957 tour he played in only two Tests without one victim, having problems with illness and injury. He took part in several other series, though, and was in the team as late as 1961–2, finishing with 139 victims at 30 each from his 36 Tests.

For much of the 1950s the two spinners were the fulcrum of the West Indies attack, and when they failed the team tended to fail too – notably at home to Australia in 1954–5 when they took only ten wickets between them and the series was lost 3–0. Yet somehow, looking back, their later failures do not seem especially important; what matters is their triumph of 1950, the fairy-tale way that, young, unknown, inexperienced, they helped their team to its first victories in England. The crucial element in the story is that they were *spinners*; a young pair of tearaway quickies would have been all well and good, but the spinner has always had an air of romance that the fast man has lacked, and the season of 1950 was definitely one for the romantics. Maybe the calypsos lost something of their rhythm over the next few years, but that first glorious summer ensured that they would always be remembered with the greatest affection.

| 1939 | Lord's | WI 277, 225; | E 404–5d, 100–2 | E 8 wkts |
| | Old Trafford | E 164–7d, 128–6d; | WI 133, 43–4 | Drawn |
| | Oval | E 352, 366–3; | WI 498 | Drawn |
| 1947–8 | Bridgetown | WI 296, 351–9d; | E 253, 86–4 | Drawn |
| | Port-of-Spain | E 362, 275; | WI 497, 72–3 | Drawn |
| | Georgetown | WI 297–8d, 78–3; | E 111, 263 | WI 7 wkts |
| | Kingston | E227, 336; | WI 490, 76–0 | WI 10 wkts |
| 1950 | Old Trafford | E 312, 288; | WI 215, 183 | E 202 runs |
| | Trent Bridge | E223, 436; | WI 588, 103–0 | WI 10 wkts |
| | Oval | WI 503; | E 344, 103 | WI Inns 56 runs |
| | Lord's | WI 326, 425–6d | E 151, 274 | WI 326 runs |

**1939 Test Series (eight-ball overs)**

**England**

| Batting | Innings | NO | HS | Runs | Average |
|---|---|---|---|---|---|
| L. Hutton | 6 | 1 | 196 | 480 | 96.00 |
| D.C.S. Compton | 5 | 2 | 120 | 189 | 63.00 |
| J. Hardstaff jr | 4 | 1 | 94 | 174 | 58.00 |
| W.R. Hammond | 6 | 1 | 138 | 279 | 55.80 |
| E. Paynter | 4 | 1 | 34 | 75 | 25.00 |

| Bowling | Overs | M | Runs | W | Average |
|---|---|---|---|---|---|
| W.H. Copson | 52.4 | 7 | 185 | 12 | 15.41 |
| W.E. Bowes | 70 | 18 | 176 | 11 | 16.00 |
| R.T.D. Perks | 30.5 | 6 | 156 | 5 | 31.20 |
| T.W.J. Goddard | 20.6 | 2 | 114 | 4 | 28.50 |
| D.V.P. Wright | 51 | 4 | 214 | 6 | 35.66 |

**West Indies**

| Batting | Innings | NO | HS | Runs | Average |
|---|---|---|---|---|---|
| G.A. Headley | 5 | 0 | 107 | 334 | 66.80 |
| K.H. Weekes | 3 | 0 | 137 | 173 | 57.66 |
| L.N. Constantine | 4 | 0 | 79 | 110 | 27.50 |
| J.B. Stollmeyer | 5 | 0 | 59 | 133 | 26.60 |
| J.E.D. Sealy | 5 | 1 | 29 | 95 | 23.75 |

| Bowling | Overs | M | Runs | W | Average |
|---|---|---|---|---|---|
| J.H. Cameron | 29 | 6 | 88 | 3 | 29.33 |
| L.N. Constantine | 71.3 | 8 | 328 | 11 | 29.81 |
| C.B. Clarke | 57 | 2 | 261 | 6 | 43.50 |
| R.S. Grant | 33.2 | 5 | 108 | 2 | 54.00 |
| L.G. Hylton | 48 | 9 | 167 | 3 | 55.66 |

Wicket-keepers: A. Wood (E) 8 dismissals  I. Barrow (WI) 1 dismissal  J.E.D. Sealy (WI) 5 dismissals

In the first match, G.A. Headley became the first batsman to score a century in each innings of a Lord's Test. In the second match, W.R. Hammond became the first non-wicket-keeper to hold 100 Test catches. In the third match, Hammond and L. Hutton put on 264 for the third wicket, then the world Test record for that wicket and still the highest in England–West Indies Tests.

## 1947–8 Test Series

### England

| Batting | Innings | NO | HS | Runs | Average |
|---|---|---|---|---|---|
| S.C. Griffith | 2 | 0 | 140 | 144 | 72.00 |
| J.D. Robertson | 8 | 1 | 133 | 390 | 55.71 |
| L. Hutton | 4 | 0 | 60 | 171 | 42.75 |
| J. Hardstaff | 6 | 0 | 98 | 237 | 39.50 |
| W. Place | 6 | 1 | 107 | 144 | 28.80 |

| Bowling | Overs | M | Runs | W | Average |
|---|---|---|---|---|---|
| H.J. Butler | 40 | 6 | 149 | 5 | 29.80 |
| J.C. Laker | 186.4 | 47 | 546 | 18 | 30.33 |
| K. Cranston | 65 | 13 | 196 | 6 | 32.66 |
| R. Howorth | 177.5 | 33 | 483 | 13 | 37.15 |
| G.O. Allen | 46 | 1 | 205 | 5 | 41.00 |

### West Indies

| Batting | Innings | NO | HS | Runs | Average |
|---|---|---|---|---|---|
| F.M.M. Worrell | 4 | 2 | 131* | 294 | 147.00 |
| J.B. Stollmeyer | 4 | 1 | 78 | 164 | 54.66 |
| G.M. Carew | 4 | 1 | 107 | 150 | 50.00 |
| E.D. Weekes | 6 | 0 | 141 | 293 | 48.83 |
| G.E. Gomez | 6 | 1 | 86 | 232 | 46.40 |

| Bowling | Overs | M | Runs | W | Average |
|---|---|---|---|---|---|
| H.H.H. Johnson | 65.5 | 24 | 96 | 10 | 9.60 |
| J. Trim | 23 | 8 | 44 | 3 | 14.66 |
| J.B. Stollmeyer | 24 | 10 | 47 | 3 | 15.66 |
| P.E. Jones | 34.2 | 7 | 83 | 4 | 20.75 |
| E.A.V. Williams | 120.4 | 33 | 218 | 9 | 24.22 |
| W. Ferguson | 214 | 40 | 567 | 23 | 24.65 |

Wicket-keepers:   C.L. Walcott (WI) 16 dismissals   T.G. Evans (E) 7 dismissals

In the first match, E.A.V. Williams scored what is still the fastest Test fifty for West Indies, in 30 minutes. In the second match, S.C. Griffith became the only player to score his maiden first-class century in his first Test innings for England. At the end of the fourth match, G.O.B. Allen was the second-oldest Test captain after W.G. Grace, at 45 years 245 days.

## 1950 Test Series

### England

| Batting | Innings | NO | HS | Runs | Average |
|---|---|---|---|---|---|
| L. Hutton | 6 | 1 | 202* | 333 | 66.60 |
| C. Washbrook | 4 | 0 | 114 | 255 | 63.75 |
| T.E. Bailey | 4 | 1 | 82* | 145 | 48.33 |
| T.G. Evans | 6 | 0 | 104 | 224 | 37.33 |
| W.G.A. Parkhouse | 4 | 0 | 69 | 130 | 32.50 |

| Bowling | Overs | M | Runs | W | Average |
|---|---|---|---|---|---|
| R. Berry | 108.5 | 47 | 228 | 9 | 25.33 |
| W.E. Hollies | 119 | 38 | 268 | 10 | 26.80 |
| A.V. Bedser | 181 | 49 | 377 | 11 | 34.27 |
| T.E. Bailey | 47.2 | 12 | 121 | 3 | 40.33 |
| R.O. Jenkins | 118.2 | 20 | 409 | 10 | 40.90 |

**West Indies**

| Batting | Innings | NO | HS | Runs | Average |
|---|---|---|---|---|---|
| F.M.M. Worrell | 6 | 0 | 261 | 539 | 89.83 |
| A.F. Rae | 7 | 1 | 109 | 377 | 62.83 |
| E.D. Weekes | 6 | 0 | 129 | 338 | 56.33 |
| J.B. Stollmeyer | 7 | 1 | 78 | 305 | 50.83 |
| C.L. Walcott | 6 | 1 | 168* | 229 | 45.80 |

| Bowling | Overs | M | Runs | W | Average |
|---|---|---|---|---|---|
| J.D.C. Goddard | 74.4 | 29 | 122 | 6 | 20.33 |
| A.L. Valentine | 422.3 | 197 | 674 | 33 | 20.42 |
| S. Ramadhin | 377.5 | 170 | 604 | 26 | 23.23 |
| F.M.M. Worrell | 98.2 | 36 | 182 | 6 | 30.33 |
| H.H.H. Johnson | 65.4 | 13 | 142 | 3 | 47.33 |

Wicket-keepers: T.G. Evans 9 dismissals  A.J.W. McIntyre (E) 3 dismissals  C.L. Walcott 7 dismissals

In the first match, A.L. Valentine became the only bowler to take the first eight wickets to fall in his first Test innings. The second match saw West Indies' first Test win in England, Valentine and S. Ramadhin each taking nine wickets in the match. In the third match, F.M.M. Worrell's 261 was at the time the highest score for West Indies in a Test in England; R.T. Simpson and C. Washbrook put on 212 for the first wicket for England, still the highest opening partnership by England in these Tests. In the fourth match, L. Hutton became the only England batsman to carry his bat through a completed innings against West Indies, and his 202 not out is the highest score by an England player to do so. Valentine's 33 wickets was the West Indies' record for a series in England until 1988. This was West Indies' first series win in England.

# 6

# Of Riots and Pads

If England's 1947–8 tour had been a self-inflicted disaster largely brought about by underestimating the opposition, they did not make the same mistake next time round. The party for the 1953–4 tour included Hutton, Compton, May, Graveney, Bailey, Evans, Laker, Lock, Trueman, Statham and Wardle so that not only was this the first time a full-strength team had gone to the West Indies, but on paper at least it was one of the strongest squads since the war. It was a historic tour in that it was the first time MCC were led abroad by an officially appointed professional captain, and also, rather less crucially, it was the first time they had travelled out by air. It was also to be a tour that would long be remembered, partly because there was some excellent cricket played by both teams as England came back from 2–0 down to square the rubber, and partly because there were a string of unpleasantries, both on and off the pitch, from the players, the spectators and, by no means least, the journalists concerned.

That first officially appointed professional captain was, of course, Len Hutton. He had been given the job for the home series against India in 1952, when naturally there were a number of critics who were appalled at seeing the old order pass; for most people, though, it was a sound and sensible move in a world that was irrevocably vastly different from what it had been just fifteen years earlier. The criticisms did not make life easier for a sensitive man who was fully aware of the burden of tradition he had to carry – and had to carry with very little leadership experience to help him, for he never was official captain of his county. As a result, his natural Yorkshire cautiousness tended to become stronger still, and there were times when he appeared to lack adventure, when it seemed that avoiding defeat was a greater priority than going for victory; yet given the delicate nature of his position, it is hard to be too critical of this. At this distance we can hardly begin to appreciate his problems, but he was aware that plenty of English people would have been pleased to see him fail, both on the field and off, as a leader, to be given confirmation that a professional could not attend to the disciplinary or diplomatic duties of a touring captain as the amateurs had throughout the years. One of the side-effects

*Sir Leonard Hutton admitted that his career was cut short by the problems and tensions on the 1953–4 tour of West Indies. Yet still no England batsman has a higher average aginst West Indies.*

of his concern for his captaincy, however, was that he introduced a tactic which has been one of the blights of the modern game, the slowing down of the over rate. Realizing that his fast bowlers were his main weapons, he decided they should be kept as fresh as possible for as long as possible, and deliberately slowed down the tempo of an innings to achieve this. Had he been able to foresee the lengths to which this would be taken, it would be charitable to assume that he would never have started it.

Yet when he retired from Test cricket in 1955, tired and unwell after the strain of responsibility, the record showed that he was one of England's most successful captains. Twenty-three matches in charge had seen eleven victories and only four defeats, with no series lost; he had some fine players at his disposal, but he must take much of the credit for the success. If the decision to appoint him had been sound and sensible then perhaps those two epithets best sum up his style of leadership, as he drew on his vast knowledge and experience and applied them with his native York-shire shrewdness. That first series against India was won easily, and was followed by an emotional recovery of the Ashes the following summer. The team that set off for the Caribbean in December 1953 was not short of confidence in its own ability.

Nor were their opponents. Since 'coming of age' in 1950, West Indies had lost heavily in Australia, won in New Zealand, and beaten India at home; and even if the latter two were not exactly at the peak of world cricket, the West Indians, after the triumphs of 1950 and with virtually the same squad, felt they were every bit the equal of the Englishmen. They were led by Jeffrey Stollmeyer, the tall, stylish opening batsman from Trinidad who had come into the team as an 18 year old in 1939, and whose partnership with Allan Rae had provided many a solid foundation on which the three Ws and their colleagues could build. He and Rae had been together since the 1948–9 tour of India when they posted two century opening partnerships in four Tests, one of them, 239, being the West Indies first-wicket record at the time. They had played an important part in the successes of 1950, never once failing to provide a sound start, with Stollmeyer's 78 on a crumbling Old Trafford pitch rated a truly outstanding innings. In the last Test of 1951–2 in Australia, Stollmeyer took over the captaincy when Goddard was unfit, and scored a fine century in a losing cause against some very hostile bowling from Lindwall and Miller. He followed this with another 150 in New Zealand and an unbeaten century against India on his home ground. He had been given the

*Jeff Stollmeyer – captain against England in 1953–4, elegant opening batsman for many years, and one of nature's gentlemen.*

captaincy for the series against India - which was won 1–0 – and showed himself to be more of a thinker than Goddard; and since two of the defeats in Australia had been narrow ones and Goddard's form had been indifferent, there was inevitably speculation on what might have been achieved had Stollmeyer replaced him earlier as captain.

Jeff Stollmeyer was the last of the white West Indies captains whose appointment did not cause a rumpus. When Atkinson and Alexander came to be given the honour ahead of Worrell, whose claim was clearly greater than theirs, there was an outcry. Stollmeyer, though, was a natural leader, a courteous gentleman who knew the game thoroughly and gave it a great deal of thought; with the selectors not yet ready to give the captaincy to Worrell, he was an ideal man to carry on the unifying process begun by Goddard. After this series against England he was named as captain against Australia the following year, but injury restricted him to just two Tests. In 1955–6 he chose not to make the tour to New Zealand, but still hoped to lead the team to England in 1957. In the event Goddard was given the job, whereupon Stollmeyer immediately announced his retirement. In view of the disaster which the tour proved to be, he was not sorry to have missed it.

His association with the game was by no means over. He served as a selector for years, was manager of the 1966 tourists to England, served on the Board of Control and finally became President of it, providing a sane voice at the time of the Packer upheaval. He also sat for years as representative of agriculture in the Trinidad Senate. Few administrators have done more for West Indian cricket than Stollmeyer, with his concern to eradicate the old rivalries and jealousies; but he was to be denied an old age in which he could quietly reflect on his achievements. In August 1989 he and his family were attacked by intruders at their home in Port-of-Spain, and he was shot five times as well as suffering various other injuries. Five weeks later he died in hospital in Florida. The tributes that were paid could have left no one in any doubt that he was an outstanding man.

The question of his team's discipline was one that was to cause Hutton a good deal of anguish, as in the early matches some of his players displayed an attitude, both on and off the field, which, in the carefully chosen words of E.W. Swanton, 'was a fair way removed from the modesty habitual to an English games-player'. As the tour went on there were further occasions when English players made it clear what they thought of some of the umpiring decisions. Perhaps these problems could have been smoothed over had the press not joined in, but some reporters, and their editors, chose to describe events less than objectively. Near the end of the first Test the observation in one English paper that England were up against eleven West Indians and two umpires was quickly made known to the West Indian people, and they were not amused. Nowadays we have become accustomed to accusations of bias against certain umpires and write about them openly, but in the 1950s the game had not become the cynical monster it now is. The British influence meant that most West Indians grew up believing in the traditional ideals of fair play and sportsmanship, and if those ideals were coming to be seen as old-fashioned in some quarters, to the ordinary West Indian cricket-lover of the time they still meant something. Thus accusations of bias – and there were others as well – from the English press were genuinely hurtful. In due course the home journalists began to counter-attack by complaining about the lack of English discipline, and a press war was under way. As reporters – not all of them, of course – from each camp championed their own team at the expense of objectivity, public opinion was influenced accordingly and the problems were steadily exacerbated.

Matters were not helped by the idea going around that the series was to decide the unofficial championship of the world, for there was the feeling that this made the crowds more volatile. Inevitably there were some racial overtones, such as members of the white community stressing to the Englishmen how important it was for them to win. There was a misunderstanding when Hutton, mindful of the excellent hospitality they would meet everywhere, asked Lord's not to arrange too many social engagements as he did not want his players to get tired by standing around making small talk; this was distorted to the belief that he had instructed his team not to fraternize with the enemy, and inevitably caused ill feeling among the West Indian players and officials. One or two of the MCC squad – Trueman had an unhappy tour in this respect – were inexperienced in touring protocol and sometimes unwittingly gave offence by their boisterousness, leading to difficult situations. And so Hutton's problems multiplied.

For the English players the trouble lay with the umpires. Of the eight umpires who stood in the five Tests, two were substitutes; the other six, wrote E.W. Swanton, 'would be welcome on the first-class list in England'. Yet as so often with touring teams, MCC felt that the bad decisions were going against them far more often than against the home sides. Probably this was true, but it was just as true that the tourists made matters worse by their aggressive responses to the poor decisions. Goddard and Stollmeyer had instilled very high standards of behaviour into their players, and there was sadness in the home ranks that the Englishmen did not always respect the umpire's decision. The issue was complicated by the English players feeling that the crowd atmosphere made the umpires' jobs even harder than they should have been, but in part at least the crowd atmosphere was caused by resentment at the English indiscipline and their tactics of slowing down the game. Perhaps if the England manager had been a strict disciplinarian the trouble could have been nipped in the bud, but Charles Palmer has always been a gentle, courteous man for whom wielding the big stick has never been an option. His way of dealing with the problem was to be as diplomatic as possible, and he worked very hard to that end, but he was confronted by a virtually unresolvable situation.

The tourists played two first-class games in Jamaica before the first Test there, winning one and drawing the second, and were pleased that their batsmen seemed to have found the measure of Valentine. West Indies for their part had a number of injury problems, Worrell in particular being unavailable, and they replaced him with George Headley; he was 44 and semi-retired, but had just scored an unbeaten 53 against MCC and Stollmeyer and his co-selectors felt he was the right choice. Inevitably the other territories saw the selection as a political one, but it was soon clear anyway that he was nothing like the batsman he had been; after making 16 in the first innings he fell for just one in the second, bowled by Tony Lock's controversial faster ball. With Worrell fit for the second match, his Test career was finally over.

All of the Tests were to be played over six days (although a day's play was shorter than in England), an arrangement that has usually meant they are slow-moving affairs. After winning the toss, Stollmeyer chose to bat, not without qualms as the wicket looked as though it might be unfriendly – so much so that England had omitted Laker in favour of a fourth fast bowler. It turned out to be fairly docile, and by the close of play they were 168 for 2, Stollmeyer and Holt, on debut, having done most of the scoring. Next day was rather more interesting: Holt fell for 94, Weekes and Walcott had good knocks, and then Gomez and McWatt rode their luck to build up a useful seventh-wicket stand. The innings closed early on the third morning for 417, whereupon England collapsed feebly, the principal tormentors being two 'little pals'. 170 all out, and then Stollmeyer upset the crowd by not enforcing the follow-on. He later wrote that he formed his own views and then consulted Headley, who agreed with him, the thinking being that the two spinners needed a rest; Ramadhin had a sore finger, and they did not fancy having to bat last against Lock on a wicket that was beginning to crack. It was sound enough reasoning, but he was given police protection as the crowd thought otherwise.

For a while England bowled tightly and took wickets, but then Weekes got on top and Stollmeyer was able to declare at 209 for 6, leaving England nine and a half hours to score 457. One significant event was that Lock became only the second bowler in Test history to be no-balled for throwing, and the first one this century (the other had been Ernie Jones in 1897–8). Watson, with a century, Hutton and May gave England a splendid start, and just before lunch on the last day they were 277 for 2 with time to reach the target; Stollmeyer had to resort to defensive leg theory to keep the runs down, as well as imitating the slow over rate which England had used. Then suddenly wickets tumbled, four with the score on 282 and two more for just three more runs. Bailey and Moss swung the bat, but 316 all out and victory by 140 runs meant the calypsos were at full volume. The bowling hero was the 37-year-old local man Esmond Kentish, with 5 for 49; his reward was to be dropped, as the selectors subsequently decided to go for speed rather than accuracy. Yet amid the celebrations came the news that both umpires had been threatened for decisions against the home players. The wife and son of Perry Burke, who had given Holt out for 94 on debut at his home ground, were attacked, and Burke himself was accosted by a man with a knife. With the home captain needing protection as well, it was an altogether turbulent start.

The pattern of the second Test, in Barbados, proved very similar. West Indies had Worrell back but had temporarily lost Weekes, while England, who had just beaten Barbados by one wicket, abandoned the four-pronged pace attack for two spinners. Hutton lost the toss for the seventh consecutive Test, on a wicket which promised bounty for the batsmen at first and the spinners later; yet before long West Indies had lost three for just 25. Enter Walcott, with an innings of massive power and authority against bowling that did not have the best of days. At the close he was not out 147 out of a score of 258 for 5, Pairaudeau having given him good support with 71. Next day he completed his double century, with 220 out of a total of 383; on this supposedly good batting wicket only he, Pairaudeau and Atkinson, with 53, had scored more than 11. At the close on the second day England stood at 53 for 2; twenty-four hours later they had advanced to 181 for 9. Ramadhin and Valentine bowled excellently, the fielding was first-class and Stollmeyer was much praised for his orchestration – but 128 runs from 114 overs, for the loss of seven wickets, on a perfectly good pitch, was undoubtedly one of England's unhappiest days. Hutton, desperately aware of his responsibility as leading batsman, ground out a very slow 72, while all of them appeared to have lost the ability to time the ball or to put away loose deliveries. The youngsters in the crowd expressd their feelings in the age-old way, and at one point Hutton briefly declined to bat because of the noise. In those far-away days people looked forward with great anticipation to a visit by England, and their disgust at what they were offered was all too understandable.

When the final England wicket fell, there were no protestations that Stollmeyer did not enforce the follow-on, for bowling last was obviously going to be helpful. With their opening partnership worth 51, Holt and Stollmeyer stranded themselves in the middle of the pitch and it was left to the umpire to say who should go. The finger pointed to the captain, upon which Holt spent the rest of the day caning the bowlers for 166, putting on 222 for the second wicket with Worrell. He went first thing next morning, and the declaration soon came; as in the first Test, England were left with nine and a half hours to get their runs, in this case 495 of them. At least they made an attempt to redress the nonsense of the first innings. After Watson went Hutton and May, and then Compton and Graveney, all batted well. At lunch on the last day these two were still together, and with some time lost to the weather a draw seemed a fair possibility. Early in the afternoon Stollmeyer put himself on; he was very much a part-time bowler and took only thirteen Test wickets, but Compton stretched right forward to his googly, missed it, and was given out lbw; not a good decision. An hour and a half later West Indies were two up in the series, as four English batsmen went for ducks and only Graveney stood firm for an unbeaten 64. 313 all out meant victory by 181 runs.

That 220 was the highest score of Clyde Walcott's Test career. The phenomenon of the three Ws is a quite unique one in cricketing history; three world-class batsmen born within a few miles of each other in Barbados, two in Georgetown and one in St Michael, within the space of eighteen months. Walcott and Worrell even made their first-class debuts together in the same match, and all three made their Test debuts in the first two games against England in 1947–8. Physically, Walcott, easy-going by nature, was the biggest of the three, standing 6 feet 2 inches (1.9 metres) and weighing some fifteen stones (95 kilograms), unusually big for the wicket-keeping that he took up early in his career when poor form with the bat threatened his place for Barbados. He was to keep wicket in his first fifteen Tests, initially retaining his place only because of his reliability in this department as he took a while to come to terms with Test batsmanship. The runs began to come in his second series, in India 1948–9, after which he had few failures – as the splendid average of 56.68, virtually identical to his career average, indicates. Forty-four Tests were to bring him 3,798 runs with fifteen centuries, but what most people seem to remember about him is his sheer power; from a crouching stance he hit the ball just about as hard as anyone ever has, favouring the drive, the square cut, the hook and the back-foot drive back past the bowler. In the early 1950s he also broadened his experience by playing in the Lancashire League.

In 1945–6, just turned twenty, he and Frank Worrell put on an unbeaten 574 for the fourth wicket against Trinidad at Port-of-Spain, then the world-record partnership for any wicket and still the West Indies record for any wicket; Walcott's 314 not out remained his highest score. In 1950 his 168 helped to set up the historic first win at Lord's, but his two best series were the present one against England when he totalled 698 runs at 87.25, and against Australia a year later when he reached 827 runs at 82.70. In this latter rubber he scored no fewer than five centuries, and achieved something no one else has ever done; only six batsmen in Test history have made a hundred in each innings of a match more than once (even Bradman only did it once) and Walcott is the only one to do it twice in the same series.

He had a less happy time of it in his last two series against England, not helped by an injury early in 1957 which, in the words of C.L.R. James, 'left a feeling of some massive piece of machinery gone wrong'. Yet even when he was not on song with the bat he was, not surprisingly as an ex-wicket-keeper, an excellent slip fielder, and was also a useful medium-pace support bowler who chipped in with 11 Test wickets at 37. From the late 1960s to the early 1980s he was manager of a number of West Indian touring teams, and was awarded the OBE for his services to the game. Jeff Stollmeyer is on record as saying that he thought Walcott was often underestimated, but that invites the question 'By whom?' – certainly not by opposing bowlers.

For the third Test they moved on to British Guiana, where MCC beat the home team by an innings thanks to Watson and Graveney each scoring a double century and putting on a stand of 402. The umpiring had been such, though, that Hutton requested that neither should officiate in the Test, and this was agreed. Since the Bourda ground had the reputation of being very easy-paced and a fast bowler's idea of hell, West Indies omitted King in favour of an extra batsman, while England brought in Wardle, thus playing three spinners and only two seamers. As it turned out, one man who was to have a happy match was Brian Statham. Hutton finally won a toss, and a slow first day's play saw England at 153 for 2. Next day they speeded up considerably, and with the captain making a virtually faultless 169 the total reached 435, with Compton, Bailey and Wardle making good runs. A notable feat occurred when Valentine bowled Laker to reach his 100th Test wicket, the first to achieve this in under four years.

It was then that Statham made his strike, taking three prime wickets on an excellent pitch with just 16 on the board. Weekes was to fall just short of a century, but apart from him the only resistance came from McWatt and Holt, the latter batting with a runner. These two had put on 98 for the eighth wicket when they went for a risky second run. May's throw was true, Evans broke the stumps and McWatt, clearly a couple of yards (2 metres) short, carried on running to the pavilion. Ramadhin had reached the crease when suddenly bottles began to rain on to the pitch behind the square-leg umpire, Menzies, who had given McWatt out. The mounted police moved in and the uproar was soon brought under control, no doubt helped by Hutton keeping his team on the field. Connoisseurs of cricket riots will not be surprised to learn that McWatt was a local man; nor to learn that under the surface there were political currents swirling, and that the run-out was just the excuse that some people were waiting for to stage a demonstration.

There were no more interruptions and soon West Indies, all out 251, found themselves following on. Whereupon England, bowling and fielding

*Johnny Wardle even managed to entertain the crowd when they were throwing bottles at him – he picked up one of them, pretended to drink, then reeled about as though drunk. It helped take the tension out of the situation.*

well, worked steadily through them, most of the batsmen getting in and then getting out. 256 all out represented a fine performance by all the bowlers on a good wicket, and left them needing just 73 with all the afternoon to get them. Only one wicket was lost before Watson ended matters with a six; and the crowd warmly applauded the English victory.

On the way to Trinidad for the next Test the MCC party stopped for a two-day match at Grenada and encountered a link with the distant past. One of the party that greeted them at the airport was W.H. Mignon, the only survivor of the 1900 touring team. When they reached Trinidad they saw off the island team by seven wickets, and went into the Test with great expectations. Hutton lost the toss yet again, though, and for the second and last time the three Ws took advantage of a beautiful wicket – the jute matting pitch made life notoriously difficult for the bowlers, and this was to be the last Test in which it was used – to run up a century apiece. By the close of the first day Weekes and Worrell had taken the score to 294 for 2, but there had been some unpleasantness when two appeals for catches were turned down – one of them after Holt had already begun to walk – and the umpires complained to Hutton about remarks made by the players. Statham also pulled a rib muscle, seriously enough to spell the end of his bowling for the tour. Next day Weekes reached his double century as he and Worrell put on 338 for the third wicket, still the West Indies record for that wicket in all Tests. Weekes's 206 was not without blemish; Fred Trueman relates that several times early in his innings the umpire turned down appeals for catches by the wicket-keeper. When at last he was out, Trueman, according to his story, grinned at him and said, 'Well played, Everton. Not bad, two hundred and six for four innings.' 'Five,' replied Weekes. 'I got a nick when I was in the sixties but nobody bothered to appeal.' With Worrell getting 167, Walcott 124 and Atkinson 74, West Indies piled up their highest home total against England: 681 for 8 declared. Trueman's opinion of jute matting pitches may easily be imagined.

532 to avoid the follow-on is a daunting target. Hutton and Bailey made a sound start before each fell in the forties, whereupon May and Compton each made a century and took the score to 301 before the third wicket fell. Graveney scored 92, and when he went 39 were needed from the last four wickets. Laker was hit above the eye and had to go off, and it was left to Trueman and Statham to squeeze their team to safety, the innings closing at 537. That effectively ended the game as a spectacle, Stollmeyer declaring the second innings at 212 for 4 and England batting out the last session. McWatt the wicket-keeper and Ferguson the bowler swopped places, McWatt having made no dismissals and Ferguson having taken

*Denis Compton – a century in the fourth Test of 1953–4 helped save the match and the series.*

1 for 155 in the first innings. Ferguson promptly held two catches and McWatt took 1 for 16, as England meandered to 98 for 3.

The 206 that Everton Weekes made in the first innings was one short of his highest Test score, against India a year earlier on the same matting pitch at Port-of-Spain. Of the three Ws, he was the shortest in height, the readiest to laugh and – although they are so much a trinity that one has the feeling that drawing distinctions among them is almost sacrilegious – arguably the finest batsman. Certainly he ended with the highest Test average, and only six of the leading run-scorers have a better figure than his 58.61; and he was the one who was most consistently compared with Bradman. His batting was unorthodox without being careless, lightning footwork giving him time to choose from a full range of strokes; the square cut, the pull and the drive off either foot were perhaps the most spectacular, but wherever the ball went it was hit with enormous power. So much so, indeed, that Frank Worrell suggested to him that he should hit the ball less hard, since with his power the fielders often did not bother to chase it; were he to ease off a bit, they would have to run after it and would quickly get tired. Weekes agreed there was something in this, but did not change his ways.

He secured his place in the national team with a century in his fourth match against Allen's side in 1947–8, following this in India a year later with four consecutive Test centuries (almost five, as he was run out for 90 in the next innings) to set a new West Indies aggregate record of 779 runs at 111. On tour in England in 1950 (like Walcott he was very successful in League cricket in England), he scored over 2,300 runs at nearly 80, with four double centuries and one treble, and in one inspired spell he made 575 runs in three innings before he was dismissed. At home to India in 1952–3, he again made over 700 runs with an average in three figures, and in this series against England he totalled 487 at almost 70. In all he totalled 4,455 runs from his 48 Tests, with fifteen centuries, and saved countless more with his brilliant fielding in the covers or at slip. There were failures in amongst all this, of course, but not many, and he was a hugely entertaining batsman to watch. He was also, according to Stollmeyer, an easy player to captain, for he had such a good knowledge of the game that he anticipated the captain's moves and knew what was coming; so it was not surprising that when he became captain of Barbados he led them well.

As well as being outstanding cricketers the three Ws were also all highly intelligent, articulate men. Walcott went on to be an excellent tour manager, while Weekes became a much-respected radio and television commentator, as well as representing his island at bridge. Like his partner, he too was awarded the OBE for his services to the game.

The final Test was played back at Kingston, where in the opening game England had played just one spinner and come a cropper. Now they played three – only for Trevor Bailey to have the best day's bowling of his Test career. Operating at slightly below top pace, he moved the ball in the air and off the seam, bowling carefully at any weaknesses he had perceived. Sixteen overs brought him 7 wickets for 34 runs, at the time England's best return against West Indies, and with good support from Trueman he had West Indies all out for 139, only Walcott reaching 50. Bailey rounded off his day by opening with Hutton, but the following morning saw them both bogged down. This day and the next were to be Hutton's, though, as the scoring rate steadily picked up and for almost nine hours he battled to press home the advantage. Admittedly the home team were without their fast bowler, King, on the third day, but it was a real captain's innings, a tale of total concentration under a fierce Caribbean sun. He was rewarded with a double century, the first one by an England captain in a Test abroad, and although none of his top batsmen got much past thirty, Wardle weighed in with 66 and the total reached 414.

He also lost his wicket because of a rumpus during the tea interval. As he left the field, concerning only with having a brief rest and freshen-up, he acknowledged the applause of the crowd in front of the pavilion; but as soon as he was in the dressing-room an official burst in crying, 'This is the crowning insult!' and complaining that he had insulted the Jamaican Chief Minister, Alexander Bustamante, by not responding to his personal congratulations. Despite Mr Bustamante subsequently assuring him that he understood that he had simply not recognized him in the crowd, the press made a front-page story out of it and called it an 'unpleasant incident', leading to speculation that as a photographer had been present it could have been a put-up job designed to discredit the MCC team. Whether this was true or not it meant that Hutton's concentration was shattered, and he was out straight afterwards for 205.

Thereafter England chipped away at the West Indies wickets, Trueman making two early strikes and Laker conceding just 71 runs from 50 overs, with four wickets. Walcott made a century and Stollmeyer 64, but 346 all out left England needing only 72, and as in the third Test they lost just one wicket getting there. It meant that one young man did not enjoy his debut as much as he had hoped, for it was in this match that the 17-year-old Garfield Sobers first trod the Test turf. Batting at number nine he scored 14 not out and 26 and took 4 for 75, his first wicket being that of Trevor Bailey – who in due course would write his biography.

Len Hutton wrote that the tour left him physically and mentally drained, and shortened his playing career by maybe two years. Yet at least some splendid cricket had been played, and the relations between the players had improved considerably as the series had gone on. Clearly there were faults and misunderstandings on both sides which were blown up out of proportion from very early on, and clearly there were lessons to be learned by many people on both sides of the Atlantic.

*

On paper, the following series should have been just as evenly fought. The West Indian team that came to England in 1957 contained most of the architects of the great victory seven years earlier: the three Ws, Ramadhin and Valentine, and the captain Goddard. They also had some young players of whom hopes were very high, such as Sobers, Kanhai and Collie Smith. Admittedly they lacked a settled pair of openers, but so did

*West Indian touring team to England in 1957. Standing left to right: W. Ferguson (scorer and baggageman), A.G. Ganteaume, N.S. Asgarali, F.C.M. Alexander, G.S. Sobers, W.W. Hall, D.T. Dewdney, B.H. Pairaudeau, R. Gilchrist, O.G. Smith, R.B. Kanhai. Seated left to right: N. Pierce (manager), S. Ramadhin, D.S. Atkinson, F.M.M. Worrell, J.D.C. Goddard (captain), C.L. Walcott, E.D. Weekes, A.L. Valentine, C. de Caires (manager).*

England. The home team were, though, in one of the most successful periods of their entire history, with a very strong team: if Peter Richardson did not have a regular opening partner he was very dependable himself, May, Cowdrey and Graveney were almost the equal of the three Ws, Bailey an outstanding all-rounder, Evans still a splendid wicket-keeper, Laker and Lock every bit as good as Ramadhin and Valentine, and Trueman, Statham and Loader a much better pace attack than the inexperienced Dewdney, Gilchrist and Hall. They had not lost a series since 1950–1 and were brimfull of confidence. On top of this, the luck went against the visitors, with injury and illness affecting several players: Weekes suffered from sinus trouble and also broke his finger, Walcott injured himself during the first Test and was below par for the rest of the summer, Valentine was ill for a while, had one good game that suggested he was back to form and then broke his nose, while Ramadhin suffered the most damaging injury of all – to his spirit. Furthermore, the West Indies Board had come up with the strange idea of appointing two tour managers, N. Pierce and Cecil de Caires, giving them both equal status. Almost inevitably this led to frictions within the party that undermined their strength.

John Goddard was now 38 and was unable to find any sort of form in

*Roy Gilchrist could have become a great fast bowler with more sensitive handling.*

the Tests. His appointment as captain had hardly been greeted ecstatically. In the last series West Indies had played, in New Zealand in 1955–6 – when, having won the first three Tests, they lost the last one to give the New Zealanders their first ever Test victory – he had actually averaged 147, thanks to being undefeated in three of his four innings, but he had been player-manager rather than captain. When Stollmeyer declined to go to New Zealand the team had been led by Denis Atkinson, despite the fact that Worrell had been vice-captain against Hutton's tourists; now all three of these were passed over in favour of Goddard. There was a school of thought which felt that Worrell was overlooked not so much because he was black but because he was a professional; maybe that was a part of it, but most people were in no doubt that his colour was altogether more important.

England had no such problems. Peter May was in the middle of his record run of leading England forty-one times, one of England's finest batsmen fortunate enough to coincide with one of their strongest teams. A classically upright, stylish batsman, six feet (1.8 metres) tall, his strokeplay was all about precision and timing, yet there was no shortage of power when needed; even the most demanding purist found him a pleasure to watch, and no one has really challenged him for the title of the most complete English batsman to emerge since the war. In character he was quiet and reserved, not ideal qualities to bring to leadership of a disparate group of men, but he seemed to have few problems with personal relation-ships within the team and there was never any question over his authority. On the pitch he succeeded in finding a balance between strict discipline and anonymity, taking the view that anyone good enough to play in a Test should not need too many instructions.

He learnt about captaincy from two people, Stuart Surridge at Surrey and Len Hutton. Surridge was one of the outstanding county captains, who took his team to triumph after triumph by positive and dynamic leadership. Hutton's captaincy of England was much more cautious, and the usual criticism of May is that he found his natural inclinations more suited to the Yorkshireman's approach; Hutton's delicate position ex-cused his lack of adventure, but in May's case it was rather more difficult to justify. He continued the idea of slow over rates as a tactical ploy, and

*Peter May on his way to 285 not out. Rohan Kanhai, on debut, is behind the stumps.*

he became noted for his reluctance to take any chance that might lead to defeat – witness the lateness of his declaration in the first Test, when someone like Surridge would have been only too eager to press home the enormous psychological advantage that had been gained. For all that, though, he was a sound and capable leader who did not lose a series until the shambles in Australia in 1958–9, and the shame was that he retired from Test cricket so early, aged just 31, worn out by the demands made upon him and with his health suffering. For now, though, he was about to play, in the first Test, the innings of his life.

The MCC game was spoiled when over half of the first day was lost to rain. West Indies batted first and, with centuries from Walcott and Sobers, were able to declare at 337 for 6; MCC replied with 284, including a hundred from Close, batting with an injured foot throughout, which ensured him a place in the first Test. Worrell was to head the bowling averages in the coming series and gave notice of that now, hitting the middle stump three times as he took 6 for 71. There was little time for anything meaningful to happen, though, and West Indies just took the opportunity for some batting practice, finishing at 193 for 3.

There had been no Test cricket at Edgbaston since 1929, and its return to favour was marked by one of the most curious games of all. In the four matches he had played before the Test, Ramadhin had taken 38 wickets and was obviously right on song, and when May won the toss and batted on a slightly damp pitch he had the best day of his Test career – 7 for 49 as England were all out for 186. West Indies then set about building a good lead. Walcott made 90 but tore a leg muscle in the process. Collie Smith, in his first Test in England, made 161, and Sobers and Worrell scored well; 474 all out. By the end of the third day Ramadhin had taken two more wickets, and at 102 for 2 the optimism was very much in the visitors' camp.

Over the weekend a group of former and current English cricketers discussed Ramadhin at length, one of them, Bill Bowes, being convinced that the best plan was to treat him as an off-spinner and play forward. Twenty minutes into the fourth day Close was out, Cowdrey joined May with the score at 113 for 3, and the plan was put into operation. It was simplicity itself: if the front leg is stretched as far forward as it can go it becomes impossible to say for certain that the ball would hit the wicket. It was not just to balls outside the line of the stumps that the batsmen went forward but to straight balls as well, secure in the knowledge that distance from the stumps meant safety. To a ball pitched around the off stump that was too short to drive, both batsmen, Cowdrey in particular, meticulously thrust their left leg forward; and there was nothing that Ramadhin, Goddard or anyone else could do about it. Since their priority was to save the game it did not make for scintillating watching; May took four hours ten minutes to reach his hundred, and Cowdrey no less than seven and three-quarter hours. Only when he had his century did Cowdrey cut loose, scoring his next fifty in almost even time. When he finally holed out they had been together for 8 hours 20 minutes and the stand was worth 411, the record English Test partnership and the record fourth-wicket partnership in all Tests. Goddard estimated that something like a hundred appeals were turned down.

West Indies were hampered by Worrell being unable to bowl and then losing Gilchrist, but Goddard still had Atkinson, Sobers and Smith as well as himself. Yet he asked poor Ramadhin to send down no less than 98 overs, the most ever bowled in an innings in any first-class match (his 129 overs in the game is also a record for Tests), when it was clear long before the torment ended that he was never going to get a wicket. Inevitably his captaincy was severely criticized, while Ramadhin, for his part, just grew more and more frustrated; he felt that the tactic was against the spirit of the game, and there were plenty of people to agree with him. Before long the lbw law would be changed, largely as a result of this stand, to make such defensive play a perilous business.

With the score at 524 England had a lead of 236, there were about three hours left and the opposition were totally demoralized. Yet May chose to make the game completely safe, putting on 59 in half an hour with Evans before declaring at 583. He himself was undefeated on 285, at the time the highest ever score by an England captain in a Test and the highest post-war Test innings. For almost ten hours he had played virtually flawlessly. Not surprisingly, West Indies then collapsed and had lost seven wickets before Goddard and Smith decided that the best way to play Laker and Lock was by stretching the front leg well forward. Smith spent 65 minutes over five runs and Goddard forty minutes without scoring, but they saved the game. A final score of 72 for 7 left everyone wondering whether that extra half-hour of bat-swinging would not have been better employed by the bowlers; although in fairness to May the concentration demanded to bat for ten hours must have taken its toll of clear thinking.

There cannot have been many people present who did not realize that they were witnessing an important moment in cricket history. Certainly, as far as this series was concerned, there was now only going to be one winner. At Lord's the match was decided when Bailey, in his fiftieth Test, had another of his inspired days, taking 7 for 44 to dismiss West Indies for

*Edgbaston 1957 – Trevor Bailey bowled by Ramadhin for 1. John Goddard thinks this a good arrangement.*

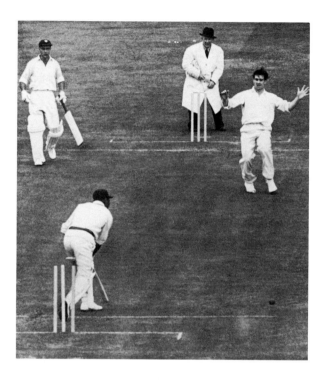

*And Everton Weekes bowled by Trueman for 9. Bruce Pairaudeau is the non-striker and Emrys Davies the umpire.*

127. Even then they might have made a fight of it had they not insisted on dropping catch after catch; May went for a duck, but Cowdrey made another 150, Richardson 76 and Evans, dropped five times, 82. A total of 424 left the visitors with a large mountain to climb, and although Weekes made a sparkling 90 – in a manner said to be reminiscent of Bradman at his best – and Sobers 66, no one else got very far. Bailey finished with 11 wickets as England won by an innings and 36 runs. Ramadhin, incidentally, took 1 for 83 from 22 overs.

An easy pitch at Trent Bridge produced a stack of runs. When England won the toss Richardson and Graveney put on 256 for the second wicket, with Graveney going on to the highest score of his career, 258. After Richardson went for 126 May also made a century, and the board showed 487 before the third wicket went down. The declaration came at 619 for 6, after which it was Worrell's turn to demonstrate great batsmanship as he became the first West Indian to carry his bat through a completed Test innings. When the last wicket fell at 372 he was undefeated on 191, without having offered a chance, and with Ramadhin he had set a tenth-wicket record of 55 against England which was to be crucial to saving the match. Following-on he was, hardly surprisingly after nine and a half

*Tom Graveney had an excellent record against West Indies, with a highest score of 258 at Trent Bridge in 1957. He was rather good to watch as well.*

hours, less successful, and five wickets were down for 89 before Collie Smith took over; supported first by Atkinson and then Goddard he stayed for seven hours to make 168 out of a second innings of 367, leaving England needing 121. Time was too short, though, and at the close they were on 64 for 1.

The last two Tests saw no West Indian batting heroics to save them. At Headingley their last four first-innings wickets fell to consecutive balls, as Trueman took a wicket with the last ball of an over and Peter Loader took the only England hat-trick in a home Test this century to dismiss them for 142. The England reply was not over-convincing as only May, Cowdrey and Sheppard got amongst the runs in a total of 279, with Worrell taking

*Godfrey Evans in regulation pose.*

7 for 70. It was very much a game for the seamers, in fact, for West Indies were then bundled out for 132, leaving England winners by an innings and five runs. If this was a miserable defeat for the visitors there was worse to come, as each innings of the third, fourth and fifth Tests got steadily smaller. At the Oval, Graveney and Richardson again made centuries to set up an England score of 412, whereupon it was Lock's turn to take some wickets – 5 for 28 as the first innings collapsed for 89, and 6 for 20 as the second innings disintegrated for 86, still their two lowest totals against England. With Laker taking five wickets in the match, cynics might have been forgiven for thinking that their home pitch had been specially prepared for them; certainly it was nowhere near Test standard. Sobers scored 81 out of 175, but England had the game won by the afternoon of the third day, an innings and 237 runs the margin.

Although they lost the Test series conclusively, these were the only defeats that West Indies suffered and 14 of their 31 first-class games were won. Ramadhin finally got some wickets in the last Test, with 4 for 107, and Sobers, although he had not yet fulfilled his promise, had done enough to suggest that he soon would. If Weekes and Walcott had struggled for much of the time, Worrell had proved again what an outstanding cricketer he was, with fine performances with both bat and ball; but perhaps the player who had most caught the eye was Collie Smith, with his two innings of over 160.

Christened O'Neil Gordon Smith, he was invariably known as Collie. Coming into the Jamaica team in 1954–5 he made 169 against the touring Australians in only his third match and found himself in the Test team as a result, where he promptly scored another hundred. Cricket being what it is, in the next Test he got a pair, and his batting faded for a while. He had an off-spinning string to his bow which helped him retain his place, though, and there were those who thought that he could have developed into a front-line spinner. As a schoolboy he had fancied himself as a speed merchant, but watching Jim Laker during the 1947–8 tour had converted him to the subtleties of spin. The centuries in England marked the resurgence of his batting and, as experience brought greater discipline, he became a fine stroke-maker, finishing with 1,331 runs at nearly 32 from his 26 Tests. His best Test performance came against India at Delhi in 1958–9, when he scored a century and took eight wickets in the match. In 1958 and 1959 he played very successfully for Burnley in the Lancashire League, and it was while travelling through the night to a charity game in London after a league match in September 1959 that he was killed in a road accident. His great friend Garry Sobers was driving, Tom Dewdney

*'Collie' Smith during his century at Edgbaston in 1957. Godfrey Evans behind the stumps.*

beside him, and Smith asleep on the back seat, when as they rounded a bend there was a lorry in front of them. Sobers swerved, but in the crash Smith was thrown off the seat and severely injured his back. He spent three days in a coma, but did not recover.

To Sobers the loss was shattering, not just because he had lost a close friend but because he had lost a stabilizing influence. For Collie Smith, though just 26, had been a wise and thoughtful companion for a young man who, at that stage in his career, did not always stop to think too closely about matters in hand. Smith had the rare talent of being able to enjoy his cricket and his life to the full, yet also to reflect upon them calmly and analytically. The tributes that came from all over the cricketing world spoke of his rich promise, his sportsmanship, his charm, his outstanding character, his spirit, his love of playing the game for the game's sake, and it was estimated that 60,000 people attended his funeral. There can be no doubt that he had the character to have matured not only into a great player but into a fine captain as well, for he had an excellent cricketing brain, was always full of ideas, and would have been highly respected. The sense of loss over what he might have achieved is still strong all these years later.

*

The 4–0 drubbing that Australia inflicted on England in 1958–9 spelt the end of the Test road for several of the stalwarts of the past decade, and as a result Peter May's team to the West Indies in 1959–60 contained a number of youngsters hoping to make strides along their own Test roads. Of the team that had come six years earlier, only May, Trueman and Statham remained, and apart from them only Cowdrey was a really experienced Test player, but Dexter, Barrington, Mike Smith, Subba Row and Pullar were all to play their parts in a successful rubber. May was still captain but his health was poor after an operation the previous summer, and after the third Test he had to return home, leaving Cowdrey in command. For West Indies, Weekes had gone and Walcott played in only the last two games, but Worrell and Ramadhin (who was to head the bowling averages) were still there, Sobers and Kanhai had established their world class, and some of the fine West Indians of the 1960s, such as Hunte, Butcher, Hall, Solomon, Nurse and Griffith had either joined the team or would do so during the series. The feeling was that West Indies were slightly the stronger team, especially with their home advantage.

It was to be the last series in which they would be captained by a white man. Worrell had actually been offered the captaincy for the visit by Pakistan in 1957–8 but had declined it as he was studying at Manchester University, and it had gone instead to F.C.M. 'Gerry' Alexander. A wicket-keeper, he had come into the team for the last two Tests of 1957, taken four catches and scored 11 runs and three ducks; yet in Worrell's absence he found himself captain for the series against Pakistan. The only other white players in the team were the Atkinson brothers and, since Denis's captaincy had not been a success and Eric was making his debut, Alexander got the job; the presence of Weekes and Walcott in the team apparently counted for nothing in captaincy terms. As a Cambridge graduate – he had won blues for cricket and soccer, had an F.A. Amateur Cup winner's medal and been capped by England at amateur soccer – he had the right credentials to satisfy the selectors, and certainly over the next four series he was to prove a sound, if not outstanding, leader. On his day he could be a fine attacking batsman, but the demands of captaincy and wicket-keeping meant that his batting was not always as strong as it might have been. It came into its own only when he had relinquished the captaincy to Worrell, for in his last series, against Australia in 1960–1, he topped the averages with 484 runs at 60, as well as making 16 dismissals. His wicket-keeping was always very dependable and at times could be quite brilliant, and in the coming rubber against England he was to equal the then world record of 23 dismissals. In all, he made 90 dismissals in 25

Tests, giving him a 'strike rate' that puts him high on the list of the leading Test keepers.

Alexander was a warm man, a courageous cricketer and, despite the racial and intercolonial problems, was generally popular with his players. At home to Pakistan (won 3–1) and then away to India (won 3–0) and Pakistan (lost 2–1) there was no Worrell in the team, so that Worrell's supporters were unable to press his case for the captaincy. With Worrell available for the England series, though, there was an outcry when he was passed over, for everyone, including the selectors, knew full well that he was a natural leader in a way that Alexander could never be, with a vastly greater store of cricketing knowledge, experience and wisdom. A year later the selectors were finally to bow to the inevitable and appoint Worrell to take the team to Australia, and Alexander, to his great credit, served as his vice-captain happily and loyally.

This 1959–60 series proved to be less than exhilarating, for one main reason: the pitches had all been over-prepared for six-day Tests (albeit of only five hours a day) and so the bowlers had little chance of disposing of the opposition twice. Only one innings was completed for less than 240, a collapse that was enough to lose the rubber. England's overall scoring rate was slightly the faster of the two, but the speed at which the overs were bowled – by both teams – left a lot to be desired. There was also an excess of short-pitched fast stuff, mostly from the young West Indians Hall and Watson, which neither Alexander nor the umpires did much to curtail and which caused some ill feeling. Furthermore, as on the previous tour, and as there would be on the next one, there was a bottle-throwing riot, with the people of Trinidad deciding it was their turn to cause some trouble.

MCC began by beating a weak team from the Windward Islands and then losing heavily to Barbados. There was a further setback when Statham withdrew injured on the eve of the first Test, and David Allen was given his first cap. The Bridgetown wicket looked good for plenty of runs, and when May won the toss he was the only one of the top batsmen not to make a score. Pullar and Cowdrey got off to a sound start, Barrington registered his first Test century, Dexter made an unbeaten 136, and on the third morning the innings closed at 482, with Alexander having set a West Indies record by taking five catches in an innings. Almost immediately there was a spot of drama: Trueman bowled a no-ball to Hunte, who hit it toward mid-on and began to run. Seeing Allen closing on it he changed his mind and sent McMorris back, but Allen, facing away from the wicket, flicked the ball back underhand and hit the stumps with McMorris – in only his second Test and without yet having scored – well out.

Hunte and Kanhai both made forties, and near the close of the third day Sobers was joined by Worrell, the latter having played no real first-class cricket since the 1957 series. It was the morning of the sixth day before they were separated. As a bald statement that sounds magnificent – the only pair to bat through two days of a Test, although an hour was lost at the end of the first day and the rest day intervened. Their partnership of 399 is the West Indian fourth-wicket Test record, the West Indian record for any wicket against England, the longest in all Tests at 9 hours 39 minutes; Worrell batted for 682 minutes and Sobers for 647, at the time the two longest innings ever played against England. The trouble was that such a scoring rate did not enthral. In the words of Alan Ross: 'There was something automatic and dream-like about the batting: these were sleep-players on a feather-bed who every now and then woke up and fired off a couple of rounds at flies on the ceiling.'

The match expired during their partnership because they did not score quickly enough to give their bowlers a target on the last day. Both had started well enough only to let the momentum drift away, apparently ignoring the captain's signals to speed things up. After Sobers went for 226, Butcher, Hall and Alexander all fell cheaply as they tried to hit out, whereupon Alexander declared with Worrell on 197, where he had been for a long, long time; in two hours he had scored ten runs. Various explanations were advanced for Worrell's slowness, none of them very convincing for, even though the field setting was defensive, there were endless singles to be picked up had he wanted to bother. It was all very sad, and when England saw out the last three hours Cowdrey made his protest by scoring just 16 runs out of 71 without loss.

The lack of excitement in Barbados was more than compensated for in Trinidad. MCC beat the island team twice and then, after May had won the toss, began the Test by losing three wickets for 57. Once again it was Barrington and Dexter to the rescue, with a hundred partnership in even time. Dexter went for 77, Barrington was hit on the head, and Hall was warned for too much short-pitched bowling. At breakfast next morning, with a fine piece of prescience, Barrington remarked, 'Crash-helmets will be worn'; he then completed his century as Watson joined Hall in the umpires' notebooks for intimidatory bowling. By the end of the day, Smith also had a hundred, the total had reached 382, and West Indies had begun their innings without alarms. Next day the series was decided, mainly by Trueman and Statham. Intelligent, controlled fast bowling, well pitched up, supported by excellent fielding, saw West Indies take lunch at 45 for 5. The afternoon produced a lot of maiden overs and one more wicket. After

*The great Brian Statham
watched by umpire Bill
Copson, another fast
bowler of distinction.*

tea, Alexander departed for his team's top score of 28, and then Singh, a local youngster in his first Test, was run out going for a quick single.

It was the signal for the bottles to come raining on to the pitch, first from one stand and then from all round the ground. There was no question of the players staying out, for apart from the sea of bottles there was soon fighting on the field which the small number of police could do nothing about. The Governor of Trinidad, Sir Edward Beetham, appealed for peace, but in vain. Desperate officials tried to turn a fire hose on the crowd but, with hardly any pressure, the water just trickled out ludicrously, and only brought forth yet more bottles. Some were deliberately broken before being thrown, and inevitably a good deal of blood was shed. The mayhem lasted three-quarters of an hour until police reinforcements, some of them mounted, dispersed the fighters, and the crowd drifted away. Thirty people ended up in hospital.

*Mike Smith's century at Trinidad in 1959–60 helped England win the series.*

Alan Ross estimated that, of the crowd of 30,000, some 500 may have actually fought or thrown bottles, and several thousand more had invaded the field. It was the biggest crowd ever to attend a sporting event in the West Indies, and the overcrowding in great heat may have contributed to the sudden eruption. Probably there were a number of causes, ranging through the poor performance of the team, an excess of rum and whisky, the fervour brought on by the gambling taking place, to the political jealousies and tensions that are an integral part of the Caribbean scene. Many knowledgeable people were in no doubt that, as was thought to have been the case six years earlier, it had been deliberately started by political activists out to discredit the local government and people, but of course nothing could be proved. In 1953–4 one element had been the unpopularity of the tourists, but here the officials were at pains to make it clear in their apologies to May's team and to MCC that the riot had nothing to do with the Englishmen. For a people renowned for their sportsmanship it was a very sad day.

Seventy-five minutes were lost and it was agreed to make these up on the remaining days. The last two home wickets soon fell on the fourth morning and they were all out for 112, whereupon May chose not to enforce the follow-on. With a lead of 270, three days left and a pitch that might be difficult on the last day, it was a reasonable decision. England did not sparkle as they built up their lead, with most of the entertainment coming from Trueman in bat-swinging mood, but on the fifth morning May declared at 230 for 9, a lead of 500. West Indies had ten hours to survive. Only two wickets were lost on that day and, with Kanhai and Sobers in harness at the close, there was hope that the game might be saved. Kanhai did go on to a century, in fact, but after Sobers went he had little real support and the last wicket went down with an hour and three-quarters to spare. 244 all out gave a victory margin of 256 runs. The wickets were shared among the bowlers, but it was Trueman and Statham who led the team off after a fine day of bowling on a good pitch.

Happily in Jamaica the excitement was confined to the cricket; not on the first day, though, as England wasted another winning of the toss by struggling to 165 for 6 by the close. Next day they were all out for 277, thanks to Cowdrey's century and some useful tailend knocks, with Wes Hall producing his best Test figures of 7 for 69 and bowling a great many bouncers in the process. West Indies' reply centred on a century from Sobers, who made 147, 73 from McMorris – which despite being hit over the heart must have been sweet after being run out off a no-ball in the first match and omitted from the second – and 70 from Nurse on his debut. At 329 for 3, things looked black for England but three wickets suddenly went for no runs, and the innings was wrapped up for 353.

Cowdrey and Pullar produced an opening stand worth 177 before both departed at that score, Cowdrey just three short of making a century in each innings. Thereafter only May's 45 made much impression on the score-book, and by the close nine wickets were down for 280. Allen followed his unbeaten first knock of 30 with an unbeaten 17 and, in a crucial last-wicket stand with Statham that was just big enough to tilt the balance, took the score to 305, leaving West Indies with 230 to win in 245 minutes; on a pitch with some crevasse-like cracks in it, there seemed every prospect of an interesting few hours. McMorris went early on, then Hunte for 40 after looking set to get the runs on his own. Good progress, then tragedy – a mix-up with Kanhai and Sobers was run out. The hundred came up in just under two hours, leaving 130 minutes in which to score as many runs. Nurse's wicket fell, Kanhai launched an assault, Scarlett departed; 90 needed in 75 minutes as fortunes fluctuated. Kanhai went down with cramp, May refused a runner, the crowd booed, Trueman scattered his stumps, the fourth time in the day he had hit the timbers. Half an hour left and West Indies clearly could not win; could England snaffle the last four wickets? Alexander and Solomon made sure they could not, and so they finished with honours even – England those four wickets short, West Indies 55 runs short. May was criticized for refusing Kanhai a runner, which he had no right to do, and he apologized; fortunately it did not affect the outcome of a match full of ebbs and flows. The way in which the advantage moved back and forth made it one of the best contests the two countries had ever had.

It was followed by one of the less exciting matches. On arrival in Georgetown, Peter May finally revealed that for several weeks he had been suffering bleeding from the abscess on which he had been operated the previous summer, and was ordered to rest. Cowdrey duly took over the side, duly won the toss, and duly continued with May's largely defensive tactics. On the deadest pitch of the series, England batted for the best part of two days for 295, only Cowdrey and Allen getting past 50, and Hall getting another six-wicket bag. With some time lost for rain, West Indies then batted until the fifth day for 402 for 8 declared, as Sobers made his third century of the rubber. There were just over eight hours left when England resumed 107 behind, with West Indies hampered by an injury to fast bowler Watson. Only early disaster could have produced any interest, but Subba Row, batting with a chipped knuckle, and Dexter helped themselves to hundreds and the game expired as England reached 334 for 8 by the close. Alan Ross maintained that it was a better match than the scores suggest, but with both sides playing slowly there never seems to have been much chance of a result. Since West Indies needed a win more than England, Alexander's slowness was less easy to understand than Cowdrey's.

After the match it was announced that May and Statham would be returning home, May because of his own illness and Statham because of his son's. Jim Parks, who had been coaching in Trinidad, was drafted into the team for the last Test, while West Indies brought in a young man named Charlie Griffith for his first game. The caravan returned to Port-of-Spain, where there had been hardly any rain for weeks, amid firm predictions that the pitch could not possibly last six days. It looked a good toss to win, and when Cowdrey won it he created the only instance of one side winning five tosses in a rubber where there has been a change of captain – and he was to go on to win all five in the forthcoming series against South Africa, too. He celebrated now by scoring another century, and with 76 from Dexter the innings reached 393, whereupon poor McMorris was again unluckily run out; this time he was backing up as Alexander drove a ball from Trueman, who stuck out a foot and saw the ball crash into the stumps. At least McMorris was to get one century before he was finished.

With time lost to the weather, it was near the end of the fourth day when Alexander declared at 338 for 8, and he must have been glad he did when Cowdrey fell immediately to a gentle half-volley; and gladder still when the sixth wicket went down for 148. Only during the evening of the fifth day, when Mike Smith and Parks came together, did the game really seem safe for England. On the last morning they took their stand to 197 – the England record for the seventh wicket in all Tests – and, though Smith fell on 96, Parks reached his first Test century. Cowdrey left his declaration till this was achieved, setting West Indies the task of scoring 406 at 140 runs an hour – they reached 209 for 5, with Walcott making 22 in his last Test innings – only to be criticized by the manager, Walter Robins, for his lack of adventure. Since his three main bowlers were injured, the pitch was still playing fairly well and the chance of winning was negligible, others took a more charitable view of Cowdrey's decision not to squander weeks of hard work and offer West Indies the chance of squaring the rubber. It was the first time England had ever won a series in the Caribbean, and, even if there had been too much slow batting on too many dead pitches, too many bouncers bowled and too little urgency in the field, they still had no intention of missing out on the celebrations.

Perhaps the most significant moment of all had come before the last Test, when it was announced that Frank Worrell would lead the West Indians on their tour of Australia towards the end of the year. Significant in that it would lead to what is recognized as one of the greatest of all Test series, but far more significant in that it meant the crumbling of the old racial barriers. From now on West Indies would have a black captain; they had set out along the road that would ultimately lead to world domination.

| 1953–4 | Kingston | WI 417, 209–6d; | E 170, 316 | WI 140 runs |
|---|---|---|---|---|
| | Bridgetown | WI 383, 292–2d; | E 181, 313 | WI 181 runs |
| | Georgetown | E 435, 75–1; | WI 251, 256 | E 9 wkts |
| | Port-of-Spain | WI 681–8d, 212–4d; | E 537, 98–3 | Drawn |
| | Kingston | WI 139, 346; | E 414, 72–1 | E 9 wkts |
| 1957 | Edgbaston | E186, 583–4d; | WI 474, 72–7 | Drawn |
| | Lord's | WI 127, 261; | E424 | E inns 36 runs |
| | Trent Bridge | E 619–6d, 64–1; | WI 372, 367 | Drawn |
| | Headingley | WI 142, 132; | E 279 | E inns 5 runs |
| | Oval | E 412; | WI 89, 86 | E inns 237 runs |
| 1959–60 | Bridgetown | E 482, 71–0; | WI 563–8d | Drawn |
| | Port-of-Spain | E 382, 230–9d; | WI 112, 244 | E 256 runs |
| | Kingston | E 277, 305; | WI 353, 175–6 | Drawn |
| | Georgetown | E 295, 334–8; | WI 402–8d | Drawn |
| | Port-of-Spain | E 393, 350–7d; | WI 338–8d, 209–5 | Drawn |

## 1953–4 Test Series

### England

| Batting | Innings | NO | HS | Runs | Average |
|---|---|---|---|---|---|
| L. Hutton | 8 | 1 | 205 | 677 | 96.71 |
| J.H. Wardle | 2 | 0 | 66 | 104 | 52.00 |
| D.C.S. Compton | 7 | 0 | 133 | 348 | 49.71 |
| P.B.H. May | 10 | 1 | 135 | 414 | 46.00 |
| T.E. Bailey | 7 | 2 | 49 | 193 | 38.60 |

| Bowling | Overs | M | Runs | W | Average |
|---|---|---|---|---|---|
| J.B. Statham | 153 | 24 | 460 | 16 | 28.75 |
| T.E. Bailey | 182 | 51 | 459 | 14 | 32.78 |
| J.C. Laker | 218.1 | 84 | 469 | 14 | 33.50 |
| F.S. Trueman | 133.2 | 27 | 420 | 9 | 46.66 |
| J.H. Wardle | 83.3 | 23 | 187 | 4 | 46.75 |

### West Indies

| Batting | Innings | NO | HS | Runs | Average |
|---|---|---|---|---|---|
| C.L. Walcott | 10 | 2 | 220 | 698 | 87.25 |
| E.D. Weekes | 8 | 1 | 206 | 487 | 69.57 |
| J.K. Holt | 9 | 1 | 166 | 432 | 54.00 |
| W. Ferguson | 2 | 1 | 44 | 52 | 52.00 |
| F.M.M. Worrell | 8 | 1 | 167 | 334 | 47.71 |

| Bowling | Overs | M | Runs | W | Average |
|---|---|---|---|---|---|
| E.S. Kentish | 43 | 15 | 72 | 5 | 14.40 |
| C.A. McWatt | 4 | 1 | 16 | 1 | 16.00 |
| G.S. Sobers | 29.5 | 9 | 81 | 4 | 20.25 |
| C.L. Walcott | 53 | 24 | 94 | 4 | 23.50 |
| J.B. Stollmeyer | 23 | 4 | 72 | 3 | 24.00 |
| S. Ramadhin | 304.3 | 133 | 559 | 23 | 24.30 |

Wicket-keepers: C.A. McWatt (WI) 8 dismissals  W. Ferguson (WI) (for one innings) 2 dismissals  T.G. Evans 6 dismissals  R.T. Spooner (E) 0 dismissals

In the third match, the eighth-wicket partnership of 99 between C.A. McWatt and J.K. Holt is still the West Indies record for that wicket against England. In the fourth match, the West Indies score of 681 for 8 declared is their highest against England at home, and E.D. Weekes and F.M.M. Worrell put on 338 for the third wicket, still the West Indies record for that wicket in all Tests. In the fifth match, L. Hutton scored the first double century by an England captain in an overseas Test, and T.E. Bailey's 7 for 34 was then the best innings analysis for England against West Indies.

**1957 Test Series**

### England

| Batting | Innings | NO | HS | Runs | Average |
|---|---|---|---|---|---|
| T.W. Graveney | 5 | 1 | 258 | 472 | 118.00 |
| P.B.H. May | 6 | 1 | 285* | 489 | 97.80 |
| F.S. Trueman | 4 | 3 | 36* | 89 | 89.00 |
| M.C. Cowdrey | 6 | 0 | 154 | 435 | 72.50 |
| P.E. Richardson | 7 | 0 | 126 | 411 | 58.71 |

| Bowling | Overs | M | Runs | W | Average |
|---|---|---|---|---|---|
| P.J. Loader | 44.3 | 17 | 100 | 10 | 10.00 |
| G.A.R. Lock | 144.2 | 59 | 163 | 15 | 10.86 |
| F.S. Trueman | 173.3 | 34 | 455 | 22 | 20.68 |
| T.E. Bailey | 117 | 37 | 277 | 12 | 23.08 |
| J.C. Laker | 246.2 | 99 | 448 | 18 | 24.88 |

### West Indies

| Batting | Innings | NO | HS | Runs | Average |
|---|---|---|---|---|---|
| O.G. Smith | 10 | 0 | 168 | 396 | 39.60 |
| F.M.M. Worrell | 10 | 1 | 191* | 350 | 38.88 |
| G.S. Sobers | 10 | 0 | 66 | 320 | 32.00 |
| C.L. Walcott | 10 | 1 | 90 | 247 | 27.44 |
| R.B. Kanhai | 10 | 1 | 47 | 206 | 22.88 |

| Bowling | Overs | M | Runs | W | Average |
|---|---|---|---|---|---|
| F.M.M. Worrell | 128.2 | 25 | 343 | 10 | 34.30 |
| S. Ramadhin | 261.3 | 78 | 547 | 14 | 39.07 |
| O.G. Smith | 89 | 14 | 223 | 5 | 44.60 |
| R. Gilchrist | 152.3 | 19 | 466 | 10 | 46.60 |
| J.D.C. Goddard | 58 | 18 | 128 | 2 | 64.00 |

Wicket-keepers:  T.G. Evans 13 dismissals   R.B. Kanhai (WI) 5 dismissals   F.C.M. Alexander (WI) 4 dismissals

In the first match, P.B.H. May's 285 not out was the highest score by an England captain in all Tests, and his partnership of 411 with M.C. Cowdrey is still England's highest for any wicket and the world Test record for the fourth wicket; S. Ramadhin bowled most balls in any first-class innings (588) and the most in any Test (774), both of which records still stand. In the third match, England's 619 for 6 declared is their highest against West Indies at home, and P.E. Richardson and T.W. Graveney put on 266 for the second wicket, still the England record for that wicket against West Indies; F.M.M. Worrell became the first West Indies batsman to carry his bat through a completed Test innings. In the fourth match, P.J. Loader took the only hat-trick in England-West Indies Tests, and T.G. Evans became the first wicket-keeper to make 200 dismissals in Tests. In the fifth match, West Indies were dismissed for what are still their two lowest totals against England, 89 and 86.

**1959–60 Test Series**

### England

| Batting | Innings | NO | HS | Runs | Average |
|---|---|---|---|---|---|
| E.R. Dexter | 9 | 1 | 136* | 526 | 65.75 |
| M.C. Cowdrey | 10 | 1 | 119 | 491 | 54.55 |
| K.F. Barrington | 9 | 0 | 128 | 420 | 46.66 |
| G. Pullar | 10 | 1 | 66 | 385 | 42.77 |
| R. Subba Row | 4 | 0 | 100 | 162 | 40.50 |

| Bowling | Overs | M | Runs | W | Average |
|---|---|---|---|---|---|
| F.S. Trueman | 220.3 | 62 | 549 | 21 | 26.14 |
| J.B. Statham | 130.4 | 42 | 286 | 10 | 28.60 |
| E.R. Dexter | 64.4 | 18 | 170 | 5 | 34.00 |
| K.F. Barrington | 106.5 | 41 | 217 | 5 | 43.40 |
| D.A. Allen | 197 | 53 | 417 | 9 | 46.33 |

**West Indies**

| Batting | Innings | NO | HS | Runs | Average |
|---|---|---|---|---|---|
| G.S. Sobers | 8 | 1 | 226 | 709 | 101.28 |
| F.M.M. Worrell | 6 | 1 | 197* | 320 | 64.00 |
| C.C. Hunte | 8 | 1 | 72* | 291 | 41,57 |
| R.B. Kanhai | 8 | 0 | 110 | 325 | 40.62 |
| C.L. Walcott | 3 | 0 | 53 | 84 | 28.00 |

| Bowling | Overs | M | Runs | W | Average |
|---|---|---|---|---|---|
| S. Ramadhin | 248.3 | 83 | 491 | 17 | 28.88 |
| W.W. Hall | 236.2 | 49 | 679 | 22 | 30.86 |
| C.K. Singh | 84.2 | 35 | 165 | 5 | 33.00 |
| C.D. Watson | 199 | 39 | 593 | 16 | 37.06 |
| F.M.M. Worrell | 115.5 | 37 | 233 | 6 | 38.83 |

Wicket-keepers:  F.C.M. Alexander 23 dismissals   R. Swetman (E) 7 dismissals   J.M. Parks (E) 3 dismissals

In the first match, G.S. Sobers and F.M.M. Worrell put on 399 for the fourth wicket, which is still the West Indies record for any wicket against England, the West Indies fourth-wicket record in all Tests, the highest fourth-wicket partnership by any country against England and the longest partnership (579 minutes) in all Test cricket; F.C.M. Alexander set a West Indies record by holding five catches in an innings. In the fifth match, M.J.K. Smith and J.M. Parks put on 197 for the record England seventh-wicket partnership in all Tests.

# 7

# The Greatest

Any captain's dream, perhaps even prayer, must be not only that he has high-class players whom he can mould into a strong team but that his resources should enable him to build a *well-balanced* side. For the 38-year-old Frank Worrell, as he brought his team to England in 1963, the dream came gloriously true; with the exception of an opening partner for Conrad Hunte the side fell perfectly into place, and proved much too strong for a rather ordinary England. Having been given the captaincy for the tour of Australia in 1960–1, Worrell had played an outstanding part in making it such a success, after which he had thrashed a weak Indian team 5–0 at home. With Hunte, Kanhai, Butcher, Solomon and himself as the batting line-up, Hall, Griffith and Gibbs for bowlers, Sobers capable of winning games almost single-handedly with bat or ball, and a young wicket-keeper named Deryck Murray who set a new West Indies record with 24 dismissals in his first series, Worrell clearly had much to be grateful about; they even had experience as well as class, for five of them had toured in 1957 and nine had played in the leagues.

Yet, since Ramadhin and Valentine had wreaked havoc in 1950, England had lost only one series at home, to Australia in 1961, and still fancied themselves in their own conditions; and this self-belief in the face of what was clearly a formidable outfit helped to redress the imbalance between the teams and turn the series into one of the most memorable of all. After a good innings in the first Test, Worrell's contribution with bat and ball was minimal; but his captaincy touched greatness, and it is one of cricket's happiest stories that he was able to end his career with a triumph of which he was the chief architect.

By the early 1960s, attendance at cricket matches in England had, for various reasons, declined considerably. The introduction in this same year of the professional one-day game was the solution adopted to stop the rot, and, financially at least, it proved very successful. Also, by the early 1960s the influx of immigrants from the Commonwealth was beginning to build up, and for the first time a West Indian touring team found themselves supported by large numbers of their compatriots. A combination of

*Ted Dexter and Frank Worrell watch film of the 1963 series before being interviewed on television.*

outstanding players and noisy, good-natured supporters did wonders for the game, and the enthusiasm that was generated spread throughout the country. The West Indies had already revitalized interest in the game in Australia and now they did it in England, too.

It takes a positive approach by both captains to make a series successful, and Ted Dexter has to take his share of the credit. He is famed as one of the great attacking batsmen since the war, a glorious striker of the ball who gave spectators an idea of what it might have been like to see the immortal names of the Golden Age in action. Tall, strong, handsome, a splendid all-round sportsman, he had come into the Test side in 1958 and begun to blossom in the West Indies in 1959–60. When in the right mood any kind of bowling was hit out of sight, and the mood was usually at its most right when some challenge was on, such as a race against the clock. The fact that his Test average of almost 48 is seven points higher than his career average says much about his character, for the wider stage clearly suited his flamboyance and panache. The shame was that he so often had to curtail his attacking instincts and play a defensive innings to rescue his team; since his batting was based on the soundest of defences the technicalities of this came easily enough, but many a spectator must have wondered at the psychological cost of it. He was also an underrated medium pace support bowler, whose body-swing at the moment of delivery generated surprising pace after a languid run-up; 66 wickets at almost 35 from his 62 Tests (to go with 4,500 runs) could have been considerably more had he been less reluctant to bowl himself.

For the most part, the flamboyance and panache failed to show up much in his captaincy. He knew the game and had the respect of his players, but he could be vague and sometimes seemed to have trouble in concentrating. He gained a reputation, which he has never lost, of being a theorist; yet since some of his ideas were decidedly unconventional – and some went disastrously wrong – it was not the most flattering of reputations. Like several captains of the period he seemed distrustful of the spinners, and was justly criticized for over-using some bowlers and under-using others. There could be a kind of uninspired flatness about his leadership – surprising in someone who in virtually everything except captaincy showed himself to be a natural buccaneer – which is reflected in the high proportion of draws in his record, fourteen out of thirty, with nine wins and seven defeats. Yet he probably suffered more than was realized from the fact that the players around him generally lacked flair, leaving him, as C.L.R. James put it, as 'a Cavalier among Roundheads', 'a good man fallen among people whose morals are not his own'; significantly, another Cavalier of the time, Fred Trueman, turned in some fine performances under Dexter's captaincy, and was outstanding in this series. Happily, though, Worrell's example brought out the best in Dexter, and, although England were well beaten three times, the crowds received admirable value for their money.

West Indies first encountered Trueman when on a dodgy Middlesbrough pitch he scored 75 for once out, took 10 for 81 and handed them their first defeat. This was followed by the game against an MCC team that was some way from the strongest line-up England could offer. The visitors dominated throughout, scoring 306 and reducing MCC to 120 for 5. Because of time lost to the weather, Cowdrey declared at this score at the beginning of the last day: Worrell then declared at 79 for 1, and MCC were left to make 266 in four and a quarter hours. After a sound start the last eight wickets fell for 53 after tea, with no one attempting to put up the shutters, and West Indies won by 93 runs with half an hour left. With big victories over Somerset and Glamorgan, the tourists went to the first Test at Manchester in a pretty cheerful frame of mind.

A little record was set in that Test which is remarkable only for the length of time it had taken to happen. For the first time in a home Test, and only the third time in all, the first three England batsmen all came from the same county: Stewart, Edrich and Barrington of Surrey. When one remembers how Yorkshire, Lancashire and Surrey had had their spells of domination it seems amazing that something as simple as this had never occurred in 83 years. Not that it helped England much. Worrell won the toss and watched contentedly as Kanhai made 90 and Hunte a century which on the second day he took to 182. 64 from Sobers and his own 74 not out – of which *Wisden* said that those who saw it would vow it was

*The long-ago – or so it seems – days of West Indian spin bowling. Note the length of Lance Gibbs' fingers.*

'the most graceful exhibition of late-cutting in the last fifty years' – enabled Worrell to declare at 501 for 6. It was the third morning that did for England. Three wickets went down for 67, and thereafter only Dexter, with 73, put up much of a fight. Stewart and Close supported him for a while but the last six wickets went for 24 and soon England were following on 296 behind.

Gibbs had 5 for 59 in the first innings and, on a pitch ideally suited to him, he improved on that on the Monday. Stewart's 87 was the best effort in a rearguard action that never looked like succeeding, and wickets tumbled steadily. Six fell to Gibbs for 98, and when the ninth wicket went down at 268 an innings victory appeared imminent. Instead, Trueman swung his bat and the total reached 296 before the last wicket fell. Hunte stroked the first ball for a single and West Indies, for the first time in their history, had won six consecutive Tests.

Those eleven wickets for 157 gave Lance Gibbs his best Test return. The almost incessant use of a four-man pace attack which has characterized West Indian cricket since 1976 has invested Gibbs's career with a kind of aura of a bygone golden age, for he played his last Test early in that year, just a few months before the great steamroller began to gather momentum. That last Test, in Australia, in which he passed Fred Trueman's Test record of 307 wickets at an average of 29, finished exactly eighteen years to the day after he had made his Test debut against Pakistan early in 1958, a period in which he had been unchallenged as his country's leading slow bowler. He is recognized as one of the best off-spinners the game has known, especially on hard pitches, yet some critics felt that had he been more willing to attack he could have been better still. Traditionally, of course, spinners have lacked the burning hostility of the fast men, but Gibbs often gave the impression – heightened by large, languid eyes – of taking quietness to almost dreamlike lengths. Certainly, he gave his bowling much thought and wove his spells subtly, varying pace and flight and extracting venom from a pitch that gave him any help at all, but for much of the time he seemed content to play the role of stock bowler, keeping one end buttoned up with his relentless accuracy and patience while Hall, Griffith, Sobers and the rest did the attacking. In his 79 Tests he sent down no fewer than 27,115 deliveries, over five thousand more than any other bowler in Test history, a record which, even allowing for the increased number of Tests, seems likely to last for a very long time.

For all that, he had some fine match-winning days. Twice he took ten wickets in a match (both at Old Trafford) and eighteen times five in an innings, his best performance coming against India in 1961–2 when he

*448 Test wickets between them. Alf Valentine (left) and Lance Gibbs discuss the grip of the ball.*

took 8 for 38 from 53.3 overs, finishing the game with the figures of 15.3–14–6–8. In Australia in 1960–1, he took three wickets in four balls in the third Test and then in the next improved even on that, with a hat-trick, although in the latter game Australia's last-wicket pair survived for 100 nail-biting minutes to earn a draw. He played in the Lancashire league and the Durham league, had a season with South Australia, and played for Warwickshire from 1967 to 1973, becoming the country's leading wicket-taker in 1971 with 131 victims. Towards the end, the knuckle on the index finger of his right hand became greatly swollen, and although at the age of forty he had two good performances in India – 6 for 76 and 7 for 98 – there was a feeling, prevalent especially in Yorkshire, that he was kept in the Test team primarily to overtake Trueman and become the first West Indian to lead the wicket-takers. He was forty-one when he achieved it and, even if he had bowled nearly 12,000 more balls than Trueman, he had earned his place in the sun by sheer hard work. His batting was that of the true number eleven, but he compensated by some outstanding gully fielding. The abiding image, though, is of him wheeling away for over after over, long, bony fingers wrapped round the ball, bouncing in off a five-pace run-up, and making life as endlessly difficult for the batsman as any bowler could.

The Lord's Test of 1963 ranks up in the galaxy alongside the 1882 game against Australia, when the closing stages were so tense that one man died and another chewed through his umbrella handle. Worrell won the toss and, after a delayed start, Hunte hit the first three balls of the game, from Trueman, to the boundary. By lunch, though, they had only 47 as Shackleton, recalled after eleven and a half years, was as accurate as ever. Two wickets fell after lunch, and then Sobers and Kanhai put on 63 in even time. Solomon had a knock of 56 to support Kanhai's 73, and at the close they were 245 for 6. Next morning the innings came to an abrupt end as Shackleton took three wickets in four balls; 301 all out, and Trueman having the last laugh after Hunte's early barrage, finishing with 6 for 100. Edrich then fell to the first ball he received, and with Stewart not lasting much longer England took lunch at 20 for 2.

That afternoon the crowd saw one of the most exciting innings of all. Statistically it was hardly enormous, but the spectacle of Dexter driving, cutting and hooking Hall and Griffith at their most ferocious was one that few who saw it can have forgotten. He made 70 off 73 balls before Sobers got him lbw, an innings worthy to grace one of the finest of matches. Barrington made 80 in more sedate fashion, Titmus an unbeaten 50 and England were all out on the third morning just four behind. That morning the gates had been closed ten minutes before the start, with people turned away for the first time in seven years; the revitalization process was clearly under way. When West Indies batted again, England were led by Cowdrey as Dexter had injured himself during his innings.

Wickets fell steadily to Trueman and Shackleton. Five went down for 104, putting England right on top; except that they had trouble with Basil Butcher, who insisted on hammering the ball all round the ground. Cowdrey later wrote that 'there seemed no possibility, in the middle, that he could keep taking such massive risks and get away with it. But he did.' By the close, he was on 129 and the lead was 218 – only for the last five wickets to crash for just 15 on Monday morning, as Trueman finished with 11 for 152. England's target was 234, but when three fell for 31 it looked, in the murky grey light, a long way away. Barrington and Cowdrey plugged away but, with Cowdrey on 19, a ball from Hall that was just short of a length reared up; he flung up his left arm to protect his face, the ball hit him just above the wrist, and the ulna bone was broken. When bad light won the day, Barrington and Close were together and the score was 116 for 3.

The weather had an important role in the drama of the last day, for as play did not begin till 2.20 p.m. an eye had to be kept on the clock in the later stages. Conditions were decidedly awkward for the batsmen, and only 18 were scored in the first hour, Barrington taking fifty-five minutes to make five before he fell for 60. Parks supported Close for forty minutes and helped take the score to 158 before he went to an appalling stroke. At tea, England were 171 for 5, effectively six, with 63 needed in eighty-five minutes. Titmus stood firm for an hour, 21 runs came in 20 minutes, and the score reached 203. He fell, Trueman came in, touched his first ball to Murray and the situation was transformed; just Allen and Shackleton, and a beplastered Cowdrey, were left, and 31 were still needed.

For over three hours Close had played with the utmost responsibility. Apart from a few overs from Gibbs, Worrell had persisted with Hall and Griffith ever since play had begun, and both had turned in performances of remarkable stamina. Close had withstood all their thunderbolts, taking ball after ball unflinchingly on his body, which was a mass of bruises by the end. Now, to the astonishment of the crowd, he began to come down the pitch to them. It seemed crazy, and it is difficult to lose the feeling that had he just continued as he had been playing he would have seen England home and been a great hero. Cowdrey wrote, however, that it was a deliberate attempt to emulate Frank Woolley's old tactics, for if the ball was well pitched up and straight it could be hit back over the stumps, and if it was wide or short it could be left alone. The only real danger was in giving a touch to the keeper – which, with 15 still required and nineteen minutes left, is what he did. His 70 was a magnificent effort, his highest score for England, and although he failed to achieve the victory it was he more than anyone who brought it so near. The headlines next morning were of the 'Mighty Close' variety.

When Hall began his final over, eight were still needed. Shackleton swung and missed. The second and third balls produced singles. At the fourth ball Shackleton lunged, missed it and looked up to see Allen almost on top of him. Murray threw the ball to Worrell at forward short leg, and he beat Shackleton to the stumps. Enter Cowdrey, left arm encased in plaster, having been practising playing backhand with his right hand and ready to do just that if needed. Hall put everything into those last two deliveries, but Allen calmly played them back to him. Any one of four results had been possible off that final ball, and when it was all over there was a great rush on to the pitch. The tension had been mind-boggling; could a simple cricket match really have produced the feeling of having been emotionally keel-hauled? A West Indian fan who found himself in court next day for getting drunk was let off by the magistrate and told, 'I don't blame you. It was worth it.'

By now it seemed that the entire country was agog with cricket, and by the end of the next game at Edgbaston the excitement was intense. The first three days were all badly affected by rain, and when play ended early on the Thursday England had lost five wickets for 157; on the Friday less than two hours play was possible, during which the rest of the wickets fell for a total of 216, with Close's 55 again giving him the honours. Before a packed house on Saturday there was just two hours forty minutes' entertainment, West Indies reaching 110 for 4 as Trueman bowled almost throughout, shortening his run-up and trying to cut the ball on the soft pitch. The morning of the fourth day saw the match begin to edge towards England as Trueman and Dexter bowled splendidly to dismiss West Indies for 186, Trueman finishing with 5 for 75 – including bowling Sobers with a ball that broke back from a good nine inches outside off stump – and the captain 4 for 38. Four England wickets down for 68 brought the visitors right back into contention, but then Dexter and Sharpe, on debut, put on 101 for the fifth wicket. Then another clatter of wickets and the score slipped to 189 for 8, at which point Tony Lock decided it was time he had a Test fifty to his name. On the last morning he and Sharpe took the score to 278, with Sharpe unbeaten on 85, before Dexter declared, leaving West Indies to make 309 in 280 minutes.

It was a good declaration; the pitch was still true and West Indies had the batsmen to do the job, but the ball had generally been on top throughout. Shackleton and Trueman got the openers cheaply, then Dexter bowled Butcher; 55 for 3 at lunch. Trueman wrote later that he noticed that Shackleton was getting the ball to come off the pitch faster than he was, an oddity that can happen on certain wickets, so he went on to his shorter run. For a while Kanhai and Sobers stood firm, until Sobers went; and then suddenly, in the space of twenty-four balls, Trueman took the last six wickets at the expense of just one scoring shot, an edged four from Gibbs. It was one of the great pieces of controlled, hostile bowling, using all his experience to make the best of the conditions. Less than an hour after lunch West Indies were all out for 91 and England had won by 217 runs.

Trueman's 7 for 44 gave him figures of 12 for 119, his best Test analysis, and he was to finish what would prove his most successful series with 34 wickets at 17.47. In New Zealand earlier in the year he had become the first bowler to reach 250 Test wickets, and of course the following year he broke the 300 barrier against Australia at the Oval. That was the icing on

*Fred Trueman helped make the 1963 series one of the best ever in England.*

the cake that rounded off a remarkable career, and it is interesting to reflect that had it not been for his habit of upsetting the authorities, especially with his strong language, he may well have played another twenty Tests and taken *four* hundred wickets. As any fan will know he was probably the most colourful cricketer of any nationality since the war, a wild young tearaway in his early days who matured into one of the greatest of all fast bowlers. His entry into Test cricket against India in 1952 was sensational, taking three of the four wickets that fell without a run on the board in the visitors' second innings; in the third match he produced what would remain his best bowling figures, 8 for 31, and ended the four-match series with 29 wickets at 13. Thereafter came setbacks, the 1953–4 West Indian tour, with its combination of poor performances and awkward behaviour, costing him especially dearly; for although he played in thirteen series at home he appeared in only six abroad.

Between 1954 and 1966 he failed only in 1956 to take 100 wickets a season, with 175 in 1960 his best effort, and he missed few home Tests. For most of the time he was Yorkshire's main strike bowler, helping them to eight championships and taking over 2,300 wickets in all. A beautiful action with a great final stride made him a joy to watch, invariably putting into practice the dictum which he has since uttered countless times on the radio: 'it's a sideways game'. He had a glorious late out-swing that brought a rich haul of wickets, but he was the master of many different deliveries. Naturally, he had his bad days, most famously against Australia at Headingley in 1964 when, given the new ball by Dexter to polish off the last three wickets, he persisted in bowling short to Peter Burge who gratefully hooked him out of sight, thereby transforming the match and the series. His good days, of course, are part of the legend of the game, especially his partnership with Brian Statham; a legend that he was never afraid to help along with his post-match raconteuring and his humour on and off the field. The anecdotes about him are endless and some of them are even true.

Having succeeded in getting the country looking at them, England then wilted under the gaze. At Lord's and Edbaston the weather had been cloudy and murky; now in the sun at Headingley West Indies felt at home and had little trouble showing their superiority. It was Worrell's fiftieth Test, and having won the toss he saw three wickets fall for 71 before Kanhai and Sobers came together with 143 for the fourth wicket. Kanhai fell for 92 but Sobers went on to a hundred, during the course of which he passed 4,000 Test runs. With a useful knock from Solomon the total reached 397, and although England began with eleven off the first over – Bolus drove his first ball in Test cricket for four – it proved to be one solitary firework rather than a display of them. The first wicket fell at 13 and the eighth at 93, and only because Lock, with another fifty, and Titmus showed some application did the innings make 174. It had been Griffith's turn for some bowling glory, taking his best Test return of 6 for 36.

As the pitch looked as though it might crack up badly, Worrell decided not to enforce the follow-on. The capacity Saturday crowd were thus treated to a splendid display of attacking batsmanship, Kanhai, Butcher and Sobers hammering the ball to all corners before, as predicted, the pitch began to take spin and Titmus picked up some cheap wickets; the last six went for just 48 for a total of 229 and a lead of 452. England's problem at this time was that Ian Botham was only seven years old and not yet ready to perform miracles, so they simply struggled to 231 and defeat by 221 runs. Close and Parks made fifties and Bolus did well, but it was all over soon after lunch on the fourth day. Despite there being only six wickets left to fall when the day began, there was a crowd of about 20,000, yet another indication of the tourists' popularity.

Worrell's Test career reached its apotheosis at the Oval, a game that has its poignancy for English fans, too, since it was the last Test in which Trueman and Statham played together. It was reckoned an important toss to win, but when Dexter did so England failed to make the most of it. Most of the batsmen got in but then got out again, the fifth-wicket stand of 101 between Close and Sharpe giving the innings of 275 most of its substance; Griffith once again took six wickets, for 71 this time, although he was warned by umpire Buller about excessive short-pitched bowling. When West Indies batted, Close kept wicket during the morning session as Parks had been hit on the foot while batting. With West Indies on 185 for 3, things looked nasty for England, but Butcher and Sobers were run out and Trueman and Statham took the new ball and went through the rest, bowling them out for 246.

Sharpe had top-scored in the first innings with 63 and he did so again in the second with 83. No one else got past 28. The editor of *Wisden* seemed to be on the verge of getting out his box of paints: 'The exuberant West Indies supporters who thronged the terrace danced with joy, twirled their coloured parasols and flung their cushions high in the air every time an England wicket fell.' When the last cushion – for the moment – was flung, England had 223 to their name, leaving West Indies to get 253 to win, and Trueman, with an injured ankle, was able to bowl just one over. Maybe if he had been fit it could have been a gripping climax; as it was, Hunte as the anchor and Kanhai as the murderer saw their team to a comfortable eight-wicket win, Hunte adding a unbeaten century to his first-innings 80. The official attendance that day was 25,350 of which some two thirds were West Indians, and when Butcher made the winning hit it seemed that most of them swarmed on to the field, everyone joyously happy and wanting to tell their heroes how much they loved them. It was a long, emotional time before the cheering finally died away.

This was the first series to be contested for the Wisden Trophy, and Frank Worrell duly raised it aloft. A few months later he became cricket's latest knight. There must have been many millions of people who were genuinely delighted for him.

Four of the team, Sobers, Hunte, Griffith and Kanhai, were cricketers of the year in the following *Wisden* in company with Close. For Charlie Griffith this was his most successful series, with 32 wickets at 16 to head the averages and 119 at under 13 for the whole tour. Six feet two inches (1.9 metres) tall and immensely strong, he formed one of the legendary fast bowling partnerships with Wes Hall, and he stays in the mind as perhaps the most *fearsome* bowler of the last thirty years; all fast bowlers do their best to look menacing, but Griffith somehow gave his menace an extra, indefinable dimension. Perhaps it was increased because there was a question mark over his action, for he had been 'called' in a game against India the year before and it would happen again in 1966. A certain volatility of temperament did not lessen the feeling of menace, either, as he was no doubt aware.

He went through virtually the full gamut as a youngster before becoming a fast bowler, starting as a wicket-keeper-batsman, switching to off-spinner, and speeding up only because his club were short of a quickie one day. Seven wickets for one run had a definite appeal, and he was under way. There came a sensational first-class debut for Barbados against the English tourists in 1959–60, taking the wickets of Cowdrey, Smith and

*A daunting sight for any batsman – the fearful Charlie Griffith with his eye on you.*

May in two overs, adding Barrington next morning, then getting Smith again and Dexter in the second innings. He made his Test debut in the last match of that series but was then dropped until this 1963 tour, after which he went on to play in a total of 28, taking 94 wickets at 28. His worst moment came not in a test but in that same match against the Indians in which he was no-balled for throwing, when Nari Contractor, the Indian captain, ducked into a ball only just short of a length and had his skull fractured. For a while it was uncertain that he would survive, and although he did he never played international cricket again.

That did not deter Griffith from bowling short, sometimes excessively so, and he was warned about it more than once; but he also had a superb yorker which brought him many wickets. The problem was that some people thought he threw it; it was a tag he was unable to lose and it undoubtedly helped to shorten his career. Garry Sobers wrote that he was convinced that Griffith's action was quite legal, and felt it unfair that, having once been called, he should be under constant scrutiny for the rest of his career. The trouble reared up again in 1966 to the extent that he felt he was being persecuted, and it obviously affected his performance. It marked the beginning of the end of his career, and he played his last Test in New Zealand early in 1969. Yet if it ended sadly for him, he had the satisfaction of knowing that he had been the most potent weapon in a splendid team that had won a very fine series.

Altogether less controversial was the career of Conrad Hunte, who headed the batting averages in this series with 471 runs at nearly 59. By temperament he was an attacking batsman, but in a team that was brim-full of stroke-makers he decided that, as an opener, he could serve the cause best by curbing his aggression and concentrating on giving the team a sound start. This was particularly important as he never found a settled opening partner, so that an inordinate share of the responsibility for a good foundation fell to him. He should have made his Test debut in England in 1957, but the letter inviting him to join the party went astray; thinking he had been overlooked, he joined Enfield in the Lancashire league, and although he later clarified his availability to the selectors he was not chosen. If England benefited from all this, Pakistan definitely did not; his debut came against them early in 1958 and was marked by a score of 142. In the third Test he made 260, putting on 446 with Sobers (who made the highest Test score of 365 not out) for the West Indies record Test partnership, and in the next match he made another century. Cricket being cricket, in the last game he became the first West Indian to be out to the first ball of a Test, but he still ended his maiden series with 622 runs at 77.

If he did not quite reach such statistical heights again he still had many fine series ahead as he developed into one of the most reliable opening batsmen, especially strong on the leg side. He played in 44 Tests over the next nine years, scoring 3,245 runs at 45 with eight centuries, and was an indispensable member of a very fine team. He was also noted for his involvement with the Moral Rearmament movement, which had begun during the 1960–1 tour of Australia when he saw a film about the life of the negro educator Dr Mary Bethune. As a committed Christian he found that the work he did for them fulfilled him in a way that nothing previously had, and he realized that his fame as a cricketer gave him an excellent oportunity to be a Christian ambassador. In this he was highly successful, but Sobers wrote that as a result he became somewhat remote from his team-mates, and felt that it was because of this that he was passed over for the captaincy when Worrell retired. Having been vice-captain, Hunte had certainly hoped that the honour would come to him and was upset when it did not; but he gave Sobers his fullest support, and played his part in maintaining West Indies' status as unofficial world champions. One famous little incident in the Adelaide Test of 1960–1 says much about him; Kanhai ran him out, and looked so unhappy at what he had done that Hunte went and consoled him. Then, lost in thought, he walked off through a gate into the crowd, some distance from the pavilion, and only realized his mistake when people began to laugh. One can think of several cricketers who might have tried that as a joke, but few others would have done it because of their concern for a team-mate. After retiring he worked full-time for Moral Rearmament.

*

One result of the success of the tour was that when Worrell and his fellow delegate John Dare put a proposal to the ICC that all countries should visit England more frequently on a shared-summer basis, there was so much enthusiasm to see West Indies back again quickly that the idea was happily accepted. Under the original plan they were not scheduled to return until 1971, which was now unthinkable. Just three years later, therefore, having played only one series in the meantime in which they beat Australia 2–1 at home – their first series victory over them – they were back. The team was virtually the same; only Worrell and Solomon had gone, their places taken by Holford and Nurse, with Hendriks and Allan sharing the wicket-keeping instead of Murray, although the problem of an opening partner for Hunte still remained. They were led by one Garfield Sobers, who was to enjoy the most phenomenally successful all-round series in the history of Test cricket: he scored 722 runs at an average of 103 with three centuries, took 20 wickets at 27 using three different styles of bowling, held ten catches and won all five tosses. Had someone rather more ordinary played instead, it might have been a closely fought rubber; but they didn't, and it wasn't.

For various reasons the team never caught the public's imagination in the way that they had under Worrell. They had to contend with a wetter summer for a start, and faced with several pitches which they felt to be below standard they steadily lost enthusiasm, and their batting lost sparkle, in the county matches. More insidiously, they came to feel that there was a campaign against Griffith because of his suspect action; he was called only once, but they felt that he was being closely watched throughout. He also received abusive, racist letters, and not surprisingly under such pressure his form declined and his behaviour was not always impeccable. The final indignity for him came when the West Indies Board withheld his bonus at the end of the tour.

England were not without their problems. They had just spent the winter drawing in Australia and New Zealand under the leadership of Mike Smith, with an anodyne team turning in, for the most part, some pretty uninspired performances. Smith was a capable captain, very popular with his players, who had some fine days both with the bat and in the field but who somehow often just did not quite convince; the fact that the proportion of draws in his record, seventeen out of twenty-five Tests in charge, is higher than any other England captain who did the job more than a handful of times, says much about his leadership and his luck with players and weather.

He was made captain in the MCC match against the tourists, and after West Indies had run up 349 for 9 declared, with a century from Butcher, Smith made sure of the Test captaincy by scoring 140 in good time. With Murray also making an unbeaten century, Smith declared on 383 for 8, and then saw his bowlers take three quick wickets. But an important catch went down, the middle order got it together, and in the end Sobers was able to make a token declaration at 246 for 9, leaving MCC under two hours to make 213, which they did not attempt. Since MCC had had the better of the game against an almost full-strength team, what followed took one or two people by surprise.

Smith was not all that good with the coin and in the first Test at Old Trafford the toss was crucial. The first ball of the series proved to be a symbol of what was to come: Jones dropped it short and Hunte square cut it beautifully for four. Thereafter, the match progressed much as it had done three years earlier, even to Hunte and Gibbs repeating their century and ten-wicket feats. Hunte, dropped on seven, went on to 135, and in the evening Sobers hammered 83 to take the score to 343 for 5 at the close. He was dropped four times before getting his hundred next morning, but reached 161 as the total climbed to 484 scored in even time. Significantly, Titmus collected 5 for 83, and it was clear that the pitch, newly prepared, was already taking spin. Gibbs thought this an admirable arrangement. England had made life difficult for themselves by picking a team with a ludicrously long tail, and then Milburn, on debut, was run out for a duck. It signalled a collapse, with only Parks and Allen getting past thirty, and on the third morning they were all out for 167, 317 behind. Gibbs took 5 for 37, having at one point had three for three off nine overs. Milburn then decided to enjoy himself, riding his luck and giving the crowd something to cheer with two sixes and twelve fours in his 94. Only Cowdrey, with 69, did much else, though, and at a quarter to six the last wicket fell at 277, leaving West Indies victorious by an innings and 40 runs. Gibbs's match figures of 10 for 106 were the principal reason for England losing their first Test inside three days since 1938; since they only started playing five-day Tests after the war, it was thus the first time they had failed to prolong the game to a fourth day out of a scheduled five. Smith was relieved of the captaincy and the job given to Cowdrey.

Lord's saw one of the most frustrating games England had endured in years. Victory was there for the taking, only for Sobers and his cousin David Holford, of whom no one had heard before the tour began and who was supposed to be primarily a bowler anyway, to come up with the record West Indies sixth-wicket partnership. There was also enough time lost to the weather, nearly five hours, to make England's run-chase at the end just too stiff; another hour and they would probably have won. The bowling hero was Ken Higgs. After three early wickets, the West Indian middle order made useful scores without any big innings, and then Higgs polished off the tail; 269 all out, Higgs 6 for 91. Then it was Tom Graveney's turn, back in the team for the first time since 1963, and on the day after his 39th birthday showing the selectors how silly they had been to ignore him. He was just four short of a century when he fell on the Saturday, and with Parks also passing ninety England reached 355 and a lead of 86.

In the soggy atmosphere the pitch sweated under the covers during the weekend, and by lunch on Monday West Indies had lost five wickets for 95. There was no way that England could fail to win. But if they still did not have Ian Botham, now aged ten, to perform miracles for them, West

Indies did have Garry Sobers. He had taken to batting at number six to allow him to wind down after bowling, and it seemed that in such a situation he would pay the penalty and run out of partners. Yet, knowing Holford was a capable batsman with a calm temperament, he made no attempt to protect him, taking the singles that Cowdrey gave him to get the young man on strike. He told Holford that the pitch was just like the Kensington Oval back home, and if he put his head down no one would get him out: good captaincy, obviously. The fact that it was his famous cousin at the other end must have helped Holford considerably, and as he grew in confidence the close fielders steadily retreated. By the close they had put on 193 and the score was 288 for 5; next morning, Sobers let Holford get a richly deserved century before he declared, with himself on 163 and the total on 369. Their unbeaten partnership of 274 is still the West Indies sixth-wicket record against all countries. England's frustration can be better imagined than described.

They were left with the task of scoring 287 in four hours. Four wickets went down for 67 when Graveney, with a badly bruised right thumb, came in to avert a hat-trick. There was still an hour and fifty minutes left for a total collapse but, batting almost one-handed, he defended while Milburn hammered the ball to distant parts. It was a much less chancy display than in his first Test, and he was rewarded with his maiden century, finishing with 126 not out with the score on 197 for 4. English fans wailed, gnashed their teeth, and hoped that their footballing heroes would not similarly trip over their bootlaces in the forthcoming World Cup.

At Trent Bridge, England again took a good first-innings lead. Higgs and Snow bowled well for four wickets each as only Nurse with 93 and Lashley with 49 made a substantial score, and West Indies closed at 235. Three England wickets went down for 13 but then Graveney and Cowdrey put on 169, with Graveney making a century and his captain falling four short. D'Oliveira chipped in with 76, and he and Underwood, on debut, put on 65 for the last wicket, an England record against West Indies that was not destined for longevity. 325 all out gave England a lead of ninety, and two wickets went down for 65 to put England right on top. Kanhai and Butcher slowly eked out Saturday, though, and then on Monday morning came the assault. In five and a quarter hours 334 runs were scored – 63 to Kanhai, 53 to Nurse, 94 to Sobers, all of whom shared in century stands with Butcher who, when Sobers declared at 482 for 5, was undefeated on 209. England made life difficult by fielding and, Higgs apart, bowling poorly, more or less handing the advantage they had gained to the opposition. It was gratefully received by Hall, Griffith and

*One of the great cavalier players, Colin Milburn shone out in the rather dour cricketing world of the 1960s.*

Gibbs, and only Boycott with 71 and d'Oliveira with 54 were able to put up much resistance; all out 253 and a win for West Indies by 139 runs.

That innings by Basil Butcher which turned the series away from England was the highest of his 44-match Test career, during which he scored over 3,100 runs at 43, with seven centuries. He made his debut in Bombay in 1958–9 in the same match as Wes Hall and by the end of the series had scored 486 runs at almost 70, with two centuries. Thereafter he struggled, and did not reappear till the opening Test of 1963. A century in the great game at Lord's cemented his place and he was a regular until the end of the 1969 tour of England, when his career ended with a disputed catch when he was on 91. In two tours of Australia, in 1964–5 and 1968–9, he finished with an identical Test record, 405 runs at 40.50 in each, a little quirk which is almost as odd as his Test bowling record – a total of 42.4 overs which produced five wickets, all taken in one spell for just 15 runs. One thinks of someone like Mike Hendrick, a fine bowler who never once took five wickets in a Test innings, and one wonders at life's injustices.

One little story says much about him. During an interval in his innings at Lord's in 1963 he opened a letter and learned that back home in Guyana (where there was a threat of civil war) his wife had had a miscarriage. Naturally he was greatly upset, but the immediate responsibility was to his team and he did not fail them. England regularly found him troublesome, for he had four good series against them and always seemed to choose a moment for a big score which was particularly annoying. Richie Benaud thought him the hardest West Indian batsman to dislodge, and that is praise indeed.

The match had a special significance for one other man as well, for when Wesley Hall had Milburn caught in the second innings he became West Indies' leading wicket-taker, passing Ramadhin's 158. In 48 Tests he was to finish with 192 wickets at 26, and the reputation of being one of the best fast bowlers of all. He was the same height as his partner, Griffith, but more lithely built and so more pleasing to watch, with great speed and a classical action; he was fearsome, but without Griffith's rather sinister air. Perhaps this was because he was one of the least malicious of all fast

*Wes Hall started out as a wicket-keeper. Many a batsman wished he had stayed behind the stumps.*

bowlers, and was enormously popular with fans everywhere for his sportsmanship and his total commitment to his team. He began as a wicketkeeper but switched to fast bowling in time to tour England in 1957, though was too inexperienced to make the Test side. His debut came against India in 1958–9; 11 for 126 in his second Test and 46 wickets at under 18 in eight games against India and Pakistan got him off to a flying start, and there was no question that he was his country's leading strike bowler for the next decade. He preferred all-out pace to pin-point accuracy, but there was much more to him than just hammering the ball down as hard as possible; an away-swinger to the right-hander brought many, many wickets, and he could bring the ball back as well. He bowled two of the most dramatic final overs in Test history, first in the tie at Brisbane when six runs were needed for victory with three wickets left (he took one wicket and there were two run-outs) and then at Lord's in 1963 after he had been bowling unchanged for well over three hours. His stamina was phenomenal.

For some reason he did not really hit the heights, statistically at least, against England, and it comes as a surprise to find that he was never one of *Wisden*'s cricketers of the year. His best series against them was in 1959–60 when he took 22 wickets at nearly 31, and his 19 games against them yielded 65 victims at 32 apiece, rather more expensive than one would expect. This is the sort of statistic that gives statistics a bad name, for there have been few cricketers who have given so much pleasure as Hall. There is probably nothing spectaors like more than a player who clearly *enjoys* his cricket and is ready to play his heart out, and few who saw Hall pounding in will surely ever forget him. After retiring, he entered politics and has sat for many years in the Barbados Parliament, at the time of writing being the Minister for Sport and Tourism. He has been known to remark that 'If you think my run-up was long, you should hear my speeches.'

Between the third and fourth Tests, West Ham United, with a spot of assistance, won the World Cup. This came at an excellent time for England, for when the fourth Test at Leeds was dismally lost the euphoria was still bubbling strongly and yet another defeat for the cricket team did not seem too important. It began tolerably well for England; after nearly half the first day was lost to the weather the fourth West Indian wicket went down next morning on 154, at which point Sobers joined Nurse. The score had moved on to 419 before they were separated, their partnership of 265 in 240 minutes being still West Indies' fifth-wicket record against all countries. Sobers scored a chanceless 174, including a hundred between lunch and tea, in the course of which he passed a string of milestones: 5,000 Test runs, 2,000 against England, 500 in the series and 1,000 for the tour. Nurse made 137 in more sedate fashion, and when the total reached 500 for 9 Sobers declared near the end of the second day. On the Saturday, England promptly collapsed, and at one point the innings stood at 83 for 6. D'Oliveira, with 88, and Higgs, with his highest first-class score of 49, dragged the total to 240. The innings came to an abrupt end when Sobers took three wickets in four balls, giving him figures of 5 for 41 taken with both pace and spin.

During the morning session, however, umpire Elliot had warned Griffith that one delivery to Graveney, a nasty bouncer, had been illegal, and that if it happened again he would have to call him. Obviously Griffith's bowling suffered as a result, though it made no difference to the result of this match. Mesmerized by Sobers and Gibbs, wickets fell steadily throughout the fourth day, only Barber and Milburn, who had had his elbow injured in the first innings, really putting bat to ball. At 205 all out, West Indies were the winners by an innings and 55 runs, thereby retaining the Wisden Trophy. Gibbs took 6 for 39 and Sobers 3 for 39, for match figures of 8 for 80 to add to his 174.

Seymour Nurse's 137 was his highest Test innings against England, although he would come within one run of it in the next series. Tall and strongly built, he was one of the most attractive players in an attractive team, a lovely stroke-player whose speciality was the drive off the back foot. In his second match for Barbados in 1957–8 he had made an unbeaten century, and scored 70 in his maiden Test against England in 1959–60. Injuries kept him out of the team for three years, but against Australia in 1964–5 he produced a double century to become a regular for the next four years. In this series in England he was second only to Sobers in the averages, with 501 runs at 62, and he also did well against England eighteen months later. In 29 Tests he scored over 2,500 runs at 47, with six centuries, and made a memorable exit from the Test stage: in Christchurch in 1968–9 he scored 258 out of his team's total of 417, the fourth highest percentage (61.87 per cent) in all Tests. Yet even such a mammoth score as this has twice been exceeded in a final Test, by Andrew Sandham (325) and Bill Ponsford (266), although both of these then had a second innings: illustrious company for an illustrious batsman.

Not surprisingly, the England team at the Oval was rather different, and for once a drastic reshuffle paid off. Cowdrey, Milburn, Parks, Titmus, Underwood and Snow were dropped, although Snow was to play when Price had to withdraw. Close was made captain for the first time, and most of the replacements did well, Murray in particular. In heatwave conditions West Indies, as ever, batted first, and lost four wickets for 83 before lunch. Kanhai and Sobers improved matters, the former making a century and the captain 81, but until Hall and Gibbs put on 45 for the last wicket no one else contributed, and the innings closed at 268. In reply, England promptly collapsed to 166 for 7 and no one could have had any doubt about the result.

Then Murray joined Graveney, a top batsman and a less accomplished one, just as it had been at Lord's with Sobers and Holford. Murray had hit a century against the tourists in the MCC game, but had never been anywhere near one in Tests; now, said *Wisden*, he 'looked every bit as good as Graveney'. Both men played calmly and determinedly, finishing the day on 330 and only being parted on the Saturday morning when Graveney was run out for 165; 217 in almost even time is England's best for the eighth wicket against West Indies and second highest overall. When Murray went for 112 the score was 399; and then one of the least expected events in England's Test history took place. Higgs and Snow came together, neither ever having scored a first-class fifty, and against the might of West Indian bowling scored 128 in 140 minutes. When Higgs finally went for 63 (Snow was on 59) they were only two short of the England tenth-wicket record set by Foster and Rhodes in 1903–4. The last three wickets had added a record 361 runs and for the first time in Test history the last three batsmen had scored a century and two fifties – against one of the best attacks. The sense of disbelief was almost as great as Headingley 81.

By the end of the day four West Indians had gone for 135, only Butcher and Nurse making a fight of it. Clearly it all hinged on Sobers – could he find a partner and bat on and on? In the second over of the day, Holford was run out and Sobers entered; Close told Snow to try a bouncer, Sobers edged a hook at it, it rebounded from his box to Close at short leg, and he left the field laughing. *Wisden* omitted the reference to his box. Griffith and Hall wagged the tail a bit but the last wicket fell at 225, West Indies' lowest of the series, to give England a win by an innings and 34 runs.

Brian Close's captaincy received great praise, especially for his intelligent handling of his bowlers; Barber in particular was given good scope to ply his leg breaks and took five wickets as a result. Close is renowned as one of the enigmas of the game, an all-rounder who became the youngest man ever to play for England but who, one always felt, could have achieved more than he did. His Test record is a fairly modest one, but there is no doubt that he was an outstanding captain; Yorkshire won four championships and the Gillette Cup in his eight years in charge, and he won six of the seven Tests he led, beating fairly weak Indian and Pakistani teams 3–0 and 2–0 in 1967. The job, it seemed, was his for some time, but controversy was never far away. Near the end of the 1967 season he was involved in a time-wasting rumpus in a Yorkshire game at Edgbaston, and refused to apologize for his actions. His Test career appeared to have come to an end, until suddenly in 1976, aged 45, he was summoned to take on West Indies once again and certainly did not disgrace himself. Yet the innings for which he will always be remembered is the 70 at Lord's in 1963, his highest Test score; he was one of the bravest of all cricketers, whether fielding near the wicket or standing up to the speed men, and the sight of him doing battle with Hall and Griffith at their most fearsome, and almost winning, is one of the great images of cricket.

For Garry Sobers it was the most astonishing series of his astonishing career. In 1959–60 he scored almost as many runs at an average over 100, in 1967–8 he made over 500 runs at 90, and against Pakistan in 1957–8 he clocked up 824 runs at 137, but in none of these was he anywhere near as effective with the ball as in 1966. As one watched him it was difficult to lose the feeling that he was so outrageously gifted that it simply was not fair. Six feet (1.8 metres) tall, lithe and strong, every action was so natural and effortless, that of the athlete who can only move gracefully; a computer buff who tried to design the perfect cricketer and came up with an answer that was not very close to Garry Sobers would simply have made a mistake. Young fans who never saw him play can get some idea of his feline grace from watching David Gower – but it is only *some* idea.

He was born in 1936 in Barbados – how *can* such a tiny island have produced so many wonderful cricketers? – the son of a seaman who was to die during the war, with an extra finger on each hand which were soon removed. Debut for Barbados came at the age of 16 against the Indian tourists in 1952–3, and Test call-up a year later in the last match of Hutton's tour, as a replacement for Alf Valentine, i.e. as a slow left-arm bowler. He was 17 years and 245 days, the second-youngest West Indian after Sealy to play Test cricket. He scored 40 runs for once out and took the wicket of Trevor Bailey with his fourth ball, finishing with 4 for 74. When Australia were the visitors the following season, he missed the first Test but then began an unbroken sequence of 85 matches that did not end till 1971–2. The runs took a little while to materialize, but eventually against Pakistan in Kingston in 1957–8 he passed three figures for the first time and went on to the record Test score, 365 not out, batting for 10 hours 14 minutes – just over three hours less than it had taken Hutton to reach 364. He followed it with two centuries in the next match, and went on to make 26 in all in his 93 Tests, a figure passed only by Gavaskar and Bradman.

Eight thousand and thirty-two Test runs at 57.78 tell their own story, but it was his manner of scoring them that seemed so remarkable, for he managed to combine power with gracefulness to a degree which has surely never been approached. Several batsmen – Jessop, Walcott, Weekes and so on – contend for the title of the hardest hitter of a cricket ball, and Sobers is among their number, but surely no one has ever hit so hard with such effortless artistry. Perhaps his left-handedness helped, for some of the most graceful stroke-makers have been left-handed, after all. Like all the best batsmen, he was basically orthodox and had an excellent defence, allied to which he had superb eyesight, marvellous timing and great speed of movement, and was always ready to play off either back or front foot as necessary. He was very strong off his legs, drove gloriously, hooked imperiously and usually safely; he would improvise wonderfully, always seeking to score runs at any opportunity, and for such an attacking batsman gave

*Another Sobers six, this one over square leg.*

very, very few chances. After ducking into a ball right at the beginning of his career he never once ducked again, determined that the bowler should not feel any psychological advantage. Many, many bowlers complained that once he was in, it became almost impossible to bowl at him.

All of this reached its peak early in January 1972 when he was leading the Rest of the World team against Australia at Melbourne. It was the third match, he was 1–0 down, 101 behind on first innings and had made a duck in that innings. Lillee and Massie were very much on song. He immediately unleashed a relentless attack on the bowling and in six and a quarter hours scored 254 murderous runs, without a chance being offered. Sir Donald Bradman rated it the best innings he had ever seen in Australia and perhaps the best that was ever played there. It was even the subject of a special film in which his batting was analysed carefully, and few sports-people can claim that distinction for any of their achievements.

Yet if his batting was his greatest glory, he would have been worth a

*Sobers the left-arm spinner. Syd Buller shows just how much an umpire needs to concentrate.*

Test place for his bowling alone. Having begun as an orthodox slow left-armer he developed left-hand wrist-spin, bowling 'chinamen' and googlies, to extend his attacking options, and also readily took to bowling fast-medium, quite good enough to open the attack for any country, with an easy action and the ability to move the ball late through the air; pace bowling proved, in fact, to be his best weapon and brought him more wickets than the others. No one else has ever been able to bowl in three such different styles with such easy mastery, and to see him switch from one to another and be instantly accurate just left one shaking one's head. His 235 Test wickets were perhaps a little expensive at 34.03 each, but as he had filled three roles in one most people were prepared to extend him a little leeway. On top of all this he was a superlative fielder, at slip, at short leg, or in his early days in the covers, with reflexes that took the breath away.

From the very beginning he was full of confidence in his own ability, an easy-going young man for whom life was about living. It took a while for the excess casualness to be worn off, a process that was helped by some years in the Lancashire league and by the paternal influence of Frank Worrell. He was also profoundly affected by the death of Collie Smith in 1959, as he had been driving the car at the time of the accident. Smith had been a calming influence on Sobers, and for a while he began to drink heavily. Not for long, though: a double century against England a few months later was followed by two more in the same series, and a marvellous century in the tied Test at Brisbane was repeated at Sydney. The catalogue of achievements just seemed to go on and on.

When he was invited to take over as captain from Worrell he hesitated for some time before accepting, since he had no experience of leadership at any level. He had been Worrell's own choice as successor, and for the first few years he handled a very strong team capably and successfully. Come the lean years in the early 1970s, though, and his captaincy faltered, perhaps because he was unable to get the best out of some less skilled players and blend them into the team. There were still some outstanding individuals, but his last victory as captain came in New Zealand in March 1969, and fifteen more Tests in charge produced plenty of draws and a few defeats. His captaincy record is, in fact, in debit, with nine victories, ten defeats and twenty draws, yet he had the advantage of winning 27 tosses out of 39 and is the only captain to win all five tosses in a rubber twice. Some felt that he was not involved enough with his team to be a really good captain, that it all came so easily to him that he could never fully understand the problems lesser mortals might have. He was also too easy-going to be a strict disciplinarian, too fond of his leisure to enforce large doses of practice on his team. Inevitably the team suffered.

There have, of course, been plenty of sportspeople with enormous natural ability who because of a flawed attitude or temperament have not done themselves justice. Sobers' attitude was faultless. He loved the game devotedly and played it very combatively, but always with great sportsmanship and enjoyment, always with laughter never far away. From the very beginning he was determined to succeed, and that determination only began to fade near the end when the grind took its toll of his knees and staleness set in; yet there was never a suggestion that he had made an enemy in the world. He was unusual among Test captains in sometimes being a gambler on the field – he has always loved horse-racing and owns a horse in partnership with Wes Hall – a characteristic that had its most famous moment against England in 1967–8 when he took a long shot and lost not only a game but a series. Posterity, of course, remembers the failed gamble and forgets the superhuman efforts he made in the next match to atone for it.

Indeed, his whole career had a superhuman quality about it. It is difficult to imagine that any other cricketer in history has given more pleasure than Sir Garfield Sobers.

| 1963 | Old Trafford | WI 501–6d, 1–0; | E 205, 296 | WI 10 wickets |
| | Lord's | WI 301, 229; | E 297, 228–9 | Drawn |
| | Edgbaston | E 216, 278–9d; | WI 186, 91 | E 217 runs |
| | Headingley | WI 397, 229; | E 174, 231 | WI 221 runs |
| | Oval | E275, 223; | WI 246, 255–2 | WI 8 wkts |
| 1966 | Old Trafford | WI 484; | E 167, 277 | WI inns 40 runs |
| | Lord's | WI 269, 369–5d; | E355, 197–4 | Drawn |
| | Trent Bridge | WI 235, 482–5d; | E 325, 253 | WI 139 runs |
| | Headingley | WI 500–9d; | E 240, 205 | WI inns 55 runs |
| | Oval | WI 268, 225; | E 527 | E inns 34 runs |

### 1963 Test Series

#### England

| Batting | Innings | NO | HS | Runs | Average |
|---|---|---|---|---|---|
| P.J. Sharpe | 6 | 1 | 85* | 267 | 53.40 |
| E.R. Dexter | 10 | 0 | 73 | 340 | 34.00 |
| D.B. Close | 10 | 0 | 70 | 315 | 31.50 |
| K.F. Barrington | 10 | 0 | 80 | 275 | 27.50 |
| M.J. Stewart | 8 | 0 | 87 | 211 | 26.37 |

| Bowling | Overs | M | Runs | W | Average |
|---|---|---|---|---|---|
| F.S. Trueman | 236.4 | 53 | 594 | 34 | 17.47 |
| E.R. Dexter | 95 | 22 | 227 | 7 | 32.42 |
| D. Shackleton | 243.2 | 73 | 518 | 15 | 34.53 |
| G.A.R. Lock | 91.5 | 24 | 230 | 6 | 38.33 |
| F.J. Titmus | 101 | 23 | 256 | 6 | 42.66 |

## West Indies

| Batting | Innings | NO | HS | Runs | Average |
|---|---|---|---|---|---|
| C.C. Hunte | 10 | 2 | 182 | 471 | 58.87 |
| R.B. Kanhai | 9 | 0 | 92 | 497 | 55.22 |
| B.F. Butcher | 9 | 1 | 133 | 383 | 47.87 |
| G.S. Sobers | 8 | 0 | 102 | 322 | 40.25 |
| J.S. Solomon | 8 | 0 | 62 | 204 | 25.50 |

| Bowling | Overs | M | Runs | W | Average |
|---|---|---|---|---|---|
| C.C. Griffith | 223.5 | 53 | 519 | 32 | 16.21 |
| L.R. Gibbs | 249.3 | 74 | 554 | 26 | 21.30 |
| G.S. Sobers | 231 | 50 | 571 | 20 | 28.55 |
| W.W. Hall | 178 | 26 | 534 | 16 | 33.37 |
| F.M.M. Worrell | 45 | 16 | 106 | 3 | 34.66 |

Wicket-keepers: K.V. Andrew (E) 1 dismissal   J.M. Parks 10 dismissals   D.L. Murray (WI) 24 dismissals

In the second match, D. Shackleton took three wickets in four balls. In the third match, F.S. Trueman, following eleven wickets in the previous game with 12 for 110, became the first bowler to take twelve wickets in a Test against West Indies in England. In the fourth Test, G.S. Sobers reached 4,000 Test runs. Trueman finished the series with 34 wickets, then a record for either side in these Tests, and D.L. Murray, in his first rubber, made 24 dismissals for a new West Indies record, and a record by either side in these Tests, both of which still stand.

## 1966 Test Series

### England

| Batting | Innings | NO | HS | Runs | Average |
|---|---|---|---|---|---|
| T.W. Graveney | 7 | 1 | 165 | 459 | 76.50 |
| C. Milburn | 8 | 2 | 126* | 316 | 52.66 |
| B.L. d'Oliveira | 6 | 0 | 88 | 256 | 42.66 |
| R.W. Barber | 3 | 0 | 55 | 97 | 32.33 |
| M.C. Cowdrey | 8 | 0 | 96 | 252 | 31.50 |

| Bowling | Overs | M | Runs | W | Average |
|---|---|---|---|---|---|
| K. Higgs | 236.4 | 49 | 611 | 24 | 25.45 |
| R.W. Barber | 51.1 | 7 | 182 | 6 | 30.33 |
| J.A. Snow | 138.5 | 29 | 451 | 12 | 37.58 |
| F.J. Titmus | 81 | 20 | 190 | 5 | 38.00 |
| B.L. d'Oliveira | 160 | 48 | 329 | 8 | 41.12 |

### West Indies

| Batting | Innings | NO | HS | Runs | Average |
|---|---|---|---|---|---|
| G.S. Sobers | 8 | 1 | 174 | 722 | 103.14 |
| S.M. Nurse | 8 | 0 | 137 | 501 | 62.62 |
| B.F. Butcher | 8 | 1 | 209* | 420 | 60.00 |
| R.B. Kanhai | 8 | 0 | 104 | 324 | 40.50 |
| D.A.J. Holford | 8 | 2 | 105* | 227 | 37.83 |

| Bowling | Overs | M | Runs | W | Average |
|---|---|---|---|---|---|
| L.R. Gibbs | 273.4 | 103 | 520 | 21 | 24.76 |
| G.S. Sobers | 269.4 | 78 | 545 | 20 | 27.25 |
| W.W. Hall | 175.3 | 35 | 555 | 18 | 30.83 |
| C.C. Griffith | 144.3 | 27 | 438 | 14 | 31.28 |
| D.A.J. Holford | 90.5 | 13 | 302 | 5 | 60.40 |

Wicket-keepers: J.M. Parks 9 dismissals   J.T. Murray (E) 3 dismissals   D.W. Allan (WI) 6 dismissals   J.L. Hendriks (WI) 7 dismissals

In the second match, the undefeated partnership of 274 between G.S. Sobers and D.A.J. Holford is still the West Indies record for the sixth wicket in all Tests, C. Milburn and T.W. Graveney put on an unbeaten 130 for the England fifth-wicket record against West Indies, and J.M. Parks reached the double of 1,000 runs and 100 dismissals. In the third match, W.W. Hall became the leading West Indian wicket-taker when he passed S. Ramadhin's total of 158. In the fourth match, G.S. Sobers reached 5,000 runs in Tests and 2,000 runs against England, and his partnership of 265 with S.M. Nurse is still the West Indies record for the fifth wicket in all Tests; he also had match figures of 8 for 80. In the fifth match, England's last three wickets produced a record 361 runs, with the last three batsmen scoring a century and two fifties for the first time in Test cricket. Graveney and J.T. Murray put on 217 for the eighth wicket, and K. Higgs and J.A. Snow put on 128 for the tenth wicket, both still the England records against West Indies. Sobers finished the series with 722 runs at 103.14, 20 wickets, 10 catches – and won every toss as well.

# 8

# England Bow Out

When England arrived in the Caribbean eighteen months later they found plenty of locals who promised them they would be thrashed. Such confidence overlooked a number of factors: that Hunte had retired, that Hall had been injured in a car crash the previous August and had scarcely recovered, that Holford had suffered a serious illness, that Griffith's star was on the wane and so on. Against this weakened team England came up with a well-balanced one which could have won the series 3–1; four of the five finishes were heart-stoppingly close but, in the event, the margin was 1–0 and the victory achieved in the most unlikely circumstances. For *Wisden* at least there was 'no doubt that justice was done'; that statement was made by an English writer, but the Almanack's impartiality has always been legendary.

England even achieved victory despite having to make do with their second-choice captain. Close had led them throughout 1967 with great success, but then blotted his copybook at Edgbaston. Colin Cowdrey was appointed instead, only to suffer the indignity of learning that Douglas Insole, the Chairman of Selectors, had admitted at a press conference that if the Edgbaston incident had not occurred, Close would have been their preference. As it happened, there was such sympathy for Cowdrey in the light of this that he received plenty of support, and his captaincy throughout the tour was admirable. After years of captaining for only a part of a series – surely no one else has had such an in-and-out tenure of the office – this was only the second time he had had a full rubber in charge, and he made the most of the opportunity.

Cowdrey was one of the finest of batsmen, polished, elegant, perfect in technique, a handsome stroke-maker who was a delight to watch. There was just one problem: sometimes, it seemed, he just could not believe in his own ability, and would scratch painfully around until some kind bowler put him out of his misery. The good days far outnumbered the stodgy ones, though, and he served England nobly for many years. Just thirteen when he appeared in a schools match at Lord's, he is still the youngest player to take the stage there; it began a career which saw him

*Colin Cowdrey led England to their last series win in West Indies in 1967–8 and batted splendidly to take advantage of Sobers' declaration. Deryck Murray watches another four runs added to the score.*

become the first man to play in one hundred Tests, finish as England's leading run-scorer, and hold more Test catches than any non-wicket-keeper had at the time. With 7,624 runs at 44, with 22 centuries, from his 114 Tests, he is ranked up there among the best. He was, furthermore, one of nature's gentlemen, charming, friendly, courteous, sporting, always ready to help, and with a zest for cricket that made him very popular.

He led Kent from 1957 to 1971, winning the championship in 1970, yet he is regarded more as a sound and capable captain than an outstanding one. He led England twenty-seven times during the decade, winning eight and losing four, but somehow he often seemed too unobtrusive to be a top-class Test captain. He had a deep knowledge of the game but frequently appeared reluctant to make quick decisions, apparently too modest or unsure to stamp his authority on the match. From the boundary it was not always clear who was meant to be directing operations, and, with the likes of Dexter, Smith and Close challenging him for the England captaincy, this was a form of invisibleness which the selectors could not ignore. He was also unlucky with illness and injury at crucial times, so that, most sadly of all, he was never invited to lead the team to Australia.

No fewer than four times he went as vice-captain, a record he would much have preferred not to hold. Happily, though, he did have a finest hour for England.

In the early stages of the tour a happy ending looked most unlikely as the visitors struggled to come to terms with the conditions. John Snow, the main strike bowler, had had a virus before Christmas and was clearly not ready for a five-day match. They were being written off by the press, and that is always an excellent state of affairs.

In the first Test at Port-of-Spain, Cowdrey won the toss and his team batted till the third morning. Boycott and Edrich provided a sound basis, the Yorkshireman actually hitting four fours in Hall's first two overs, as much a symbol of what was to come as Hunte's boundary from the first ball of the previous series. He went for 68, Cowdrey for 72, and then Barrington and Graveney put on 188 for the fourth wicket, both making centuries. The total of 568 was England's second highest in the Caribbean. West Indies' response centred on 85 from Kanhai and 118 from Lloyd, in his first Test against England, but there was little other support, and when Jones took three wickets in four overs just before the tea on the fourth day they found themselves all out for 363 and following on for the first time under Sobers' captaincy. A crucial hour and forty minutes was lost to rain, but Nurse, Camacho, Kanhai and Butcher all played solidly and, at 164 for 2 on the last afternoon, the game was moribund. Then Hobbs caught and bowled Kanhai, and in one marvellous over just before tea David Brown disposed of Butcher, Murray and Griffith and missed Hall's stumps by a whisker. Lloyd and Holford both departed quickly but Boycott, in the unfamiliar position of short leg, put down a difficult catch off Hall that was decisive. He and Sobers stood firm for the rest of the session and, with the score on 243 for 8, the match was saved.

Snow came in for the Kingston Test at the expense of Hobbs and made an immediate impression. It was an important toss for Cowdrey to win, for the pitch, never good, was at its best on the first day. In the game against Jamaica, he and Edrich had put together a big stand, Cowdrey just making a hundred and Edrich just missing out. The same thing happened in the Test, and, with Barrington chipping in too, the total reached 376. By the time West Indies batted, though, a ridge had developed at one end and Snow took full advantage of it with 7 for 49, shooting them out for 143. By the afternoon of the fourth day, only Nurse had batted well in the follow-on and West Indies had reached 204 for 4 when Butcher got a thin edge to a ball from d'Oliveira and Parks took the catch. This meant that, with just five wickets left, 30 were still needed to avoid an innings defeat.

According to Cowdrey, Butcher did not see the catch taken and quite justifiably paused to see whether he was out, and it was his hesitation that proved disastrous. For the third successive England tour a Test was marred by a bottle-throwing riot, and this one was particularly nasty. Cowdrey tried to calm them down but was clearly wasting his time, so the players left the pitch. The police produced tear gas and turned it on the demonstrators, only to see them laughing as the wind blew it away from them and over the rest of the ground. Many of the crowd tried to get out in a hurry and several were injured, while in the dressing-room many of the players sat with wet towels around their heads to lessen the discomfort.

There was no way of knowing whether political tensions were to blame or whether it was simply the fact that defeat seemed inevitable and tasted unpleasant. The Jamaican authorities were very apologetic, of course, and after some discussion England agreed to continue that evening, with the seventy-five minutes that were lost to be made up on the sixth morning if necessary. This was irregular, but in the circumstances was felt to be the best thing. The problem for England was that the interruption had upset their rhythm completely. All the impetus was gone, and Sobers and Holford made the most of their new freedom. In the last hour that evening not a ball passed the bat; on the next day, Sobers, playing brilliantly on such a brutal pitch, and having been missed before the riot when he had made only seven, hit an unbeaten 113 and declared at 391 for 9. His innings had turned the tide completely and England were now thoroughly demoralized; the first four batsmen went for 19 – two wickets to Sobers – and at close of play he claimed the extra seventy-five minutes the following morning. In the event, with the umpiring not beyond criticism, first Graveney and then d'Oliveira held out just long enough, and the game ended with the score on 68 for 8. There was a nasty moment when Parks was struck in the throat by a ball from Hall, but it proved not to be serious. Had England lost, it really would have been one of the great injustices of the game's history, but the record books tend not to list injustices.

Before the next match, England suffered a severe blow when Fred Titmus was badly injured in a boating accident in Barbados. A group of players were bathing just offshore, holding on to a small motor boat which, unknown to them, had the propeller under the centre of the hull rather than at the stern. Titmus let his legs float up under the boat and suddenly he had lost four toes. Fortunately his big toe was not affected and, according to the surgeon who operated on him, he was lucky in that had the propeller struck half an inch further up the foot he would have had to amputate at the ankle. As it was, Titmus not only played for Middlesex again but even in four more Tests, although as these were in 1974–5 when Lillee and Thomson were wreaking havoc he may well have wished he had not. Pat Pocock took his place for the third Test and Tony Lock was summoned from Australia.

It fell to the good people of Barbados to draw the short straw and get the one Test of the rubber that was a non-event. Sobers won the toss and batted, but on a day shortened to three hours fifty minutes by rain his batsmen could manage only 86 runs. After ten overs, two runs had been scored and two no-balls delivered. Camacho was especially slow, and when he finally went next day for 57 it was after 81 overs. Butcher and Sobers improved things a bit, but it was mid-morning on the third day before the innings closed at 349, Snow taking 5 for 86. Boycott and Edrich put on 172 for the first wicket, with Boycott falling for 90 on the fourth day while Edrich went on to 146 in almost as many overs. Graveney and d'Oliveira made fifties and once again England took a good lead, this time of exactly 100. Had West Indies collapsed, there was time for England to force a win, and hope sprang eternal when Snow took the first three wickets with 79 on the board; but 60 from Butcher and an unbeaten century from Lloyd condemned the game to a draw, and the innings closed at 284 for 6.

In contrast, the good people of Trinidad had to endure an extremely exciting finish when they would have preferred the match to end sleepily. When Sobers won the toss Camacho was in a quite different mood and made a fine 87. Then Kanhai put together a brilliant 153, sharing a third-wicket stand of 273 with Nurse, who made 136, and the declaration came at 526 for 7. Boycott and Edrich made a solid start, but at 260 for 5 the follow-on target seemed some way away. Then Knott joined Cowdrey, was dropped early on, but went on to 69 not out; with Cowdrey making 148, the total reached 404. This was the match in which Butcher took his five wickets all at once – Cowdrey and the tail – and they were enough to put him top of the averages for the whole series. Maybe it was this spell that made Sobers feel the Englishmen were vulnerable to leg-spin, for during the afternoon, with the score on 92 for 2, he declared, setting England a target of 215 in 165 minutes. Hall had been dropped and Griffith was unable to bowl because of an injured thigh muscle, so with depleted resources he was taking a calculated gamble; but he hoped that leg-spinner Rodriguez, on his home ground, would prove difficult if the batsmen were chasing runs against the clock – although he did not expect England to go for the runs – and that a couple of early wickets would trigger a collapse. It was later revealed that Everton Weekes, then the team manager, agreed that a declaration was preferable to a stagnant finish, but characteristically Sobers took all the criticism himself and mentioned nothing of any support he had had when the decision was made.

The standard version of what happened in the England dressing-room before the innings began is that Cowdrey was fearful of losing the game if they went for the runs and had to be persuaded by the others, Barrington especially, that he was a good enough batsman to see it through. Cowdrey insists there was no dispute, and that he was simply cautious because he had so often seen run chases develop into desperate battles for survival. In the event, Boycott and Edrich gave them a good start with 55 in 19 overs before Edrich fell, and then Boycott and Cowdrey played beautifully. Gibbs, Rodriguez, Sobers and the others were dispatched to all corners, a hundred runs coming in 18 overs of high-class batsmanship. Cowdrey went for 71 with the score on 173 and Graveney soon followed, but d'Oliveira stayed with Boycott – whose 80 was paced to perfection – and the victory was achieved by seven wickets with three minutes to spare. In an instant all Sobers' achievements were forgotten and he was pilloried mercilessly, even hung in effigy in Port-of-Spain. Anyone researching into crowd psychology must have been delighted.

Inevitably, this brought out the best in Sobers for the final Test at Georgetown, and during the match he became the first West Indian to score 6,000 Test runs. He won the toss, then with three wickets down for 72 he and Kanhai put on 250 for the fourth wicket, both scoring 150s. Replying to 414, once again it was Boycott and Cowdrey who supplied the backbone of the innings; Cowdrey went for 59, but Boycott finally reached the century he had been threatening all series. Yet when the eighth wicket went down, England were way adrift on 159, at which point Pocock joined Lock. Eighty-two minutes later Pocock got off the mark, the second-longest instance in Test cricket. Lock, meanwhile, in his last Test, was heading for his highest score, and when he finally departed for 89 he had changed the match considerably; 371 all out meant a deficit of only 43 when a much larger one had loomed. Their stand of 109 is the England record for the ninth wicket against West Indies.

By now it was the morning of the fifth day, but as neither side had an unassailable lead in the series this was a six-day match. Quick runs were clearly in order, but apart from Nurse only Sobers provided very many. Wickets fell steadily – six of them to Snow for match figures of 10 for 142 – and Sobers ran out of partners just five short of another century. England had to bat throughout the final day to draw the match or score 298 to win. The pitch was still playing well and they began steadily, reaching 33 without loss. Eight runs later they had lost five wickets. Knott was with Cowdrey and there were still two full sessions to survive. All through the afternoon they stood firm, but with seventy minutes left Cowdrey was out for 82. It was up to Knott and the tail. As the clock ticked round, first Snow then Lock departed. Pocock defended resolutely, then fell to what *Wisden* described as a 'first-bounce catch'. Poor Jeff Jones, the last man, who had been sitting in the dressing-room praying he would not have to bat, found himself facing the final over of the game. Cowdrey gave him no instructions for there were none to give. He and Knott met in the middle and appeared to be talking; in fact, they were singing the opening lines of 'We'll Keep a Welcome in the Hillsides'. It sounds like Beau Geste defending the beleaguered fort.

Gibbs, already with 6 for 60 under his belt, tried everything he knew. Jones, whose Test batting average would be 4.75, was totally surrounded by fielders, while in the dressing-room most of his colleagues were simply unable to watch. His stature as a batsman may be gauged from his figures for the series; including this over he had six innings and scored four runs, and had an average of 2 thanks only to four 'not outs'. Yet somehow he survived, and for once millions of people in England were grateful to a Welshman. The series was England's, although some of the locals were so upset at this that they attacked the team as they were leaving the ground, and Tony Lock was hit on the head by a stone.

The batting heroes of the rubber were Cowdrey (534 runs) and Boycott (463 runs), both of whom averaged 66, and Knott, who came into the team for the last two Tests and, in three innings, scored 149 vital runs for only once out. Cowdrey had led very much by example and had orchestrated his bowlers splendidly, and they had responded excellently. It was the three speed men who got most of the wickets, Brown and Jones each taking 14 and John Snow, despite missing the first Test, setting a new England record in the West Indies by taking 27 at under 19 each. This was the first of Snow's two outstanding series, the other coming in Australia in 1970–1 when he took 31 wickets to help win the Ashes. He had made his debut against New Zealand in 1965 and went on to play in 49 Tests and take 202 wickets at 26, but he suffered badly from the lack of a regular opening partner. On this tour he clicked with Brown and Jones and the results were startling. He was renowned for his moodiness and there were times when he seemed to be lounging around on the boundary with no interest in what was happening in the middle; yet on his good days he was a really hostile fast bowler who won many matches.

*Poets are usually thought of as gentle souls. John Snow was an exception.*

An easy action off a relatively short run culminated in a powerful delivery which could move the ball either way, and he was able to get some response out of most pitches. He was adept at varying his pace, and rarely would a whole over be bowled at full speed. When the pitch suited him, as in Jamaica, he was quite lethal, probably more so than any English fast bowler since Trueman and Statham. He was one of those players whom controversy follows doggedly: disciplined a number of times by Sussex, dropped by England after a collision with Gavaskar which looked as though he had deliberately charged him, numerous clashes with umpires, and so on. He called his autobiography *Cricket Rebel* and it summed him up well; perhaps had he caused his captains fewer headaches he would have been an even better bowler, but it could as well be argued that it was his mean streak that made him so hostile. Snow was always an individualist, and he proved it by publishing two volumes of poetry. Fearsome fast bowlers are not renowned for doing that sort of thing.

*

In May 1969 Colin Cowdrey, having at last seen off all his challengers and settled into the England captaincy, suffered a disaster: batting in one of the first of the new Sunday league matches, he snapped an Achilles tendon and had to miss the rest of the season. The man appointed in his place was to bring England one of the most successful periods in her history.

After nineteen years with Yorkshire, Ray Illingworth had taken over the captaincy of Leicestershire only at the beginning of that season, and perhaps if he had not done so the England job would not have come his way. For years he had been a vital member of a highly successful York-shire team, taking many hundreds of wickets with his off-spin and batting determinedly in the lower middle order. He had played in thirty Tests since his debut in 1958, never commanding a regular spot as he was fighting for a place with several other spinners, and it seemed as though he would remain a high-class player who had not really made it as a true Test cricketer. The call to the captaincy came more or less out of the blue, but for once the selectors got it absolutely right; tough, shrewd, immensely knowledgeable about the game, he immediately showed himself to be a natural leader. He talked to his players, learned how to get the best out of them, showed them he was fully committed to their interests, and so fashioned a group of moderately talented individuals into a formidable team. It was one of the most remarkable cricketing achievements since the war.

Along the way his own batting developed into real Test class and he several times saved his team, twice scoring a century and finishing with over 1,800 runs at 23 from his 61 Tests, to add to his 122 wickets at 31. Of thirty-one games as captain, twelve were won and just five lost, his greatest moment being the recapture of the Ashes in 1970–1. England were unbeaten for his first nineteen games in charge, taking them to a new Test record for any country of twenty-six matches without defeat. He did it mainly through his tactical expertise, putting his wealth of experience, gained under some fine Yorkshire leaders, to best use, turning the screw at any opportunity and showing what could be done by determination and competitiveness. Only Mike Brearley, a very different type of leader, vies with him as the best England captain since the war, and though in 1969 he was new to the job he soon proved himself more adept than his opposite number.

Sobers' problem seemed to be staleness. After eighteen months with little respite he looked very ordinary with both bat and ball, although a chipped bone in his shoulder did not help. His team had just come from a tour of Australia and New Zealand which saw them lose 3–1 and draw

1–1, and had they but known it they would not enjoy another Test victory for four years. It was an inexperienced team that Sobers brought, missing the likes of Hall, Griffith, Kanhai, Hunte and Nurse, and only five of the party had played a Test in England before. They were also unlucky with the early-season weather, for though it later turned into a fine summer they had little chance for practice when they needed it most.

They had the best of things in the match against a strong MCC team, for all that. Only Edrich passed 20 for MCC, but he did so by some way, making 125 out of a total of 200. Sobers had begun the tour poorly, but now he hit 74, helping the score to 285. The weather had the last word, though, after Edrich and Boycott had made a good start on the last morning; at 127 without loss, the rain came down and any chance of an exciting finish disappeared. As had happened three years earlier, the team having the better of this match was to have decidedly the worst of the Test series.

By the time of the Old Trafford Test the weather was fine, and it proved a good toss for Illingworth to win. Thanks to some dropped catches, Boycott and Edrich kicked off with a century stand, the former going on to 128. Graveney, in what was to be his last Test as he played in a benefit match on the Sunday and was promptly suspended, made 75, d'Oliveira 57 and the tail, which had looked too long, did well, taking the total to 413. This took them till nearly tea on the second day, and the rest of that day was the crucial period of the game: Snow got Fredericks first ball, Brown yorked Carew in the next over, and with their tails so quickly up they bowled splendidly, the fielders did their stuff, and by the close West Indies were 104 for 6. Next morning they polished off the rest for just 147, and Illingworth had the happy task of enforcing the follow-on in his first Test in charge.

This time Fredericks and Carew put on 92, and *Wisden* blamed Carew's departure on a 'fatuous loud-speaker announcement' which broke his concentration, so that he lashed out at the very next ball from d'Oliveira, whose OBE had been announced that morning, and was caught. Butcher, Davis and Sobers all made runs, but at the close West Indies were still 51 adrift with just six wickets left. On the Sunday night there were thunderstorms, and Monday's play was badly interrupted by rain. Three more wickets went down, and on the last morning it was only the eighth-wicket pair who passed England's total; when the innings closed at 275 England needed just ten runs. Boycott and Edrich managed to cope.

Lord's saw a fascinating match played in lovely weather to packed houses, and was significant for West Indies in that it marked the debuts of two players from Caribbean cricketing outposts, Mike Findlay from St

Vincent and Grayson Shillingford from Dominica, the first players from outside the 'big four'. Camacho and Fredericks gave their team a good start with 106 for the first wicket, and then Davis settled down to make a very patient first Test century, determined to atone for having helped run out his captain when Sobers was on 29. *Wisden*, incidentally, complained that England bowled only 99 overs on the first day, a figure that now seems the height of luxury. The total made 380, whereupon England promptly collapsed to 61 for 5 and it was time for the first of four Yorkshiremen in the team to grab some glory. Jack Hampshire and Alan Knott put on 128 for the sixth wicket and, after Knott had gone, Hampshire pressed on to become the first Englishman to make a hundred in his first Test, that match being at Lord's. It had taken England 78 years longer to achieve this than it took Australia, as Harry Graham had done it in 1893 – and by one of those little quirks both men scored 107. When Hampshire departed it was Illingworth who carried on, but when the ninth wicket went down England were still 119 adrift. With Snow holding up the other end, Illingworth blossomed: 97 not out on Saturday evening, he soon had his century, and when he was out for 113 the deficit was only 36. With a previous highest Test score of 50, it was a great triumph for the new captain.

Again Fredericks and Camacho put on a sound start, and Lloyd then

*Geoff Boycott made five centuries against West Indies. The stroke off his legs through mid-wicket was one of his most productive.*

produced a sparkling 70. Sobers had had to go off with a leg injury on Saturday evening, only the second time in 75 Tests he had needed a substitute, and now he batted for an unbeaten 50 with Camacho as a runner. On the last morning he declared at 295 for 9, setting England a target of 332 in four hours plus 20 overs. Edrich fell immediately, and Boycott and Parfitt made little attempt to go for the runs. West Indies did their best to make a game of it by bowling 21 overs an hour, and when Sharpe joined Boycott they stepped up the pace, putting on 126 in ninety minutes. Boycott became the game's third Yorkshireman to make a century and Sharpe was only 14 away from being the fourth, but when they both went in quick succession 61 were still needed off the last ten overs; at the end they were 295 for 7, 37 short of the target. Sobers, having batted with a runner, bowled 29 overs, and whether you saw this as a heroic effort or some kind of sharp practice probably depended on your nationality.

Leeds suffered from a slow pitch after several days of rain, and with the weather overcast at first the ball was mostly in command. Only Edrich, with 79, could come to terms with the conditions until d'Oliveira and Knott made forties and the total struggled to 233. Illingworth, of course, knew all about bowling at a cloudy Headingley and handled his attack beautifully, with Knight in particular finding things to his liking. West Indies simply could not get going and, lacking the injured Shepherd, were all out for 161 as only Butcher and Holder passed 30. Yet England found it very difficult to capitalize on their lead, as Sobers bowled splendidly to take 5 for 42 from 40 overs; all the batsmen except Boycott got in, struggled and then got out again, with the last three wickets putting on a crucial 93 runs, including 37 for the tenth from Brown and Snow.

West Indies' target was 303 with nearly two days left, and although Fredericks soon went Camacho played steadily for 71, Davis made 29 and Butcher, in what was his last innings, struck out gloriously. He had made 91 in two and a half hours, and at 219 for 3 the match was definitely in the visitors' grasp, when he was given out to a catch by Knott that was disputed. Enter Sobers, the obvious man for the situation – only to drive recklessly at Knight and be bowled for a duck. Lloyd and the strapped-up Shepherd soon followed and the overnight score had become 228 for 7. It took England eighty minutes next morning to polish off the last three wickets, the all-out total of 272 giving them victory by just 30 runs.

It was the first time they had won two matches in a series against West Indies since 1957. It is also historic as the last time England took a series off West Indies. Not only does it *seem* a long time ago; it was.

*

West Indies have dominated world cricket for so long now that it becomes increasingly difficult to remember a time when they did not. Yet when they came to England in 1973 they had not won a match since beating New Zealand in March 1969. Twenty matches (fifteen of them at home) had seen six defeats and fourteen draws, despite the presence at various times of such as Sobers, Kanhai, Lloyd, Gibbs, Fredericks, Rowe, Kallicharran, Boyce, and so on. And not only had they been defeated, but they had been defeated, and held to draws, by countries they would have expected to demolish, drawing 1–1 in New Zealand, losing 1–0 at home to India and drawing 0–0 at home to New Zealand. When, early in 1973, they went down 2–0 at home to Australia, the entire Caribbean virtually went into mourning. The main problem, remarkable as it now sounds, was the lack of a pace attack.

Sobers had missed the series against Australia with a knee injury, the first time he had been absent from the Test side for eighteen years. Rohan Kanhai, by some way the senior member of the side, had assumed the captaincy, and it was he who now brought the team to England. He was 37 and already greying, approaching the end of a career that had seen him described as having come nearer than anyone, even Everton Weekes, to batting like Bradman. The difference between him and Bradman, and between him and Weekes for that matter, is that they had more discipline than he did, for there were a fair number of occasions when Kanhai simply got himself out. If it seems hard to criticize someone who scores 6,227 runs at 47.53 in 79 Tests, there were undoubtedly times when – through impatience, boredom, even arrogance – he did not do himself justice; for a batsman of his class to score 'only' fifteen Test centuries in 137 innings seems wrong, somehow. Yet when he really applied himself, his batting was one of the great spectacles of cricket, full of bold, inventive stroke-play of which the boldest and most inventive was the falling hook shot – a full-length ball would be swung to leg with such violence that he would land on his back and the ball would land a very great distance away. A small man, always neatly turned out, he was also a very safe slip and lightning-fast at cover.

The story of his entry to the first-class game reads like something from schoolboy fiction. Cricket was enormously popular in his home town in British Guiana, Berbice, and competition amongst the boys to progress up the ladder was intense. When he went for an important trial there were so many hopefuls that four of them from Berbice had to draw lots for two places. Kanhai missed out, but then one of the 'lucky' ones sprained his ankle and he was given his chance; he impressed the coaches, was given a

*Rohan Kanhai's falling hook shot, not found in many coaching manuals. Murray and d'Oliveira look on.*

game against the Australian tourists in which he scored 51 and 27, and was under way. Two years later, in 1957, he came into the Test side, first as wicket-keeper but after three games solely as a batsman. His maiden Test century took thirteen games to arrive but was worth waiting for; 256 in just six and a half hours at Calcutta in 1958–9 helped his team record the second-largest victory margin in all Tests. Just three months later his second Test century, against Pakistan, was also a double, and after this there were few series in which he failed. Among his outstanding feats were his two hundreds in the dramatic match at Adelaide in 1960–1, becoming the first West Indian to achieve that in a Test in Australia, and his 150s in each of the last two Tests against England in 1967–8. His first 61 Tests were played consecutively, the sequence interrupted only by injury.

He played league cricket in England and Scotland, for Western Australia in 1961–2, for Tasmania in 1969–70, and, most significantly, for Warwickshire from 1968 to 1977. His very best batting was for his county, reaching 1,000 runs in each of his ten seasons and featuring in two

*Chris Old takes the new ball, Rohan Kanhai, captain on the 1973 tour, despatches it back over his head.*

outstanding partnerships. In 1968, he (with 253) and Billy Ibadulla put on 402 for the fourth wicket against Nottinghamshire, then the county record, and, in 1974, he (with 213 not out) and John Jameson passed this with an unbeaten 465 against Gloucestershire for the world record second wicket, scored in 312 minutes of what *Wisden* called 'brutal and ruthless' batting.

Perhaps if Sobers had not had trouble with his left knee the captaincy would never have come to Kanhai, for, although Sobers' leadership during West Indies' lean period had been criticized, his position was so sacrosanct that deposing him as captain was hardly a realistic option. Kanhai learned well from his tough first series against Ian Chappell's Australians, so that by the time he came to England in 1973 he had welded together a power-ful team by instilling the discipline that had slipped away under Sobers, and replacing the staleness that had crept in with a new dynamism and self-belief. No fewer than eleven of his squad had played county cricket in

England, and he was able to orchestrate their experience and enthusiasm with some imaginative and intelligent captaincy. With players eager to prove themselves, he had a unit altogether too powerful for an England team that was slipping away from the triumphs of recent years.

Ray Illingworth was still at the helm, for what would be his last series. He had achieved his great triumph in Australia and then retained the Ashes in 1972, but there had been reverses as well; and earlier in the 1973 season England had been surprised by the spirited opposition they had encountered from New Zealand. Given West Indies' poor form, England had to be favourites before the series began, but there must have been plenty who wondered whether the cracks that the New Zealanders had opened up would become gaping holes under a Caribbean onslaught. They soon found out.

Early in the afternoon of the first day at the Oval, England captured the third West Indian wicket for just 64. This brought Kallicharran in to join Lloyd – two of the six left-handers in the team – and in 200 minutes they put on 208 runs. Kallicharran fell at 80 and next morning Lloyd went for 132, whereupon 72 from number nine Boyce helped the last three wickets put on over 100 runs; 415 all out. Boycott, as usual, was England's bastion, eventually falling on 97. Greig and Illingworth took the score to 247 for 5 but, in graphic contrast to West Indies' innings, the last five wickets went for just ten runs as Boyce finished with 5 for 70. The English faithful thought back to 1966 and had a nasty feeling as to what was coming.

Yet for a short while their heroes made a good attempt to get back into the match; three wickets down for 52. Then along came Kallicharran with another score of 80, and with a fifty from Sobers the total reached 255. Earlier in the summer, New Zealand and England had both made well over 400 second innings runs, and England now needed 414 – could they do it again? When Boycott went for 30 everyone knew the answer and, although Frank Hayes played well to become only the fifth Englishman since the war to score a century on Test debut, he had little support. In the end, both teams' second innings made 255, so that West Indies won by the 158-run margin they had opened up half-way through.

Six wickets for 77 gave Keith Boyce match figures of 11 for 147, at the time the second-best West Indies Test figures and, with a total of 83 runs as well, he had rather dominated matters. There must have been many English fans who were pleased that Boyce had had his hour, for spectators appreciate players who do their best to give them their money's worth and there have been few more whole-hearted cricketers than he. There was a dynamism about him that could be electrifying. A hostile fast bowler, an

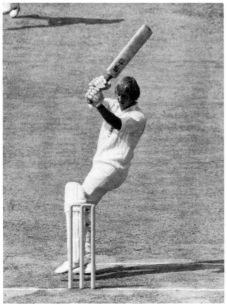 

*Frank Hayes scores his century on Test debut at the Oval in 1973.*
*Congratulations are in order.*

aggressive batsman who was never content with a four if he could get a six and a splendid fielder, he had joined Essex in 1966 at the behest of Trevor Bailey and turned in some memorable performances. The most sensational was still two years in the future, when against Leicestershire in their title-winning season he scored the fastest championship hundred for 38 years in 58 minutes and then took 12 wickets for 73.

He had made his Test debut in 1970–1 against India and played 21 matches in all, averaging 24 with the bat and taking 60 wickets at 30, figures that perhaps do not fully reflect his value. He just missed out on a Test century, running out of partners when on 95 at Adelaide in 1975–6 after he had been on 65 when the last man joined him. One-day cricket was ideally suited to his talents, and in 1971 he set a record in the John Player League by taking 8 for 26, admittedly when Lancashire were throwing the bat in a rain-affected match; more significantly, he was the first player to reach 1,000 runs and 100 wickets in professional one-day cricket. He also played an important part in West Indies' World Cup final victory in 1975, with a powerful 34 and 4 wickets for 50. In short, he was very much one of those players whose departure leaves the feeling that something special has gone out of the game.

*The superb rhythmic follow-through of Keith Boyce, his body like an arrow as the right arm goes down after delivery. One of the most successful limited-overs bowlers of all, he usually bowled a yard faster in Tests – and knew which end of a bat was which as well.*

The second Test at Edgbaston – notable as the first time all eleven of a touring Test side had played English county cricket – was less than inspiring. Old and Arnold soon had West Indies in trouble at 39 for 3, but Fredericks curbed his attacking instincts and ground out 150 in eight and a half hours to help the total to 327, with Illingworth at one stage bowling 27 overs for just 18 runs. Early in England's innings there was an appeal against Boycott for a catch at the wicket, but it was turned down by umpire Arthur Fagg. Kanhai was displeased and wanted the world to share his displeasure, spending the rest of the day making it clear what he thought of the umpire. At the close of play, Fagg requested an apology from the West Indians, but got only a statement that they were 'fully satisfied with Mr Fagg's umpiring'. He therefore threatened to withdraw from the match, and the first over on Saturday morning saw Alan Oakman, a former umpire and Test player, on in his place. Fagg relented and

*Trouble brewing at Edgbaston in 1973. Umpire Arthur Fagg turned down the appeal for a catch by Murray and Boycott lived on, but Kanhai (at first slip) showed such dissent that in protest Mr Fagg did not appear for the first over next morning.*

resumed, and before long the umpires had to tell Kanhai to speed up the over rate as only 26 had been bowled during the morning. West Indies had scored at just over two runs an over; England meandered to 305 at just under two an over, apparently oblivious to the fact that they needed a win to get back into the series. West Indies' second innings was a bit more interesting as Lloyd made 94 and Sobers 74, but Kanhai, reasonably enough, saw no need for a declaration and they were finally all out for 302, leaving 227 minutes for England to reach 325. They simply had some batting practice and strolled to 182 for 2. It was one of those games which are better forgotten.

Many a famous player has ended his Test career on a low note, and now it was Ray Illingworth's turn. At Lord's Kanhai won his third toss of the series and, helped by Fredericks, Lloyd and Sobers, proceeded to put the game out of England's reach. By the close of the first day, he had passed 6,000 Test runs, was undefeated on 156 and his team were 335 for 4. Next day Sobers also reached 150 and Bernard Julien, in his third Test, came up with his maiden first-class century off just 127 balls, their seventh-wicket partnership of 155 in just 113 minutes being a record for

*150 not out at Lord's in 1973. The effortless grace of Sir Garry.*

West Indies against England and ending only when Sobers had to leave with a stomach upset. The total had reached 652 for 8, their highest score in a Test in England, before Kanhai called a halt; for the second time in Test history five bowlers had conceded a hundred runs, and only the young Bob Willis, with 4 for 118, had any credit against his name. Since the pitch had had both pace and bounce and was described by *Wisden* as 'a credit to the Lord's groundsman, Jim Fairbrother', it was a particularly dismal performance by the English bowlers.

Before long their batsmen were performing pretty dismally, too. Three wickets went down for 29 before Amiss and Fletcher, and then Fletcher and Greig, steadied things, but a clatter of wickets saw them at 205 for 8. At this point, at about a quarter to three on the third afternoon, there was one of the more unexpected events of cricket's long history – it was announced that a telephone call had been received saying there was a bomb in the ground. The IRA were currently involved in one of their bombing campaigns on the British mainland and obviously no chances could be taken, so the ground – with a 28,000 capacity crowd – had to be cleared. Many spectators decided that the safest place was on the playing area, the England team went to a tent behind the pavilion and the West Indies returned to their hotel in Maida Vale. The call proved to be a hoax and, at 4.30, play resumed with the majority of the spectators still there. It was agreed that the time lost would be made up and a start was made that evening, but by the close the match was as good as over. All out for 233, England followed on 419 behind and then lost Amiss, Knott and Boycott, the last-named in the most uncharacteristic way – hooking a short ball down the throat of deep square leg *in the final over*, and for his pains being jostled by a bunch of rowdies as he left the field. Only Fletcher and Extras got past 15 in England's innings, the Essex man being unbeaten on 86 when the final curtain fell at 193, leaving West Indies victorious by an innings and 226 runs. It was their largest winning margin over England.

England had been at their most unenterprising. Of the last match Illingworth said, 'We were outbatted, outbowled and outfielded. There are no excuses.' His captaincy had taken a knock, but his integrity was unblemished.

*

*Bernard Julien was pretty handy with the bat as well as the ball. Arthur Fagg is on duty.*

*Bomb scare at Lord's in 1973. The covers are put on to protect the wicket and the spectators take to the field. A figure sits on the covers – who else could it be but Mr H.D. Bird?*

*Lord's 1973 and the series won, Rohan Kanhai drops a bottle of champagne to the crowd below. The big bongo drum player takes the prize and victory tastes good.*

When England arrived in the Caribbean a few months later it was to defend a remarkable record: they had not lost a Test there since early in 1954, during which time they had won four and drawn nine. After the drubbing of the previous summer, though, there cannot have been many who thought they would survive intact for another series, even if West Indies had now gone twenty-two home Tests without a win. Kanhai was entrusted with the job of ensuring that this sequence was not extended, while England's affairs were put in the hands of Mike Denness.

Denness's main problem was a lack of experience at Test level, for he had played only nine games before the tour, eight of them as vice-captain to Tony Lewis in India and Pakistan the previous winter. He was a fine batsman without being a really top-class one, strong against the spinners but susceptible to extreme pace, attractive to watch but with the annoying habit of building the foundations of an innings only to get himself out. Because his career was overshadowed by the carnage inflicted by Lillee and Thomson in 1974–5, there is a tendency to overlook his successful days and think of him as a failed Test batsman, but in twenty-eight matches he averaged only just under 40 – higher than nearly all the leading batsmen who have played for England since – and scored four centuries, one of which is the highest ever made by an England captain in Australia.

The same point applies to his captaincy yet, despite that Australian tour, his record is in credit, with six wins and five defeats in his nineteen games in charge. Perhaps one of the reasons for the impression of failure is that he did not enjoy good relations with the media, a difficulty that was exacerbated by the fact that Tony Greig, his vice-captain, could charm every pressman in sight. The press were aware that his quiet and reserved nature rarely permitted him to unwind as one of the boys and felt that Greig's more informal relations with the players, and greater cricketing ability, made him better suited to the job.

Denness suffered from having to succeed the much revered Illingworth – revered both by the press and the players – and from the fact that most of his team were more experienced at Test level than he was, a difficult situation which seemed often to cause him trouble. Yet he was certainly a shrewd and enterprising leader, who had taken over from Cowdrey as Kent captain in 1972 and in five years led them to six one-day trophies and second place in the championship. Maybe this highlights another of his problems: that one-day cricket is vastly different from Test cricket, and few captains have been able to switch fluently from one to the other. As far as this tour was concerned, his contribution with the bat was fairly modest and, as he was in charge for the first time, his captaincy took a while to settle down; in the last Test, though, he led the team exceptionally well and fully deserved his share of the credit for the result.

In the first Test at Port-of-Spain, Kanhai won the toss and on a damp pitch put England in. It was a good move; after a quarter of an hour Boycott hooked and was caught at long leg, and the procession began. Greig got 37, Extras 21, and with no one else passing 12 they were all out for 131. Yet the bowlers then did well, sending back six batsmen for 196. Only Kallicharran stood firm, passing the hundred mark and reaching 142 at the end of the second day. There then occurred an incident which might easily have provoked a riot, for the disturbances in the three previous tours had all been sparked off by much less inflammatory happenings. Off the last ball of the day Julien played the ball to Greig at silly point and turned towards the pavilion. Knott pulled up the stumps. Kallicharran walked down the pitch, whereupon Greig threw the ball at the bowler's stumps, appealed and, quite correctly under the laws, umpire Sang Hue ruled that Kallicharran was run out. It was recognized that Greig's action was impulsive rather than malicious, but the West Indian officials were worried that it might be the catalyst to trouble. Eventually, after a long and fraught meeting, agreement was reached that in the interests of the game as a whole and the tour in particular the appeal would be withdrawn and Kallicharran would bat on. Greig apologized and was soon forgiven by the crowds, and potential disaster was avoided.

Kalli went for 158 next morning but Julien finished undefeated on 86, the final score being 392. The pitch was easing but England had a mountain to climb – and Boycott and Amiss took them a good way up it. The first wicket had made 209 before Boycott went for 93, and Denness then helped Amiss take the score to 328 early in the afternoon of the fourth day. It seemed that England would save the match, maybe even win it if the home team became demoralized in the face of a big score. Then Denness was run out, and by tea the score was 378 for 8. The lbw decision that did for Amiss for 174 was not one of the best, but the rest just collapsed to Gibbs and Sobers. In a short time, Gibbs's figures changed from 99 for 1 to 108 for 6. The innings ended on 392, leaving the non-mathematicians an easy job, and the 132 needed to win was polished off for the loss of three wickets.

Jamaica saw a rearguard action to rank alongside that of Sobers and Holford at Lord's in 1966. On an easy pitch it was a good toss for Denness to win, yet his batsmen failed to make the best of it. Wickets fell steadily, with three batsmen giving catches off long hops that should have been despatched to the rope. Only Boycott with 68 and Denness with 67 got

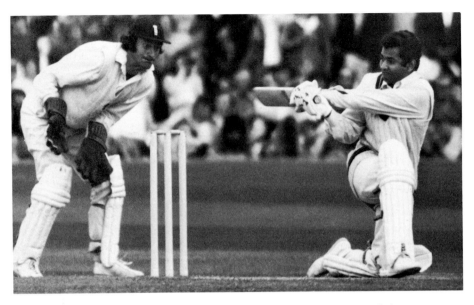

*Alvin Kallicharran sweeps Underwood to the rope. 'Popeye' Knott can't believe it.*

past fifty, Underwood and Pocock contributed as much as some of the top order, and the innings closed on 353. The rearguard action really began from there, for on such an easy pitch the bowlers were soon trying to contain rather than take wickets. Rowe and Fredericks put on 206 for the West Indies first-wicket record against England, Fredericks falling for 94 but his partner going on to a century. Kallicharran reached 93 before he went, but the England bowlers had stuck to their task well and the scoring had been relatively slow. Only on the fourth morning when quick runs were needed did Julien cut loose, scoring 66 off 58 balls and putting on 112 in 75 minutes with Sobers, during which stand Sobers became the first man to pass 8,000 Test runs. At lunch Kanhai declared at 583 for 9, a lead of 230 and ten hours left.

Boycott soon went when a bouncer from Boyce just clipped his glove. Jameson helped take the score past 100 before he departed, and then Amiss ran out Hayes for a duck, taking on Lloyd at cover point for a quick single and seeing him score a direct hit on the stumps. Since Lloyd was the best cover fielder in the world at the time, this was a strange lapse; yet he did exactly the same thing next day to run out Knott. Five wickets had gone before the close on the fourth day, but Underwood, sent in as night-watchman, stayed there for seventy-five minutes on the last morning in the face of a great many bouncers from Boyce. Knott's run-out certainly made Amiss even more determined to stay there, but he had been very lucky right at the beginning of the day when he turned a ball straight into the hands of Sobers, one of the greatest of close fielders, at backward short leg. Perhaps the third ball of the day was just too early for his concentration to have settled down, and he dropped it.

When Knott went England were 41 ahead with three wickets left. Old stayed there, again subjected to a deluge of bouncers, for an hour and forty minutes, helping Amiss put on 72 for the eighth wicket. Then it was Pocock's turn, contributing just four runs of the 49 that the ninth wicket brought but keeping his castle intact till after tea. By now England's lead was 162 and the match was saved, but for good measure Willis held out for over fifty minutes and at the end the score was 432 for 9. Had he fallen, Amiss would have become the fourth man to carry his bat through a completed innings for England, with the highest score of anyone to achieve the feat in Test history. As it was, his 262 not out was his first first-class double century, and it remained the highest score of his career. He had batted for nine and a half hours, for most of the time knowing that if he made a mistake England would probably lose the game. It was, simply, one of the really heroic innings of Test cricket.

West Indies did seem to be Dennis Amiss's favourite opponents. His full Test record was 3,612 runs from 50 games at an average of 46, with eleven centuries; in ten games against West Indies, he scored 1,130 runs at an average of 70, with four centuries of which two were doubles. He had made his debut against them in 1966 but it had taken him a long time to secure his place in the team; the vital century finally came in Pakistan in 1972-3 and the floodgates duly opened. In twenty games between March 1973 and August 1974 he scored 2,140 runs at an average of 71, and if he then had a disastrous time against Lillee and Thomson he did at least make a come-back with a double century against Holding, Roberts and Daniel in 1976. He was mostly a front-foot player, with a cover-drive that was a real glory, but if he rarely scored really quickly he certainly had the shots when he chose to unleash them. His confidence benefited greatly from the introduction of the helmet and he went on to serve Warwickshire admirably for years; when all ended happily with his hundredth century in 1986 there was much genuine pleasure in the cricketing world, for his career had seen more than its share of crises. Somehow with Amiss there was always the feeling that he ought to have played for Gloucestershire or Somerset, a rural county rather than one based in the concrete and asphalt of Birmingham, for the disciplined, calm, unhurried, determined, diligent way in which he accumulated his runs seemed much more suited to a countryman than a townee. Or perhaps it was just the pipe that created that impression.

Before the next Test, MCC lost dismally to a Barbados team lacking Sobers and Boyce. They then spent much of the Bridgetown Test looking as though they were going to lose that as well, for the pattern of the game closely followed the previous one. Again Kanhai put England in on a damp pitch and wickets tumbled, four down for 68, five for 130. Then Greig and Knott came together, and their 163 set an English record for the sixth wicket against West Indies. Knott fell for 87, but Greig went on to 148 and, with some help from the tail, the total reached 395. On the third day, most of the population of Barbados decided they wanted to see some cricket, and thousands of people climbed over walls, on to roofs, etc. They must have had a premonition that big events were afoot, for they saw Rowe and Kallicharran put on 249 for the second wicket, the West Indies record against England at the time. Next day Rowe passed Headley's 270 for the highest West Indies score against England and, after ten hours ten minutes, during which only 140 overs had been bowled, he was finally dismissed for 302, the eleventh Test triple century. Wickets had been falling and only Murray, with 53 not out, had had a good knock, but Kanhai was able to declare at tea on the fourth day with 596 for 8 on the board. If England were despondent then Greig at least had something to celebrate, as 6 for 164 meant that he was the first England player to score a century and take five wickets in an innings of the same Test. He had also caught Sobers for 0 off Willis, the first time the great man had registered a Test duck on his home ground.

To Greig's dismay he was out in the middle again before the day was over. With the pitch wearing and cracked, four wickets went down for 40, and with Amiss back in the pavilion there cannot have been many people who thought England could escape again. One who did was Keith Fletcher; after Greig went with the score on 106, he and Knott defied the bowlers for most of the day, helped by a leg injury to Gibbs which hampered him. On such a pitch both played with great skill and application; Fletcher's 129 not out gained him the star heroic billing, but without Knott it would probably not have been possible, for if the tail-enders had survived for long on that pitch it would have been remarkable. The game saw one unwanted record amid all the fine performances – 99 no balls were called, of which 20 had runs scored from them. By the close England were 277 for 7.

The triple century was the second peak of Lawrence Rowe's career, the first having come on Test debut against New Zealand two years earlier when he made 214 and 100 not out, a feat which seems unlikely to be repeated. A superbly balanced batsman, he had wonderful timing which, like Sobers, enabled him to hit the ball very hard without appearing to bludgeon it. *Wisden* spoke of his 'languid ferocity' and how 'there was always more poetry than brutality about his play'. He was primarily a back-foot player, but always seemed to have so much time to move forward for the drive. The 302 was an especially important innings for him as his previous ten first-class centuries had all been scored at Sabina Park, and such home dependence had brought some criticism. But now that he had laid that little bugbear to rest, it was assumed he would go on to become one of the greats, particularly as this series produced two other centuries and saw him head the averages with 616 runs at 88. In the event, he had problems with injury, trouble with his eyes, and even developed an allergy to grass, all of which obviously curtailed his career. After another hundred in the first Test in Australia in 1975–6, his form steadily drifted away and, like most people who do not fulfil their potential, he came to be regarded as an enigma by those who do not understand the pressures. He played in a total of thirty Tests and scored just over 2,000 runs at 43, with

*Rohan Kanhai accepts the Wisden Trophy from MCC President Mr A.M. Crawley after the 1973 series.*

seven centuries, before debarring himself from any more by going to South Africa. It seemed a sad end to a career that had begun so brightly.

England's two successful rearguard actions had undoubtedly sapped the vitality from the home team. The fourth Test in Guyana was a washout, but not before England had taken a decent grip on the game. Sobers withdrew through tiredness, leaving a bowling attack that looked too ordinary to cause much trouble on a docile pitch. England batted first again, but this time of their own volition, and Amiss and Greig both scored centuries. With Knott making another good score, the total reached 448. They then bowled better than West Indies, containing the batsmen well so that at the end of the third day they were 110 for 2. Time had already been lost to rain and now it came down in earnest, so that it was the last afternoon before play resumed. The only interest lay in whether Fredericks could get his century; he had scored two of them in the recent Guyana v. MCC match, but now he fell just two short. At 198 for 4, the curtain came down and everyone trooped back to Trinidad for the last match. At this point the tourists had played ten first-class matches and had lost two and drawn eight. It had not been a distinguished tour.

The final Test was scheduled for six days and, since England felt that the Port-of-Spain pitch offered them their best chance of bowling the opposition out twice, it was clearly a good toss to win. Denness won it well enough, but only Boycott took much advantage. It took him six hours twenty-five minutes to score 99, but since only Amiss and Knott got past thirty and the last six wickets fell for 63, it was invaluable; 267 all out was very much a squandering of the pole position. Fredericks and Rowe replied with 110 for the first wicket, and early in the afternoon of the third day the score was 224 for 2. Suddenly, in the space of twenty balls, Greig, bowling off-spin, had Lloyd, Sobers, Kanhai and Murray back in the pavilion for just six runs. Rowe, who was to bat over seven hours for 123 of which Boycott would have been proud, took the score to 270 with Julien and 300 with Boyce, but the last three wickets fell quickly and they were all out for 305. For Greig it was a splendid triumph; in 19.1 overs bowled that day he took 8 for 33, for figures of 8 for 86.

Once again, England's innings centred on Boycott. Thus far in the rubber he had fallen below his own high standards, but he came good at the crucial time. It took him six and three-quarter hours to reach his hundred, but he made it, with only 45 from Fletcher giving him much support. Wickets fell regularly at the other end, and again it was Knott who showed the higher order how it should be done. His 44 proved vital, taking the total to 263 and setting West Indies a target of 226. At the beginning of the last day they were 30 for none and they reached 63 before things began to happen: in nine balls Rowe was lbw to Birkenshaw, Kallicharran went second ball for a pair, and Fredericks was run out attempting a second run. Now the tension was tangible, and both Lloyd and Kanhai, for all their experience, succumbed to it; 85 for 5 and two more wickets for Greig. Sobers came in on a pair, and played easily to share a 50 stand with Murray. He had made 20 when Underwood bowled him a full toss and, trying to find the gap, he missed it. 135 for 6, then 138 for 7 as Julien went. When Murray was eighth out there were only 166 on the board and England had surely won, but Boyce and Inshan Ali shrugged off the tension and batted well. The deficit was halved, and Denness decided to take the new ball; not without qualms, one imagines, for the new ball has often shown itself a two-faced ally. But Greig had Ali caught and two runs later Arnold bowled Gibbs; 199 all out and England had won by 26 runs, mainly, thought *Wisden*, because they withstood the tension better. Boycott and Greig were the heroes, the latter taking 5 for 70 for match figures of 13 for 156, the best for England against West Indies.

For Kanhai and Sobers it made a sad end to their Test careers, Kanhai scoring two and seven and Sobers nought and twenty. Indeed, one important reason why England were able to draw the series was that three leading batsmen, Sobers, Kanhai and Lloyd, all had a thin time, averaging only in the twenties. Yet, if West Indies had shown themselves the better team in the first three matches, England deserved much credit for refusing to capitulate and for taking the chance of victory when it came their way. It was the last English win over West Indies for what appeared at one point to be for ever.

| | | | | | |
|---|---|---|---|---|---|
| 1967–8 | Port-of-Spain | E 568; | | WI 363, 243–8 | Drawn |
| | Kingston | E 376, 68–8; | | WI 143, 391–9d | Drawn |
| | Bridgetown | WI 349, 284–6; | | E 449 | Drawn |
| | Port-of-Spain | WI 526–7d, 92–2d; | | E 404, 215–3 | E 7 wkts |
| | Georgetown | WI 414, 264; | | E 371, 206–9 | Drawn |
| 1969 | Old Trafford | E 413, 12–0; | | WI 147, 275 | E 10 wkts |
| | Lord's | WI 380, 295–9d; | | E 344, 295–7 | Drawn |
| | Headingley | E 233, 240; | | WI 161, 272 | E 30 runs |
| 1973 | Oval | WI 415, 255; | | E 257, 255 | WI 158 runs |
| | Edgbaston | WI 327, 302; | | E 305, 182–2 | Drawn |
| | Lord's | WI 652–8d; | | E 233, 193 | WI inns 226 runs |
| 1973–4 | Port-of-Spain | E 131, 392; | | WI 392, 132–3 | WI 7 wkts |
| | Kingston | E 353, 432–9; | | WI 583–9d | Drawn |
| | Bridgetown | E 395, 277–7; | | WI 596–8d | Drawn |
| | Georgetown | E 448; | | WI 198–4 | Drawn |
| | Port-of-Spain | E 267, 263 | | WI 305, 199 | E 26 runs |

**1967–8 Test Series**

England

| Batting | Innings | No | HS | Runs | Average |
|---|---|---|---|---|---|
| A.P.E. Knott | 3 | 2 | 73* | 149 | 149.00 |
| M.C. Cowdrey | 8 | 0 | 148 | 534 | 66.75 |
| G. Boycott | 8 | 1 | 116 | 463 | 66.14 |
| J.H. Edrich | 8 | 0 | 146 | 340 | 42.50 |
| K.F. Barrington | 7 | 0 | 143 | 288 | 41.14 |

| Bowling | Overs | M | Runs | W | Average |
|---|---|---|---|---|---|
| J.A. Snow | 165 | 28 | 504 | 27 | 18.66 |
| D.J. Brown | 162 | 32 | 458 | 14 | 32.71 |
| R.N.S. Hobbs | 28 | 3 | 78 | 2 | 39.00 |
| F.J. Titmus | 68 | 24 | 165 | 4 | 41.25 |
| I.J. Jones | 198.2 | 31 | 656 | 14 | 46.84 |

West Indies

| Batting | Innings | NO | HS | Runs | Average |
|---|---|---|---|---|---|
| G.S. Sobers | 9 | 3 | 152 | 545 | 90.83 |
| R.B. Kanhai | 10 | 1 | 153 | 535 | 59.44 |
| C.H. Lloyd | 9 | 2 | 118 | 369 | 52.71 |
| S.M. Nurse | 10 | 0 | 136 | 434 | 43.40 |
| B.F. Butcher | 9 | 1 | 86 | 301 | 37.62 |

| Bowling | Overs | M | Runs | W | Average |
|---|---|---|---|---|---|
| B.F. Butcher | 34 | 17 | 67 | 5 | 13.40 |
| C.C. Griffith | 93.1 | 29 | 232 | 10 | 23.20 |
| L.R. Gibbs | 318.3 | 114 | 610 | 20 | 30.50 |
| G.S. Sobers | 228.5 | 72 | 508 | 13 | 39.07 |
| W.W. Hall | 122 | 29 | 353 | 9 | 39.22 |

Wicket-keepers:  D.L. Murray 14 dismissals  J.M. Parks 9 dismissals  A.P.E. Knott (E) 4 dismissals

In the first match, England's total of 568 was their second highest in the West Indies. In the third match, J.M. Parks became the second English wicket-keeper to hold 100 catches. In the fourth match, England, set to make 215 in 165 minutes, won with three minutes to spare. In the fifth match, G.S. Sobers became the first West Indian to score 6,000 Test runs; G.A.R. Lock and P.I. Pocock put on 109 for the record English ninth-wicket partnership against West Indies. J.A. Snow's 27 wickets (in only four Tests) are the most for England in a series in the West Indies.

**1969 Test Series**

England

| Batting | Innings | NO | HS | Runs | Average |
|---|---|---|---|---|---|
| G. Boycott | 6 | 1 | 125 | 270 | 54.00 |
| R. Illingworth | 5 | 1 | 113 | 163 | 40.75 |
| J.H. Edrich | 6 | 1 | 79 | 169 | 33.80 |
| J.H. Hampshire | 4 | 0 | 107 | 135 | 33.75 |
| B.L. d'Oliveira | 5 | 0 | 57 | 162 | 32.40 |

| Bowling | Overs | M | Runs | W | Average |
|---|---|---|---|---|---|
| D.L. Underwood | 53 | 29 | 101 | 6 | 16.83 |
| D.J. Brown | 110.3 | 25 | 288 | 14 | 20.57 |
| B.R. Knight | 120.1 | 29 | 279 | 11 | 25.36 |
| J.A. Snow | 139.3 | 26 | 406 | 15 | 27.06 |
| B.L. d'Oliveira | 75 | 25 | 169 | 4 | 42.25 |

### West Indies

| Batting | Innings | NO | HS | Runs | Average |
|---|---|---|---|---|---|
| G.S. Camacho | 4 | 0 | 71 | 187 | 46.75 |
| B.F. Butcher | 6 | 0 | 91 | 238 | 39.66 |
| C.A. Davis | 6 | 0 | 103 | 208 | 34.66 |
| R.C. Fredericks | 6 | 0 | 64 | 204 | 34.00 |
| C.H. Lloyd | 6 | 0 | 70 | 183 | 30.50 |

| Bowling | Overs | M | Runs | W | Average |
|---|---|---|---|---|---|
| J.N. Shepherd | 137.5 | 44 | 266 | 12 | 22.16 |
| G.C. Shillingford | 59.4 | 12 | 160 | 6 | 26.66 |
| G.S. Sobers | 145 | 47 | 318 | 11 | 28.90 |
| C.A. Davis | 30 | 8 | 32 | 1 | 32.00 |
| V.A. Holder | 148.5 | 52 | 335 | 9 | 37.22 |

Wicket-keepers:  A.P.E. Knott 11 dismissals   J.L. Hendriks (WI) 1 dismissal   T.M. Findlay (WI) 9 dismissals

In the second match, J.H. Hampshire became the first England player to score a century on debut, the game being at Lord's. The rubber was historic in that it was the last series in which England beat West Indies.

## 1973 Test Series

### England

| Batting | Innings | NO | HS | Runs | Average |
|---|---|---|---|---|---|
| K.W.R. Fletcher | 6 | 2 | 86* | 266 | 66.50 |
| G. Boycott | 5 | 1 | 97 | 202 | 50.50 |
| D.L. Amiss | 6 | 1 | 86* | 231 | 46.20 |
| F.C. Hayes | 6 | 1 | 106* | 159 | 31.80 |
| A.W. Greig | 5 | 0 | 44 | 122 | 24.40 |

| Bowling | Overs | M | Runs | W | Average |
|---|---|---|---|---|---|
| G.G. Arnold | 149.1 | 37 | 390 | 15 | 26.00 |
| R.G.D. Willis | 35 | 3 | 118 | 4 | 29.50 |
| C.M. Old | 44 | 3 | 151 | 4 | 37.75 |
| D.L. Underwood | 133 | 38 | 330 | 8 | 41.25 |
| J.A. Snow | 49 | 12 | 133 | 3 | 44.33 |

### West Indies

| Batting | Innings | NO | HS | Runs | Average |
|---|---|---|---|---|---|
| G.S. Sobers | 5 | 1 | 150* | 306 | 76.50 |
| C.H. Lloyd | 5 | 0 | 132 | 318 | 63.60 |
| R.C. Fredericks | 5 | 0 | 150 | 251 | 50.20 |
| R.B. Kanhai | 5 | 0 | 157 | 223 | 44.60 |
| B.D. Julien | 5 | 0 | 121 | 220 | 44.00 |

| Bowling | Overs | M | Runs | W | Average |
|---|---|---|---|---|---|
| K.D. Boyce | 98.1 | 22 | 294 | 19 | 15.47 |
| V.A. Holder | 80 | 24 | 174 | 7 | 24.85 |
| L.R. Gibbs | 135.1 | 46 | 227 | 9 | 25.22 |
| G.S. Sobers | 82.1 | 24 | 169 | 6 | 28.16 |
| B.D. Julien | 110 | 27 | 266 | 7 | 38.00 |

Wicket-keepers:  A.P.E. Knott 7 dismissals   D.L. Murray 8 dismissals

In the first match, F.C. Hayes scored a century on debut for England, and K.D. Boyce's match figures of 11 for 147 were then the best for West Indies against England. In the third match, West Indies gained their biggest ever victory over England, their 652 runs being then their highest total in England. G.S. Sobers and B.D. Julien made an unbeaten 155 for the record West Indies seventh-wicket partnership against England and R.B. Kanhai became the second West Indian to score 6,000 Test runs.

## 1973–4 Test Series

### England

| Batting | Innings | NO | HS | Runs | Average |
|---|---|---|---|---|---|
| D.L. Amiss | 9 | 1 | 262* | 663 | 82.87 |
| A.W. Greig | 9 | 0 | 148 | 430 | 47.77 |
| G. Boycott | 9 | 0 | 112 | 421 | 46.77 |
| A.P.E. Knott | 9 | 1 | 87 | 365 | 45.62 |
| K.W.R. Fletcher | 7 | 1 | 129* | 262 | 43,66 |

| Bowling | Overs | M | Runs | W | Average |
|---|---|---|---|---|---|
| A.W. Greig | 207.1 | 46 | 543 | 24 | 22.62 |
| J. Birkenshaw | 40 | 9 | 96 | 2 | 48.00 |
| R.G.D. Willis | 73 | 15 | 255 | 5 | 51.00 |
| P.I. Pocock | 200 | 50 | 550 | 9 | 61.11 |
| C.M. Old | 87.4 | 15 | 313 | 5 | 62.60 |

### West Indies

| Batting | Innings | NO | HS | Runs | Average |
|---|---|---|---|---|---|
| L.G. Rowe | 7 | 0 | 302 | 616 | 88.00 |
| R.C. Fredericks | 7 | 1 | 98 | 397 | 66.16 |
| A.I. Kallicharran | 7 | 0 | 158 | 397 | 56.71 |
| B.D. Julien | 5 | 1 | 86* | 172 | 43.00 |
| D.L. Murray | 5 | 2 | 53* | 113 | 37.66 |

| Bowling | Overs | M | Runs | W | Average |
|---|---|---|---|---|---|
| B.D. Julien | 174 | 50 | 378 | 16 | 23.62 |
| C.H. Lloyd | 56 | 21 | 71 | 3 | 23.67 |
| K.D. Boyce | 118.4 | 23 | 324 | 11 | 29.45 |
| G.S. Sobers | 223.2 | 92 | 421 | 14 | 30.07 |
| L.R. Gibbs | 328.3 | 103 | 661 | 18 | 36.72 |

Wicket-keepers:   D.L. Murray 15 dismissals   A.P.E. Knott 4 dismissals

In the first match, L.R. Gibbs became the first West Indian to take 250 Test wickets. In the second match, the partnership of 206 betwen R.C. Fredericks and L.G. Rowe was the record for the first wicket for West Indies against England, and G.S. Sobers became the first player to reach 8,000 runs in Test cricket. In the third match, A.W. Greig and A.P.E. Knott set the English sixth-wicket record against West Indies with a partnership of 163, and Greig became the first player to score a century and take five wickets in an innings in the same Test for England; L.G. Rowe became the first West Indian to score a treble century against England. In the fourth match, D.L. Amiss became the first English batsman to score three centuries in a series against West Indies. In the fifth match, Greig's innings analysis of 8 for 86 and match analysis of 13 for 156 are the best for England against West Indies.

# 9

# Sun, Rain and Speed

1976: the year of the drought, of cricket fields that turned brown or white through the absence of water, and of Tony Greig's announcement that his team were going to make the West Indies grovel. It was not one of the shrewdest remarks ever made.

A few months earlier, West Indies had encountered any number of problems in Australia and had lost the series 5–1; they had then beaten India 2–1 at home, the last match being won when no fewer than five Indians were unable to bat in the second innings. England had lost two series to Australia and looked a fairly ordinary outfit; despite their experience in Australia, West Indies looked to have the better all-round team, and Greig's 'forecast' seemed altogether ill-advised. Presumably he intended it to fire up his own team, but predictably it did just that to the opposition.

It was, though, a gesture that was pretty much in character, for he never lacked confidence from the moment he scored 156 in his first county match for Sussex. Almost six feet eight inches (2 metres) tall, he seemed larger than life in most of his actions, blond, handsome, with great charisma that was much better suited to the Test arena than to the county grind; a Test batting average of 40 compared to a career average of 31 shows this perfectly. In his maiden Test in 1972, he top-scored in both innings and took five wickets, an all-round performance he was able to sustain for the whole of his Test career of 58 consecutive matches, scoring almost 3,600 runs with eight centuries and taking 141 wickets at 32 with fast-medium (or, as in 1973–4 when he had an outstanding series, off-spin) bowling. Strong and brave – his 110 against Lillee and Thomson on an uneven Brisbane pitch in 1974–5 was an innings of real courage – he loved to drive off the front foot, could hit the ball vast distances and was very much a crowd-pleaser. There were one or two controversial incidents, such as the Kallicharran run-out, over the years, but it was generally agreed that these arose from misplaced exuberance rather than any darker motives; and despite his South African origins, there were few complaints when he replaced Denness as captain in 1975.

*Tony Greig. When the stumps only come up to your knees you have to be larger than life.*

After the battering the team had taken in Australia, he realized that the first job was to restore morale, and he did manage to instil some of his own determination into his players. There was a warmth and a charm about him that made for easy relations with most people, even the press, and they helped him build up the confidence that was needed all round. He was unfortunate to come up against West Indies, playing four fast bowlers for the first time, when he was still an inexperienced leader and the memory of Lillee and Thomson was still raw. Perhaps if he had met them after the confidence gained by a successful tour of India in 1976–7, when his captaincy was much praised, the story might have been different. In this 1976 series he was still unsure of himself tactically, gave the impression that he had little plan of campaign thought out, and often seemed to be changing his bowling and field settings more on a whim than on a good tactical basis. Yet after the success in India, it apperaed that the job was his for the foreseeable future – only for the news to break at the beginning of the 1977 season that, when in Australia for the Centenary Test, he had used his position to recruit players to Kerry Packer's World Series Cricket. The outrage was enormous, he was stripped of the captaincy and, although he played in the Tests of that year, his career was over. In retrospect, it seemed almost inevitable that someone as colourful as Greig should find a wholly novel way of bringing about his own downfall.

His opposite number, Clive Lloyd, had already been through the two formative experiences of his captaincy. During the heavy defeat in Australia he was criticized for not being able to instil spirit into a losing team, and was fully aware of his shortcomings. But, for one thing, the sheer size of the defeat made him and his players determined that it would never happen again and, for another, the power of Lillee and Thomson made him realize just what a potent weapon a battery of fast bowlers would be. Just a couple of months afterwards, playing India in Trinidad with three spin bowlers in his team, he saw them reach 406 for 4 to win the match, only the second time a team had passed 400 runs to win a Test. The spinners Padmore, Jumadeen and Imtiaz Ali did the bulk of the bowling and, as far as Lloyd was concerned, it was they who had let him down. The fact that Holding (who had 6 for 65 in the first innings) and Julien conceded four an over from 34 overs and the spinners only just over two an over from 105 was of less significance than the spinners' inability to bowl batsmen out. His long-held belief that spinners could not be trusted had been vindicated, and from now on Test cricket would take on a new dimension. Whether you think that dimension has been for the good of the game will probably depend on your nationality.

Lloyd, a cousin of Lance Gibbs, made his Test debut against India in 1966–7 and scored 82 and 78 not out. Eighteen years and 110 Tests later he bowed out, with Nemesis unable to resist shaking her fist at him. In his last Test at Sydney in 1984–5, having wrapped up the series with three victories in the first three games and not having lost for 27 Tests since 1981–2, his team suddenly collapsed to an innings defeat, the architects of which were Bob Holland and Murray Bennett – spinners both. Clive Lloyd is one of the best-loved cricketers ever to walk on to a field, but after the relentless domination of his four-man pace attack there must have been many people who permitted themselves a smile at the news. Obviously, the pitch had been prepared for the spinners, but since West Indies had prepared many of their own pitches for their speed merchants they could hardly complain. Even then, Lloyd went down fighting with 72 in his last innings; it took him to a total of 7,515 runs at 46, with nineteen centuries.

His batting could be awesome in its power. Six feet five inches (1.9 metres) tall, left-handed, bespectacled, with a loose, ambling walk that always seemed so relaxed, he wielded a three-pound (1.35-kilo) bat with enormous strength and delighted in sending the ball vast distances. So often there was an explosive quality about his batting which was very difficult to contain, and his driving in particular was magnificent. David Lloyd, his captain at Lancashire, tells a story that once in a Gillette Cup

*The fearsome tale of the gigantic bat, sucking the blood of bowlers and fielders alike. Clive Lloyd in full flow.*

match against Gloucestershire at Old Trafford, Clive Lloyd edged a ball from Mike Procter so hard that it went for six. Procter's anger at this annoyed Lloyd so much that he told his captain he was going to hit him over the pavilion; and he did just that – next ball. Until his knees failed him and the cartilages were removed, he was also one of the finest of all cover fielders, with electrifying speed and a pin-point throw that seemed barely credible. After the knee operation he moved to the slips, and of course proved pretty useful there, too.

He had made his debut for Guyana (then British Guiana) in 1963–4 as a nineteen year old, and joined Lancashire in 1968. The association with Lancashire lasted until 1986 and was always a happy one, for he was enormously popular with the fans and with his team-mates. His contribution over the years was massive, especially in the one-day competitions, and his loyalty and dedication to his adopted county became legendary. Off the pitch he gave much time to helping young players, while on it his play was never selfish, always for the team rather than his average; and there were times when he batted in great pain rather than let the side down. He even played his part as a support bowler, whose right-arm leg-breaks or medium pace could be quite economical.

Lloyd's Test career was not quite the succession of personal triumphs that Sobers had enjoyed. At the end of 1971, playing for a World XI in Australia, he badly injured his back when diving to attempt a catch and spent a month in hospital. At first it seemed that his career might even be over, but he fought back. It took a while to establish himself back in the team as his form was poor and he was not originally selected for the visit of the Australians in 1972–3. When Sobers dropped out with knee trouble, Lloyd took his place, and on his home ground in the fourth Test made 178; thereafter he would miss one or two games through injury but, apart from the Packer hiatus, his position was secure. It was clear, too, that Kanhai, who had taken over the leadership from Sobers, was coming to the end of his career and that whoever took over from him would have the opportunity for an extended run in the job if he were successful. Lloyd believed that the lean years at the end of Sobers' tenure were the result of an unprofessional approach, with not enough thought given to the problems; under Kanhai this improved somewhat, but after he had failed to beat Denness's team the job was given to Lloyd.

Since his experience of captaincy was limited, he had not believed he would be appointed; but he had had his hopes, and had thought a lot about the team's problems. The first priority was to re-establish the team unity that had been allowed to dwindle, with the result that there had been much arguing and bickering The old inter-island rivalries that Worrell had eradicated had surfaced again, and he knew the team would accomplish little until these disappeared. He asked his players for their loyalty to him, in return for which he would do his best to improve their conditions. He asked them to adopt a more professional approach, to harden their attitude and not capitulate when things became tough, as they had sometimes been prone to. He decided that the only way to become the best team in the world was to adopt a killer instinct; to play fairly and sportingly, but to be tough and uncompromising. He wanted to be a winner rather than a good loser. Obviously he was then lucky that a lot of outstanding players began to come into the team at the same period, men like Richards, Greenidge, Roberts, Holding, Croft, Garner, and he had material of the highest class on which to work. But there had been unsuccessful sides in the past that had been packed with outstanding individuals who had not coalesced, or been moulded, into a good *team*. The credit for West Indies' world domination from the mid-1970s onwards must lie very largely with Lloyd.

The emphasis on pace bowling meant that he found himself in a rather curious position. On the one hand, he was loved for his own great ability, his loyalty to his teams, his concern for youngsters and all the other good work he did off the pitch, and for his warm, relaxed character that made him friends in many places. On the other hand, his determination to win became such that he frequently appeared to condone his fast men bowling in an intimidating fashion, which obviously led to criticism from press and public. The prime requirement for opposing batsmen became courage rather than skill, and it was all unnecessary since they were such fine bowlers that they could dismiss teams cheaply when bowling in an orthodox manner. When they gave quite unacceptable displays of dissent, such as Holding kicking down the stumps or Croft deliberately barging into an umpire who had no-balled him, Lloyd did nothing to discipline them in public view.

Then again, his fast-bowling policy, more than any other factor, has hastened the decline of the spinner, a decline that has been hugely to the game's detriment; and with a seemingly inexhaustible supply of young speed men reaching the Test team and creating further successes, there is little sign that the decline might be halted. One of the attractions of the game has always been its diversity, and, whatever success they bring, a relentless stream of fast bowlers ultimately becomes boring. By the time of the 1988 tour of England, there were signs that the fans were realizing this, for Test attendances were well down on those of the 1984 tour. Admittedly, the weather was worse, English fortunes were at a low ebb, and the higher charges may well have deterred many people, especially the Caribbean fans; but one suspects that some thousands of people simply could not face the prospect of yet another day almost entirely given over to fast bowling.

Lloyd captained West Indies 74 times, winning 36 and losing just 12, and he twice won the Prudential World Cup. He was the most successful Test captain of all time and one of the greatest as well. He accomplished the most difficult of all sporting tasks: not just taking his team to the top but keeping it there. If only he could have been just a little less ruthless about it along the way.

Two of the first three games of the 1976 tour were easily won, so that any English optimist who thought that their Australian experiences might have knocked the stuffing out of West Indies had to ponder anew. After the MCC match there was no longer much reason to hope. Greenidge and Lloyd top-scored as West Indies declared at 251 for 9, and then Holding, Roberts and Holder, restricted MCC to 197, only Gilliat, the captain, having a substantial knock, and Amiss ducking into a bouncer which left him with four stitches in his scalp. Injuries to two MCC bowlers helped Richards and Gomes both make centuries, and Lloyd declared at 248 for 3, setting a target of 303. Then, in *Wisden*'s delightful words, 'it was the turn of the three pace bowlers to wreak havoc and so produce a feeling of contentment in the minds of their colleagues for the Test series ahead'. In other words, they bowled them out for 83, Extras top-scoring with 21; since most of the team either were or would be Test players, that feeling of contentment must have seemed well justified.

England sprang a surprise by recalling 45-year-old Brian Close for the first Test at Nottingham. The centre-piece of the match, though, was a wonderful innings of 232 off just 313 balls by Viv Richards, who was in the middle of his *annus mirabilis*. It was his fifth Test century of the year, and he passed 1,000 runs for the year in his eighth match. With Kallicharran, who made 97, he put on 303 for the third wicket, with some wonderful strokes all round the wicket that culminated in 36 runs off his last 13

*Brian Close recalled to the colours in 1976 at the age of forty-five. Murray and Kallicharran watch him play a ball from Julien.*

*In his first innings against England, at Trent Bridge in 1976, Viv Richards made 232. Tony Greig is despatched to the cover boundary.*

balls before holing out on the boundary. The rest of the wickets fell fairly quickly for a total of 494. Brearley, on debut, went for nought, but Steele, first with Edrich and then with Woolmer, made a century and took the score to 226 for three. Then wickets tumbled, and sixteen were still needed to avert the follow-on when the eighth went down; but Old with a bruised wrist, and Snow saw them to safety and the innings made 332.

Needing to score quickly, West Indies made 176 at nearly five an over, despite some fine bowling from Snow, when Lloyd declared with five wickets down, setting England the task of surviving for five and a quarter hours or scoring 339 to win. Brearley stayed for a while but, after Steele failed, Edrich and Close, two experienced old soldiers, came together and stayed together. In due course, Lloyd conceded the draw and gave the ball

*The redoubtable David Steele – courage, determination, skill and runs against Lillee and Thomson in 1975 and the West Indies pacemen in 1976. A brief Test career but a glorious one.*

to his batsmen, and the match petered out with England at 156 for 2. No one was in any doubt who had controlled it.

England then had the best of the Lord's Test; true, West Indies lacked Richards, who was ill, but Edrich was absent too. Greig won the toss but England then batted poorly, scraping their way to 197 in the first day, although only 80.4 overs were sent down in six hours, Close's 60 being the best effort. Underwood then had a good day, making 31 and with Old taking the score to 250, then taking 5 for 39 as West Indies were all out for 182. Only Greenidge and Lloyd kept them afloat as Snow and Underwood bowled really well and the fielders backed them up. On Saturday morning the gates were closed early with thousands locked out, only for the whole day to be lost to the weather; had just an hour or two's play been possible there would almost certainly have been a result. As it was, on the fourth day England batted steadily but without much conviction, Steele and Close the top scorers, and were all out on the last morning for 254, leaving West Indies to make 323 runs in a minimum of 294 minutes. Roberts finished with 10 for 123, and then watched his colleagues make little

*Lord's 1976. A balletic leap from Alan Knott to dismiss Clive Lloyd.*

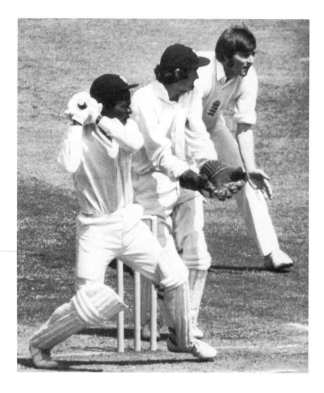

*Roy Fredericks always favoured the square cut. Knott and Old watch Pat Pocock receive the treatment at Lord's in 1976.*

attempt at first to get the runs. Kallicharran took nearly two and a half hours over 34, while Fredericks was grafting away at the other end. Only when Lloyd came out did the runs begin to flow, but when the final twenty overs began another 154 were still needed. Lloyd claimed the last half hour, but when he was out at 233 for 4 he indicated that as far as he was concerned that was that. Greig, characteristically, decided differently and insisted on playing on; two more wickets fell and the match finally ended at 241 for 6 when, with only three balls left, a win became impossible.

Before the Old Trafford Test, West Indies had four games and won them all, one of which involved bowling out Yorkshire for 90 when only 110 were wanted to win. For the Test, Richards and Edrich returned and, with various fast bowlers injured, Mike Selvey was called up for England. He celebrated by taking a wicket with his sixth ball and two more by the time he had bowled twenty; when Hendrick got Lloyd, West Indies were 26 for 4. It was up to Greenidge and, apart from being dropped on 26, he did them proud. King's 32 was the only other score in double figures, while Greenidge's 134 out of 211 represented 63.5 per cent of his team's total, a proportion that has only once been exceeded in all Tests. England

*England press for victory at Lord's in 1976. Murray refuses to be intimidated by the ring of fielders.*

were thus faced with the task of scoring twelve to avoid the follow-on and they achieved this – just. 37 for 2 overnight became 71 all out after eighty-five minutes next morning, with Holding finishing with 5 for 17. The difference in the bowling attacks then became rather noticeable; by soon after tea on the third day, West Indies had rattled up 411 for 5 when Lloyd declared, with 50 from Fredericks, 135 from Richards, and Greenidge becoming only the second West Indian after Headley to score a century in each innings against England.

With a deficit of 552 and thirteen and a quarter hours left, obviously only the weather was going to save England, so there was not the least justification for the barrage of short balls that Holding and Roberts hurled at Edrich and Close. It was intimidatory bowling of the worst sort against two brave batsmen who, as it turned out, were both playing their last Test innings. Umpire Alley eventually warned Holding, but there must have been many Lancastrians who were sad to see Lloyd, on his home ground, do nothing about it. He did admit afterwards that they had been carried away by trying to make a quick breakthrough and had bowled badly, but it still left an unpleasant taste. On the Monday they showed how easy it was for top-class bowlers to pitch the ball up and get wickets. Edrich and Close soon went, and on two occasions Roberts found himself on a hat-trick; the second time, Selvey edged to Greenidge at slip – and he dropped

*The infamous barrage of bouncers at Close and Edrich, Old Trafford 1976.*
*Close sways away from another one from Michael Holding which Murray takes*
*above his head.*

it. Rain washed out the last session with England 125 for 9, but the next
morning was fine and only one more run was added. The margin of 425
runs was the largest runs victory West Indies have had over England, and
for the only time in Test cricket Extras had a bigger match aggregate (44)
than any batsman. It was not felt to be a good idea to mention the word
'grovel' in the presence of the England captain, especially as he had scored
only 38 runs in five innings.

Headingley saw a cracking match, and anyone lucky enough to be there
on the first day is unlikely to have forgotten it. Greenidge and Fredericks
immediately laid into the bowlers, bringing up 50 in 8.3 overs, 100 in 18.2
overs, and at lunch after 27 overs they were 147 without loss. Fredericks
reached his hundred soon after, and when he was out Greenidge and
Richards took 95 off twelve overs. Greenidge went for 115, Rowe joined
Richards, and at tea the score was 330 for 2. After tea the batsman
continued to play their shots and the runs came, but the ball began to
move around and wickets fell, too. By the close, the score was 437 for 9
from just 83 overs, surely one of the best days of cricket since the war. The
last wicket fell at 450, whereupon England promptly collapsed to 32 for 3.

*Headingley 1976. Holding beat Greig four times in one over and the two faces tell the story. Greig went on to a century but West Indies won the match.*

*Alan Knott has been second only to Les Ames as an England wicket-keeper/ batsman.*

Willey and Balderstone, both on debut, stemmed the tide for a while, and then Greig and Knott came together at 169 for 5 with the follow-on a distinct possibiliy. They put on 152 before they were separated, first attacking well and then being contained. When Greig went for 116, Snow supported Knott, who spent over an hour in the nineties before reaching the same score as his captain, and when the tail went quickly the total was 387.

A shower livened up the pitch and the West Indian openers soon fell. On the Monday morning two more wickets went down and, at 72 for 4, the excitement began to mount. The crucial innings then came from King, who hammered 50 off 39 balls to help the score to 196; England needed 260 to win, with time not a problem. Willis's 5 for 42 clearly inspired Roberts, who in his first four overs sent back Steele, Hayes and Balderstone: Woolmer and Willey took the score to 80 before the former departed, and Willey and Greig then looked as though they might turn the

*At Headingley in 1976 Deryck Murray took five catches in the second innings. Alan Knott was one of them off Wayne Daniel's bowling. Collis King joins in the appeal.'*

match England's way. But at 140 Willey went to a superb catch by Roberts, and at the close they were on 146 for 5, needing another 114. Clearly much would depend on whether Knott could stay with Greig but, after nightwatchman Underwood went, Knott and Snow both followed quickly, all dismissed by Daniel inside four overs. Greig's response was to throw the bat, and Ward hung on while 46 were added; but, with the score on 204, he was caught behind off Holding and Willis was lbw first ball, leaving Greig unbeaten on 76 and West Indies winners by 55 runs. Greig was gracious in defeat, saying that their play on the first day deserved every credit.

Roy Fredericks's second century helped him pass 500 runs for the series, although Richards and Greenidge still finished above him in the aggregates and averages. Short, left-handed and aggressive, he was an opener who hit the ball extremely hard, played every shot in the book with great relish and was always looking to attack from the first ball. Not only the Headingley crowd would testify to this; Lillee, Thomson and their friends saw him reach his century from 71 balls against them in 1975–6, and go on to his highest Test score of 169. He came into the Guyana team as a 20 year

*Headingley 1976 and Gordon Greenidge at second slip practises for the high jump. In the first picture he catches John Snow off Daniel's bowling and in the second he celebrates as Murray catches Alan Ward off Holding. Collis King is at first slip.*

*He might have been small but Roy Fredericks hit the ball exceptionally hard. Alan Knott is denied the chance to pounce.*

old in 1963, made his Test debut against Australia in 1968–9, got into the runs straight away, and remained a permanent fixture. In all, he played 59 Tests and scored 4,334 runs at 42 with eight centuries, took a handful of very expensive wickets with his left-arm spinners and was a quite brilliant close leg fielder. He played for Glamorgan in 1971 and 1972 (and briefly the following year before joining the touring party), scoring a thousand runs in both seasons and, with Alan Jones, putting on a county record opening stand of 330 against Northamptonshire in 1972. Perhaps the best way to describe him is as a typical West Indian batsman, fundamentally very reliable and dependable yet always looking to attack if possible, always full of attractive stroke-play. He had the occasional run of poor form, but when the runs came they came thick, fast and gloriously.

Four players had especial reason to remember the Oval game: two scored double centuries, one took fourteen wickets and one became the leading Test wicket-keeper. Lloyd won his fourth toss and, after Greenidge had gone for a duck, Richards shared in three century stands. Fredericks made 71, and Rowe had reached 70 when he was stumped by

Knott, overtaking Godfrey Evans with his 220th dismissal. By the end of the first day, Richards was on 200 and the score was 373 for 3. Nothing much changed next morning as 141 were scored, but early in the afternoon Richards was finally out. 291 made off 366 balls, with 38 fours, in just under eight hours does rather speak for itself. It meant that he had scored 1,710 Test runs in eleven matches in 1976 at an average of 90, still the record aggregate for a calendar year. Lloyd soon followed for 84, but then King and Murray continued the torment, and, when the declaration came on the second evening, the score was 687 for 8, still the West Indies record against England.

Next day it was a question of who would stay with Amiss, playing his first Test of the summer. Steele did for a century partnership and then Willey did the same; but when Greig was out near the close of play, with the board on 303 for 5, there was a pitch invasion by, for the most part, West Indian fans. This caused a delay of nine minutes, but play was able to restart for the last couple of overs. Most of the wickets had been falling to

*Dennis Amiss on his way to a double century at the Oval in 1976. Cherish the fact that he is wearing a cap; the days of the anonymous helmet were drawing near.*

Holding, and when he finally bowled Amiss for a splendid 203 it was clear that the follow-on would not be avoided. Knott and Miller, on debut, had a useful stand, but when the innings closed at 435 the deficit was 252. Daniel, though, was injured and Holding, having taken 8 for 92, clearly deserved a rest, so Lloyd decided to bat again. Fredericks and Greenidge thought this an excellent idea and hammered 182 in two hours twenty minutes without being separated, by which time England were just demoralized. They had six hours twenty minutes to survive, but the first hour of the last day saw five wickets crash for 78. Knott did his best with another fifty but it was all over with eighty minutes to spare; all out 203 and victory by 231 runs. Holding's figures this time were 6 for 57 for match figures of 14 for 149, the first West Indian to take more than twelve wickets in a Test.

The remarkable thing about Holding's performance was that it was achieved on a batsman's pitch from which no other bowler got any response at all. He did it in the classic manner, by pitching the ball well up and bowling very, very quickly, and the fact that he needed help from his

*'Whispering Death'. The superbly smooth delivery of Michael Holding, eye fixed on the spot he is going to hit, head steady as a rock. A wonderful athlete in action.*

colleagues for only two of those wickets shows just how accurate he was. Tall and slim, without the usual broad shoulders of the pace man, he had excelled at athletics as a youngster, with the result that he was a fast bowler like virtually no other; his approach to the wicket was so soft and silky that he hardly seemed to touch the ground at all, and several umpires said that they were not able to hear him running in. Until he cut it down in later years, his run-up was extremely long – and his saunter back to his mark extremely slow – but the speed that it generated undoubtedly justified the length, and the grace of it all was an aesthetic delight. As the years passed, he sacrificed a little speed for greater control, especially of away-swing, but that run-up never for a moment lost its beauty.

His career was not without its less attractive moments, and it is sad that many fans will remember the famous picture in the 1981 *Wisden* of him kicking down the stumps after having an appeal refused in New Zealand almost as readily as they will recall his wonderful bowling; yet even in dissent he was physically graceful, and the picture is positively balletic. The fact that he could get such good results by orthodox bowling also left one wondering why he occasionally indulged in a bouncer war, for it obviously did his reputation no good and was not as a rule very product-ive. His debut in the disastrous series in Australia was not a happy one, but things improved at home to India and then he really came into his own against England, finishing with 28 wickets at under 13. By the time he called it a day, he had played in 60 Tests and taken 249 wickets at 23, and like all of his fast-bowling collagues had benefited from being one of a quartet as he could operate in short spells and rest more often. Since he did not have the physical strength of most of the others, this was important for him and must have contributed a lot to his effectiveness. On that basis, then, we have a reason to be glad that Clive Lloyd adopted his strategy of all-out pace, for had he not done so perhaps we would have seen less of one of the most watchable of all bowlers.

Holding's 28 wickets were equalled by Andy Roberts. The first Anti-guan to play Test cricket, Roberts had made his debut during Denness's tour, the first of the unending stream of top-class fast bowlers which has transformed modern cricket. He played only once in that series but was then brought back for the rubber in India and made a big impact, so that when he had Steele's wicket at Headingley he chalked up his hundredth Test wicket in the record time of two years 144 days. Tall and strong, with very broad shoulders, he would go on to claim 202 victims at 25 from his 47 Tests, of which 50 came in a dozen games against England. From a fairly economical run-up he bowled with great pace, usually very

*Perfect balance in the leap before the delivery stride. Andy Roberts set the Caribbean fast bowling conveyor belt in motion.*

accurately, and could move the ball both in the air and off the pitch; sometimes, as at Old Trafford, he would overdo the bouncers, and he had his share of injured batsmen to his credit – or rather debit. More often, though, he preferred to pitch the ball up and get his wickets in less intimidating fashion.

He played for Hampshire from 1973 to 1978, had a season with New South Wales, and appeared for Leicestershire between 1981 and 1984. For Hampshire he had a very successful first full season, taking 119 wickets at only 13 in 1974, and having some good days in limited-overs cricket as well. Thereafter the relationship became steadily more strained and he left during the 1978 season. He gained a reputation as the Buster Keaton of the cricket world, a man who rarely seemed to have any expression on his face and who was not one for the excited cavortings that greet the fall of a wicket; yet behind the mask a good deal of thought was given to his bowling, and he was liked and respected by his fellow players. In 1985 he was awarded the CBE.

During this 1976 tour, West Indies played twenty-six first-class matches and won eighteen of them, losing only to Middlesex, the champions, and T.N. Pearce's XI (which contained eight Middlesex players) at the

Scarborough festival when they omitted their leading strike bowlers. Clearly they were helped by having hardly any matches affected by the weather, but it was still a wonderfully sustained performance. Perhaps for many of the fans the best moment of all came at the end of the fifth Test, when Tony Greig went out and 'grovelled' before them.

*

Before the teams met again the Great Schism had occurred, as Kerry Packer inserted his spanner into the gently revolving works. For nine Tests against Australia and India, West Indies were led by Alvin Kallicharran, with some names alongside him which now look very unfamiliar. England had lost fewer players than most countries to World Series Cricket and had won a number of rubbers as a result but, when the armistice was signed, England's limitations were soon exposed. To mark the return to normal, a totally abnormal arrangement was made, whereby West Indies and England were both in Australia at the same time, playing alternate Tests against the home team. Since England lost 3–0 and West Indies won 2–0, there was not much doubt who was Top Team, though, having said that, West Indies then lost a very bad-tempered series in New Zealand, going down by one wicket in the only Test to see a result. Shortly afterwards, in May 1980, Clive Lloyd and Co. arrived in England with a squad that included Holding, Roberts, Garner, Marshall and Croft. There was a spinner in the party, Derek Parry, but needless to say he did not play in any of the Tests.

After the series in Australia, Mike Brearley announced that he would not be able to tour in 1980–1 as he wanted to continue his studies in psychoanalysis, and the England selectors decided to appoint a new captain for the start of the 1980 rubber. They chose Ian Botham, their young hero – he was then twenty-four – who had already performed great deeds in the twenty-five Tests he had so far played. The feeling among press and public was that he was too young, too inexperienced, and too much was being asked of him too soon. Yet he had been Brearley's choice to succeed him, for he had perceived that Botham was an intelligent, tactically aware player and believed that he offered 'tremendous hope for a new, vital start'. His initial appointment was for just two Tests, a demonstration of lack of faith that cannot have helped his confidence and seemed to many to be ludicrous. In the event, his twelve Tests proved a singularly unhappy period as he lost four and drew eight; he insisted that the responsibility did not affect him but his form declined – partly at least through a back injury – and his performances varied from moderate to dismal.

Any present-day fan will be familiar with the Botham story, for it has been told too often to need repeating. No one would suggest that he rivals Sobers as the greatest of all-rounders, for, although he has taken more wickets, his batting has been much less consistent and his Test average is some twenty-three points lower than Sobers'. Compared with the other great all-rounders of his time, Imran Khan, Richard Hadlee and Kapil Dev, he is certainly the best batsman and best slip fielder, but Hadlee and Imran are more dangerous bowlers, and much less likely to have a bad day. Perhaps no player has ever been quite as competitive as Botham, and if his combativeness has led him into trouble off the field it has generally worked in his favour on it – except when he has refused to part with the ball despite not bowling well, or when he has holed out in the deep when a more circumspect approach was required. As a public figure hero-worshipped by countless youngsters, his drug-taking was a sad business, but few people in any field have ever used their fame better than his long-distance walks which have raised vast sums for charity. One of his regrets is that in four series against West Indies his record is very ordinary – one innings in which he took eight wickets, but little else of note – and he is aware that not having proved himself against the best team in the world will be held against him when reputations come to be assessed.

His captaincy suffered by having to succeed Brearley, for the Middlesex man's wonderful understanding of the psychological needs of each of his players was something that Botham could never hope to emulate. By nature he is very much 'one of the boys', which must have made it hard to assert himself, he does not find it easy to take advice and is readily upset by criticism. There were times when his own belief in himself as a great player could backfire on him if he failed to realize that he was having an off day, and he could look stubborn and bloody-minded as a result. Since he was not a natural captain he had to lead by example, and when the mighty deeds failed to materialize he was very much up against it. Nor was he helped by being up against the mighty deeds of the West Indies in his first two series, and perhaps if he had been able to cut his teeth on something less difficult the story might have had a happier turn to it.

The story came desperately close to beginning with a victory. On a Trent Bridge wicket that saw the ball moving around off the seam and in conditions that helped the swing bowlers, Botham won the toss and bat-ted. Before long England were benefitting from the first of a string of catches dropped by both sides, and their total of 263 was over a hundred more than it would have been had Boycott, Woolmer and Botham not had a second chance. Botham's 57 was top score, so at least his captaincy got off to a bright start. In reply, Greenidge and Richards hammered 88 in even time, but then only Murray made a substantial score, his 64 being joint top with Richards and 41 more than it should have been had a catch been accepted; 308 all out. By the beginning of the fourth day, England were well placed at 145 for 2, although both Boycott and Woolmer had once again been missed; but they batted slowly and then four wickets fell quickly. Willey held things together for a while and the total reached 252, helped by no fewer than 52 extras since the ball was moving around so much that Murray had a very hard time behind the stumps. West Indies had over eight hours to make 208, but on that pitch it never looked easy.

*What he lacked in aesthetic grace Bob Willis made up in speed, determination and sheer guts. Despite appearances, umpire David Constant is not asleep.*

Greenidge soon went, leaving Richards to lay into the bowling. In 56 minutes he made 48 before Botham got him, and by the close of play just 99 were needed with eight wickets left. Next day Bacchus was caught behind off Hendrick's first ball, and suddenly England began to think they might do it. Willis had one of his inspired days and, after taking four wickets in the first innings, went one better this time, with 5 for 65. Kallicharran, Lloyd (with an injured hand), Murray and Marshall all went, and when the seventh wicket fell 28 were still needed. The crucial moments had occurred earlier, though, when Haynes was twice dropped at slip – first by Tavaré on 23 and then by Hendrick on 49, both fairly straightforward chances. Haynes was eventually run out for 62 and left the field in tears thinking he had lost his team the match, but by then only three more were needed and Roberts was striking the ball well. He had been dropped off a hard chance when just twelve were needed, but went on to hit the winning four off Botham, and his eight wickets and two useful knocks earned him the Man of the Match award. England were left to reflect on one of the game's oldest sayings, the one about catches winning matches. It is interesting to think that had they snatched – or preferably caught cleanly – that victory, the pattern of English Test cricket might have been changed for years ahead, for, as the other four matches were all drawn, a victorious first series might have given Botham's captaincy the shove it needed to get airborne.

At Lord's, England were almost certainly saved by the weather. Their first innings, though, was marked by a wonderful display from Gooch, who at his thirty-sixth attempt finally produced a Test century, and it was very much worth waiting for. His 123 came out of 165 off 162 deliveries in 211 minutes; a few months earlier in Australia he had run himself out on 99 in his desperation to reach the magic figure, but one would never have guessed it from the effortless way he swept there now. Unfortunately, his team-mates did not provide much support; Tavaré managed an incredibly laborious 42 but everyone else failed. 269 did not look anything like enough; and when West Indies reached 260 for 1 it looked positively minute. For Richards it was another triumph, with 145 coming off just 159 balls, a display even more spectacular than Gooch's – although the Englishman had had to contend with rather more hostile bowling. Richards also had the benefit of solid support at the other end as Haynes steadily made his way to 184, the highest West Indian innings at Lord's, and with Lloyd chipping in a fifty the total reached 518. By now it was near the close on the third day; Gooch and Boycott made a confident start, but much of the Monday was lost to rain and the game was then abandoned on the last afternoon with

Answers on a postcard to . . . Desmond Haynes poses for a 'supply your own caption' picture.

Haynes in more familiar pose – on his way to 184 at Lord's in 1980, at the time the highest West Indian Test innings at headquarters.

almost ten hours having been lost. At 133 for 2, England might have fought back for an honourable draw; or they might not.

The honourable draw had to wait till Old Trafford, although over eleven hours were lost to the weather. Lloyd won the toss and put England in despite the pitch looking good for runs, and before four o'clock had supervised their dismissal for 150. Brian Rose was brought in for his first home Test and promised he would attack the bowling; he was as good as his word and made 70, but 33 from Gatting was the only other contribution as the last seven wickets went for 24 in fifty-two minutes. England soon struck back, though, and had three wickets down for 25, only for Richards to launch into Willis. 65 came from 68 balls, with 53 of them debited to the Warwickshire man. Time was lost on the first two days and then the Saturday was washed out altogether, so it was Monday before Lloyd was able to complete his first Test hundred at his adopted home, in what many thought would be his last opportunity. He held the second half of the innings together, passed 5,000 Test runs, and saw the total to 260.

Faced with a deficit of 110, England actually got their heads down and battled. Boycott led the way with 86 and everyone made a contribution of sorts, but soon after lunch on the final day they were 290 for 6 and defeat was still possible. It was Willey, supported by Emburey, who kept it at bay, the final score being 391 for 7; admittedly, Roberts had hardly been able to bowl on the last day, but the home team had shown themselves that they could bat a bit if they tried.

There were times at the Oval when both sides had thoughts of winning; at one point the bookmakers quoted 100 to 1 against a West Indies victory, but a day later they were 5 to 4 when England's Pythonesque second innings was at its nadir. Their first innings was marked by an over rate of 12.3 an hour against which Gooch scored 83, Rose and Boycott made fifties, Gatting almost did, and with the help of 57 extras the total reached 370. Once again, the Saturday's play was washed out, but on Monday morning five wickets were down for 105 and, with Lloyd having badly pulled a hamstring while fielding, the follow-on definitely loomed. It

*The Oval 1980 saw one of the more remarkable Test scorecards – after being 92 for 9 when Bob Willis joined Peter Willey, the innings was declared on 209 when Willey reached his maiden Test century. He is congratulated by partner and fans alike.*

was Bacchus who saved the day with 61, Marshall and Garner both made forties, and the final total reached 265.

England then collapsed in wonderfully spectacular fashion; Rose made 41, but until Willis joined Willey everyone else had failed dismally and nine wickets had gone down for 92. Garner and Croft were by now both injured, but West Indies suddenly found themselves up against some determination. When Willis came out, England were 197 ahead with 151 minutes and twenty overs left and there cannot have been many who doubted West Indies would win, but with Willis lunging his left leg forward and Willey protecting him from the strike as much as possible, they began to put together a remarkable stand. By the end of the second Test, Willey's last nine Test innings had produced 90 runs, and, had he been caught when on 13 at Old Trafford, his Test days would almost certainly have been over; as it was, his 62 not out there and his reputation as a battler persuaded the selectors to press on with him, and he justified their faith now. Their unbeaten stand of 117 was only thirteen away from the England tenth-wicket record when, with Willis on 24, he reached his maiden Test century, Botham declared and the match ended. From 92 for 9 to 209 for 9 represented one of the oddest innings in Test cricket.

After a fine spring, the summer of 1980 became a big disappointment and the weather reached something of a soggy climax for the fifth Test at Headingley. After two days of almost non-stop rain, the first day was washed out completely, since the lakes dotted around the ground were not thought to be conducive to good cricket. Hard work by the ground staff enabled play to begin on Friday afternoon, whereupon Richards, leading West Indies for the first time because of Lloyd's injury, gleefully put England in. Before long they were 59 for 6; Botham swung the bat for 37 off as many balls, and Bairstow, replacing the runless Knott, made 40 to take the total to 143.

Next day, according to *Wisden* in poetic mood, 'thick grey cloud hung sullenly over the ground from start to stumps, creating an atmosphere straight out of *Wuthering Heights*'. In conditions quite alien to them, the West Indies batsmen performed altogether more creditably than their opponents, Greenidge and Haynes producing their best opening stand of the series, 83, and Richards, Kallicharran and Holding all making useful knocks in a score of 245. When the Monday's play was then completely washed out too, England had to accept that they were not going to square the series and could hope only for another draw. Gooch became the only player to score a fifty in the match and put on 95 for the first wicket with Boycott, but when the fifth wicket fell just before tea they were only 72 ahead and could still have lost. Rose had pulled a thigh muscle while fielding but now, batting with a runner, made an unbeaten 43 to steer England to safety. After having lost over fourteen hours to the weather, the game was called off with the score at 227 for 6 declared, and a series that had promised so much with its exciting start fizzled out meaninglessly, with almost seven of the twenty-five playing days lost. Botham did not even have much luck with the weather during his captaincy.

This was Deryck Murray's last Test after a career spanning seventeen years which had seen him play in 62 Tests and make 189 dismissals, at the time the West Indian record by a street. He was only twenty when he made his debut in England in 1963, promptly setting a West Indian record with 24 dismissals in the series. If he did not touch such heights again, he remained a thoroughly reliable keeper right to the end, small, neat and quiet, and rarely given to histrionics. He interrupted his cricketing career to go to Cambridge, whom he captained, and then Nottingham University to take a degree in business studies, playing for the county from 1966 to

*Deryck Murray, fresh from the shower, celebrates his seven victims in the Headingley Test of 1976.*

1969 while he was there. A few years later, between 1972 and 1975, he had a spell with Warwickshire, during which time he returned to the Test team against Australia in 1972–3 – he had played only one other series in the meantime, against England in 1967–8 – and remained a fixture for the rest of the decade. He was a very handy and determined batsman, good enough to score almost 2,000 Test runs at nearly 23, even opening the batting a few times, and over 13,000 during his career, including 1,000 a season three times. For much of the 1970s he was Lloyd's vice-captain and led the team once, against Australia in the first match after Packer's 'circus' had left town.

He was also a prime mover in the bid to get better pay for West Indian cricketers, putting in much work as the first secretary of the West Indian Players' Association. Quiet and reserved he may have been, but his determination to succeed has been of great importance to his colleagues, both on and off the field.

Although they had recently lost narrowly to New Zealand, there was no question that West Indies were now the outstanding team in the world, and they were to continue that way throughout the 1980s. To paraphrase the last chapter of Sellar and Yeatman's classic *1066 And All That*, West Indies were thus clearly top nation, and History came to a . That chapter, incidentally, is entitled 'A Bad Thing'.

*

A few months later, England were in the Caribbean for a tour that, in the problems they encountered, lacked only a riot to round it off. For a start, the weather was atrocious when they most needed to acclimatize, and in their first seven weeks they had only seventeen days of cricket. Finding decent practice facilities was a constant headache, leading to some crazy situations; in St Vincent, for example, Ken Barrington, the assistant manager, hunted all over for a place for Boycott to practise, and eventually found a piece of flat ground near the airport which had ducks waddling around and a donkey at long leg. There was the cancellation of the second Test after the Guyanese government decided to deport Robin Jackman because of his South African connections; and then came the real tragedy, when Ken Barrington had a heart attack and died during the third Test in Barbados. By the end of that Test they were two down with two to play, and it is difficult to think of any England tour where such a low point had been reached. Yet in the last two Tests they fought back well, with some help from the weather which few could have grudged them, to earn draws, several batsmen contributing excellent fighting innings. Botham retained the England capaincy but, although he topped the bowling averages, his form with the bat was wretched. In contrast Clive Lloyd, back after his injury, had a splendid series with a lowest score of 58 in five innings.

England did actually begin with a victory, Miller and Willey rather unexpectedly bowling out the Young West Indies XI on the last afternoon. Thereafter rain restricted them to one-day games and half of a four-day game, so they went into the first Test in Trinidad very under-prepared. It soon showed, even in their team selection, for they left out Gatting and played three spinners. The start was delayed for three hours partly because the bowlers' run-ups were damp and partly because vandals, protesting about the omission of Deryck Murray, the local captain, had left wet patches on the pitch – and thrown a good few bottles around as well. With this in mind, Botham chose to field first, only for Greenidge and Haynes to put on 168 for the first wicket. On the second day, Emburey bowled forty overs for 81 runs and five wickets, but Lloyd, David Murray and Roberts all batted well. Roberts's fifty included an over from Botham from which he hit twenty-four runs (462660), a new Test record for a six-ball over, and Lloyd finally declared on the third morning at 426 for 9. The rest day, incidentally, was taken after two days for the lovely Caribbean reason of avoiding a clash with a steel-band festival.

It was Croft who claimed the bowling honours in England's first innings as only Gooch and Gower passed forty in a total of 178. With time lost to the weather, England were faced with surviving for eight and three-quarter hours to draw the match, but Gooch and Rose fell quickly. Boycott stayed over five hours for 70 but had no lengthy support, Botham holed out in the deep when his responsibility as captain was to put his head down, and England never looked as though they were going to make it. Botham's dismissal was the result of fine captaincy by Lloyd, for when it seemed he was going to bat sensibly Lloyd put on Richards, knowing full well Botham would not be able to resist trying to hit his friend out of the ground, and sure enough the sucker punch worked. Even with more time lost, it was all over before the last hour. 169 all out gave West Indies a win by an innings and 79 runs, the first time they had beaten England by an innings at home since 1934–5; by coincidence, it was the first time an England captain had chosen to field first in the Caribbean since Wyatt did in the same series.

While in Trinidad, Bob Willis had been injured and returned home. His replacement was Robin Jackman who arrived in Guyana on 23 February, with the Test scheduled to begin on 28 February. It would seém that the mischief was started by a Jamaican radio commentator, who suggested that as Jackman had coached in South Africa the Guyanese government was contravening the Gleneagles agreement by admitting him. The British Minister for Sport, Hector Monro, pointed out that the Gleneagles agreement was irrelevant here as it made no reference to actions by one country against the nationals of another, but on 26 February the British High Commissioner in Georgetown was notified that Jackman's visitor's permit had been withdrawn and he must leave the country. At the same time, Alan Smith, the England manager, announced that England would not play the second Test as it was 'no longer possible for the Test team to be chosen without restrictions being imposed'. The following day, the English party left for Barbados and, after lengthy discussions with representatives of the governments of Barbados, Montserrat, Antigua and Jamaica, the other scheduled venues, it was stated on 4 March that the tour would continue.

Informed sources in the Caribbean thought it likely that the political maneouvrings behind all this were by way of a reprisal for a report by Lord Avebury criticizing Forbes Burnham's ruling party for election-rigging. The point, though, which takes the whole affair into the realms of the ludicrous is that other members of the England party, such as Boycott and Bairstow, had also played and coached in South Africa but no objection was made to them. There seems to be no logical reason for ignoring some and then picking on one, but one can only suppose that, having missed, for whatever reason, their first opportunity of causing trouble, the authorities were just glad to get a second chance. Much sympathy went Jackman's way as many felt that he had been humiliated; and went also to the cricket fans of Guyana, deprived of a Test match and also, because of the weather, of any game against the tourists apart from a one-day international. On England's next tour in 1985–6, Guyana was carefully omitted from the itinerary, and it would be nine years before they returned – only for the Test to be washed out completely.

There was a warm welcome from the people of Barbados, but their sympathy did not prevent them from preparing a pitch to suit the fast bowlers when the Test took place. One little piece of history was made when Roland Butcher became the first black man to play for England, and by a neat coincidence it was on the ground just fourteen miles from his birth-place. He did not have an outstanding game but was given the warmest of receptions by the crowd when he batted and was helped on his way by reassuring words from Desmond Haynes, a fellow Barbadian. Once again, Botham won the toss and chose to field as the pitch looked as though it would be most lively on the first morning, and for the second time his decision could not really be criticized. Jackman had Greenidge caught with his fifth ball in Test cricket, and shortly before lunch the fourth wicket went down for 65. Gomes, on 7, was bowled by Dilley off one of just two no-balls delivered all day and, on 17, was dropped by Bairstow off a straightforward chance. He went on to 58, putting on 154 with Lloyd, the captain batting beautifully for a century to take his team out of trouble. On the second morning, the innings was finished off for 265, only for England to collapse dismally. Holding started it with a blistering over of flat-out speed that accounted for Boycott, after which no one passed 26 and they were all out for 122, with Croft again the leading wicket-taker. Late that evening, Ken Barrington suffered a heart attack and died.

It does not take much to imagine the effect of this on a group of already dispirited players, all of whom held him in the warmest affection. Many a tear was shed that night, and after the minute's silence at the beginning of the next day the play had an unreal feel to it. It was dominated by a century from Richards, which on the fourth morning he took in explosive style to 182 not out when Lloyd declared on 379 for 7. Faced with a deficit of 522, Boycott and Gatting fell in successive balls with the score on 2; Gooch and Gower put on 120, but when Gower went for 54 Gooch found little company. He completed his century next day but the last wicket fell at 224, leaving West Indies victors by 298 runs. It all seemed very irrelevant.

Out of these depths the England players fought back well, some of them showing just the qualities that Barrington would have wanted. Led by Geoff Miller as Botham was attending Viv Richards' wedding – to which fifty people were invited and two thousand turned up – they beat the Leeward Islands and then moved on to Antigua for the inaugural Test at St John's, West Indies' first new Test ground since the opening series of 1929–30. When they inspected the wicket, they found it being rolled by some prisoners from the local jail, one of whom looked familiar to Boycott. 'I remember you from seven years ago,' he said. 'I'll still be here in ten years,' replied the man. 'I'm doing life!'

On what was described as an old-style West Indian pitch, Botham again won the toss and at last chose to bat; a good start was ended when Gooch ran himself out, and soon wickets were tumbling. 135 for 3 became 138 for 6 and the writing was in its usual place on the wall. Enter Peter Willey, determined to take on the bowlers. Downton and Emburey kept him company for a while, and when number eleven Dilley joined him he had 69; when Dilley was out for 2 next morning Willey had completed his century, a splendid 102 not out that took England to 271, Croft finishing with 6 for 74. West Indies soon lost Haynes, but Richards, on his home ground, and Greenidge set off at an explosive pace with 45 off the first seven overs. This became slower and slower as the day went on, and although Richards reached his hundred after tea he then scored only three in an hour. 236 for 2 overnight became 296 for 7 next morning as England bowled themselves back into the game, but Lloyd and Garner put on 83 for the eighth wicket and then Holding and Croft an unbeaten 67 for the tenth as the bowlers tired, enabling Lloyd to declare on 468.

With twelve and a half hours left, England were clearly up against it, so when the rain fell on the fourth day they were not too upset. After having had it ruin so much of their practice time, it seemed only fair that it should come to their aid when they needed it. Boycott and Gooch then batted steadily for three hours before Gooch departed for 83, after which Gower and Boycott took their team to safety. Both fell before the end but Boycott had another century under his belt as the score reached 234 for 3. If the people of Antigua had not seen the victory they wanted, they had at least enjoyed some good fighting cricket.

The Kingston match had a similar pattern, except that England batted first because they had been put in by Lloyd. The first day belonged very much to Gooch, who made a fine 153 that was to earn him the Man of the Match award. In support, though, only Boycott reached 40 and the overnight score was 278 for 6; next morning they were all out for just another seven runs. The last three West Indian wickets were also to fall cheaply, but before that the batsmen had done rather better; Greenidge and Haynes posted another century partnership and Lloyd and Gomes both reached the nineties. 442 all out for a lead of 157, leaving England again with two days to survive. In an hour they were 32 for 3 and that was clearly that, but now it was Gower's turn for the heroics. They were lucky to lose almost three hours to rain, but Gower was still there at the end of the last day, having batted seven and three-quarter hours for 154 not out. He had two principal supporters; Willey made 67 in a stand of 136 for the fourth wicket, but when the sixth wicket fell there were nearly four hours left and the lead was only 58. The man for the crisis proved to be Downton, who stayed with Gower till the end, which came when Botham declared on 302 for 6; they were helped by Marshall not being able to bowl, but it was still a fine piece of concentration of which Ken Barrington would have been proud.

In the light of what was to happen in the next few years, defeat by just 2–0 may be seen as something of a triumph, especially in view of the two traumas that occurred. One man who emerged from the tour with much credit was Alan Smith, the manager, who had been diplomacy personified during the political crisis and sensitive and supportive at the time of Barrington's death. Of the players, Gooch in particular had had a good tour and was really beginning to fulfil his potential, but the difference between the two bowling attacks seemed just to be increasing. The home bowler of the series was Colin Croft with twenty-four wickets at under 19, and few English batsmen will have been sorry that he played in only two rubbers against them. Tall and strong, he was unusual in regularly bowling from wide of the crease, sometimes even so wide that his hand could not be seen against the sightscreen, which obviously caused the batsman trouble. If this reduced the likelihood of an lbw decision the unfamiliar angle made the batsman's job that much more difficult.

*Colin Croft – took 8 for 29 against Pakistan in only his second Test, the second-best West Indian Test figures of all.*

Croft began his Test career against Pakistan in 1976–7 with 33 wickets in the rubber, including 8 for 29 in his second match, the best ever analysis by a West Indian fast bowler. He was one of the Packer defectors, but immediately returned to the team when that problem was resolved and was a regular until he joined the rebel tour to South Africa in 1982–3, bringing his West Indies career to an end before he was thirty. One hundred and twenty-five wickets at 23 each in only 27 Tests shows just how dangerous he was, and he had a reputation for meanness as well. He bowled a great many short balls, and the feeling among the batsmen was that he did not seem worried whether he hit them or not. Certainly one sometimes felt that he was not too bothered about sporting ethics, and causing half a dozen batsmen to retire hurt in just 27 Tests seems an unacceptably high 'strike rate'. Perhaps if he had been English one might feel differently.

| 1976 | Trent Bridge | WI 494, 176–5d; | E 332, 156–2 | Drawn |
| | Lord's | E 250, 254; | WI 182, 241–6 | Drawn |
| | Old Trafford | WI 211, 411–5d; | E 71, 126 | WI 425 runs |
| | Headingley | WI 450, 196; | E 387, 204 | WI 55 runs |
| | Oval | WI 687–8d, 182–0d; | E 435, 203 | WI 231 runs |
| 1980 | Trent Bridge | E 263, 252; | WI 308, 209–8 | WI 2 wkts |
| | Lord's | E 269, 133–2; | WI 518 | Drawn |
| | Old Trafford | E 150, 391–7; | WI 260 | Drawn |
| | Oval | E 370, 209–9d; | WI 265 | Drawn |
| | Headingley | E 143, 227–6d; | WI 245 | Drawn |
| 1980–1 | Port-of-Spain | WI 426–9d; | E 178, 169 | WI inns 79 runs |
| | Georgetown | Cancelled | | |
| | Bridgetown | WI 256, 379–9d; | E 122, 224 | WI 298 runs |
| | St John's | E 271, 234–3; | WI 468–9d | Drawn |
| | Kingston | E 285, 302–6d; | WI 442 | Drawn |

**1976 Test Series**

**England**

| Batting | Innings | NO | HS | Runs | Average |
|---|---|---|---|---|---|
| J.H. Edrich | 4 | 1 | 76* | 145 | 48.33 |
| D.B. Close | 6 | 1 | 60 | 166 | 33.20 |
| D.S. Steele | 10 | 0 | 106 | 308 | 30.80 |
| A.W. Greig | 9 | 1 | 116 | 243 | 30.37 |
| A.P.E. Knott | 9 | 0 | 116 | 270 | 30.00 |

| Bowling | Overs | M | Runs | W | Average |
|---|---|---|---|---|---|
| R.G.D. Willis | 57.3 | 11 | 234 | 9 | 26.00 |
| J.A. Snow | 106.4 | 16 | 423 | 15 | 28.20 |
| A. Ward | 24 | 2 | 128 | 4 | 32.00 |
| D.L. Underwood | 224 | 59 | 631 | 17 | 37.11 |
| C.M. Old | 68.3 | 11 | 248 | 6 | 41.33 |

**West Indies**

| Batting | Innings | NO | HS | Runs | Average |
|---|---|---|---|---|---|
| I.V.A. Richards | 7 | 0 | 291 | 829 | 118.42 |
| C.G. Greenidge | 10 | 1 | 134 | 592 | 65.77 |
| R.C. Fredericks | 10 | 1 | 138 | 517 | 57.44 |
| L.G. Rowe | 3 | 0 | 70 | 126 | 42.00 |
| C.L. King | 5 | 1 | 63 | 167 | 41.75 |

| Bowling | Overs | M | Runs | W | Average |
|---|---|---|---|---|---|
| M.A. Holding | 159.3 | 54 | 356 | 28 | 12.71 |
| A.M.E. Roberts | 221.4 | 69 | 537 | 28 | 19.17 |
| W.W. Daniel | 108 | 28 | 317 | 13 | 24.38 |
| V.A. Holder | 158 | 48 | 367 | 15 | 24.46 |
| C.L. King | 39 | 11 | 95 | 2 | 47.50 |

Wicket-keepers:   A.P.E. Knott 6 dismissals   D.L. Murray 19 dismissals

In the first match, A.P.E. Knott became the first wicket-keeper to hold 200 Test catches and J.H. Edrich reached 5,000 Test runs. In the third match, C.G. Greenidge scored 63.5 per cent of his team's first-innings total, a percentage that has only once been exceeded in Tests, and he also became the second West Indian to score a century in each innings against England; England's total of 71 is the lowest by either side in England v. West Indies Tests. In the fourth match, J.A. Snow took his 200th Test wicket and D.L. Murray equalled the West Indian record of five catches in an innings. In the fifth match, West Indies made their highest total against England (687 for 8 declared); I.V.A. Richards totalled 829 runs for the series for a West Indian series record and took his aggregate for the calendar year to 1,710 runs, the world Test record; M.A. Holding's 8 for 92 is the best by a West Indian bowler against England, and his 14 for 149 made him the first West Indian to take more than 12 wickets in a Test; Knott became the leading Test wicket-keeper when he claimed his 220th victim.

### 1980 Test Series

**England**

| Batting | Innings | NO | HS | Runs | Average |
|---|---|---|---|---|---|
| B.C. Rose | 6 | 1 | 70 | 243 | 48.60 |
| G. Boycott | 10 | 1 | 86 | 368 | 40.88 |
| G.A. Gooch | 10 | 0 | 123 | 394 | 39.40 |
| P. Willey | 9 | 2 | 100* | 262 | 37.42 |
| R.A. Woolmer | 4 | 1 | 46 | 109 | 36.33 |

| Bowling | Overs | M | Runs | W | Average |
|---|---|---|---|---|---|
| J.E. Emburey | 39.3 | 13 | 83 | 6 | 13.83 |
| G.R. Dilley | 74 | 19 | 183 | 11 | 16.63 |
| G.A. Gooch | 25 | 7 | 59 | 3 | 19.66 |
| R.G.D. Willis | 110.1 | 27 | 407 | 14 | 29.07 |
| I.T. Botham | 131 | 41 | 385 | 13 | 29.61 |

**West Indies**

| Batting | Innings | NO | HS | Runs | Average |
|---|---|---|---|---|---|
| I.V.A. Richards | 6 | 0 | 145 | 379 | 63.16 |
| D.L. Haynes | 6 | 0 | 184 | 308 | 51.33 |
| C.H. Lloyd | 4 | 0 | 101 | 169 | 42.25 |
| M.A. Holding | 6 | 4 | 35 | 61 | 30.50 |
| A.M.E. Roberts | 4 | 1 | 24 | 78 | 26.00 |

| Bowling | Overs | M | Runs | W | Average |
|---|---|---|---|---|---|
| J. Garner | 212.4 | 73 | 371 | 26 | 14.26 |
| A.M.E. Roberts | 105.2 | 24 | 262 | 11 | 23.81 |
| M.D. Marshall | 172.3 | 42 | 436 | 15 | 29.06 |
| M.A. Holding | 230.5 | 56 | 632 | 20 | 31.60 |
| C.E.H. Croft | 104 | 25 | 306 | 9 | 34.00 |

Wicket-keepers: A.P.E. Knott 11 dismissals  D.L. Bairstow (E) 2 dismissals  D.L. Murray 14 dismissals

In the first match, West Indies' 2-wicket win is the narrowest margin of victory by either side in these Tests. In the third match, C.H. Lloyd became the third West Indian to reach 5,000 Test runs. In the fourth match, P. Willey and R.G.D. Willis made an unbeaten 117 for the tenth wicket, only the third English century partnership for the tenth wicket in their Test history. In the fifth match, I.T. Botham became the first England player to complete the double of 1,500 runs and 150 wickets.

### 1980–1 Test Series

#### England

| Batting | Innings | NO | HS | Runs | Average |
|---|---|---|---|---|---|
| G.A. Gooch | 8 | 0 | 153 | 460 | 57.50 |
| D.I. Gower | 8 | 1 | 154* | 376 | 53.71 |
| P. Willey | 8 | 3 | 102* | 244 | 48.80 |
| G. Boycott | 8 | 1 | 104* | 295 | 42.14 |
| R.O. Butcher | 5 | 0 | 32 | 71 | 14.20 |

| Bowling | Overs | M | Runs | W | Average |
|---|---|---|---|---|---|
| I.T. Botham | 145.2 | 31 | 492 | 15 | 32.80 |
| R.D. Jackman | 73.2 | 15 | 198 | 6 | 33.00 |
| G.B. Stevenson | 33 | 5 | 111 | 3 | 37.00 |
| G.R. Dilley | 129.4 | 25 | 450 | 10 | 45.00 |
| J.E. Emburey | 185 | 62 | 419 | 7 | 59.85 |

#### West Indies

| Batting | Innings | NO | HS | Runs | Average |
|---|---|---|---|---|---|
| I.V.A. Richards | 5 | 1 | 182* | 340 | 85.00 |
| C.H. Lloyd | 5 | 0 | 100 | 383 | 76.60 |
| H.A. Gomes | 5 | 1 | 90* | 199 | 49.75 |
| D.L. Haynes | 5 | 0 | 96 | 234 | 46.80 |
| C.G. Greenidge | 5 | 0 | 84 | 223 | 44.60 |

| Bowling | Overs | M | Runs | W | Average |
|---|---|---|---|---|---|
| M.A. Holding | 132.2 | 38 | 315 | 17 | 18.52 |
| C.E.H. Croft | 157.5 | 34 | 455 | 24 | 18.95 |
| J. Garner | 151.2 | 48 | 303 | 10 | 30.30 |
| A.M.E. Roberts | 104 | 28 | 251 | 8 | 31.37 |
| I.V.A. Richards | 100 | 35 | 206 | 5 | 41.20 |

Wicket-keepers: D.A. Murray (WI) 13 dismissals  P.R. Downton (E) 6 dismissals  D.L. Bairstow 5 dismissals

In the first match, A.M.E. Roberts set a Test record by scoring 24 runs off one over from I.T. Botham. The second match was cancelled when the Guyana government withdrew R.D. Jackman's visitor's permit and issued a deportation order on him. In the third match, R.O. Butcher became the first black player to appear for England. In the fourth match, M.A. Holding and C.E.H. Croft made an unbeaten 67 for the tenth wicket, the West Indies record against England. Croft's 24 wickets were a record for a home series against England.

# — 10 —

# Black Washes Best

We now reach the part of this history where English fans, if they can bear to continue, will really need to grit their teeth. The summer of 1984 was a glorious one, the West Indian team was one of their strongest and had just beaten Australia 3–0; the England team, with some of the top players banned after going to South Africa, was one of their most ordinary and had just lost series to Pakistan and New Zealand for the first time, and it was all rather one-sided. The tourists lost only one match all season, a one-day international, and England hardly looked convincing in that. Clive Lloyd still had, it appeared, dozens of ultra-fast bowlers to call on, while England's slender resources were entrusted to the charge of a fellow with blond curly hair and a pleasing batting style.

As a young man, David Gower prophesied that he would be England captain by the age of 25. He made it, too, taking over against Pakistan in 1982 for one match when Willis was injured – and, given the most tooth-less of bowling attacks, losing heavily. In Pakisan in 1983–4 he took over again when Willis had to return home sick and gained two creditable draws, after which he was officially appointed to lead England against the West Indies in 1984, at the age of 27. With the easy grace and dignity associated with the old amateur tradition there was never any doubt that the job would come to him, and so gifted was he as a batsman that one somehow assumed he would slip easily into it once he had learned the ropes. The fact that many another highly gifted player has not found captaincy easy tended to be overlooked.

He arrived on the Test arena in memorable style against Pakistan in 1978, hooking his first ball for four with nonchalant ease. Thereafter he took heed from being dropped once or twice, and soon established a permanent place in the team. As England's leading batsman of the 1980s he has borne a heavy responsibility and perhaps because of this has never completely fulfilled his potential; few batsmen can have been blessed with so much natural ability, yet he often looks vulnerable until he has settled down and even then has succumbed countless times to an infuriating nibble or waft outside the off stump. When things are not right he can be

*If David Gower's captaincy against West Indies left something to be desired, his batting has given endless pleasure to millions of people.*

almost static, but when in full flow his grace, elegance and timing have been beautiful to behold. He is famed for his 'laid-back' attitude, his apparent unconcern about his actions both at the crease and at press conferences, and such an easy-going approach led many people to believe that he had little real commitment. In this they were wrong, for he has shown many times that he can fight as well as anyone. If as a captain he was not authoritarian enough, that was just not his style; given opposition that were not vastly superior he could lead a team well enough, and chalked up two notable series wins against India and Australia. His record is singularly unhappy, though, with five victories and eighteen defeats in his thirty-two games in charge, culminating in the ignominy of the 1989 Ashes series. In anyone's book that is failure of some magnitude, but the fact for English cricket was simply that there were very few players of real Test class around at the time; after all, when Mike Gatting, one of the best of the county captains, got his chance he won only twice in twenty-two Tests.

The Test series began at Edgbaston as it was to continue – with a thumping. After half an hour the first English injury occurred, Andy Lloyd going into the record books as the possessor of the briefest of all Test careers. He had scored ten in thirty minutes before he was hit on the temple of his helmet by a ball from Marshall that lifted sharply; with his

*Edgbaston 1984 and the shortest career in Test cricket is just ending. After only half an hour Andy Lloyd was felled by a Malcolm Marshall bouncer and played no more that season.*

*Physiotherapist Bernard Thomas tells Lloyd to touch his nose, and it is soon clear that his vision is impaired.*

vision blurred it was several days before he left hospital, and he did not play again all season. Since he had been hailed as the new John Edrich and had already shown himself capable of taking on that mantle, it was a bad blow for England. Four more batsmen had departed without the board showing fifty before Botham, dropped before he had scored, chanced his luck for 64, and 33 from Downton helped the score to 191.

West Indies soon lost their openers, but then Gomes went glory-chasing; with Richards, he put on 206 for the third wicket and, with Lloyd, 124 for the fifth. By the time the eighth wicket went down the lead was already 264, so perhaps it was unkind of Baptiste and Holding to hammer 150 in 113 minutes for West Indies' ninth wicket record against England. The final total was 606, scored in only ten hours of excellent batsmanship, although it was widely felt that the England selectors had helped them along by omitting Foster and playing two spinners, Cook and Miller, on a

pitch of low bounce. England duly subsided a second time, the honours
going to Downton who was promoted to open in place of Andy Lloyd and
made a solid 56, but wickets fell steadily and 235 all out meant that the
victory margin was an innings and 180 runs. For many people the saddest
aspect was the selectors' policy of playing Randall at number three; every
fan in the country could have told them that he should have batted down
the order and that exposing him so early was almost certain to fail. There
was much wrath that he had been meaninglessly sacrificed and a Test
career that had given so much pleasure needlessly brought to a premature
end.

Lord's celebrated its centenary of Test cricket and produced a match
worthy of the occasion. England were put in, but Fowler, with a good
fighting hundred, and Broad, with 55 on debut, gave England the rare
luxury of a century opening stand. Unfortunately, the next biggest con-
tributor was Extras, and 286 all out looked very thin; until, that is, I.T.
Botham produced one of his more inspired performances. He captured
three quick wickets before Richards and Lloyd (who passed 7,000 Test
runs) steadied the ship, but then had Richards lbw, although umpire
Meyer later admitted that he may have made a mistake and had

*Viv Richards shows his
reaction at Gower's exit as
the ritual dance begins.*

considered recalling the batsman. Botham had the first six wickets before Marshall and Baptiste held him up for while, Marshall being lucky not to be on the wrong end of a legendary catch when Don Topley, a groundstaff boy who went on to play for Essex, brilliantly caught him one-handed on the square leg boundary, only to put one foot over the rope. Even so, Botham took 8 for 103, the second-best return of his Test career, as West Indies were all out for 245.

England's second innings, after three wickets had gone cheaply, centred on Lamb and Botham. The 128 they made for the fifth wicket actually saw the visitors go on the defensive, although not for long. Botham went for 81, but with less than an hour left of the fourth day Lamb accepted an offer of bad light, which most people thought was a mistake. He had been batting steadily and was well set, and since England, 328 ahead with three wickets left, were apparently in control they should have used all the time available to build up their score. Thus ran the argument. Instead, he was out first thing next morning for 110 and Gower declared at 300 for 9, leaving West Indies to make 342 in four and a half hours and twenty overs. It was a perfectly good declaration, but before long the older spectators were recalling Headingley 1948, when Yardley set Australia over 400 to win and Morris and Bradman saw them home. Now the hero was

*Another version of the ritual dance at the fall of a wicket. Here Milton Small and friends celebrate Gower's exit at Lord's in 1984.*

Ian Botham's 4,000 Test run came with this boundary off Marshall
at Lord's in 1984. In the same match he became the first bowler to
take eight wickets in an innings in a Test against West Indies in
England.

*A satisfying way to bring up your double century – Gordon Greenidge hooks Neil Foster off the end of his nose to move from 197 to 203. His unbeaten 214 at Lord's in 1984 made David Gower's declaration, which had seemed a good one, look rather whimsical.*

*Larry Gomes contributed 92 not out as he and Greenidge made an undefeated 287, a new second-wicket record by either side in these Tests.*

Gordon Greenidge, very ably assisted by Gomes. How could anyone have guessed that the movement the bowlers had found throughout the game would suddenly disappar? Yet it did, and the batsmen made the most of the conditions. Haynes fell with the score on 57, Gomes was missed immediately and Greenidge was missed when he had 110; apart from that it was batsmanship of the highest quality. When the target was reached with 11.5 overs to spare, Gomes was on 92, while Greenidge, in one of the great pieces of batting, had 214 to his name, the first West Indies double century at Lord's. It took him just five hours, included 29 fours, and took him past 4,000 Test runs (a milestone Botham had passed earlier in the game). 344 for 1 meant a nine-wicket victory in a match that England had thought they might win.

That proved to be the high point of England's summer. For a while in the third match at Headingley they were in contention, but the possibility of victory never remotely reappeared. The first casualty of the match was, for a change, a West Indian fast bowler, when Marshall fractured his left thumb trying to stop a shot from Broad; yet even this worked against England, for it simply inspired him to his best Test figures when he bowled in the second innings. Once again, the backbone of the innings came from Lamb and Botham, and just before the close on the first day Lamb became the first England batsman since Barrington in 1960 to score centuries in consecutive Test innings against West Indies. He went first thing next morning, though, and the innings closed on 270 as Holding became the fourth West Indian to take 200 Test wickets. By the end of the second day the visitors had reached 239 for 7, only Gomes and Lloyd making an impression as Allott, recalled after a two-year absence, headed for his best Test return of 6 for 61. Near the close, Holding began to lay about him and was dropped off a skyer; next morning he continued in the same vein to ensure his team a first innings lead, and ensure, too, that Bob Willis's Test career would end on an unhappy note as it was he who took most of the stick. His 59 came off only 55 balls, but when he and then Garner departed, Gomes was apparently stranded on 96 since Marshall was not expected to bat. Not only did he do so, one-handed, but he scored a four, and allowed Gomes to reach his century. West Indies reached 302.

When his hand was being plastered up Marshall was advised not to play again for ten days. Instead he opened the bowling with Garner and soon had a wicket. Fowler and Gower held him up for a while with 91 for the third wicket, but by the close of play he had two more – including a caught and bowled – and on Monday morning, cutting down his run-up, he polished off the tail to finish with 7 for 53. It was mightily impressive

*1984 was Allan Lamb's* annus mirabilis, *with three centuries against West Indies and one against Sri Lanka. Here he sends Eldine Baptiste to the rope at Headingley.*

*Bob Willis's Test career came to a sad end at Headingley in 1984, as Michael Holding hit him for five sixes. Willis got him in the end, his last Test wicket.*

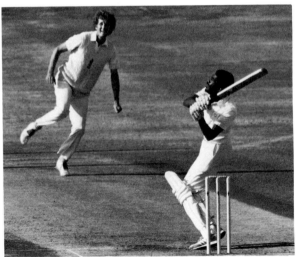

*In the same match Malcolm Marshall, having
fractured his left thumb, came in to see Larry
Gomes, on 96, to his century, and scored a
four batting one-handed – with a straighter
bat than some of the Englishmen had shown.
He then took 7 for 53, including a caught and
bowled. Useful commodity, courage.*

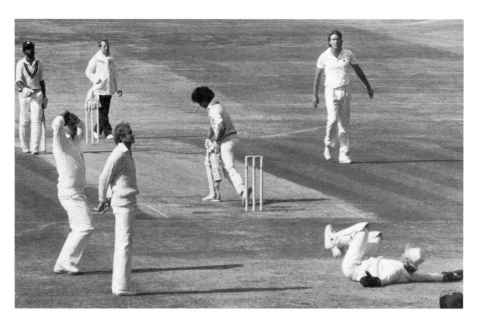

*Every picture tells a story. Paul Downton has just failed to reach
a snick by Larry Gomes off Derek Pringle, and the response of
Botham and Gower says it all. Gomes went on to an unbeaten century,
thanks to Malcolm Marshall.*

bowling by any standards, and with his left hand in plaster it was quite
remarkable. England were all out for 159, leaving West Indies the modest
target of 128. Three years before on this ground, of course, Australia had
failed to reach something similar, but now there were 106 on the board
before the openers were separated, and there were still eight wickets in
hand when the victory came. It was the first time since 1921 that England
had lost the first three Tests of a home rubber.

There cannot have been any English fans who had expected their team
to win the series, but the manner in which they were just being steam-
rollered seemly scarcely credible. The worst thing was that it appeared
there was nothing they could do to stop it; the players had hardly a shred
of belief left in themselves, and Gower was unable to instil any. And so the
procession unfolded.

Like Lord's, Old Trafford was celebrating its centenary of Test cricket,
and, as before, Gordon Greenidge marked the occasion by scoring a
double century. The first morning of the match did actually belong to
England, West Indies' lunchtime score being 77 for 4; but then Botham
bowled poorly, and Greenidge and Dujon accepted this beneficence grate-

*West Indies take the 1984 series 3–0 after three matches. One young fan*
*shows the world what he thinks of it.*

fully. Their fifth-wicket stand realized 197 before Dujon went for 101 just before the close, bringing in Winston Davis as nightwatchman, replacing Marshall for his only Test of the series. Next morning Davis laid about himself for 77, his highest first-class score, Botham again bowling poorly and being punished for it. In fact, Botham did have an excuse, in that before the match he had received a death threat. When Greenidge was finally caught behind, he had made 223 in nine and three-quarter hours, a phenomenal effort of concentration on a pitch of uneven bounce, for he gave not one chance throughout. West Indies reached exactly 500, with Pocock, recalled after a gap of 86 Tests, finishing with four wickets.

Fowler and Broad then got off to a good start with 90 for the first wicket before things began to go wrong. After Fowler went, Davis broke Terry's left arm, the uneven bounce having deceived the batsman, and then once again it was all left to Lamb. Allott supported him for a while, and at 278 for 7, with Lamb on 98, there seemed a chance that the follow-on might be saved. Then Pocock and Cowans departed in one over and the

*Like Marshall in the previous Test, Paul Terry came in at Old Trafford*
*in plaster to help a team-mate reach his century. Allan Lamb duly got there,*
*but Joel Garner produced the perfect yorker to end the innings.*

West Indians began to troop off, only for Gower to wave them back since Terry, arm in sling beneath sweater, was returning. For the second Test running we were treated to the sight of a batsman in plaster coming out to help a colleague reach his hundred, and both were successful. What was not clear in this case, though, was whether he would attempt to stay there while Lamb got the twenty-three needed to avoid the follow-on. When Lamb played five balls of an over defensively and then ran two off the last, it was clear that he was just settling for his hundred, and since Terry immediately succumbed Lamb was criticized for exposing him, rather than trying to keep the strike. He said afterwards that he had understood Terry had come out just to allow him to reach his goal, but it was an unfortunate end to a splendid innings, which made him the first English batsman since Barrington in 1967 to score three consecutive centuries in a series.

The confusion about the ending simply unsettled England even more. Gower at last reached fifty and finished unbeaten on 57, but wickets tumbled steadily and early on the final morning it was all over. 156 all out gave West Indies victory by an innings and 64 runs, but at least in this instance England were not blasted out. There was much pleasure that Roger Harper played throughout the series, and here his off-spin received its best reward with 6 for 57.

At Lord's Greenidge had to share the Man of the Match award with Botham, but here there was no question of his undisputed right to it. The irony for England was that had he decided differently he would have been playing *for* them rather than against them, for his parents had brought him from Barbados at the age of twelve to live in Reading, and he had played for England schoolboys. He joined Hampshire in 1970 and a couple of years later the selectors were enquiring after him, but he chose to await his chance with West Indies. It came in India in 1974–5 when he began with 93 and 107; this proved to be something of a false dawn and he had an unhappy time in Australia in 1975–6, but he worked on his technique and finally established himself in England in 1976 with 592 runs at 65, including a century in each innings on a poor Old Trafford pitch. Thereafter, he was a fixture in the team apart from the World Series interlude, with these two double centuries in 1984 representing the peak of his career.

For some eight years he opened the innings for Hampshire with the great Barry Richards, a daunting prospect for many a young bowler hoping to establish himself – and many an older one who already had. When he first came into the Hampshire team, Greenidge's natural inclination

*Gordon Greenidge gives a perfect demonstration of the square cut,
generating power with the right leg as the body goes to meet the ball.
A fielder with any sense would simply get out of the way.*

was to attack every ball, and it was Richards more than anyone who taught him restraint, taught him to wait for the bad ball. Greenidge was happy to admit that playing alongside the South African was 'an education and an inspiration', but he also conceded that while they both had many outstanding days individually they did not score as many runs in partnership as they might have done, since they were both attacking players and therefore risk-takers. Naturally, Greenidge tried to emulate Richards which, when things went well, was fine, but when they did not it meant that, for a while, he gained a reputation for not being over-reliable; perhaps he suffered from trying to hit the ball too hard, for there were plenty of people who felt that he would have been a better player had he not tried to 'bury the ball into the wall of some distant building' (his own words) at every opportunity. Yet it was a wonderful pairing, one of the most exciting in the game's history, and it helped Hampshire to the championship in 1973 and the John Player League in 1975 and 1978.

Naturally the passing of the years brought a more responsible approach which made him even more formidable, for he still had all the strokes and all the power but now he was less likely to get out unnecessarily. He also gained the lovely reputation of being particularly dangerous when he was limping, since an injury to his leg simply made him hit more fours to cut down on the running. When he was joined in the Test team by Desmond Haynes, one of the most dependable and successful of all opening partnerships was created, and as the senior member in his late twenties Greenidge matured at just the right time. During England's tour of 1989–90 he celebrated his hundredth Test by scoring his eighteenth century, passing 7,000 runs in the process, and at the end of the series his total stood at 7,134 at an average of 46. To have continued to be so dependable and at the same time so exciting a batsman for so long, shows him to have been one of the greats of the game.

Before the last Test at the Oval, Gower exhorted his troops to 'one last, big effort' to avoid completely ignominy, and for a while it seemed that they might. After Lloyd chose to bat on a pleasant sunny day, Botham somehow managed to get the ball to swing and took 5 for 72, including his three hundredth wicket in Tests. West Indies actually succumbed to 70 for 6 and England were cock-a-hoop. Lloyd spoilt it, of course, with an unbeaten 60 that helped his team to 190 all out, but having dismissed them for their lowest total in years England had to feel confident. By the close of the first day, though, they had lost Broad, and Pat Pocock, going in as nightwatchman, had told the England physiotherapist Bernard Thomas that he had cleaned his teeth and gargled in case Thomas had to give him

*Being a West Indian spinner in recent years hasn't been the safest of occupations, but Roger Harper played throughout the 1984 series.*

Ian Botham's 300th Test wicket, the Oval 1984. Jeff Dujon has tried to take evasive action from a ball that has climbed from just short of a length, but has gloved it. Chris Tavaré at first slip gets in on a piece of history.

*The Oval 1984. It might be raining but a 'blackwash' is not far away.*

the kiss of life. Next morning the humour in this wore decidedly thin, as Marshall in particular sent down bouncer after bouncer, unchecked by umpire Constant and apparently unconcerned at the damage he might do – such as badly bruising Fowler's arm and causing him to retire for a while. Pocock was not spared the treatment, and he and at least three colleagues fell to balls that flew to throat height. Marshall took 5 for 35 as wickets toppled at regular intervals, and the board reached only 162.

A flicker of hope came when three West Indian wickets went down for 69, but then it was Haynes' turn to come good after a disappointing series. Supported by Lloyd and then Dujon, he batted for more than seven hours for 125, helping the total to 346 and leaving England ten hours to survive or score 375. For a while Broad and Tavaré defended well, but then suddenly Holding, for the first time in over a year, decided to go back to his full-length run-up, without even having told Lloyd what he intended to do. It came like an electric shock. Broad, Gower and Lamb fell in quick succession and then it was just a case of mopping up. Botham delayed the inevitable with a fifty, but Holding finished with 5 for 43 and England were all out for 202. At least defeat by a mere 172 runs represented something of an improvement on earlier games.

There was no doubt, though, that the banner proclaiming 'Blackwash' said it all.

*

From these depths, England went to India and pulled off a remarkable triumph after losing the first Test, and then beat Australia 3–1 in 1985. After the Oval Test David Gower murmured that West Indies must be 'quaking in their boots' at the thought of England's forthcoming visit, a characteristically ironic piece of Gower humour. Faced by the weakest bowling attack ever to leave Australia, the England batsmen had made hay, none more so than the captain, and some people felt that the confidence this built up would give them a lift in the Caribbean. Then they awoke, and behold it was a dream.

When Clive Lloyd retired at the end of the 1984–5 tour of Australia, the captaincy passed to Viv Richards. To an outsider this seemed a quite natural progression, but within the West Indies it was not greeted with unmitigated delight. Even after so much success, the inter-island rivalries are never far from the surface, and other players had their advocates. Lloyd's great achievement had been to weld all the factions into a united team, and doubt was expressed that Richards could maintain the unity. Yet he got off to a good start against New Zealand, and no one in England could have been in any doubt that even without Lloyd around their heroes were in for a tough time.

Viv Richards has been rated the world's number one batsman since 1976 when he scored a record 1,710 Test runs in the year. Since then, despite having played cricket almost endlessly, he has been astonishingly consistent, averaging over fifty both in Tests and overall. When he has had quiet periods one simply got the feeling that he was having a rest, a feeling reinforced by his ability to produce a big innings apparently at will, especially on the grand occasion or when his team is struggling. Fundamentally, he is an orthodox batsman who can be totally unorthodox, the possessor of every stroke in the book and an improviser who can create any number of others.

His speed at getting into position is breath-taking, almost as breathtaking as the power with which he murders the ball. He walks to the crease with a swagger, totally confident, undoubtedly one of the few batsmen to whom the word 'unforgettable' could be applied without risk of hyperbole. With his splendid physique and proud, noble head his presence is such as to give him an instant advantage over any bowler, and he has rarely failed to put that advantage to use; spinners in particular have suffered at his hands, but when he decides that he wants to score runs it is virtually impossible to bowl to him. From the spectators' viewpoint, not only does he provide wonderful entertainment but he does it without encasing himself in a helmet, now so rare as to be a treat in itself. Such disdain for something that has become almost universal in the first-class game clearly helps in his psychological battle with the bowlers; disdain is, in fact, an important part of his armoury, combining with his might and skill to cement his authority. As he is also a useful off-spinner, occasional medium-pacer, and excellent slip fielder, the cumulative result is the most formidable cricketer of the 1970s and '80s.

Strangely, his career began with a considerable upset. He came from a cricketing family – his father was a leading fast bowler in Antigua – and his great talent was evident very early on, so that he was already popular

*'The world's greatest batsman' – Viv Richards demonstrates the on drive.*

with the fans as a youngster. At the age of seventeen he was playing for Antigua in the Leeward Islands tournament when he was given out caught behind. He gestured his dissent at this and in no time the crowd were clamouring for the umpire to reverse the decision, which he did. As a result he was suspended for two years, which of course delayed his entry into first-class cricket; but it taught him a lot.

His Test debut came in the same match as Gordon Greenidge against India in 1973–4, Greenidge totalling 200 runs and Richards 7; in the next game he made 192 not out and was under way. He made 829 runs in four matches (he missed the Lord's Test through illness) in 1976, which was statistically his best performance, and if he has never made quite so many since that must just be because of the demands, physical and psychological, of playing so much top cricket. Two of his most memorable innings came in one-day internationals, the 138 not out in the 1979 World Cup final and the 189 not out at Old Trafford in 1984 which single-handedly transformed a desperate situation into a winning one, and which will surely never be forgotten by anyone who saw it. In 1980–1, in the first Test to be played on his home ground in Antigua, there was never any doubt that he was going to mark the occasion with a century, and, as we shall see, when England returned five years later he marked that occasion in the most spectacular fashion. At Sydney in 1988 against New South Wales he became the twenty-second batsman and the first West Indian to score a century of centuries. All of this has been achieved with an inevitability which few batsmen since Bradman have been able to suggest, and in 111 Tests at the end of the 1989–90 series he was just ten runs short of 8,000 at an average of 51.

In 1974, at the age of 22, he joined Somerset, and with Joel Garner was to play a very important part in their one-day successes between 1979 and 1983. Helped in the crucial early years by Brian Close, his – and Garner's – loyalty to their adopted county became every bit as great as Clive Lloyd's to Lancashire. His colleague Vic Marks wrote that 'we willed opposition fast bowlers to bounce him so that we could witness the majesty of his hooking', and there can be very few batsmen of whom that could be said. In 1985 his batting reached its peak at Taunton against a Warwickshire team who bowled and fielded well but who could not stop him making 322, the highest first-class innings in England for thirty-six years; after a slightly uncomfortable start, the second and third hundreds came off sixty-seven and sixty-three balls respectively, and only tiredness after a drive from Leeds the evening before caused his downfall. Thus, the decision by the county at the end of the following season not to re-engage him and Garner came as an enormous surprise and caused a furore; from the emotional angle it was poor reward for years of devoted service, but rationally, since the opportunity to sign up Martin Crowe of New Zealand, who promised so much, had either to be taken or lost, it was a sensible move. It is impossible for the outsider to appreciate what this meant to a man as proud as Richards, but it was noticeable that in the Test series against Pakistan and New Zealand which followed his form was very ordinary.

Pride has always been an important part of his make-up. The usual epithet applied to his bearing is patrician, and his batting, as a matter of course, is liberally endowed with arrogance. At the wicket he is a Roman general, unquestioning of his own ability to defeat the barbarians; yet because the pride and haughtiness are justified by having repeatedly proved himself to be the best, one cannot resent them, especially since he usually leaves them on the field of combat. Off the field he is mild-mannered and dismissive of his achievements – though his verbal attack on an English journalist at the end of the 1989–90 tour was fulminating stuff – while at the same time he is intensely proud of his humble background, is very much a man of his people. He was offered enormous sums to go to South Africa but would never contemplate it; it would have meant a betrayal of everything he stood for, a soul-selling of Faustian proportions. Instead, he wanted to meet his final challenge, to take over the West Indies captaincy from Lloyd and continue their triumphal march through the record books.

England began their tour in miserable fashion, handing Windward Islands their first ever win over a touring team. They then lost Gatting, who had been in better form than anyone, in the first one-day international when his nose exploded after coming into contact with a ball from Marshall that he failed to hook. The optimists tried to suggest that Garner and Holding might be on the wane; the realists knew better. Home advantage meant that pitches could be prepared especially to suit fast bowlers, and come the first Test in Jamaica it was soon evident this is what had happened. Matters were not helped by the Sabina Park authorities providing one sightscreen that was too low to be of much use if the bowler was over six feet (1.8 metres) tall, and when England complained after the game against Jamaica the reply was that it could not be raised without obscuring the view of some two hundred people who had already bought tickets. Admittedly, as the tour went on England did little to help their own cause, but there were all kinds of things workings against them.

The first Test lasted two days and five hours on a pitch that was very hard, very fast and some way from flat. It was a happy debut for the latest model to drop off the fast-bowling conveyor belt; Patrick Patterson had played for Lancashire the previous summer without making much impression, but now on his home patch with the sun on his back he hit Test cricket with a bang. Gooch and Robinson began carefully after Gower won the toss, but then Patterson got Robinson and the collapse was under way. The best England could offer was 51 from Gooch and 49 from Lamb, and just before tea they were all out for 159. Greg Thomas came close to a wicket three times in his first over in Test cricket, but Greenidge and Haynes survived to give their usual start before Greenidge had to retire with a cut forehead after mishooking Botham. That slowed things down a bit and on the second day England made some progress through the wickets. Greenidge, Gomes and Dujon all made fifties, but Ellison bowled well for 5 for 78, and restricting the total to 307 was hailed as a mini-triumph.

On the first day the West Indian bowlers had been sparing with the bouncer, for on such a pitch there was no need for it. On the third day there was no such respite, Patterson in particular giving the impression that he knew, and cared, nothing about Law 42 and the intimidatory bowling of fast short-pitched balls. Only Willey, who seemed to play his best Test innings against West Indian thunderbolts, made a fight of it with 71; Botham hammered a quick 29, but the last wicket went down for 152, leaving West Indies needing five to win. One yearned for Richards to make the romantics smile by sending in two bowlers to polish them off, reflecting that when Percy Chapman did it with fifteen needed against Australia in 1928–9 (and lost two wickets!), West Indian Test cricket was just six months old. What a hope.

Before the second Test in Trinidad, England actually won a one-day international thanks to a superb unbeaten century from Gooch. In the Test, on a less malign pitch than in Kingston, he was out fourth ball, and three wickets were soon down for 30. Gower and Lamb both produced sixties and actually managed a century stand, but no other batsman passed eight and the total was no more than 176. Botham then bowled dismally to allow Greenidge and Haynes to make a good start, after which Richardson clocked up a steady hundred. Emburey and Edmonds, however, made them work for their runs and took wickets as well, Emburey finishing with 5 for 78. It was Marshall who took the game right away from England, holding together the tail for 62 not out and stretching the total to 399. At least England made a slightly more respectable fist of their second innings. Gooch, Gower and Lamb made forties, only for the ball to start shooting and wickets to fall. When the eighth wicket went down England were still nine behind, only for two unlikely heroes to emerge. Richards took the new ball – which did not shoot – and Ellison and Thomas played quite contentedly for two hours, putting on 72 for the last wicket, a new England record in the West Indies, taking the total to 315. This left West Indies to make 93, and early on the fifth morning they duly got there, having lost three wickets to Emburey and Edmonds, both of whom bowled well throughout. The margin was narrower than before; were England turning the corner?

At the end of the second day of the Barbados Test, it seemed that perhaps they had. After Gower won the toss and put them in, West Indies had a good first day as Haynes made a patient 84 and Richardson his second successive century; 269 for 2 at the close reflected the lack of life that Botham and Thomas had been able to extract from the pitch and the catches that had gone. Then on the second day, when the pitch should have been easier, only Richards, with 51, looked convincing and the last eight wickets fell steadily. The total was 418, and there was better still to come from England. Robinson soon went, but Gooch and Gower batted well and took the overnight score to 110 for 1; only another 119 to avoid the follow-on and clearly England's best day of the series so far. Soon after two o'clock the next afternoon they were all out for 189, the atmosphere helping the ball to move and swing around. Fifteen wickets were to go down in all that day, and although Gooch and Robinson made a sound start, once they were separated the procession continued as normal. They were 132 for 6 at the close and it was clearly time to pray for rain; but it came on the rest day by mistake, and although Emburey and Downton battled for a while, the end was not long delayed. 199 all out meant victory by an innings and 30 runs; it also meant that West Indies had emulated Australia's feat in 1920–1 and 1921 of recording eight successive Test victories over England. It seemed that only the weather could stop another blackwash.

The fourth Test in Trinidad was simply a repeat of the first. On a pitch of uneven bounce England were put in and shot out before the end of the day for 200, David Smith, Lamb and Botham the only ones to make an impression. Next day, Thomas, who had had a good tour so far, bowled poorly and paid the price; Botham, by contrast, had had an awful tour, but now he bowled well and took five wickets as a result. This did not stop West Indies taking a firm grip on the match, as Greenidge reached 5,000 Test runs and Richards 6,000, warming up for his achievement in the next match with 87. 312 all out was hardly the big total they would have wanted, but it was quite enough. Smith, in his second Test, top-scored in the second innings as well as the first, but it was all totally predictable; 150 all out left West Indies 39 to win, and less than six overs sufficed. As at Kingston, the margin was ten wickets; the only difference was that the match lasted a quarter of an hour less.

Before the last Test it seemed that Gooch would return home, annoyed at an article written about his South African connections by Lester Bird, the Deputy Prime Minister of Antigua, and tired of the hostile receptions he had been getting from press and public. Only an appeal by Gower to his loyalty persuaded him to stay, and he was to have his best game of the series. St John's, Antigua did, in fact, see something approaching a Test match, and it was only in the final hour that England lost. Yet even then they did not play particularly well. Gower won the toss and inserted West Indies, only for Haynes to hold the innings together as his partners got in and then out. On the second day, Haynes reached his century and England paid the penalty of having Botham poised one behind Dennis Lillee's 355 Test wickets. Inevitably, he bowled relentlessly on, never looked like getting anywhere, and the last four wickets put on 183 as Marshall, Harper and Holding enjoyed themselves at almost five an over. 474 set England a stiff target but the pitch was less malicious than the earlier ones and Gooch and Slack put on 127 for the first wicket. Twice Richards complained about the ball, each time causing a lengthy hold-up to upset the batsmen's concentration, and behaving with such arrogance that after the match he apologized to the umpires for it. When the openers were parted it was Gower who held the innings together with 90, and thanks to 51 Extras the follow-on target was passed with three wickets in hand, and the total made 310.

By now it was the morning of the fourth day and West Indies had a lead of 164; clearly quick runs were needed to make sure they had plenty of time to bowl England out again. Haynes and Richardson opened and put on exactly 100, then Richards, on his home ground, marched out, the first time he had batted at number three for some while. English hearts sank even further than they already were, for it would not have needed a weather forecaster to predict that Hurricane Viv was about to strike. Fifty minutes later he had 53 from 35 balls, and thirty-one minutes after that, from another 21 balls, he had 103; the fastest century in terms of balls received in the history of Test cricket, 56 balls to Jack Gregory's 67 against South Africa in 1921–2, although Gregory took only 70 minutes while Richards took 81 minutes. He hit six sixes and seven fours in his hundred, then one more six to take him to 110 before he declared, and the scribes were simply stuck for superlatives to convey the majesty of it. The domination of the bowlers was total, put the ball wherever they might. Most striking of all was the sheer inevitability of it: the game was being played in front of his beloved Antiguans, quick runs were needed, King Viv decided he was going to get them, and that was that.

The declaration at 246 for 2 left England 410 runs behind, with five hours fifty minutes plus the last twenty overs to survive. Two wickets fell on the fourth evening, but Ellison stayed with Gooch for some time next morning, as did Gower. Wickets fell during the afternoon and, with the final twenty overs approaching, there were three wickets left and it was up to Gower and Downton. The captain had defended solidly for hours, but now Harper got one to bounce and he was caught behind. That was that, and when the last wicket fell – to a poor piece of umpiring – there were 14.5 overs left, England had 170 and the winning margin was 240 runs.

So it was another blackwash, another disaster, for England. They went without a hope and they came back, it seemed, without a friend, perilously close to reaching mother-in-law status as the comedians' favourite butt. There were some valid defences, particularly the poor state of most of the pitches and the injuries to Gatting (having returned from getting his nose repaired he promptly had a thumb broken and played in only the final Test), but some of the criticisms were very valid, too. Principal among these was their attitude to practice, which was almost entirely voluntary. It seemed to most onlookers that the first step to take to correct the disparity between the teams was to practise as hard as possible, especially as the West Indians were doing just that themselves; Gower and Tony Brown, the manager, however, enforced no such ruling. Admittedly, the practice facilities were often poor, but the preference for relaxation as an antidote to the cannon-balls suggested that deep down the fighting spirit was lacking. With an authoritarian captain to instil some pep into them, a draw or two may have been salvaged and it would have been just another defeat rather than an abject cave-in, but Gower was not able to pick them up. For all that, the way in which he was publicly rebuked by Peter May, the Chairman of Selectors, after returning home, and appointed only for the first Test against India, annoyed many people by its insensitivity and seemed to be about as productive as the shooting of Admiral Byng on his quarterdeck. It was a sad time for English cricket; sadder still was the fact that, apart from one series, things would simply continue to get ever worse.

For West Indies, two bowlers, Garner and Marshall, shared the honours at the top of the averages with 27 wickets each, Garner's being slightly the less expensive at just 16 apiece. Joel Garner was, in fact, almost at the end

*For such a tall man Joel Garner had a beautiful follow-through with a great deal of athletic grace.*

of his Test career, with only a couple more games to come, a career that had begun back in 1976–7 against Pakistan when he made his debut in the same game as Colin Croft. He was to play 58 Tests in all, taking 259 wickets at just under 21, a lower average than any of the top West Indian bowlers except Marshall. A clue to his role may be found in the fact that only seven times did he take five wickets in an innings and never once ten in a match. For most of the time the 'Big Bird' preferred to sacrifice the flat-out pace of his team-mates for accuracy and control, taking wickets by making the ball swing and cut, and so in Tests was for some years used as first or second change bowler. Only with the retirement of Roberts did he get promotion to the new ball, whereupon he stepped up his speed and took 31 wickets against Australia in 1983–4, although he then reduced it again. His accuracy and stinginess with runs made him almost without equal as a one-day bowler, for he could both contain and attack at the same time since the bounce he got from his great height and the control he had over the ball gave him the extra penetration that brought wickets. Two of his greatest performances came in 1979, with 5 for 38 in the World Cup final and 6 for 29 in the Gillette final for Somerset, although both times Richards pipped him for the match award.

In many ways Garner was the model professional, totally dedicated and loyal to his teams, an intelligent man who gave much thought to his game. If it is stretching the imagination to describe any West Indian fast bowler as a gentle giant he is nevertheless mild-mannered and easy-going, and it is significant that while the likes of Croft and Marshall were doing unpleasant things to batsmen's heads, the damage that Garner inflicted was mostly confined to arms and hands; obviously any broken bone is bad and obviously he sent down his share of bouncers, but there was never the suggestion that he was using his physical advantages maliciously; six feet eight inches (2 metres) tall and weighing seventeen stones (108 kilograms), the prospect of the carnage he might have caused had he been of an aggressive nature hardly bears thinking about. As it is, he has gone down as a highly skilled bowler who, because he lacked the flamboyance of some of his colleagues, attracted less attention than many of them; but who consistently, almost stealthily, got on with the job of collecting three or four wickets in innings after innings after innings.

*

By 1988 West Indies were going through what England had been going through for as long as anyone could remember: a period of transition. Holding, Garner and Gomes had retired and youngsters such as Ambrose, Hooper, Arthurton and Bishop were on their first tour of England. At the end of 1987 they had failed to reach the semi-finals of the World Cup and then played two drawn series against India and Pakistan, in the latter case coming close to defeat before squeezing a two-wicket victory to square the rubber. England's fortunes under Mike Gatting had been varied, losing relentlessly at home, carrying all before them in a triumphal tour of Australia, narrowly losing a World Cup final they should have won and then having their captain, under great provocation, address naughty words to a Pakistani umpire. Gatting's altercation with Shakoor Rana was to have a considerable effect on the West Indies Test rubber.

When England convincingly won all three one-day games, the country was seized with a spasm of excited optimism. Had the mighty champions really reached the end of the road? Was the underdog about to have his day? When, in the first Test at Trent Bridge, Gooch and Broad put on 125 for the first wicket the smiles were widening all the time; when the last wicket fell with just 245 on the board we knew where we really were. When a sound start was then followed by a sparkling 80 from Richards, a classical 84 from Hooper and a thumping 72 from Marshall, with even Ambrose making 43, we knew exactly what was what, and when Richards declared on the fourth evening at 448 for 9, leaving England with a day plus 31 overs to survive, there were probably not many people who thought they would make it. But the last day belonged to Gooch and Gower, with Gatting also fighting well; Gooch finished with 146 and Gower 88 not out, greatly helped by Marshall having to go off injured. It was a day to reassure English hearts, for not only was the sequence of defeats brought to an end but the fight was sturdily fought and morale given a welcome boost. There had not been a crisis for about six months, though, so it was clearly time for one.

The tabloid newspapers decided it was their duty to reveal that Gatting had invited a barmaid to his hotel room during the Test match, and that he and other players had taken part in 'sex romps' with girls from the hotel; though how the newshounds, scrabbling around in the bushes outside, could see what was happening in the rooms was not really clear. Perhaps if it had not been for the Shakoor Rana affair the TCCB might have handled this quietly and sensibly by issuing a non-committal statement and letting the fuss die down. Instead, they got themselves into a thoroughly embarrassing mess, saying they accepted Gatting's statement that nothing improper had taken place but sacking him all the same. Since the logic of this eluded most people, it seemed reasonable to conclude that he was belatedly paying the price for arguing with an umpire. England captains must not do things like that, but they had not been able to sack him at the time because of the provocation he had been under; now that he had stepped out of line again he gave them a heaven-sent opportunity to administer the axe. The rights and wrongs of it were debated for some time and the feeling seemed to be that the TCCB had come out of it in a worse light than Gatting; as the Melbourne newspaper *The Age* put it, 'Gatting, caught rumour, bowled hypocrisy, 0'. It meant that the Test career of a man aged just 31, who still had a great deal to offer his country, was almost over; true, it would be terminated by his own decision to go to South Africa, but this came about only because of his disillusion with cricket's establishment.

So John Emburey was handed the captaincy that could well have been his years earlier if he had not gone to South Africa in 1982, thereby losing the Middlesex captaincy to Gatting after Mike Brearley retired. He had been in and out of the England team for ten years and had played 55 Tests, probably the best off-spinner in the world for much of this time. In the last year or two his wicket-taking ability seemed to have deserted him, and his Test average crept up noticeably, a year later finishing after 60 Tests with 138 wickets at 37. He became especially good as a one-day containing bowler, playing a big part in his county's successes, and contributing many

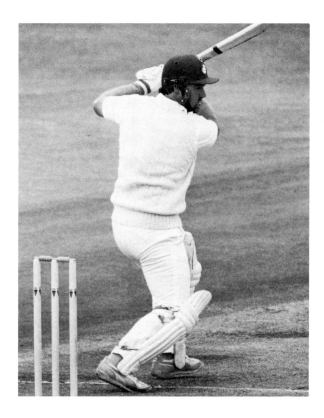

*Mike Gatting, first of a long line of England captains in 1988.*

useful, if very idiosyncratic, lower middle order runs; while his Test bowling average was declining, his batting figure was improving all the time, and reached a handy 21. A very thoughtful cricketer, with a much greater knowledge of the game's history than most players, one had the impression that he could have made a fine Test captain had the chance come earlier.

With Gatting dropping out of the Lord's Test at his own request, Emburey could hardly have made a better start. Richards won the toss and took a long time to decide to bat; when he did so Dilley bowled superbly, and five wickets went down for just 54. Could this be true? No, of course not. Logie, on 10, was dropped at slip and went on to put on 130 for the sixth wicket with Dujon, a crucial stand in view of the end result. Still, 209 all out seemed a fair performance by England, or it would have done had more of their batsmen scored some runs. Only Gooch and Gower passed forty, neither by any margin, and, with Marshall taking 6 for 32, the last wicket fell at 165. Here we go again, said everyone, and they were right; on the first two days there had been plenty of cloud to help the bowlers, but on the Saturday the sun shone and West Indies made the most of it. Greenidge, hit on the knee, began to limp, so making a century inevitable – and passing 6,000 Test runs in the process – while Richards hammered 72 from eighty balls. When Hooper went they were 240 for 5 and perhaps just catchable if the rest of the wickets tumbled. Logie and Dujon, once again, had other ideas, and exceeded their first innings partnership by one run. It was the first time two West Indian batsmen had made a century stand for the sixth wicket in each innings of a Test and it took the game right away from England; when the last wicket fell, Logie was left un-beaten on 95, the score was 397, and England had to survive for the best part of two days.

Thanks to an over rate of 11.2 and the time lost to the weather being made up at the end, that fourth day became the longest in Test history, not finishing until 7.40. By then England were 214 for 7, only Allan Lamb, desperately needing a big score to stay in the team, having given the scorers much exercise. Lamb was on 99 and it took him an age next morning to reach the hundred, his first since 1984. The tail showed more application than the top of the order, and when Lamb was run out for 113 Jarvis and Dilley batted well to put on 53 for the last wicket. Had England held a few more catches, that could have won them the match; as it was, an all-out total of 307 meant victory for West Indies by 134 runs. At least the accountants were happy, as for the first time in England match receipts passed the £1 million mark. Just for the record, 77,923 people paid £1,031,262.50; twenty-five years earlier 110,287 people had paid £56,300.

Marshall took 10 for 92 in that match but arrived at Old Trafford for the third Test reportedly with a rib injury. In a game that went to the fifth day only because many hours were lost to the weather – the actual playing time was two and two-thirds days – one was left wondering what he might have done had he been fully fit. On the first morning, England crashed to 55 for 4 and there was never any doubt about the result; by the close, it had become 135 all out, and in three overs West Indies batted, two catches were dropped. Next day, John Childs, nearly 37 and England's oldest Test debutant for over forty years, took a wicket in his third over, but only three were down when the England total was passed. For the third consecutive innings Dujon featured in a substantial sixth-wicket stand, this time putting on 94 with Harper, and, given the va-garies of the weather, Richards' problem was when to declare. He did so when play was about to resume after a stoppage early in the last session of the fourth day, with the score 384 for 7, and he could hardly have timed it more precisely; 60 for 3 overnight, and, as next morning it looked as though it might rain at any time, Marshall decided to polish the rest off quickly. In just over an hour he took five wickets, Ambrose chipped in with the other two, and England were all out for 93. One was reminded of some hapless Victorian consumptive, fading away and unable to do anything about it. Marshall's figures were 7 for 22 off 15.4 overs, giving him a strike rate of a wicket every 26 balls throughout the series. So West Indies won by an innings and 156 runs; yet had England managed to hold on for just another three or four minutes they would have got a draw, for the heavens opened and further play would have been impossible. Obviously, they deserved to be beaten out of sight, but since the weather had looked almost certain to save them if someone could have stayed there, the collapse became even more abject.

Before the next match, the selectors debated long and hard over the England captaincy, the problem being that Emburey's form had declined and his place in the team could hardly be justified; their solution was to drop him and appoint Chris Cowdrey in his place, whose enthusiastic style of leadership had taken an ordinary Kent side to the top of the table. He had played five Tests on the 1984-5 tour of India without any marked success, leaving the impression that he was not quite up to Test standard. For some people the choice was an imaginative one, for others it was yet another piece of selectoral nonsense, made worse by the fact that he was Peter May's godson. In the event, the most important repercussion of the appointment was to deprive Kent of the championship, for it proved such a traumatic time for Cowdrey that his team lost their way for a few weeks, and missed the title by just one agonizing point. Curiously, his father had also been one of three captains in a series against West Indies; he, though, had not suffered the indignity of being refused admission to the car park at the ground because the attendant did not recognize him.

At Headingley, David Gower, thirty-three years old, became the youngest player to reach one hundred Test matches – or, as Don Mosey put it on the radio, he reached his hundredth Test in fewer games than anyone else. The feat was marked by a drain bursting under the pitch soon after play began and flooding one of the run-ups; inevitably, the umpire concerned was 'Dickie' Bird, famed for his wariness about the weather, and now having to contend with water coming from below as well as above. England were soon losing wickets when play began, four going down for 80; but then Lamb and Robin Smith, on debut, showed what could be done, and on the Friday morning posted a century partnership and looked good for plenty more. Then tragedy: after a quick run Lamb's right calf muscle seized up and he had to leave the field – and from 183 for 4 the score suddenly became 185 for 8, then 201 all out. One's heart bled for Cowdrey, for he looked desperately nervous and soon succumbed without scoring. The bowlers, though, did well in favourable conditions and, if they had been better supported at slip, could have made a match of it. As it was, with most of the Saturday lost to rain the total reached 275 thanks to Harper holding the tail together.

Gooch and Curtis made a solid start and the deficit was passed for the loss of just one wicket. Then the statutory collapse. Gower needed just two runs to reach 7,000 in his hundredth Test and got them, only to fall immediately to a quite unnecessary flick down the leg side. Only Lamb, coming in at number eight and hitting fours off one leg, averted total disgrace, 138 all out leaving just 65 needed for victory. As so often, the openers, this time Haynes and Dujon, had no problems.

The changes that were made for the Oval game took the number of England players used in the series to twenty-three and, as Cowdrey had to withdraw with a bruised foot, Graham Gooch was appointed the fourth captain of the series. For a couple of days or so England were actually in the match. Their first innings made only 205, with 57 from Smith and 43 from debutant Bailey (whose reward, after failing in the second innings, was to be dropped against Sri Lanka, one of the most astonishing pieces of selectoral crassness for years); but on the second morning, in real sunshine for about the first time in the rubber, Foster bowled splendidly to decapitate the order. As at Lord's, it was Logie and Dujon who got the runs, but with Foster taking 5 for 64 they were all out for 183, the first time England had taken a first-innings lead since the Lord's game of 1984. When Gooch and Curtis opened with 50 one began to wonder – would we see an upset as we had in 1966? Then Curtis fell, and in quick succession so did Bailey and Smith. Foster did well as nightwatchman but otherwise only Gooch, in one of his slowest innings, stood firm; he batted over seven hours with the ball moving around awkwardly and had 84 to his name when he was last out, having seen the total to 202. It set West Indies a target of 225, which everyone knew was about three hundred too low, and inevitably Greenidge and Haynes began with a century partnership. Gooch damaged a finger as soon as the innings began and had to go to hospital, Pringle taking command; but he could work no miracles and victory was gained for the loss of just two wickets. For most English people it was just a case of sighing with relief that it was all over.

When Marshall took Curtis's wicket in the second innings he had 35 for the series (the average finishing at 12.65 each), beating Fred Trueman's

*The destroyer – Malcolm Marshall took 35 wickets in the 1988 series.*

England-West Indies record of 34 set in 1963 (admittedly set against a much stronger team) and the West Indian record of 33 for most wickets in any Test rubber. No fewer than 19 of those 35 were taken without assistance from his team-mates, and on average he took a wicket every 35 balls. His overall strike rate, in fact, is lower than any other major bowler, confirming his position as number one in the world rankings. Unlike some of his colleagues, he does not have the build or the strength of an American footballer, being under six feet (1.8 metres) tall and weighing twelve stones (76 kilograms). Instead, he has relied on great fitness and stamina to enable him to keep sprinting in at full pace, and speed of arm and perfect balance to capitalize on the momentum; combined with an unrelenting desire to keep on taking more and more wickets, it has all proved irresistible. Like Harold Larwood long before him, he used his relative shortness (in fast bowling terms) to make the ball skid through at great pace, always difficult for a batsman to deal with. Over the years, a good many bouncers have been sent down and several batsmen have been injured, especially around the head; this is because, unlike most of his colleagues, his bouncers usually go through at head height rather than above it and so are particularly awkward. Thus, it was rather ironic that in this, his best series, he bowled hardly any; instead, he took his wickets by adapting his bowling to the slow conditions of a rainy summer, reducing his pace a fraction and making the ball move around more.

His Test debut had come against India in 1978–9 aged only twenty, but, with so many other top bowlers in competition, it was a few years before his place was secure. Being signed by Hampshire as replacement for Andy Roberts just a few months after his Test debut gave him the chance to impress Clive Lloyd in county matches and in 1982 he really came good with 134 wickets, the best season's haul since the reduction in championship matches in 1969. This cemented his place in the Test team, although it would be another year or so before he was given the new ball, and then it was just a question of piling up the scalps as the main strike bowler. By the end of the 1989–90 series against England, he had 329 wickets at under 21, by some way his country's leading bowler. He also had claims to be considered a genuine all-rounder, having played many attacking innings in the lower middle order. Of the great West Indian bowlers from Roberts on, he is the most successful, perhaps because, with the exception of Croft, he has been the most difficult to play. Yet off the pitch he has a reputation as a dressing-room joker, an easy-going character who likes his soul and reggae music and has a smile never far from the surface. Just give him a cricket ball and watch the transformation.

One of West Indies' other heroes of the summer, and a stalwart for much of the decade, was wicket-keeper Jeffrey Dujon, with over 300 runs and twenty dismissals in the rubber. If he is not the greatest gloveman the game has known, he is a very successful wicket-keeper-batsman; in his first two Tests in Australia in 1981–2 he appeared solely as a batsman before taking over from David Murray, and by the end of the 1989–90 series he had played in 68 Tests, made 223 dismissals (a miserly five stumpings tells a sad tale) and scored almost 3,000 runs at an average of 35 with five centuries. If some have found his wicket-keeping style too flashy, others see it as artistic; he is a naturally graceful man who would be hard put to look clumsy. Whatever one's opinion, he has missed remarkably little considering he has had to cope with such an endless barrage of fast bowling. His batting has been a pleasure to watch, elegant, artistic and poised, strong on both sides of the wicket, equally happy using his feet to the spinners or hooking the fast men. In 1983 he took over the captaincy of Jamaica when Rowe went to South Africa but found it a difficult business, perhaps because he is too quiet and introspective for cricket leadership.

\*

By and large, the 1980s were a very unhappy time for the England Test team, with only the occasional series victory to relieve the encircling gloom. This culminated in the misery of the 1989 Ashes rubber, after which the tour of the Caribbean early in 1990 seemed to be about to take its place alongside St Bartholomew's Day, Glencoe and other great massacres of history. There was much discussion as to who should captain the ship, and when Graham Gooch was appointed anyone of a cynical disposition found it hard to escape the feeling that it was in the hope that, with his South African connections, at least one government would refuse to let him in, thus avoiding another 5–0 blackwash. By not only relieving David Gower of the captaincy, which was inevitable, but omitting him altogether the selectors provoked an uproar; they came up with a party that had only two specialist openers, an inexperienced middle order, and some fast bowlers who were virtually untried, injury-prone and had a reputation for speed but not accuracy. The official pronouncement was that they intended to fight fire with fire. It seemed crazy; suicidal, even. But in the weeks before they left they worked extremely hard at their fitness,

*Jeff Dujon in action against Worcestershire early in 1984, warming up for a century in the Old Trafford Test.*

*The creator of the 'miracle' at Sabina Park, 1989–90, Graham Gooch has four centuries to his name against West Indies.*

were coached by Geoff Boycott to improve their batting technique, and insisted to the press that people back home in England were going to be pleasantly surprised. This series, incidentally, was to introduce English fans to Bishop Ambrose, the most quaintly named fast bowler since Lillian Thomson.

Gooch was the leading run-scorer in first-class cricket for the 1980s, with over 21,000 at 49, and in view of this his Test record – 4,724 runs at just under 37 from 73 Tests before the tour began – is something of a disappointment, and illustrates clearly the difference it makes to a player to belong to a successful side. Tall and powerful, he is naturally an attacking batsman who loves to play his shots, and his Test average has no doubt suffered from having often had to play defensively to shore up the innings. For Essex there have been few such problems, and his batting has been, after Keith Fletcher's captaincy, probably the chief reason for their successes. In 1986 he took over the captaincy from Fletcher and led them to their third championship in four years, but early in 1987 he suffered a bad loss of form and the team slipped right down the table. Deciding that captaincy was affecting his batting, he stood down in favour of Fletcher for a season, resuming again in 1989 when the county did well but his own form was fairly ordinary. His first taste of Test captaincy came at the Oval in 1988; he was unable to stem the West Indian flood, but produced a battling second innings to make a game of it. He was rewarded with a victory over Sri Lanka, and then chosen to lead the team to India, only for the tour to be cancelled because of the South African connections of himself and several members of the party. When the Australians arrived in 1989, he seemed scarcely to be considered for the leadership, and appeared to have few advocates beyond the purlieus of Chelmsford and Colchester. Yet in February 1990 he pulled off one of cricket's all-time miracles.

Early in the tour one of the fast bowlers, Ricardo Ellcock, had a recurrence of a back injury and went home. After indifferent form in the early games, the first Test at Sabina Park, where four years earlier they had been annihilated in three days, was upon them. West Indies had lost only one home Test in the previous decade, and had not lost in Kingston since Australia beat them in 1954–5.

The pitch had recently been relaid and proved itself slow but uneven. When Richards won the toss he decided, after some thought, to bat, and Greenidge and Haynes were soon strolling along. They had reached 62 and looked good for 200 when Greenidge played the ball to long leg and, seeing Devon Malcolm fumble his fielding, came back for a second. Malcolm's throw was superb, thundering into Russell's gloves at the top of the stumps, and Greenidge was on his way. And then, against tight bowling and good catching, wickets just slipped away. When Richards was fifth out only 124 were on the board, and immediately after tea the innings collapsed totally. In six overs Fraser took five wickets for six runs for figures of 5 for 28 off twenty overs, and West Indies were all out for 164. People listening in England must have thought there was something wrong with their radios.

By the close, England were 80 for 2, and next day came the only big partnership of the match. Lamb, dropped by Dujon on 30, played splendidly thereafter, putting on 172 for the fourth wicket with Robin Smith, reaching his tenth Test century and fifth against West Indies, and finally falling for 132. The score was 288 when Smith departed for 57, and if the last wickets did not pile on the pressure they did enough to give England a lead of exactly 200. It was the third day that clinched it. Malcolm disposed

'Our West Indian bowlers are better than your West Indian bowlers.' Gladstone Small, Barbados-born, had a successful tour in 1989–90.

of Haynes with a very fast, dipping full toss, and then after Greenidge and Richardson seemed to be settling down, wickets began to go. Four were down for 112 before Best and Richards took the score to 192. Then Malcolm bowled Richards, and after Best fell to Small the tail soon went. 240 all out left England just 41 to get after the rest day. Since Malcolm, a local boy, and Small, Barbados-born, each took four wickets, the joke in England was that 'our West Indian bowlers are better than your West Indian bowlers'.

During the rest day it rained. That night it came down in buckets. The fourth day became one of intense frustration for England as the ground staff, with little of the equipment of their English counterparts, did not fall over themselves to get play started. By next morning, though, the sun was back and England could be denied no longer. It took them all of the pre-lunch session to get the runs as Walsh and Bishop made life difficult, and Gooch fell just before the end; but with three balls left before lunch

Larkins drove the winning run and one of the most remarkable Test victories of all had been achieved. West Indians of a literary turn of mind might have thought of W.B. Yeats: 'Things fall apart; the centre cannot hold; Mere anarchy is loosed upon the world.'

Slowly people began to realise it was not a miracle after all, but the reward for an enormous amount of hard work, planning and discipline which ensured they were the fittest and best-prepared England team ever; a very professional approach which saw them practising endlessly; high-class line and length bowling, backed up by excellent fielding, which had the West Indian batsmen constantly under pressure; sound batsmanship to build on the bowlers' successes; and a crackling team spirit fostered by Gooch which one could not remember seeing in an England team in years. As the series went on, it became clear that the players would happily follow Gooch through fire, flood, armies of tarantulas or anything else he might choose, if at the end of it there was the chance of winning a Test match. For a man who always looks so morose when batting – 'I know I look a miserable sod out there, but I can't help it,' he once said – and whose captaincy had previously seemed rather ordinary, it was a revelation.

No one could have doubted that West Indies would fight back. Yet England had played so well that, equally, there was no reason to think it would prove to be a flash in the pan. The series was alight – only for it to be thoroughly dampened in Guyana when relentless rain washed out the second Test completely, for only the fifth time in Test history. Would this mean that England had lost their momentum?

Not at all. In Trinidad, West Indies were without Richards and were led for the first time by Desmond Haynes. Gooch won an important toss, put West Indies in, and before long five wickets were down for 29. Logie, however, was dropped on 17 and, with Hooper, set about a rescue. But then more wickets fell, and the eighth was down for 103; only for Logie and Bishop to put on 74 for the ninth wicket, and when Logie was last man out just two short of a well-deserved hundred, the score was 199. In reply, England, against a very slow over rate, scored just 146 in a slightly shortened day, with Gooch and Larkins putting on a century opening stand. When they resumed on the third afternoon after time lost for rain, they lost quick wickets, and at 214 for 6 seemed to have wasted the advantage. Capel and Russell dug in, though, and a total of 288 gave them a handy lead. The next day belonged to Devon Malcolm, a man who came into the Test team a few months earlier against Australia with a reputation for being able to bowl extremely quickly but rarely accurately, who, with less than perfect eyesight, was a total rabbit with the bat, and who could be a joke as a fielder. After Greenidge and Haynes had put on 96 for the first wicket, Fraser had Greenidge lbw; immediately after the interval Haynes hit Malcolm's second ball for four, only for the next ball to leap up at him and give Lamb an easy catch. Two balls later, Best fell lbw to a shooter, and the next ball clipped Dujon's off-stump. Three wickets in four balls seemed a pretty good response to the unkind things written about Malcolm in the press.

Richardson and Logie steadied the ship for a while till Malcolm had Logie caught. At 200 for 6, Malcolm got Moseley and Ambrose ran out Hooper, only to make amends by putting on 34 for the ninth wicket with Bishop which would prove vital. First thing next morning, Malcolm had Walsh lbw, giving him 6 for 77 and match figures of 10 for 137 and leaving England all day to make 151. Just before lunch they were 73 for 1 when it began to rain – hard. Worse, they had lost Gooch after a ball from Moseley had reared up and struck him on the left hand, breaking a bone, although until the match was over even his team thought it was only bruised. On that moment England's whole tour turned.

Play resumed just after four o'clock, the pitch having been sweating under the covers in the meantime, and the light decidedly dingy. Stewart, who had been playing well, hammered his first ball down the throat of third man, and with West Indies taking time-wasting tactics to the extreme – 16.5 overs in around two hours – England did not really have a hope. Smith and Bailey fell quickly, and when Lamb went with the score on 106 England's last realistic chance went with him. It all ended in something like farce, with Capel and Russell unsure whether to press on or come off, but there were still 31 to get and the light was wretched when Gooch called them in. Since there was no sparing of the short-pitched stuff, and no intervention from the umpires, to continue would probably only have resulted in an injury anyway. It could be argued that had England scored faster on the second day they would have won comfortably, but having controlled the game from the beginning they were desperately unlucky to lose out to the weather; and for the fans listening at home it was especially frustrating that it was a beautiful evening in England. There was also bad feeling that Haynes had resorted to 'sledging' Stewart to upset his concentration, and there would be more bad feeling before long.

Desmond Haynes' first taste of Test captaincy was not a very happy experience, going for a duck in the first innings, dropping a catch and demeaning himself with the sledging as the match slipped away. It did little for the image of a man who has been part of the backbone of the team for so long, and was playing in his eighty-seventh Test. The first came in 1977–8 against Australia and he began with fifties in his first three innings, only to join the Packer brigade and miss out for a couple of years. Since things returned to normal, he and Gordon Greenidge have formed the most prolific opening partnership Test cricket has known; before the series they had opened the innings over 120 times, about twice as many as any other Test first-wicket partnership, although they had produced only thirteen century partnerships. Since they are both high-class batsmen this comes as quite a surprise, but looking through the records one sees that one of them has failed fairly often; their strength is that when that has happened the other has usually gone on to a big score, thereby relieving the pressure on the middle order. Haynes has tended to be the less adventurous of the two and does not quite have his partner's determination to hammer the ball into a distant wall, but before the series began he had 5,340 runs at 41, with twelve centuries, to his name all the same. England have usually been favoured opponents, and before the series ended he would have two more hundreds against them.

Both sides had injury problems during the series, West Indies missing Logie and Ambrose from the first Test, Richards and Marshall from the second, Best, Marshall and Moseley from the fourth. England lost their most important batsman and bowler from the last two Tests, for apart from Gooch's broken hand Fraser pulled a rib muscle, and his accuracy was very sorely missed. Allan Lamb took over the captaincy and did his best, but it soon became clear that without Gooch they were nothing like the same team. Lamb had taken over the Northamptonshire leadership the previous season and had shown himself enthusiastic if inexperienced, but had then missed a good deal of the season through injury. A fine attacking batsman, he had been in the England team for much of the time since making his debut in 1982, but after his four centuries in the summer of 1984 he had disappointed too often and his average scarcely reflected his ability – in 57 Tests he had made just over 3,000 runs at 34 before the tour began. Always the man of action type rather than the deep thinker, he is a captain who leads by example; if he showed himself rather insensitive to the needs of his bowlers, he showed his batsmen just what to do.

David Smith was flown in from England as cover for Gooch, only to have his thumb badly bruised in the one-day international in Barbados and so miss the Bridgetown Test. Lamb won the toss and chose to field, but although Haynes was soon dismissed there was altogether more resistance from the West Indian batsmen than before. Lacking Fraser, the English attack found itself being hit around, and in the afternoon Richards launched into Malcolm, taking 18 off one over. Yet the bowler could have had him three times, two sixes just clearing the fielder and a top edge over the wicket-keeper falling harmlessly. Lamb immediately took Malcolm off, which one felt Gooch would not have done, and West Indies built up their innings. Richards fell on 70 but Best, on his home ground, soldiered on and was rewarded with his first Test century, going on to 164. A total of 446 gave England plenty to do, and as before it was Lamb and Smith who did the bulk of the work. 193 for the fourth wicket, with Lamb equalling Colin Cowdrey's record of six Test centuries against West Indies, ensured a reasonable score, and 358 all out left them with a fair chance of saving the match.

On the fourth day, England hardly surprisingly, bowled extremely slowly in an effort to delay the declaration. It was time for Haynes to enjoy himself, though and, aided by some dropped catches, he reached a century as West Indies headed for 267 for 8 declared. Malcolm, incidentally, after being the man of the match in Trinidad, took 0 for 188 here, partly at least because he persisted in bowling short whereas before he had pitched the ball up. The feeling was that Richards should have declared before he did as the last hour's batting produced few runs, but when England set about playing out time, Larkins, having gone first ball in the first innings, lasted only one more this time. This brought in Bailey, who had recorded his own pair in Trinidad. He had reached six when he played at a ball down the leg side which hit him on the thigh, with the bat some inches away, and was taken by Dujon. Umpire Barker made no response to the appeal, whereupon Richards – who at slip was in precisely the wrong place to see what had happened – danced down the pitch waving his right hand frantically, giving every appearance that he was about to remonstrate forcefully with the umpire; whereupon Mr Barker raised his finger and Bailey was on his way.

The television replay showed clearly that Bailey had not touched the ball, and from the English point of view it was difficult to escape the feeling that Mr Barker – whose umpiring, and that of his colleagues, had been first-class, with, if anything, England getting the benefit of the doubt in several close decisions – had been pressurized into giving him out. When Mr Barker heard that Christopher Martin-Jenkins had said in his radio commentary that 'a very good umpire cracked under pressure' he denied it and issued a writ against Martin-Jenkins for defamation. As he suggested that Richards had been less than sporting, Martin-Jenkins found himself banned from the local airwaves and Public Enemy Number One in Barbados; since he is renowned as a courteous, generous-spirited chap, it brought home to English fans just how fervently Richards is regarded in the Caribbean, although any English supporter who watched the incident on television would have been hard pushed to disagree with Martin-Jenkins's assessment of it. Richards insisted he was not pressurizing the umpire but doing a celebratory dance, which seemed odd since as the umpire had not raised a finger at the time he had nothing to celebrate.

In the excitement after Bailey's departure, nightwatchman Small also fell, leaving England 15 for 3 overnight, Stewart and Russell at the crease. The hero next day was Russell, defending for over five hours without giving a chance; not bad for a man whose entry into the Test team was delayed because he supposedly could not bat. Stewart stayed with him for about an hour and a half and Lamb hung around for a while, but Smith was his main ally and, as the day ebbed away, it seemed as though only the new ball stood between England and a draw. Sure enough, when Ambrose took it he did for Russell with a shooter and then disposed of the rest. There was over an hour left when Malcolm came in, and had some of the others defended as well as he did the game might have been saved. He survived about half that time before Ambrose got him, finishing with 8 for 45; all out 191 meant a win by 164 runs.

The match finished on a Tuesday. On the Thursday morning another began, everyone having decamped to Antigua. It was an astonishing piece of planning, especially as the Friday, being Good Friday, was the rest day. In theory the teams started equal, with everything to play for – but the tide was now running West Indies' way. Sure enough, after Lamb had won the toss the batsmen got in only to get out, and the innings ended on the second day for 160. Greenidge, in his hundredth Test, and Haynes then produced an opening stand of 298, beating their own West Indian record by two runs.

On that third morning, though, it had been Haynes who led out the home team, since Richards was in the press box breathing fire at *Daily Express* journalist James Lawton who had asked him for an explanation of the V-sign he had given to his own crowd. His outburst, it would seem, was the culmination of much anger at press criticism of West Indian bowling, both the excessive use of bouncers and the slow over rate; but it was an astonishing way for a Test captain to behave, and he apologized to his team for not leading them out. It cannot have done his concentration any good, for after the Greenidge-Haynes partnership and a knock from Richardson wickets fell rapidly, Richards being caught off Malcolm for just one. All out 446 meant that England had a lot of batting to do in the last two days, and when Larkins went at the end of the third day to a ball that he did not see in the shadows, one felt they just were not going to make it. Sure enough, next day saw a procession, only Lamb and Hussain passing thirty, although Smith batted for an hour with a broken finger and it was revealed that Hussain had been playing for five weeks with a broken bone in his wrist and Lamb had a cracked elbow. All the same, 154 all out gave West Indies victory by an innings and 32 runs.

If it was a sad end for England, they at least had the knowledge that only the weather deprived them of a draw. Had Gooch not been injured who knows what would have happened in the last two games; but then, West Indies had their share of injuries, too. It was also sad that no English spinner had been seen throughout the rubber, and that both sides blatantly and cynically ignored the ruling about bowling 90 overs in a day, so that play just continued until the light faded every day of the series; those two factors left many people fearful for the game's future. For English fans, though, there was pleasure that their team had begun to show heart and direction and purpose, all of which had been missing since the Ashes tour of 1986–7; while West Indian fans were just happy that their heroes had shown that, after all, W.B. Yeats had got it wrong and the centre could hold. The steamroller had hit a bump, but for the time being it was back on course.

| 1984 | Edgbaston | E 191, 235; | WI 606 | WI inns 180 runs |
| | Lord's | E 286, 300–9d; | WI 245, 344–1 | WI 9 wkts |
| | Headingley | E 270, 159; | WI 302, 131–2 | WI 8 wkts |
| | Old Trafford | WI 500; | E 280, 156 | WI inns 64 runs |
| | Oval | WI 190, 346; | E 162, 202 | WI 172 runs |
| 1985–6 | Kingston | E 159, 152; | WI 307, 5–0 | WI 10 wkts |
| | Port-of-Spain | E 176, 315; | WI 399, 95–3 | WI 7 wkts |
| | Bridgetown | WI 418; | E 189, 199 | WI inns 30 runs |
| | Port-of-Spain | E 200, 150; | WI 312, 39–0 | WI 10 wkts |
| | St John's | WI 474, 246–2d; | E 310, 170 | WI 240 runs |
| 1988 | Trent Bridge | E 245, 301–3; | WI 448–9d | Drawn |
| | Lord's | WI 209, 397; | E 165, 307 | WI 134 runs |
| | Old Trafford | E 135, 93; | WI 384–7d | WI inns 156 runs |
| | Headingley | E 201, 138; | WI 275, 67–0 | WI 10 wkts |
| | Oval | E 205, 202; | WI 183, 226–2 | WI 8 wkts |
| 1989–90 | Kingston | WI 164, 240; | E 364, 41–1 | E 9 wkts |
| | Georgetown | Abandoned – rain | | |
| | Port-of-Spain | WI 199, 239; | E 288, 120–5 | Drawn |
| | Bridgetown | WI 446, 267–8d; | E 358, 191 | WI 164 runs |
| | St John's | E 260, 154; | WI 446 | WI inns 32 runs |

## 1984 Test Series

### England

| Batting | Innings | NO | HS | Runs | Average |
|---|---|---|---|---|---|
| A.J. Lamb | 10 | 1 | 110 | 386 | 42.88 |
| I.T. Botham | 10 | 0 | 81 | 347 | 34.70 |
| G. Fowler | 10 | 0 | 106 | 260 | 26.00 |
| B.C. Broad | 8 | 0 | 55 | 195 | 24.37 |
| P.R. Downton | 10 | 1 | 56 | 210 | 23.33 |

| Bowling | Overs | M | Runs | W | Average |
|---|---|---|---|---|---|
| R.M. Ellison | 44 | 10 | 94 | 5 | 18.80 |
| P.J.W. Allott | 104.5 | 26 | 282 | 14 | 20.14 |
| I.T. Botham | 163.2 | 30 | 667 | 19 | 35.10 |
| P.I. Pocock | 53.3 | 17 | 145 | 4 | 36.25 |
| D.R. Pringle | 71.3 | 10 | 257 | 5 | 51.40 |

### West Indies

| Batting | Innings | NO | HS | Runs | Average |
|---|---|---|---|---|---|
| C.G. Greenidge | 8 | 1 | 223 | 572 | 81.71 |
| H.A. Gomes | 8 | 3 | 143 | 400 | 80.00 |
| C.H. Lloyd | 6 | 1 | 71 | 255 | 51.00 |
| I.V.A. Richards | 7 | 1 | 117 | 250 | 41.66 |
| P.J.L. Dujon | 6 | 0 | 101 | 210 | 35.00 |

| Bowling | Overs | M | Runs | W | Average |
|---|---|---|---|---|---|
| M.D. Marshall | 167.4 | 50 | 437 | 24 | 18.21 |
| J. Garner | 217.5 | 60 | 540 | 29 | 18.62 |
| R.A. Harper | 128.4 | 47 | 276 | 13 | 21.23 |
| M.A. Holding | 122.2 | 24 | 343 | 15 | 22.87 |
| E.A.E. Baptiste | 125 | 39 | 265 | 8 | 33.13 |

Wicket-keepers:   P.R. Downton 10 dismissals   P.J.L. Dujon 13 dismissals

In the first match, I.V.A. Richards became the fourth West Indian to score 5,000 Test runs, and E.A.E. Baptiste and M. Holding put on a record West Indies ninth-wicket partnership against England of 150 (in only 114 minutes). In the second match, C.H. Lloyd became the second West Indian to score 7,000 Test runs, and C.G. Greenidge and I.T. Botham each reached 4,000 Test runs; Greenidge became the first West Indian to score a double century at Lord's, and his partnership of 287 with H.A. Gomes is the record for the second wicket by either side in these Tests. In the third match, M.A. Holding reached 200 Test wickets, and R.G.D. Willis ended his Test career with the English record of 325 wickets and the world record of 55 'not out' innings. In the fourth match, West Indies became the first visiting team to win the first four Tests of a series in England, extending this in the final match to five victories. In that last match, Botham became the fifth bowler to reach 300 Test wickets, thereby becoming the first player to do the double of 3,000 runs and 300 wickets.

## 1985–6 Test Series

### England

| Batting | Innings | NO | HS | Runs | Average |
|---|---|---|---|---|---|
| D.I. Gower | 10 | 0 | 90 | 370 | 37.00 |
| G.A. Gooch | 10 | 0 | 53 | 276 | 27.60 |
| A.J. Lamb | 10 | 0 | 62 | 224 | 22.40 |
| D.M. Smith | 4 | 0 | 47 | 80 | 20.00 |
| P. Willey | 8 | 0 | 71 | 136 | 17.00 |

| Bowling | Overs | M | Runs | W | Average |
|---|---|---|---|---|---|
| J.E. Emburey | 153 | 34 | 448 | 14 | 32.00 |
| N.A. Foster | 83.5 | 8 | 285 | 7 | 40.71 |
| R.M. Ellison | 82.3 | 19 | 294 | 7 | 42.00 |
| J.G. Thomas | 86 | 13 | 364 | 8 | 45.50 |
| I.T. Botham | 134.5 | 16 | 535 | 11 | 48.63 |

**West Indies**

| Batting | Innings | NO | HS | Runs | Average |
|---|---|---|---|---|---|
| D.L. Haynes | 9 | 3 | 131 | 469 | 78.16 |
| I.V.A. Richards | 6 | 1 | 110* | 331 | 66.20 |
| R.B. Richardson | 9 | 2 | 160 | 387 | 55.28 |
| R.A. Harper | 3 | 1 | 60 | 100 | 50.00 |
| M.D. Marshall | 5 | 1 | 76 | 153 | 38.25 |

| Bowling | Overs | M | Runs | W | Average |
|---|---|---|---|---|---|
| J. Garner | 156.1 | 30 | 436 | 27 | 16.14 |
| M.D. Marshall | 169.3 | 36 | 482 | 27 | 17.85 |
| C.A. Walsh | 33 | 6 | 103 | 5 | 20.60 |
| B.P. Patterson | 118.1 | 19 | 426 | 19 | 22.42 |
| M.A. Holding | 102.4 | 16 | 385 | 16 | 24.06 |

Wicket-keepers: P.J.L. Dujon 16 dismissals  T.R.O. Payne (WI) 5 dismissals  P.R. Downton 8 dismissals

In the second match, M.D. Marshall reached 200 Test wickets. In the third match, P.J.L. Dujon equalled the West Indies record of five catches in an innings by a wicket-keeper. In the fourth match, I.V.A. Richards passed 6,000 Test runs, C.G. Greenidge passed 5,000 Test runs, H.A. Gomes passed 3,000 Test runs and I.T. Botham took his 350th Test wicket. In the fifth match, West Indies completed their tenth successive victory and their second successive 5–0 series win over England, Richards scored the fastest-ever Test century in terms of balls received (56), and J. Garner and M.D. Marshall both broke the West Indies record for wickets taken in a home series against England, each taking 27.

**1988 Test Series**

**England**

| Batting | Innings | NO | HS | Runs | Average |
|---|---|---|---|---|---|
| G.A. Gooch | 10 | 0 | 146 | 459 | 45.90 |
| A.J. Lamb | 8 | 2 | 113 | 254 | 42.33 |
| D.I. Gower | 8 | 1 | 88* | 211 | 30.14 |
| R.A. Smith | 4 | 0 | 57 | 106 | 26.50 |
| P.R. Downton | 5 | 1 | 27 | 84 | 21.00 |

| Bowling | Overs | M | Runs | W | Average |
|---|---|---|---|---|---|
| G.R. Dilley | 136.1 | 26 | 403 | 15 | 26.86 |
| N.A. Foster | 73.2 | 12 | 250 | 9 | 27.77 |
| D.R. Pringle | 119 | 33 | 326 | 11 | 29.63 |
| G.C. Small | 37.5 | 6 | 140 | 4 | 35.00 |
| P.W. Jarvis | 57.1 | 6 | 217 | 6 | 36.16 |

**West Indies**

| Batting | Innings | NO | HS | Runs | Average |
|---|---|---|---|---|---|
| A.L. Logie | 7 | 2 | 95* | 364 | 72.80 |
| P.J.L. Dujon | 7 | 1 | 67 | 305 | 50.83 |
| R.A. Harper | 3 | 0 | 74 | 147 | 49.00 |
| C.G. Greenidge | 6 | 0 | 103 | 282 | 47.00 |
| D.L. Haynes | 7 | 2 | 77* | 235 | 47.00 |

| Bowling | Overs | M | Runs | W | Average |
|---|---|---|---|---|---|
| W.K.M Benjamin | 67 | 17 | 151 | 12 | 12.58 |
| R.A. Harper | 29 | 11 | 63 | 5 | 12.60 |
| M.D. Marshall | 203.1 | 49 | 443 | 35 | 12.65 |
| C.E.L. Ambrose | 203.1 | 56 | 445 | 22 | 20.22 |
| C.A. Walsh | 157.2 | 40 | 412 | 12 | 34.33 |

Wicket-keepers: P.R. Downton 9 dismissals  C.J. Richards (E) 3 dismissals  P.J.L. Dujon 20 dismissals

In the second match, C.G. Greenidge reached 6,000 Test runs, and A.L. Logie and P.J.L. Dujon shared century partnerships for the sixth wicket in each innings, a unique Test feat for West Indies; the total match receipts passed £1,000,000 for the first time in England. In the fourth match, D.I. Gower reached 7,000 runs in his hundredth Test. In the fifth match, M.D. Marshall took his tally of wickets in the series to 35, a West Indies record for any Test series; this also beat F.S. Trueman's record of 34 wickets in an England-West Indian series, set in 1963. By the end of the series, West Indies had beaten England in 14 of the previous 15 encounters.

### 1989–90 Test Series

#### England

| Batting | Innings | NO | HS | Runs | Average |
|---|---|---|---|---|---|
| A.J. Lamb | 7 | 0 | 132 | 390 | 55.71 |
| G.A. Gooch | 4 | 1 | 84 | 128 | 42.66 |
| R.A. Smith | 7 | 2 | 62 | 186 | 37.20 |
| W. Larkins | 8 | 1 | 54 | 176 | 25.14 |
| A.J. Stewart | 8 | 1 | 45 | 170 | 24.28 |

| Bowling | Overs | M | Runs | W | Average |
|---|---|---|---|---|---|
| A.R.C. Fraser | 71.1 | 18 | 161 | 11 | 14.63 |
| G.C. Small | 161 | 33 | 505 | 17 | 29.70 |
| D.E. Malcolm | 161.4 | 21 | 577 | 19 | 30.36 |
| P.A.J. DeFreitas | 78.5 | 11 | 242 | 6 | 40.33 |
| D.J. Capel | 124 | 17 | 436 | 9 | 48.44 |

#### West Indies

| Batting | Innings | NO | HS | Runs | Average |
|---|---|---|---|---|---|
| D.L. Haynes | 7 | 0 | 167 | 371 | 53.00 |
| C.A. Best | 5 | 0 | 164 | 242 | 48.40 |
| C.G. Greenidge | 7 | 0 | 149 | 308 | 44.00 |
| A.L. Logie | 5 | 0 | 98 | 212 | 42.40 |
| I.V.A. Richards | 5 | 0 | 70 | 141 | 28.20 |

| Bowling | Overs | M | Runs | W | Average |
|---|---|---|---|---|---|
| C.E.L. Ambrose | 132 | 32 | 307 | 20 | 15.35 |
| I.R. Bishop | 162.1 | 35 | 419 | 21 | 19.95 |
| C.A. Walsh | 93.2 | 14 | 243 | 12 | 20.25 |
| E.A. Moseley | 87 | 12 | 261 | 6 | 43.50 |
| M.D. Marshall | 59 | 17 | 132 | 3 | 44.00 |

Wicket-keepers: P.J.L. Dujon (WI) 15 dismissals  R.C. Russell (E) 14 dismissals

In the first match, England beat West Indies for the first time since April 1974. In the fourth match, A.J. Lamb became only the second England captain (the first being A.C. MacLaren) to score a century in his first match as captain. In the fifth match, C.G. Greenidge was playing in his hundredth Test, passed 7,000 Test runs and with D.L. Haynes set a West Indian first-wicket record of 298.

# — 11 —

# Instant Entertainment

## A FAMILIAR STORY

When England won the last Test of 1973–4 the teams had met only twice in one-day internationals. By the time England won another Test they had played a further thirty, plus two that were rain-restricted and one washed out altogether. Not surprisingly, West Indies dominated these, winning seventeen of the first twenty-two played up to the end of 1985–6. Then a curious thing happened – England suddenly began to win, with nine of the next ten meetings going their way, and even while their Test form was wretched somehow turned themselves into perhaps the best one-day side in the world. The danger with this was that the longer it went on the more likely it became that both players and fans would get their priorities wrong, so that the feeling of 'we may as well concentrate on what we're good at and not bother too much about Tests' would become steadily more predominant. There were signs, especially in 1988, that the players appeared to be trying harder in the one-day internationals than in the Tests, and the traditionalists – who of course regard themselves as the real cricket lovers – feared for the future.

Back in 1973 such fears would have seemed absurd. The first limited-overs international, between Australia and England, had taken place only two years earlier, and the Prudential Trophy had then been introduced with great success in 1972. Earlier in 1973, the matches against the New Zealanders had been rather an anti-climax to their tour, with the second spoiled by rain, but no one doubted that they were now a permanent addition to the summer. West Indies had won the three-Test series 2–0, yet so far had never played a one-day international against anyone, so the balance between form and experience seemed a neat one; and so it proved.

The first meeting, at Leeds, was one of the most exciting. West Indies made a good start and with 132 for 3 at lunch looked ready to blossom. Then Willis bowled Lloyd, four more wickets fell cheaply – Sobers made a duck in his only one-day international – and the final score was 181. The England selectors, having said goodbye and thank you to Illingworth, had appointed Denness captain, and he immediately came good with a steady 66 to hold the innings together. When he was out England had ten overs to score 39, with five wickets left, and by the beginning of the penultimate over needed just seven with three wickets left. Then Greig went, having made 48, Hendrick followed next ball, and the last over began with four still required. Sobers bowled to Willis, was clumped back over his head for two then steered to third man for two, and England were home with three balls to spare. If the one-day series was then to prove one-sided for years to come, at least it got off to a good start.

There was something of a contrast at the Oval. In good batting conditions England did not distinguish themselves as 63 from Fletcher was the only substantial knock. 189 was clearly nowhere near enough, and Fredericks alone accounted for 105 of the reply. With Kallicharran making 53, there were only four more needed when the second wicket fell, and as there were also more than thirteen overs in hand West Indies won the Prudential Trophy on a faster run rate over the two games. It had not been hard to predict that the Caribbean style of attacking play would be greatly suited to one-day cricket.

The joys – and the financial rewards – of the instant game had not reached the West Indies when Denness led his troops there a few months later and, as the two sides were drawn in separate groups in the 1975 World Cup, it was 1976 before they met again. Tony Greig had already failed in his attempt to make the West Indies 'grovel', and never looked like doing it now. Indeed, in the first game at Scarborough they lost a wicket first ball and had three down for 23 before Barlow, on his first representative appearance, held the innings together with 80 not out, helping the total to 202. There was one lovely freak occurrence near the end: Knott played the ball down to fine leg and Holding's throw hit the stumps with Barlow well home, whereupon he called Knott for a second run. With both batsmen in the middle of the pitch, the ricochet beat Barlow to the bowler's end and broke the stumps there as well; Lloyd appealed, but umpire Jepson gave 'not out'. When West Indies batted, Richards was soon laying into them, hammering a six and twenty fours in 119 not out. No one else scored very many but no one needed to, and there were still six wickets and fourteen overs in hand when King finished things off with a six.

Rain caused delays at Lord's so that the match had to be carried over till Sunday, but it made no difference to Richards. He fell three short of his century this time, and once again no one else got out of the twenties, but 221 still proved too much for England. With six wickets going down for

62 they were never in the hunt, but Randall did his best to keep the game alive, supported by Knott and Jackman. He was to have many fine one-day knocks over the years and now he hit 88; only when he was ninth out was the match definitely lost, West Indies eventually winning by 36 runs.

More rain at Edgbaston washed out the Bank Holiday Monday, and when the game was played on Tuesday afternoon it was limited to 32 overs. West Indies duly hammered everything in sight. Richards failed, but Lloyd hit 79 off 57 balls and Greenidge and Rowe made quick forties, taking the total to 223. England never had a chance; Amiss, Randall and Wood scored a few, but in the end they fell 50 short. Barlow followed his good first match with two ducks, but one notable thing about the game was the international debut of I.T. Botham. He was walloped for 31 for 1 in three overs and scored 20.

The next meeting was in the dramatic setting of the 1979 World Cup Final at Lord's. Brearley won the toss and put West Indies in, and the England bowlers did well; the fourth wicket went down on 99 and they were clearly on top. They had not yet got Richards, however, and when Collis King joined him they decided it was time to entertain the crowd. With Willis having been injured in the semi-final, England had chosen to play an extra batsman, Larkins, and make up their fifth bowler by combining Gooch, Boycott and Larkins, and it proved ill-judged. Probably they would have lost all the same, but another bowler might have made it much closer. Richards and King put on 139 for the fifth wicket in just seventy-seven minutes, King annihilating the bowlers to the tune of three sixes and ten fours in his 86, most of them from the three part-time bowlers who conceded, by coincidence, 86 between them. After King went, Richards reached his century and was on 138 not out at the close, having seen the total to 286. Inevitably, he won the Man of the Match award.

In reply, Boycott and Brearley put on no less than 129 for the first wicket – jolly good in a Test, but they took thirty-eight overs about it, with Boycott not getting into double figures until the seventeenth over. With 158 still needed from the last twenty-two overs, the later batsmen never had a chance, perishing quickly as they threw the bat. Poor Larkins was one of four ducks as Garner took five for 38, and the innings subsided to 194 all out. Victory by 92 runs meant that Clive Lloyd was holding aloft the Prudential World Cup for the second time.

A few months later, both England and West Indies were in Australia, each playing three alternating Tests against the home team to 'celebrate' the armistice drawn up with Kerry Packer. England lost all three of their Tests and West Indies won two of theirs, but neither side liked the

*Collis King – 86 in 77 minutes in the 1979 World Cup Final. This was one of his three sixes.*

arrangement of interspersing them with one-day games that were part of the new Benson and Hedges World Series Cup. Switching between one-day and five-day mode was unpopular with the players, and the new showbiz-style razzmatazz that accompanied the games seemed specifically designed to cater for the drunken yobbos who turned up by the cartload. The important thing, though, was that they paid their admission fee *before* they became totally paralytic and abusive; that seemed to be all that really mattered.

The teams played four matches, spread over several weeks, against each of the others, with the top two then going through to a best-of-three final. England's first game, at Sydney, was also their first under floodlights, and they won it. Randall and Brearley made a good start, Gower and Willey pressed on well, and at the end of fifty overs they were on 211. A brief shower reduced West Indies' target to 199 from 47 overs, and Greenidge, Rowe and Kallicharran looked to have this well under control. Then the wickets went, and Croft, the last batsmen, was left needing to score three

*World Cup Final, 1979. Richards, Croft, Garner, King, Holding, Kallicharran, Lloyd, Murray and Greenidge display the silverware.*

off the final ball. Brearley pushed all the fielders, including wicket-keeper Bairstow, back to the boundary – and Botham bowled him.

Any English people in Brisbane had rather less to get excited about. England made a decent 217, with 68 from Boycott and 59 from Gower; but after Greenidge and Haynes had got half-way to the target, Richards, who had missed the first match, played as only he can. The second wicket, like the first, produced 109 runs and he made 85 of them off 77 balls. With Greenidge also on 85 not out, the nine-wicket win was rather comprehensive.

The third match at Melbourne was then completely washed out, but at Adelaide West Indies produced another drubbing. Richards made another 88, Greenidge and Kallicharran got fifties and 246 was clearly going to be hard for England to beat. In front of a full house they steadily disintegrated, no one passing 24 as Roberts took 5 for 22. 139 all out left West Indies 107 ahead. Remarkably, however, England had won all their matches against Australia, and Australia had won three of theirs against

West Indies; England therefore finished well clear at the top of the table, with 11 points to West Indies' 7 and Australia's 6. So it was back to Melbourne for the first of the final matches.

If England had held any one of the three catches they put down they would have won, since the three top-scoring West Indies batsmen all had a 'life'. Greenidge was dropped on 6 and made a further 74, Kallicharran on 25 and went on to 42, and King was unbeaten on 31 after giving a chance on 5. 215 was the kind of score to promise a close finish, and Boycott, Willey and Larkins saw them well on the way. The innings lost momentum when Willey and Larkins were run out in quick succession, and as the final over began 15 were still needed. Brearley did his best, but four were still needed off the last ball and he could manage only a single.

A two-run defeat seemed set fair to demoralize England, but their batsmen did not do badly in the second game at Sydney. Boycott's 63 held the innings together, Gooch and Gower got a few, Botham walloped 37 off 39 balls and 208 seemed a reasonable total on a pitch helpful to bowlers. Yet Greenidge and Haynes found few problems, and when Haynes went Richards merely carried on as before. He and Greenidge made 119 in 27 overs, and although Richards went near the end for 65 Greenidge remained unbeaten on 98. An eight-wicket win meant that Lloyd was hoisting yet another trophy to the heavens.

The treadmill ground on. Another few months and West Indies were back in England for a Test series that lost much of its interest to the weather. The one-day games were now held before the Test series rather than after, an *hors d'oeuvre* rather than a stodgy pudding served up when everyone was full, but the first game at Headingley was distinctly uninspiring. In poor light and on a tricky pitch, West Indies, put in by Botham, had to work hard to reach 198, with 78 from Greenidge the major contribution and Old's figures being a remarkable 11–4–12–2. Time had been lost to rain and bad light, and by the close England had struggled to 35 for 3; next morning, the conditions were better and Tavaré, on his international debut, reached 82 not out. The problem was that no one stayed with him, and England subsided to 174 all out.

By contrast, Lord's was actually blessed with sunshine. Botham again put them in and all the bowlers did well – except him. Being carted for 71 off his eleven overs allowed West Indies to reach 235, with most of the batsmen making a useful score. Boycott and Willey opened with 135 off 33 overs, but then the wickets clattered. It was Botham who redeemed his poor bowling and got the crowd going with 42 not out, hitting the winning four off the third ball of the last over. This was one of only two occasions Botham tasted victory as England captain, the other being in a one-day game against Australia a year later, and each time he was there at the death. West Indies still won the Prudential Trophy on the faster run rate.

At this period the players must have been getting sick of the sight of each other, for just another few months and England were playing their first one-day games in the West Indies. The opening encounter took them to the small island of St Vincent, where the pitch was some way from international standard. The home team were without Richards but fielded a young man named Everton Mattis who, on representative debut, accomplished a rare feat: his 62 was more than all the other batsmen put together and, since Haynes got 34, it will be seen that the others had a collective off-day *par excellence*. A target of 128 should not have been beyond England, but four wickets went down for 15 and it was left to Gower and Botham to make a game of it. When Botham was eighth out the score was 114 and there were more than five overs left. Emburey and Stevenson nudged their singles, but Holding had the last word. He bowled Emburey at 123, and Old two runs later. It was the third time in eight games that the margin of victory had been just two runs.

The second one-day game in Guyana was played against a background of uncertainty over whether Robin Jackman was about to be asked to vacate the premises. England simply never got going. Only three batsmen got past twenty and none got to thirty, and a total of 137 was clearly a waste of everyone's time. Greenidge and Richards went cheaply, but only two more wickets were lost in strolling to victory. Jackman did not play in the match, but no sooner was it over than official statements were buzzing, and cricket was staggering through yet another crisis.

Happily there was now a break of over three years. Yet little had changed: Richards was still executioner-in-chief and England still seemed mesmerized at the prospect of playing the world champions. By 1984, the Prudential Trophy had metamorphosed into the Texaco Trophy, and the first game at Old Trafford contained the finest dish ever served up in a one-day international.

Lloyd won the toss and decided to bat, only to see seven wickets crumble for 102. Richards was not among them. Baptiste kept him company for a while as he blazed away, but when the ninth wicket fell with the score on 166 and fourteen overs still unused, it seemed that his effort would be in vain. Holding, though, stood firm, his share of an unbeaten last wicket stand being 12. Richards's share was rather larger, 93 to be precise, the fourteen overs yielding 106 runs as Richards hammered 21

*Another victory draws near. Gower is caught by wicket-keeper Dujon off*
*Roger Harper at Headingley 1984. Lloyd, Greenidge and Richards close in.*

fours and five sixes – one of them out of the ground – in all, for 189 not
out off 170 balls. He might have been stumped on 44 but that was the only
chance he gave. It was one of the truly marvellous innings, one that no one
who saw it could ever forget; since it has been shown on television virtually every time rain has stopped play in any match since, it would be
almost impossible to have forgotten it anyway. Faced with a total of 272,
England were simply demoralized. Lamb made 75 but there was little
from anyone else, and the tourists won by 104 runs.

At Trent Bridge, the first part of the story was the same except for one
detail – Richards went for just three. Lloyd made 52 but the rest of the
batting disappointed, and, with rain reducing the game to fifty overs each,
West Indies managed only 179. Fowler and Andy Lloyd made a good
start, Gower chipped in well, and the rest of the batsmen did enough to see
England home by three wickets. They hardly looked ready to slug it out in
a Test series, but at least they had a victory under their belts. Any euphoria
this produced was very short-lived. At Lord's, Fowler and Lloyd and
Gower again made some runs, but it took thirty Extras to help their total
to 196. Their only chance was to get Richards cheaply; instead he made 84
not out off 65 balls, and, with Gomes also getting fifty, the margin was
eight wickets. Another trophy for Clive Lloyd's collection.

During 1985–6 in the Caribbean the script-writer was still West Indian.
The centre-piece of the first mini-drama in Kingston was Mike Gatting's

exploding nose as he missed an attempted hook off Marshall. Psychologically this did England no good at all, of course, and the batsmen struggled to 145 off 46 overs, the reduction in the number of overs caused by West Indies bowling so slowly. If any sweat was lost in reaching this target it was not noticeable, and a six-wicket win was duly recorded.

Yet after being annihilated in the first Test, England showed they could still fight. The one-day game in Trinidad was, according to *Wisden* 'described by many as the best one-day international played in the West Indies', and England won it off the final ball. Rain reduced it to 37 overs a side and the home team were soon rattling along. Haynes made 53 and Richardson finished unbeaten on 79, but once again it was Richards who dominated. Off just 39 balls he made 82 astonishing runs, and the innings closed on 229, setting England a run rate of 6.2 an over. It proved to be Gooch's day; with Slack he put on 89 for the second wicket in seventeen overs, setting the foundations for the later onslaught. Yet his partners contributed relatively little as the runs were steadily knocked off and his century was passed; come the last over and nine were needed, and it was a leg-bye off the final delivery that earned England their win. Gooch finished on 129 not out, made without a chance, a superb innings. Three days later in the Test he was out fourth ball.

Barbados enjoyed no such entertainment. Gower put West Indies in and watched them score 249 in 46 overs, thanks in part to a very fast outfield. Richards was missed when 5 and went on to 62, the same score as Richardson, with all the batsmen making useful contributions. When England batted, Gooch was given out caught behind and it seemed to dispirit his team-mates; without their hero of the previous game they looked lost, and folded for 114 all out. At least the crowd went home happy.

*Wisden* had some strong words to say about the fourth game, back in Trinidad: 'England put up a performance which exposed to the crowd of 21,000 what depths of incompetence they had reached . . . after two days off following the Test defeat, the first practice was made optional – and Gower himself was one of the six who failed to attend.' They made 165 from their 47 overs, with Robinson top-scoring on 55, and Haynes, Richardson and Richards had no trouble in knocking off the runs for the loss of two wickets. 'England's batting, fielding and – apart from Emburey and Edmonds – their bowling proclaimed the lack of practice and resolve on a slow pitch which, had they been in the right frame of mind, would have given them an even chance of levelling the series,' asserted *Wisden*. In one-day matches England were now just about at rock bottom; within a year they were very much on top.

# THE MOTHERLAND STRIKES BACK

Mike Gatting has proved himself an excellent one-day captain, winning several trophies with Middlesex during the 1980s. He was soon bringing his skills to bear for his country, too, especially in Australia in 1986–7. Not content with just the interminable Benson and Hedges World Series Cup, the players also had to fit in the Benson and Hedges Challenge between the fourth and fifth Tests, a jamboree dreamed up to latch on to the sporting frenzy which the TV and marketing people had decreed would seize the nation when the America's Cup yacht races were staged off Fremantle. At least there was no travelling as all the games were played in Perth. Australia, England, West Indies and Pakistan would play each other mercifully just once, and the two top teams would then meet in a final. Since Gatting and his troops had retained the Ashes just a few days beforehand, they were ready to take on all comers.

By the time they played West Indies, they had already beaten Australia and West Indies had lost to Pakistan. England were put in and saw half their wickets fall for 96 in half their overs before they were rescued by 71 from Lamb and 50 from Jack Richards, with the spinners chipping in as well. 228 looked better when three West Indian wickets went for 51 and better still when Richards was caught. Logie and Dujon were steering the game their way when Dujon was bowled as he stepped back for a cover drive, and that was the turning point. The rest of the wickets slipped away, 209 all out gave England a win by 19 runs and, as Pakistan had already beaten Australia, ensured that the final would be between them and England. Good, tight bowling enabled England to do this comfortably, giving them their second trophy in ten days.

There was just time for England and Australia to fit in the final Test before getting on with the serious business – serious to those for whom dollar signs are important – of dashing round the country playing game after game after game of the Benson and Hedges World Series Cup. Just two days after losing the splendid fifth Test in Sydney, England were in Brisbane playing West Indies, and beating them convincingly. Moisture in the pitch made the toss an important one, and when Gatting won it the bowlers did their stuff beautifully. Only Haynes and Logie put up much resistance and 154 all out, with conditions improving all the time, presented England with few problems; had the situation been reversed, one knew that West Indies would have won by eight or nine wickets, but English fans were happy enough to have six still in hand.

The itinerary for this competition appeared to have been worked out with the sole aim of maximizing the profit of the air operators who did the transporting. Australia, for instance, having finished the Test in Sydney on 15 January, played in Brisbane on 18 January, Melbourne on 20 January, Sydney on 22 January, Adelaide on 25 and 26 January, Sydney on 28 January and so on. By any stretch of anyone's imagination it was insane and, coming at the end of a tough Test series, it was extremely tiring for the players. England's second encounter with West Indies was at Adelaide, where they were given a good start of 121 by Broad and Athey. They capitalized on this well enough by reaching 252 in their fifty overs, and then took two quick wickets when West Indies batted. In good batting conditions, the English bowlers performed well, and with some good catches being held the innings never really threatened. When Emburey went through the lower order with four wickets in thirteen balls, England were left winners by 89 runs.

Never before had England beaten West Indies in two consecutive one-day games, let alone three, and West Indies went into the next match at Melbourne, clearly determined that it would not be four. On an uneven pitch, English wickets were soon tumbling, Broad not helping the cause by running out Lamb. Only 34 from Emburey gave the bowlers any sort of target to defend, although 147 was obviously nothing like enough. De Freitas and Small were extremely economical and there were only nine balls left when the total was passed, but with Richards on song – and becoming the first man to score 5,000 runs in one-day internationals – only four wickets went down.

That was as far as their success went, though. The pitch at Devonport was of more interest to bowlers than batsmen, and only a steady 76 from Broad, with some support from Lamb, gave England a reasonable total of 177. Normally that should present no problem to the team batting second, but none of them could dominate the bowling and the low total seemed to spur England to some brilliant fielding; when Botham got Gomes and Richards in successive overs, the game moved England's way, and the rest of the wickets drifted away for a total of just 148. *Wisden* records that 'on five of the eight occasions on which Gatting changed the bowling, the man brought on took a wicket in the first over of his spell'. Such inspiration on the captain's part was to help him towards an OBE, for with England then beating Australia in the first two games of the final, their clean sweep of three trophies out of three was accomplished. Gatting made the point that they had to win the final two games as after so much cricket they simply did not have the strength left for a third. It was the most successful tour

England had ever made, all the more satisfying as it began with them being written off as a bunch of no-hopers.

Later the same year, the teams were again in opposition in the 1987 Reliance World Cup staged in India and Pakistan. Drawn in the same group, they had to play each other twice, and the first game at Gujranwala produced a memorable finish. The last ten overs of each innings saw over 90 runs scored; West Indies batted first and had made 151 for four from forty overs when Logie and Dujon, and then Harper, swung the bat. 243 looked a useful score from fifty overs. England began slowly, and then as Gatting and Gooch were accelerating they both fell in quick succession. Before much longer two more wickets had gone, with the score on 131 for 6 and the game seemingly lost. But Lamb was still there, and with Emburey and then DeFreitas swinging merrily he brought England back in contention. With three overs left 35 were still needed; Walsh was duly hammered for 16, all but one to Lamb, but the penultimate over from Patterson yielded only six. That left 13 from the last; Lamb struck a two and a four, and then Walsh sent down a dreadful ball that shot through for four leg-side wides. Now thoroughly rattled, he bowled a no-ball, from which Lamb curiously took a single and so lost the strike; but when Walsh now sent down a full toss, Foster gleefully walloped it to the rope and England had won. A week later, poor Walsh was involved in another traumatic final over as Pakistan despatched him for 14 to win off the final ball.

With Pakistan making the running in the group, the second England-West Indies game was crucial as it virtually assured the winners of a semi-final place. Having put England in, West Indies then bowled poorly and after 30 overs England were happily placed at 131 for 2. It was captain Richards who put the brakes on with some neat off-spin, only for the last ten overs to realize another 83. Gooch was chief hero with 92 and Lamb again showed what a good one-day player he is, but 22 of the total of 269 were wides that West Indies could ill afford. With West Indies on 147 for 2 and Richards and Richardson in full flow, the game had West Indies' name on it; Richards, with 51 from as many balls, had already struck Hemmings for two sixes, but now the Notts man flighted in a superb ball that deceived him completely and took his off-stump. It proved the turning-point. Hemmings took a catch to dismiss Logie, who was beginning to look dangerous, and then the wickets slithered away – including Harper run out by a fine throw from Hemmings, who was having a wonderful time. Richardson made 93, but with the last six wickets going for just 30 West Indies were all out 235, leaving England winners by 34 runs. They duly disposed of India in the semi-final, only to lose to Australia in a game they should have won.

It was a good six months before they had to meet again, this time in the Texaco Trophy matches in England. The home selectors had been ridiculed in the press for the squad they chose, and it hardly seemed a match for the mighty West Indies; yet by steady bowling and sound batting, England won all three games convincingly, and chemists did a good trade in indigestion tablets as much humble pie had to be eaten. They won by applying themselves to the job in hand and, if they had continued to do the same in the Tests, it might have been an interesting summer.

At Edgbaston, West Indies got off to a good start as the first wicket produced 34 runs in just six overs, but three fell cheaply and it was left to Logie and Hooper to make fifty apiece and give the innings its backbone. But, on a slow wicket, their partnership of 97 used up 29 overs, and 217 off 55 overs did not look enough. After a sound start from Gooch and Broad, England's response belonged primarily to Gatting, and his 82 not out saw his team home with six wickets in hand. The Headingley game was played on an uneven pitch that made batting difficult. West Indies bowled better this time and at 83 for 5 had England in trouble, with only Gooch having looked confident. Then Richards chose to bowl himself and Simmons (who had begun with two quick wickets) for a long spell and England were let off the hook, Pringle and Downton putting on 66 in thirteen overs. The total reached 186, and West Indies never threatened it. In the face of excellent bowling, wickets fell steadily, and with 31 from Richards the top score they were all out for 139, giving England a 47-run victory. It was their first series win against West Indies in England.

The pattern of the Lord's match was similar to the first one. Rain and bad light brought several interruptions, made batting difficult, and took the game into a second day. With West Indies 125 for 6 off fifty overs at the close of the first day, things looked good for England, but next morning Marshall and Dujon threw the bat and took the total to 178, which in the conditions was not that bad. But England only had to bat steadily and they were home, and Gooch, Broad, Gatting and Lamb did just that. Walsh set a record for the most economical bowling in a one-day international between Test-playing countries with just eleven runs off eleven overs, but 21 no-balls and wides sent down by his chums did not help the struggle, especially as Gooch was 'out' twice to no-balls. There were seven wickets and five overs in hand when victory was completed, the word 'whitewash' being gleefully bandied about. Gatting in particular had had a good series, batting well and leading the team excellently; with the first

Test then drawn under his leadership, how different the rest of the summer might have been had he not invited the famous barmaid to his room.

England's resurgence could not last. In 1989–90, while the Test series was producing surprises, the one-day games reverted to type. The first two at Port-of-Spain were spoiled by the weather; in the opening one, West Indies had made 208 and England 26 for 1 when the rain came, while the second got no further than West Indies being 13 without loss. At Kingston, though, after England had won the Test, there was plenty of excitement. England batted first and, thanks mainly to Lamb and Smith, reached 214. Yet the bowlers defended well, and only Richardson mastered them so that the closing overs were tense. Richardson reached his century during which three hard chances were missed, and from Fraser's final ball Bishop needed two to win on fewer wickets lost. He swung it to the extra-cover boundary and Sabina Park, where everyone had been generous in Test defeat, could not have celebrated more had the World Cup been won.

In Georgetown, things were more one-sided. On a good pitch, England struggled after Gooch and Larkins had made a solid start, and 188 for 8 was disappointing. When Haynes and Best put on 113 for the first wicket it all became academic, the main interest being whether Best would get his hundred. He did, but ran himself out trying to make it 101; still a six-wicket victory all the same. In Barbados, with Haynes leading West Indies and England led by Lamb, England repeated their Kingston score of 214, though off only 38 overs after morning rain. As so often on this tour, Robin Smith and Lamb were the main architects, both playing aggressively after David Smith, flown out to replace the injured Gooch, had hung around for some time to get accustomed to the conditions only to get a bruised thumb in the process. When Haynes and Richardson played even more aggressively, and then Best joined in again, the game was heading West Indies' way; falling wickets slowed things down, though, and in the end the target was reached with three balls and four wickets to spare. 3–0 to West Indies set the tour back on its path towards normality after the Test aberrations in Jamaica and Trinidad.

| 1973 | Headingley | WI 181; | E 182–9 | E 1 wkt |
|------|------------|---------|---------|---------|
|      | Oval | E 189–9; | WI 190–2 | WI 8 wkts |
| 1976 | Scarborough | E 202–8; | WI 207–3 | WI 7 wkts |
|      | Lord's | WI 221; | E 185 | WI 36 runs |
|      | Edgbaston | WI 223–9; | E 173 | WI 50 runs |
| 1979 | Lord's* | WI 286–9; | E 194 | WI 92 runs |

| 1979–80 | Sydney** | E 211–8; | WI 196 | E 2 runs†† |
| | Brisbane** | E 217–8; | WI 218–1 | WI 9 wkts |
| | Melbourne** | Match abandoned | | |
| | Adelaide** | WI 246–5; | E 139 | WI 107 runs |
| | Melbourne** | WI 215–8; | E 213 | WI 2 runs |
| | Sydney** | E 208–8; | WI 209–2 | WI 8 wkts |
| 1980 | Headingley | WI 198; | E 174 | WI 24 runs |
| | Lord's | WI 235; | E 236–7 | E 3 wkts |
| 1980–1 | St Vincent | WI 127; | E 125 | WI 2 runs |
| | Berbice | E 137; | WI 138–4 | WI 6 wkts |
| 1984 | Old Trafford | WI 272–9; | E 168 | WI 104 runs |
| | Trent Bridge | WI 179; | E 180–7 | E 3 wkts |
| | Lord's | E 196–9; | WI 197–2 | WI 8 wkts |
| 1985–6 | Kingston | E 145–8; | WI 146–7 | WI 6 wkts |
| | Port-of-Spain | WI 229–3; | E 230–5 | E 5 wkts |
| | Bridgetown | WI 249–7; | E 114 | WI 135 runs |
| | Port-of-Spain | E 165–9; | WI 166–2 | WI 8 wkts |
| 1986–7 | Perth† | E 228; | WI 209 | E 19 runs |
| | Brisbane** | WI 154; | E 156–4 | E 6 wkts |
| | Adelaide** | E 252–6; | WI 163 | E 89 runs |
| | Melbourne** | E 147; | WI 148–4 | WI 6 wkts |
| | Devonport** | E 177–9; | WI 148 | E 29 runs |
| 1987 | Gujranwala* | WI 243–7; | E 246–8 | E 2 wkts |
| | Jaipur* | E 269–5; | WI 235 | E 34 runs |
| 1988 | Edgbaston | WI 217; | E 219–4 | E 6 wkts |
| | Headingley | E 186–8 | WI 139 | E 47 runs |
| | Lord's | WI 178–7; | E 180–3 | E 7 wkts |
| 1989–90 | Port-of-Spain | WI 208–8; | E 26–1 | Rain |
| | Port-of-Spain | WI 13–0 | | Rain |
| | Kingston | E 214–8; | WI 216–7 | WI 3 wkts |
| | Georgetown | E 188–8; | WI 191–4 | WI 6 wkts |
| | Bridgetown | E 214–3; | WI 217–6 | WI 4 wkts |

West Indies: 21 wins    England: 14 wins    No result: 3

* World Cup
† Benson and Hedges Challenge
** Benson and Hedges World Series Cup
†† In this match rain reduced WI's target to 199

Centuries
England: G.A. Gooch 129*

West Indies: R.C. Fredericks 105  I.V.A. Richards 119*, 138*, 189*  R.B. Richardson 108*  C.A. Best 100

4 wickets in an innings
England: D.L. Underwood 4–44  G.R. Dilley 4–46, 4–23  J.E. Emburey 4–37  G.C. Small 4–31

West Indies: A.M.E. Roberts 4–32, 4–27, 5–22  V.A. Holder 5–50  J. Garner 5–38, 5–47  C.L. King 4–23  C.E.H. Croft 6–15  M.D. Marshall 4–23, 4–37  I.R. Bishop 4–28

# 12

# Sir Frank

Of all the wonderful cricketers to come from the West Indies, it is fair to say that five have been of outstanding importance. George Headley and Learie Constantine were the giants of the early Test years who did most to establish the team; Garfield Sobers was for twenty years the supreme all-rounder of the game's history; Clive Lloyd devised the concept of a quartet of pace bowlers who would carry all relentlessly before them. Few would argue, though, that the most important person in the history of West Indies cricket was Frank Worrell, for as the first regular black captain it was he who united all the old discordant factions and created one of the most glorious of teams. He is the central, pivotal figure in the story.

Because of his death, aged just forty-two, he is also thought of as a tragic figure, a man who was unable to fulfil the important public service to his people that seemed to be his destiny. It is easy to let this feeling of tragedy overshadow his story, but that would be wrong. He must be celebrated as a superb cricketer and one of the great captains.

He was born in Barbados on 1 August 1924 into a middle-class family, at a time when class boundaries on the island, having been modelled on the English system, were very rigid. His parents, brother and sister emigrated to the United States when he was a youngster and he was brought up by his grandmother, and it was only the lack of cricket in America which later deterred him from joining them. Because of the better opportunities in the States emigration from the West Indies was common at this time, and one cannot help wondering how many more outstanding players might have graced their cricket had their parents not left. By the age of thirteen, Worrell's ability was obvious and, still in short trousers, he was playing top-grade cricket in his school first team, modelling himself on Derek Sealy, who was one of his masters. Yet he was hardly a budding saint and his success made him unpopular with both masters and boys. He was regarded as a 'big-head', he played truant, got into trouble for telling a lie, and was lectured by the headmaster in front of the whole school because of the complaints there had been about him. He said this was the worst moment of his life, and the various carpetings he received ultimately

*Sir Frank Worrell – his captaincy touched even greater heights than his batsmanship.*

had their effect; years later the memory of them would have a deep effect on his attitude to captaincy.

Worrell must be understood against his political background. Barbados was British through and through, and one of his friends said of him many years later: 'He was as English as can be. He always admired the culture, manners and civilization of the better type of Englishman.' The class system was inflexible, though, and the white upper classes held the power, both economic and political. The black middle classes were allowed to become professional people – doctors, lawyers, civil servants, etc. – but that was their limit. This created the problem that their English-style education taught them liberal principles, while the system then denied them that same liberal advancement to the higher echelons of power and social prestige. This was more or less the case throughout the West Indies, although attitudes in Barbados were undoubtedly narrower than elsewhere. It was a system that could not endure, and agitations for greater democracy grew steadily louder. As Worrell's career came at the same period, the stature he acquired both as a man and a leader gave added impetus and credibility to the black independence movement, especially as cricket is such an important part of Caribbean life.

Early in his career he was thought of primarily as a left-arm spinner, and made his debut for Barbados in 1941–2 as such. The following season he made 64 not out as nightwatchman against Trinidad, was moved up the order in the second innings, and responded with 188; a year later, in 1943–4, also against Trinidad, he and John Goddard put on an undefeated 502 for the fourth wicket, at the time the third highest partnership in first-class cricket. Worrell's share was 308, which remained his highest score. Two more years and, in company with Walcott, he would have the first-class record outright, putting on an unbeaten 574 for the fourth wicket in Port-of-Spain, his contribution this time being 255. The record was beaten just a year later, but Worrell is still the only batsman to share in two partnerships of over 500 runs in first-class cricket.

By now, though, he was tired of Barbados, particularly its narrowness of spirit; they expressed their appreciation of his runs by refusing to allow him, as a black man, to practise at Kensington Oval, and he believed there were still those who resented his success and thought him the same 'big-head' as at school. In some quarters, of course, he was enormously popular, and it may have been that as a young man in his early twenties he found it difficult to cope with the adulation of the fans. For various reasons, therefore, he moved to Jamaica and, although he returned to Barbados many times, it was never with any great enthusiasm for the place. Ultimately, he came to realize that this persecution complex existed only in his own mind, and that his unpopularity in Barbados arose from his walking out on them. Remarkably, even after he became captain of the Test team, he was booed when he went out to bat at Bridgetown.

Test call-up came during England's 1947–8 tour. He was chosen for the first match but had to drop out with food poisoning. In the second Test at Port-of-Spain, he duly became the third 'W', Weekes and Walcott having already made their debuts, and scored 97 and 28 not out. He also showed his inexperience by asking Gerry Gomez, his captain, if he could be substituted so that he could go to the airport to meet his sister. He was duly reprimanded for his arrogance, providing him years later with another memory that would help make him a sympathetic captain. The first century was not long delayed, 131 not out in the third Test helping his team to a seven-wicket win, and he ended his first Test series with an average of 147. Obviously, he was now quite a celebrity, and in 1948 was signed up

*The unique phenomenon of the three Ws. Left to right: Frank Worrell, Clyde Walcott, Everton Weekes. Just what is it about Barbados that produces so many wonderful cricketers?*

by Radcliffe in the Central Lancashire League; he stayed with them until the end of 1952, set batting records which have never been beaten, even by Sobers, and was hugely popular, for his personal qualities as much as his cricketing skills. Around this time he was a heavy drinker although, as a conscientious professional, he did not let it affect his game.

In the West Indies the incident of wanting to go to the airport, and the fact that he turned up late for matches a number of times, had gained him a reputation for lack of discipline. The next upset came when he was chosen for the 1948–9 tour of India but asked, as a professional, to be paid £250; the WICBC refused, Worrell declined to back down, and he did not go. He felt that, with a wife and child to support, he should be paid what he was worth, and he made it clear that he was not prepared to give in when he thought he had a good case. It was not the last argument he would have with the authorities over pay, though this was the only series he missed for that reason. (By contrast, he was very generous to people who had less than he did, and often gave away money and cricket equipment.) He was delighted, therefore, when the following year he was invited to join a Commonwealth team touring India; feeling he had a point to prove he made plenty of runs, and was invited on two similar tours in the coming years. On the second of these, the captain, Leslie Ames, was injured for much of the time and Worrell was appointed his deputy. He took to it like the proverbial fish to water.

The triumphant tour of England in 1950 saw Worrell way out on top of the averages, scoring 539 runs in four matches at almost 90, and making his highest Test score of 261 at Nottingham. He played in six series against England and only in the last, in 1963, did he fail with the bat; other big scores included 191 not out, again at Nottingham, carrying his bat to help save the third Test of 1957, and 197 not out at Barbados in the first match of 1959–60, again to ensure a draw after a big England

*Worrell's grace captured against Warwickshire in 1950. Hafeez Kardar at gully watches Fred Gardner miss the ball as Worrell scores off the bowling of Charlie Grove. Don Taylor of New Zealand is at silly mid-on.*

innings. This latter was, at 682 minutes, the longest Test innings ever played for West Indies, and he had become so becalmed towards the end that his captain declared before he reached his double century. His overall average against England is a splendid 54.97, with almost 2,000 runs scored in 25 games; before the last series he was even averaging 63, although he was never one to get too bothered about statistics. That last series cost him a Test average over 50 as he dipped to 49.49, finishing with 3,860 runs from his 51 Tests, with nine centuries. Six feet (1.8 metres) tall, slim and athletic, his right-handed batting was less ferocious than that of Walcott and Weekes, relying on superb timing and balance, lightning footwork and an uncanny judgement of where the ball was going to pitch. His coaching had been minimal, but all his strokes came from the text-book and he was never once known to play across the line. His glory was the late cut, rated by C.L.R. James as 'one of the great strokes of our time', but apart from the hook, which he did not play, all the other strokes were there, elegant, graceful, polished, a joy to watch. He was also the most relaxed of batsmen, often having been asleep in the dressing-room before going out to the middle.

Having begun as a left-arm spinner he turned himself into a fast-medium bowler who frequently took the new ball and who at times could be decidedly nippy. In reality, he was more of a third seamer than a strike bowler, and did the job only in the absence of a faster man, but he once took 6 for 38 in Australia and at Leeds in 1957 had his best Test figures of 7 for 70. His 69 Test wickets cost 38.72 each, and against England he took 28 wickets at 43 – expensive, but good enough to put him high on the list of all-rounders. He was also a first-class close fielder, especially in the gully or at short leg, with 43 Test catches to his name.

In October 1956, Worrell joined Manchester University as a mature student to read for a BA in Economics, changing in his second year to a BA Administration, which included social anthropology. According to his professor, he was thorough and conscientious rather than brilliant, taking his studies very seriously since he wanted both to improve himself and gain a qualification for when he finished playing. It was during his second year at Manchester that he was offered the West Indies captaincy for the visit by Pakistan, but decided that his studies had to come first; he had a strong sense of predestination and apparently felt that the leadership would be his eventually. Completing his degree would ensure that he was better equipped to do the job, especially as by studying social anthropology he would be better able to understand his players. Yet had the visitors been England or Australia he may well not have been able to resist the temptation, and this was only partly because they were the leading lights in world cricket; there was also the racial aspect, in that he passionately wanted to prove that a team of black players led by a black captain was the equal of, if not better than, the white teams.

No doubt it is difficult for young people now to appreciate the complexities and the rigidities of the social structure in colonial days. Looking back, it seems remarkable that only in the 1950s did white people come to accept – grudgingly for the most part – that black people did not need white people in positions of authority to lead and guide them. The situation changed steadily during the 1950s as more and more black men came to high office, and naturally the West Indian people could see no reason why the same should not happen on the cricket field. Worrell had been vice-captain against England in 1953–4, but when Australia toured a year later the selectors' feet, apparently, had turned cold; Denis Atkinson, who had little captaincy experience, was made Stollmeyer's deputy, and as Stollmeyer then missed three Tests through injury, found himself pitched in at the deep end. There was little support for the white captain among the black players and the series was disaster. Yet a year later Atkinson was appointed again – with another white man, Bruce Pairaudeau, as his deputy – to take the team to New Zealand. Worrell did not go on that tour, but when West Indies went to England in 1957 under Goddard he was annoyed that the vice-captaincy went to Clyde Walcott; Worrell and Walcott, while friends, were never all that close, in fact, whereas Worrell and Weekes were.

When Worrell declined the captaincy after the 1957 tour, it was given to Gerry Alexander and the series against Pakistan was well won. A year later, as Worrell was still at university, Alexander was appointed to take the team to India and Pakistan, winning the first series but losing the second. One problem during the tour had centred on the young fast bowler Roy Gilchrist, who had been sent home from India for disciplinary reasons; after the tour, opinion was divided as to whether his misdemeanours should mean the end of his Test career or whether he should be helped back into the fold by someone such as Worrell, whom he worshipped. In the end, the WICBC's attitude that they could not accept any individual who did not uphold their tradition of sportsmanship prevailed, and Gilchrist played no more Tests. So far, with Worrell having turned down the chance, no one had been able to complain about the captaincy; but by now Worrell had his degree, was very much available, and Alexander himself expected him to be made captain for the tour by England in 1959–60. Instead, Alexander was reappointed. Perhaps it was a show of support for his disciplining of Gilchrist; perhaps there was the feeling that Worrell had drifted away from the hub of West Indies cricket; or perhaps once again the selectors simply could not bring themselves to appoint a black man.

The belief that Worrell should have been appointed was extremely strong throughout the Caribbean, and it found its expression through C.L.R. James, then editor of the Trinidad newspaper *The Nation*. He ran a relentless campaign based on the argument that 'there was not the slightest shadow of justification for Alexander to be captain of a side in which Frank Worrell was playing'. He concentrated on the cricketing angle rather than the racial one, emphasizing Worrell's greater experience and status and highlighting the errors of judgement he felt Alexander had made. He conceded that it was hard on Alexander, and later came to respect him greatly for the way in which he gave Worrell his fullest support as vice-captain. When the WICBC met to discuss the captaincy for the visit to Australia in 1960–1, it was Alexander himself who pressed Worrell's claims, and in due course the announcement was made that Worrell would lead the team. Everyone, it seemed, joined in the celebrations.

That tour has, of course, gone down as the most exciting series of the century. After the drama of the tied first Test, Australia won the second by seven wickets and West Indies the third by 222 runs; as the fourth neared its close, West Indies appeared to have the game in their hands, only for the last Australian pair to survive for an hour and forty minutes and earn a draw; and the final Test was won by Australia with just two wickets left. Cricket in Australia had been declining in popularity for some years, not helped by an abject England team two seasons before, and the excitement that West Indies generated by their enterprising play was unbounded, culminating in a vast ticker-tape send-off when the tour was over. Naturally, Richie Benaud and the home players took their full share of the credit, but it was Worrell who was hero number one. What was it about his captaincy, then, that was so special?

For one thing, he was lucky to have some outstanding players under him, and fortunate, too, in the Board's choice of manager for the tour. He had grown close to Gerry Gomez since the day he had asked if he could meet his sister at the airport, and they now worked together admirably. Good public relations were made a priority, so that the atmosphere surrounding the team was always cordial, which obviously had a beneficial effect on the players. He was determined to be thorough in his preparations, and made sure there were plenty of games before the Tests began so that the players could get used to the conditions. He also made sure that all players were kept informed of decisions about team selection, which had not always happened before. At team meetings anyone was welcome to have his say, thereby building cohesion and a feeling that everyone belonged to the unit. Discussion was encouraged as much as possible, and from this he learned much about each man. Younger players in particular were looked after, since not knowing the ropes on a tour has blighted more than one career.

He watched over his players and made sure they knew he was doing so. He looked carefully for antagonisms and smoothed them out as unobtrusively as possible. He was a strict disciplinarian whose word was law and, while players could argue with his views and put their own ideas to him freely, he would tolerate no arguing with umpires; when Sobers once disputed an lbw decision he was reprimanded in front of the team. At the same time, he took great trouble over the team's welfare, even to the extent of helping them when they signed their contracts. In other words, he combined paternalism, very careful attention to detail, and the traditional values of the English public school. His players respected and loved him as a result.

They respected him, too, of course, as one of the greatest players since the war, and knew that, as a top-flight batsman and a bowler who could be both slow and fast-medium, he would not be asking them to do things he had not already achieved himself. He was aware that a captain with a record such as his has a big advantage, since any troops will respond better to a leader they know has been through the fire himself, and so he knew just what he could ask of his bowlers. For the most part, the fast men were used in short bursts to conserve their strength and responded well to this; but when the occasion demanded, as on the final day at Lord's in 1963, they could keep going for hour after hour just because the captain asked them to. Hall said afterwards that he had not realized himself capable of such sustained accurate bowling, but kept at it simply because Worrell wanted him to; he also said that he was physically and mentally shattered at the end of it. Similarly, in the Oval Test, Sobers put in a prodigious spell of bowling, keeping at it because his captain felt he was the right bowler for the situation. Worrell had achieved any captain's dream of knowing that his players would give their last drop of sweat just for him.

After so many years, there was little about the game that he did not know, and tactically he was a highly skilled operator who, his players knew, would stay calm in a crisis. Undoubtedly, he was a conservative captain rather than an adventurous one – James records that Worrell once said to him 'In cricket you leave well alone', which, James felt, went deep into his method as a captain – but, for all that, he was not afraid of making changes if he felt they were needed. A famous one was dropping Ramadhin before the third Test in Australia and replacing him with Gibbs, whose Test career thus far had been fairly ordinary; Gibbs took eight wickets in the match to see his team home and was under way as a real Test bowler. James gives an account of one of these wickets which shows Worrell's tactical ability. Chasing 464 in the last innings, O'Neill and Harvey were approaching 200 and looking good. Harvey, though, was suffering from a pulled muscle in his right leg, which Worrell knew could be a handicap against spinners. He therefore brought Sobers close in at cover and told Gibbs to flight the ball at Harvey. Gibbs did so and Harvey went out to drive, but with his injured leg could not get to the pitch and holed out to Sobers. That was the third wicket down; fifty runs later the match was over, Gibbs having taken 5 for 66.

When he returned from the tour of Australia, Worrell was offered the position of Warden at Irvine Hall, part of the University of the West Indies in Kingston. This involved helping students with their problems, welfare administration, some tutoring and, in particular, helping in the promotion of sport in the university. It was strange for him at first but he soon came to enjoy it and did his best to improve the sporting standards and attitudes. Soon after this, his name was put forward for the Jamaican Senate and he became a member, but although he attended regularly it was not something he took to. He was altogether too dignified and courteous for the rough and tumble of politics, was not a good debater, and left after less than eighteen months. In 1964, he moved to Trinidad to become Dean of Students, which was a promotion, at the UWI campus there, continuing the work he had begun in Kingston by stressing to the students the importance of discipline, physical fitness, responsibility and such like – in other words, all the values that had made him such a successful captain.

A year after the Australian tour, India visited West Indies and were annihilated, not helped by losing their captain, Contractor, whose skull was fractured by a ball from Griffith in the match before the third Test. Worrell averaged 83 with the bat, leading his team to only the fourth 5–0 clean sweep in Test history. If it was sad that in England in 1963 his form finally drifted away, he did at least give his last fine Test innings, an unbeaten 74, to the Manchester crowd, a happy choice of venue in view of his connection with Radcliffe and the university. By the end of the tour, his captaincy record was, out of fifteen Tests, nine victories and three defeats, outstanding by any yardstick. In Australia, he had rejuvenated a sport that had been declining for years; in England, he did exactly the same, leaving people exhilarated by his team's play wherever they went and creating a great new surge of interest in the game. The adulation when it was all over was something that had hardly been seen before in England, even on momentous Ashes-winning occasions, and early in 1964 his efforts were rewarded with a knighthood, conferred by the Queen at Buckingham Palace.

At the end of 1966, he was invited by the Indian government to spend six weeks there, visiting universities, watching some of the West Indies tour matches, and receiving an honorary Doctor of Law degree from the University of the Punjab. As the trip went on he began to feel unwell, and when he left he returned to Kingston, rather than Trinidad, as he knew the hospital staff there. He was diagnosed as having leukaemia, his wife was called from Trinidad, and when she arrived was told he had no more than six weeks to live. It was not an uncommon illness in the West Indies at the time, and the variety which Worrell had was particularly virulent. He knew he was dying and retained his dignity to the end; it came on 13 March 1967, and the cricketing world, quite simply, was devastated. Flags were lowered, tributes flooded in, memorial services were held, culminating in the first one ever for a cricketer at Westminster Abbey. It was desperately hard to accept that this serene man, so calm, so dignified, such a majestic cricketer, could have been taken in this way.

He had taken a group of talented individuals and moulded them into a superb team, ridding them of their old factions and weaknesses, and showing the disbelievers that black men were every bit as good as white. West Indies had had their triumphs before, of course, but now things were different; they were no longer inferior to whites, they were unified, they were strong and the future was theirs. There would be further set-backs as one lean spell caused the factions to surface again, but now they were truly under way and in due course their supremacy would become complete. Worrell passionately believed in the unity of the West Indian people, and realized that the foundations of such unity could be laid more readily through cricket than any other means. It was the richest legacy he could possibly have bequeathed to his people.

# Afterword

West Indian cricket has been strong for so long principally because it is looked upon almost as a religion in the Caribbean. Nowhere else in the world can match the fervour of it. Children have long played it everywhere, often in dreadful conditions – on the beaches, in the roads, on any bit of rough ground. The batsmen all attack like Greenidge or Richards, except that they do it virtually all the time and there is little idea of defensive play when the bowling demands it. The bowling, needless to say, is as fast as possible. Few of the youngsters will have been to a big match; what they are emulating is what they have seen on television in shop windows and heard on their transistors. Those transistors are an essential element in West Indian life, keeping everyone who does not have the time or, more likely, the money, to go to a game in touch with what is happening. When Richards is batting people just stop work and listen. In England even when Botham was working one of his miracles people at work did not stop; if they did not have a radio they just rang the Test score, on the works phone of course, a bit more frequently. There is, quite simply, no comparison in the attitudes to the game of British people and Caribbean people.

How an area with such a small population could have produced so many world-class cricketers is beyond the comprehension of most Britons. Barbados, which even now has little more than a quarter of a million people, has led the way with a roll of honour of mind-boggling proportions. Trinidad, which now has around a million inhabitants, has also produced far more than its fair share, and it is interesting to note the differences between the two. In Barbados (and other places such as Jamaica and Antigua), the wickets are fast and so the bowlers have traditionally bowled fast, while the batsmen have looked to attack at every opportunity, to hit the ball as hard and as gleefully as possible. Trinidad, on the other hand, used matting wickets for decades, producing batsmen who relied on timing and placing for their runs rather than power, men such as Stollmeyer and, more recently, Gomes, who were closer in style to their English opponents than to some of their team-mates. The bowling has been more different still; there is a sizeable East Indian population in Trinidad that has produced bowlers with oriental wiles and subtleties unthought-of in Barbados, with Achong and Ramadhin the obvious examples. There have been exceptions, naturally, such as Learie Constantine and George John, but the differences are broadly true. There are no comparable differences in Britain, where any kind of player may turn up just about anywhere.

There are signs, though, that cricket may be sliding slowly off its pedestal in the Caribbean. In the past, there were few other sports apart from football and swimming, and neither of these represented much of a challenge. Now, as the British influence wanes, it is replaced by an American one; television has brought along the delights of basketball and its popularity has quickly soared. Easy to play, fast-moving, athletic, it is very much a game for the modern world. And with the brightest students, who would have gone to Britain until the Thatcher government started charging them substantial fees, now studying in the US, it seems likely that the trend away from cricket to American sports will steadily continue. Maybe in twenty or thirty years time England will take a Test series off them.

If the last two decades have been just a trifle one-sided, before that the competition was excellent, with first one side holding sway and then the other, which is as it should be. With the racial differences there have inevitably been problems, such as injudicious behaviour by English tourists, racist taunts by English crowds, touchiness by West Indian officals over imagined slights, and the odd riot or three. English fans feel that the emphasis on fast bowling in the last fifteen years has been greatly to the game's detriment, leading to the continuing decline of the spinner, a lack of variety, slow over rates, broken bones and a situation where batting is more about courage than skill. Many English fans even regard West Indian cricket as boring, but it is more impossible to know, as defeat follows defeat follows defeat, to what extent this is an objective judgement or to what extent it is just sour grapes. There was naturally much rejoicing in Britain that the worm was turning in 1989–90, but there would have been more had there been a spinner or two in the team.

West Indies, for their part, are simply playing their own game and, since it has made them the most powerful team in the world, cannot see why they should deprive themselves of their trump cards just because other countries cannot produce trump cards of their own. It has long been the case that the fact of winning is far more important than the manner of doing so, and since they have found a winning formula they have a powerful argument for keeping it, especially now that the financial rewards are considerable. The whingeing, as they see it, that takes place in the British press angers many West Indians, as Viv Richards demonstrated with his outburst in Antigua during the last Test of 1989–90.

What British people so often fail to understand is that the old inter-island divisions and prejudices that have always dogged Caribbean life are still present, and that a successful cricket team is the one thing that transcends this fragmentation. Jeffrey Dujon, in an interview for a magazine, summed it up: 'We're the only example of Caribbean unity that exists, when the team performs we're the only thing the entire Caribbean focuses on. We're an example of the excellence, as well as the unity, the Caribbean is capable of.' English cricket does not have this capacity for internal strife in the same way, the periodic Yorkshire blood-lettings being of a different order; but West Indian cricket has grown strong precisely because it has risen above its problems, and on that basis England cannot find the same sort of strength since they do not have the same problems to overcome. However passionate a follower of England's fortunes might be, it is unlikely he will be able to match the fervour of the average West Indian.

Presumably the well of fast bowlers will one day run dry and then West Indies will have to devise a new strategy; after all, India did not fare too badly in the 1960s and '70s with a quartet of spinners. By the time that happens, England may have her own supply and the roles may become reversed. One hopes not; the best series between the two was that of 1963, and in those days cricket teams had a balanced attack. The game was more enjoyable for everyone that way.

# Statistical Highlights of the Test Matches

| | Captains | | Results | | | | |
|---|---|---|---|---|---|---|---|
| | England | West Indies | Tests | E | WI | D | |
| 1928 | A.P.F. Chapman | R.K. Nunes | 3 | 3 | 0 | 0 | |
| 1929–30 | F.S.G. Calthorpe | E.L.G. Hoad (1st) | 4 | 1 | 1 | 2 | |
| | | N. Betancourt (2nd) | | | | | |
| | | M.P. Fernandes (3rd) | | | | | |
| | | R.K. Nunes (4th) | | | | | |
| 1933 | D.R. Jardine | G.C. Grant | 3 | 2 | 0 | 1 | |
| | R.E.S. Wyatt (3rd) | | | | | | |
| 1934–5 | R.E.S. Wyatt | G.C. Grant | 4 | 1 | 2 | 1 | |
| 1939 | W.R. Hammond | R.S. Grant | 3 | 1 | 0 | 2 | |
| 1947–8 | K. Cranston (1st) | G.A. Headley (1st) | 4 | 0 | 2 | 2 | |
| | | G.E. Gomez (2nd) | | | | | |
| | G.O.B. Allen | J.D.C. Goddard | | | | | |
| 1950 | N.W.D. Yardley | J.D.C. Goddard | 4 | 1 | 3 | 0 | |
| | F.R. Brown (4th) | | | | | | |
| 1953–4 | L. Hutton | J.B. Stollmeyer | 5 | 2 | 2 | 1 | |
| 1957 | P.B.H. May | J.D.C. Goddard | 5 | 3 | 0 | 2 | |
| 1959–60 | P.B.H. May | F.C.M. Alexander | 5 | 1 | 0 | 4 | |
| | M.C. Cowdrey (4th, 5th) | | | | | | |

| | The Wisden Trophy | | | | | | Held by |
|---|---|---|---|---|---|---|---|
| 1963 | E.R. Dexter | F.M.M. Worrell | 5 | 1 | 3 | 1 | WI |
| 1966 | M.J.K. Smith (1st) | G.S. Sobers | 5 | 1 | 3 | 1 | WI |
| | M.C. Cowdrey | | | | | | |
| | D.B. Close (5th) | | | | | | |
| 1967–8 | M.C. Cowdrey | G.S. Sobers | 5 | 1 | 0 | 4 | E |
| 1969 | R. Illingworth | G.S. Sobers | 3 | 2 | 0 | 1 | E |
| 1973 | R. Illingworth | R.B. Kanhai | 3 | 0 | 2 | 1 | WI |
| 1973–4 | M.H. Denness | R.B. Kanhai | 5 | 1 | 1 | 3 | WI |
| 1976 | A.W. Greig | C.H. Lloyd | 5 | 0 | 3 | 2 | WI |
| 1980 | I.T. Botham | C.H. Lloyd | 5 | 0 | 1 | 4 | WI |
| | | I.V.A. Richards (5th) | | | | | |
| 1980–1 | I.T. Botham | C.H. Lloyd | *4 | 0 | 2 | 2 | WI |
| 1984 | D.I. Gower | C.H. Lloyd | 5 | 0 | 5 | 0 | WI |
| 1985–6 | D.I. Gower | I.V.A. Richards | 5 | 0 | 5 | 0 | WI |
| 1988 | M.W. Gatting (1st) | I.V.A. Richards | 5 | 0 | 4 | 1 | WI |
| | J.E. Emburey (2nd, 3rd) | | | | | | |
| | C.S. Cowdrey (4th) | | | | | | |
| | G.A. Gooch (5th) | | | | | | |
| 1989–90 | G.A. Gooch | I.V.A. Richards | †4 | 1 | 2 | 1 | WI |
| | A.J. Lamb (4th, 5th) | D.L. Haynes (3rd) | | | | | |
| | In England | | 54 | 14 | 24 | 16 | |
| | In West Indies | | 45 | 8 | 17 | 20 | |
| | Totals | | 99 | 22 | 41 | 36 | |

* One Test cancelled
† One Test abandoned because of rain

**Batsmen with 500 Runs**

| England | Tests | Innings | NO | HS | Runs | Average |
|---|---|---|---|---|---|---|
| G. Boycott | 29 | 53 | 5 | 128 | 2205 | 45.94 |
| M.C. Cowdrey | 21 | 36 | 2 | 154 | 1751 | 51.50 |
| G.A. Gooch | 21 | 42 | 1 | 153 | 1717 | 41.88 |
| L. Hutton | 13 | 24 | 3 | 205 | 1661 | 79.10 |
| T.W. Graveney | 19 | 31 | 5 | 258 | 1532 | 58.92 |
| A.J. Lamb | 18 | 35 | 3 | 132 | 1254 | 39.19 |
| D.I. Gower | 19 | 38 | 3 | 154* | 1149 | 32.83 |
| D.L. Amiss | 10 | 18 | 2 | 262* | 1130 | 70.63 |
| K.F. Barrington | 17 | 30 | 0 | 143 | 1042 | 34.73 |
| A.P.E. Knott | 22 | 38 | 4 | 116 | 994 | 29.24 |
| E.H. Hendren | 9 | 17 | 3 | 205* | 909 | 64.93 |
| P.B.H. May | 13 | 21 | 2 | 285* | 986 | 51.89 |
| E.R. Dexter | 10 | 19 | 1 | 136* | 866 | 48.11 |
| A.W. Greig | 13 | 23 | 1 | 148 | 795 | 36.16 |
| J.H. Edrich | 14 | 25 | 2 | 146 | 792 | 34.43 |
| P. Willey | 15 | 29 | 5 | 102* | 757 | 31.54 |
| I.T. Botham | 19 | 36 | 0 | 81 | 757 | 21.03 |
| L.E.G. Ames | 11 | 18 | 3 | 149 | 748 | 49.87 |
| W.R. Hammond | 13 | 20 | 2 | 138 | 639 | 35.50 |
| T.G. Evans | 16 | 25 | 2 | 104 | 625 | 27.17 |
| A. Sandham | 4 | 8 | 0 | 325 | 592 | 74.00 |
| D.C.S. Compton | 9 | 14 | 2 | 133 | 592 | 49.33 |
| D.B. Close | 11 | 20 | 1 | 70 | 574 | 30.21 |
| J.M. Parks | 12 | 22 | 1 | 101* | 563 | 26.81 |
| B.L. d'Oliveira | 12 | 19 | 2 | 88 | 555 | 32.65 |
| K.W.R. Fletcher | 7 | 13 | 3 | 129* | 528 | 52.80 |

| West Indies | Tests | Innings | NO | HS | Runs | Average |
|---|---|---|---|---|---|---|
| G.S. Sobers | 36 | 61 | 8 | 226 | 3214 | 60.64 |
| I.V.A. Richards | 31 | 42 | 3 | 291 | 2493 | 63.92 |
| C.G. Greenidge | 32 | 48 | 2 | 223 | 2318 | 50.39 |
| R.B. Kanhai | 33 | 57 | 3 | 157 | 2267 | 41.98 |
| C.H. Lloyd | 34 | 51 | 4 | 132 | 2120 | 45.11 |
| F.M.M. Worrell | 25 | 42 | 6 | 261 | 1979 | 54.97 |
| G.A. Headley | 16 | 29 | 3 | 270* | 1852 | 71.23 |
| D.L. Haynes | 27 | 42 | 5 | 184 | 1852 | 50.05 |
| C.L. Walcott | 20 | 36 | 5 | 220 | 1391 | 44.87 |
| B.F. Butcher | 20 | 35 | 3 | 209* | 1373 | 42.91 |
| R.C. Fredericks | 16 | 28 | 2 | 150 | 1369 | 52.65 |
| E.D. Weekes | 17 | 30 | 1 | 206 | 1313 | 45.28 |
| S.M. Nurse | 11 | 20 | 0 | 137 | 1016 | 50.80 |
| C.C. Hunte | 15 | 26 | 3 | 182 | 1005 | 43.70 |
| A.I. Kallicharran | 16 | 24 | 1 | 158 | 891 | 38.74 |
| J.B. Stollmeyer | 14 | 25 | 2 | 78 | 858 | 37.30 |
| H.A. Gomes | 16 | 22 | 4 | 143 | 801 | 44.50 |
| C.A. Roach | 11 | 22 | 1 | 209 | 756 | 36.00 |
| L.G. Rowe | 7 | 10 | 0 | 302 | 732 | 73.20 |
| P.J.L. Dujon | 18 | 24 | 3 | 101 | 709 | 33.76 |
| D.L. Murray | 28 | 41 | 7 | 64 | 654 | 19.24 |
| R.B. Richardson | 12 | 20 | 2 | 160 | 653 | 36.28 |
| G.E. Gomez | 14 | 22 | 3 | 86 | 587 | 30.89 |
| A.L. Logie | 8 | 12 | 2 | 98 | 576 | 57.60 |
| L.N. Constantine | 13 | 23 | 0 | 90 | 563 | 24.48 |
| G.S. Camacho | 7 | 14 | 0 | 87 | 515 | 36.79 |

**Highest Batting Averages**

Qualification: 8 innings

| England | Tests | Innings | NO | HS | Runs | Average |
|---|---|---|---|---|---|---|
| L. Hutton | 13 | 24 | 3 | 205 | 1661 | 79.10 |
| A. Sandham | 4 | 8 | 0 | 325 | 592 | 74.00 |
| D.L. Amiss | 10 | 18 | 2 | 262* | 1130 | 70.63 |
| E.H. Hendren | 9 | 17 | 3 | 205* | 909 | 64.93 |
| T.W. Graveney | 19 | 31 | 5 | 258 | 1532 | 58.92 |
| J.S. Robertson | 4 | 8 | 1 | 133 | 390 | 55.71 |
| K.W.R. Fletcher | 7 | 13 | 3 | 129* | 528 | 52.80 |
| C. Milburn | 4 | 8 | 2 | 126* | 316 | 52.66 |
| P.B.H May | 13 | 21 | 2 | 285* | 986 | 51.89 |
| M.C. Cowdrey | 21 | 36 | 2 | 154 | 1751 | 51.50 |
| L.E.G. Ames | 11 | 18 | 3 | 149 | 748 | 49.87 |
| D.C.S. Compton | 9 | 14 | 2 | 133 | 592 | 49.33 |
| E.R. Dexter | 10 | 19 | 1 | 136* | 866 | 48.11 |
| P.E. Richardson | 6 | 9 | 0 | 126 | 427 | 47.44 |
| G. Boycott | 29 | 53 | 5 | 128 | 2205 | 45.94 |
| J. Hardstaff jr | 6 | 10 | 1 | 98 | 411 | 45.67 |
| G. Pullar | 5 | 10 | 1 | 66 | 385 | 42.77 |
| G.A. Gooch | 21 | 42 | 1 | 153 | 1717 | 41.88 |
| A.J. Lamb | 18 | 35 | 3 | 132 | 1254 | 39.19 |
| P.J. Sharpe | 6 | 11 | 1 | 86 | 387 | 38.70 |
| A.W. Greig | 13 | 23 | 1 | 148 | 795 | 36.16 |
| W.R. Hammond | 13 | 20 | 2 | 138 | 639 | 35.50 |
| K.F. Barrington | 17 | 30 | 0 | 143 | 1042 | 34.73 |
| G. Gunn | 4 | 8 | 0 | 85 | 276 | 34.50 |
| J.H. Edrich | 14 | 25 | 2 | 146 | 792 | 34.43 |
| D.I. Gower | 19 | 38 | 3 | 154* | 1149 | 32.83 |
| B.L. d'Oliveira | 12 | 19 | 2 | 88 | 555 | 32.65 |
| R.A. Smith | 6 | 11 | 2 | 62 | 186 | 32.44 |
| P. Willey | 15 | 29 | 5 | 102* | 574 | 31.54 |
| T.E. Bailey | 11 | 15 | 4 | 82* | 343 | 31.18 |
| D.S. Steele | 5 | 10 | 0 | 106 | 308 | 30.80 |
| D.B. Close | 11 | 20 | 1 | 70 | 574 | 30.21 |
| **West Indies** | | | | | | |
| L.G. Rowe | 7 | 10 | 0 | 302 | 732 | 73.20 |
| G.A. Headley | 16 | 29 | 3 | 270* | 1852 | 71.23 |
| I.V.A. Richards | 31 | 42 | 3 | 291 | 2493 | 63.92 |
| G.S. Sobers | 36 | 61 | 8 | 226 | 3214 | 60.64 |
| A.L. Logie | 8 | 12 | 2 | 98 | 576 | 57.60 |
| F.M.M. Worrell | 25 | 42 | 6 | 261 | 1979 | 54.97 |
| J.K. Holt | 5 | 9 | 1 | 166 | 432 | 54.00 |
| R.C. Fredericks | 16 | 28 | 2 | 150 | 1369 | 52.65 |
| S.M. Nurse | 11 | 20 | 0 | 137 | 1016 | 50.80 |
| C.G. Greenidge | 32 | 48 | 2 | 223 | 2318 | 50.39 |
| D.L. Haynes | 27 | 42 | 5 | 184 | 1852 | 50.05 |
| E.D. Weekes | 17 | 30 | 1 | 206 | 1313 | 45.28 |
| C.H. Lloyd | 34 | 51 | 4 | 132 | 2120 | 45.11 |
| C.L. Walcott | 20 | 36 | 5 | 220 | 1391 | 44.87 |
| H.A. Gomes | 16 | 22 | 4 | 143 | 801 | 44.50 |
| C.C. Hunte | 15 | 26 | 3 | 182 | 1005 | 43.70 |
| B.F. Butcher | 20 | 35 | 3 | 209* | 1373 | 42.91 |
| R.B. Kanhai | 33 | 57 | 3 | 157 | 2267 | 41.98 |
| C.A. Best | 6 | 9 | 1 | 164 | 320 | 40.00 |
| O.G. Smith | 5 | 10 | 0 | 168 | 396 | 39.60 |
| A.I. Kallicharran | 16 | 24 | 1 | 158 | 891 | 38.74 |
| J.B. Stollmeyer | 14 | 25 | 2 | 78 | 858 | 37.30 |
| G.S. Camacho | 7 | 14 | 0 | 87 | 515 | 36.79 |

| West Indies | Tests | Innings | NO | HS | Runs | Average |
|---|---|---|---|---|---|---|
| R.B. Richardson | 12 | 20 | 2 | 160 | 653 | 36.28 |
| C.A. Roach | 11 | 22 | 1 | 209 | 756 | 36.00 |
| D.S. Atkinson | 6 | 11 | 2 | 74 | 314 | 34.89 |
| R.A. Harper | 10 | 12 | 2 | 74 | 343 | 34.30 |
| P.J.L. Dujon | 18 | 24 | 3 | 101 | 709 | 33.76 |
| B.D. Julien | 10 | 14 | 1 | 121 | 430 | 33.08 |
| C.A. McWatt | 5 | 8 | 2 | 54 | 198 | 33.00 |
| J.E.D. Sealy | 9 | 15 | 1 | 92 | 448 | 32.00 |
| G.E. Gomez | 14 | 22 | 3 | 86 | 587 | 30.89 |

## Record Partnerships for each Wicket

### England
| | | | | |
|---|---|---|---|---|
| 1st | 212 | C. Washbrook and R.T. Simpson | Trent Bridge | 1950 |
| 2nd | 266 | P.E. Richardson and T.W. Graveney | Trent Bridge | 1957 |
| 3rd | 264 | L. Hutton and W.R. Hammond | Oval | 1939 |
| 4th | 411 | P.B.H. May and M.C. Cowdrey | Edgbaston | 1957 |
| 5th | 130* | C. Milburn and T.W. Graveney | Lord's | 1966 |
| 6th | 163 | A.W. Greig and A.P.E. Knott | Bridgetown | 1973–4 |
| 7th | 197 | M.J.K. Smith and J.M. Parks | Port-of-Spain | 1959–60 |
| 8th | 217 | T.W. Graveney and J.T. Murray | Oval | 1966 |
| 9th | 109 | G.A.R. Lock and P.I. Pocock | Georgetown | 1967–8 |
| 10th | 128 | K. Higgs and J.A. Snow | Oval | 1966 |

### West Indies
| | | | | |
|---|---|---|---|---|
| 1st | 298 | C.G. Greenidge and D.L. Haynes | Antigua | 1989–90 |
| 2nd | 287* | C.G. Greenidge and H.A. Gomes | Lord's | 1984 |
| 3rd | 338 | E.D. Weekes and F.M.M. Worrell | Port-of-Spain | 1953–4 |
| 4th | 399 | G.S. Sobers and F.M.M. Worrell | Bridgetown | 1959–60 |
| 5th | 265 | S.M. Nurse and G.S. Sobers | Headingley | 1966 |
| 6th | 274* | G.S. Sobers and D.A. Holford | Lord's | 1966 |
| 7th | 155* | G.S. Sobers and B.D. Julien | Lord's | 1973 |
| 8th | 99 | C.A. McWatt and J.K. Holt | Georgetown | 1953–4 |
| 9th | 150 | E.A.E. Baptiste and M.A. Holding | Edgbaston | 1984 |
| 10th | 67* | M.A. Holding and C.E.H. Croft | St John's | 1980–1 |

## Best Batting

### England
| | | | |
|---|---|---|---|
| A. Sandham | 325 | Kingston | 1929–30 |
| P.B.H. May | 285* | Edgbaston | 1957 |
| D.L. Amiss | 262* | Kingston | 1973–4 |
| T.W. Graveney | 258 | Trent Bridge | 1957 |
| E.H. Hendren | 205* | Port-of-Spain | 1929–30 |
| L. Hutton | 205 | Kingston | 1953–4 |
| D.L. Amiss | 203 | Oval | 1976 |
| L. Hutton | 202* | Oval | 1950 |
| L. Hutton | 196 | Lord's | 1939 |
| D.L. Amiss | 174 | Port-of-Spain | 1973–4 |
| L. Hutton | 169 | Georgetown | 1953–4 |
| L. Hutton | 165* | Oval | 1939 |
| T.W. Graveney | 165 | Oval | 1966 |
| T.W. Graveney | 164 | Oval | 1957 |
| J.B. Hobbs | 159 | Oval | 1928 |
| D.I. Gower | 154* | Kingston | 1980–1 |
| M.C. Cowdrey | 154 | Edgbaston | 1957 |
| G.A. Gooch | 153 | Kingston | 1980–1 |
| A. Sandham | 152 | Bridgetown | 1929–30 |
| M.C. Cowdrey | 152 | Lord's | 1957 |

**West Indies**

| | | | |
|---|---|---|---|
| L.G. Rowe | 302 | Bridgetown | 1973–4 |
| I.V.A. Richards | 291 | Oval | 1976 |
| G.A. Headley | 270* | Kingston | 1934–5 |
| F.M.M. Worrell | 261 | Trent Bridge | 1950 |
| I.V.A. Richards | 232 | Trent Bridge | 1976 |
| G.S. Sobers | 226 | Bridgetown | 1959–60 |
| G.A. Headley | 223 | Kingston | 1929–30 |
| C.G. Greenidge | 223 | Old Trafford | 1984 |
| C.L. Walcott | 220 | Bridgetown | 1953–4 |
| C.G. Greenidge | 214* | Lord's | 1984 |
| B.F. Butcher | 209* | Trent Bridge | 1966 |
| C.A. Roach | 209 | Georgetown | 1929–30 |
| E.D. Weekes | 206 | Port-of-Spain | 1953–4 |
| F.M.M. Worrell | 197* | Bridgetown | 1959–60 |
| F.M.M. Worrell | 191* | Trent Bridge | 1957 |
| D.L. Haynes | 184 | Lord's | 1980 |
| I.V.A. Richards | 182* | Bridgetown | 1980–1 |
| C.C. Hunte | 182 | Old Trafford | 1963 |
| G.A. Headley | 176 | Bridgetown | 1929–30 |
| G.S. Sobers | 174 | Headingley | 1966 |
| G.A. Headley | 169* | Old Trafford | 1933 |
| C.L. Walcott | 168* | Lord's | 1950 |
| O.G. Smith | 168 | Trent Bridge | 1957 |
| F.M.M. Worrell | 167 | Port-of-Spain | 1953–4 |
| J.K. Holt | 166 | Bridgetown | 1953–4 |
| G.S. Sobers | 163* | Lord's | 1966 |
| O.G. Smith | 161 | Edgbaston | 1957 |
| G.S. Sobers | 161 | Old Trafford | 1966 |
| R.B. Richardson | 160 | Bridgetown | 1985–6 |
| A.I. Kallicharran | 158 | Port-of-Spain | 1973–4 |
| R.B. Kanhai | 157 | Lord's | 1973 |
| R.B. Kanhai | 153 | Port-of-Spain | 1967–8 |
| G.S. Sobers | 152 | Georgetown | 1967–8 |
| G.S. Sobers | 150* | Lord's | 1973 |
| R.B. Kanhai | 150 | Georgetown | 1967–8 |
| R.C. Fredericks | 150 | Edgbaston | 1973 |

**Highest Innings Totals**

| | | | |
|---|---|---|---|
| England in England: | 619–6 dec | Trent Bridge | 1957 |
| England in West Indies: | 849 | Kingston | 1929–30 |
| West Indies in England: | 687–8 dec | Oval | 1976 |
| West Indies in West Indies: | 681–8 dec | Port-of-Spain | 1953–4 |

**Lowest Innings Totals**

| | | | |
|---|---|---|---|
| England in England: | 71 | Old Trafford | 1976 |
| England in West Indies: | 103 | Kingston | 1934–5 |
| West Indies in England: | 86 | Oval | 1957 |
| West Indies in West Indies: | 102 | Bridgetown | 1934–5 |

**Most Runs in a Series**

| | | | |
|---|---|---|---|
| England in England | 489 (ave 97.80) | P.B.H. May | 1957 |
| England in West Indies | 693 (ave 115.50) | E.H. Hendren | 1929–30 |
| West Indies in England | 829 (ave 118.42) | I.V.A. Richards | 1976 |
| West Indies in West Indies | 709 (ave 101.28) | G.S. Sobers | 1959–60 |

## Bowlers with 20 Wickets

| England | Tests | Balls | Mdns | Runs | Wkts | Average |
|---|---|---|---|---|---|---|
| F.S. Trueman | 18 | 4584 | 176 | 2018 | 86 | 23.46 |
| J.A. Snow | 14 | 3594 | 111 | 1917 | 72 | 26.63 |
| I.T. Botham | 19 | 3447 | 118 | 2079 | 58 | 35.84 |
| J.C. Laker | 13 | 4093 | 239 | 1549 | 51 | 30.37 |
| J.B. Statham | 12 | 3137 | 113 | 1422 | 42 | 33.86 |
| G.A.R. Lock | 13 | 3408 | 181 | 1323 | 39 | 33.92 |
| R.G.D. Willis | 13 | 2164 | 71 | 1381 | 38 | 36.34 |
| D.L. Underwood | 17 | 3877 | 203 | 1656 | 38 | 43,58 |
| G.R. Dilley | 11 | 2039 | 70 | 1036 | 36 | 28.78 |
| A.W. Greig | 13 | 2462 | 73 | 1281 | 36 | 35.58 |
| J.E. Emburey | 14 | 2637 | 123 | 1178 | 30 | 39.27 |
| T.E. Bailey | 11 | 2078 | 100 | 857 | 29 | 29.55 |
| D.J. Brown | 8 | 1803 | 61 | 830 | 28 | 29.64 |
| K. Higgs | 5 | 1420 | 49 | 611 | 24 | 25.45 |
| A.P. Freeman | 3 | 840 | 50 | 302 | 22 | 13.72 |
| P.I. Pocock | 10 | 1383 | 105 | 1144 | 22 | 52.00 |
| G.C. Small | 5 | 1193 | 39 | 645 | 21 | 30.71 |

| West Indies | Tests | Balls | Mdns | Runs | Wkts | Average |
|---|---|---|---|---|---|---|
| M.D. Marshall | 21 | 4757 | 196 | 1994 | 107 | 18.64 |
| G.S. Sobers | 36 | 8753 | 410 | 3324 | 102 | 32.59 |
| L.R. Gibbs | 26 | 8844 | 497 | 2887 | 100 | 28.87 |
| M.A. Holding | 21 | 4486 | 188 | 2031 | 96 | 21.16 |
| J. Garner | 19 | 4428 | 211 | 1650 | 92 | 17.93 |
| S. Ramadhin | 18 | 7154 | 464 | 2201 | 80 | 27.51 |
| W.W. Hall | 19 | 4271 | 139 | 2121 | 65 | 32.63 |
| C.C. Griffith | 15 | 2913 | 112 | 1291 | 57 | 22.65 |
| A.M.E. Roberts | 12 | 2886 | 133 | 1174 | 50 | 23.48 |
| L.N. Constantine | 13 | 2788 | 110 | 1339 | 50 | 26.78 |
| C.E.L. Ambrose | 8 | 2011 | 88 | 752 | 42 | 17.90 |
| A.L. Valentine | 9 | 3836 | 282 | 1140 | 40 | 28.50 |
| E.A. Martindale | 10 | 1605 | 40 | 804 | 37 | 21.72 |
| C.E.H. Croft | 7 | 1571 | 59 | 761 | 33 | 23.06 |
| V.A. Holder | 10 | 2573 | 136 | 981 | 33 | 29.73 |
| K.D. Boyce | 7 | 1301 | 45 | 618 | 30 | 20.60 |
| H.C. Griffith | 8 | 1860 | 69 | 850 | 30 | 28.33 |
| C.A. Walsh | 9 | 1702 | 60 | 758 | 29 | 26.14 |
| F.M.M. Worrell | 25 | 3165 | 134 | 1211 | 28 | 43.25 |
| B.D. Julien | 10 | 2220 | 105 | 812 | 25 | 32.48 |
| W. Ferguson | 5 | 1566 | 47 | 722 | 24 | 30.08 |
| B.P. Patterson | 8 | 1284 | 35 | 781 | 24 | 32.54 |
| R.A. Harper | 10 | 1174 | 73 | 394 | 22 | 17.91 |
| I.R. Bishop | 4 | 973 | 35 | 419 | 21 | 19.95 |

## Lowest Averages

### Qualification: 10 wickets

| England | | Balls | Mdns | Runs | Wkts | Average |
|---|---|---|---|---|---|---|
| C.S. Marriott | 1 | 247 | 8 | 96 | 11 | 8.72 |
| A.P. Freeman | 3 | 840 | 50 | 302 | 22 | 13.72 |
| A.R.C. Fraser | 2 | 427 | 18 | 161 | 11 | 14.63 |
| W.H. Copson | 2 | 420 | 7 | 185 | 12 | 15.41 |
| W.E. Bowes | 2 | 560 | 18 | 176 | 11 | 16.00 |
| M.W. Tate | 3 | 762 | 43 | 246 | 13 | 18.92 |
| R.W.V. Robins | 2 | 382 | 5 | 220 | 11 | 20.00 |
| P.J.W. Allott | 3 | 629 | 26 | 282 | 14 | 20.14 |

| England | Tests | Balls | Mdns | Runs | Wkts | Average |
|---|---|---|---|---|---|---|
| E.W. Clark | 2 | 504 | 22 | 233 | 11 | 21.18 |
| W.E. Hollies | 3 | 558 | 24 | 217 | 10 | 21.70 |
| G.T.S. Stevens | 2 | 412 | 9 | 241 | 11 | 21.91 |
| F.S. Trueman | 18 | 4584 | 176 | 2018 | 86 | 23.46 |
| K. Higgs | 5 | 1420 | 49 | 611 | 24 | 25.45 |
| J.A. Snow | 14 | 3594 | 111 | 1917 | 72 | 26.63 |
| G.A.E. Paine | 4 | 1044 | 43 | 467 | 17 | 27.47 |
| G.R. Dilley | 11 | 2039 | 70 | 1036 | 36 | 28.78 |
| T.E. Bailey | 11 | 2078 | 100 | 857 | 29 | 29.55 |
| D.J. Brown | 8 | 1803 | 61 | 830 | 28 | 29.64 |
| B.R. Knight | 4 | 1027 | 32 | 448 | 15 | 29.87 |
| C.I.J. Smith | 4 | 714 | 30 | 329 | 11 | 29.91 |
| D.E. Malcolm | 4 | 970 | 21 | 577 | 19 | 30.36 |
| J.C. Laker | 13 | 4093 | 239 | 1549 | 51 | 30.37 |
| G.C. Small | 5 | 1193 | 39 | 645 | 21 | 30.71 |
| G.G. Arnold | 6 | 1192 | 48 | 538 | 17 | 31.65 |
| D.V.P. Wright | 4 | 726 | 20 | 353 | 11 | 32.09 |
| R.M. Ellison | 4 | 759 | 29 | 388 | 12 | 32.33 |
| N.E. Haig | 4 | 888 | 50 | 360 | 11 | 32.73 |
| E.R. Dexter | 10 | 958 | 40 | 397 | 12 | 33.08 |
| J.B. Statham | 12 | 3137 | 113 | 1422 | 42 | 33.86 |
| G.A.R. Lock | 13 | 3408 | 181 | 1323 | 39 | 33.92 |
| W. Voce | 4 | 1130 | 35 | 584 | 17 | 34.35 |
| A.W. Greig | 13 | 2462 | 73 | 1281 | 36 | 35.58 |
| I.T. Botham | 19 | 3447 | 118 | 2079 | 58 | 35.84 |
| R.G.D. Willis | 13 | 2164 | 71 | 1381 | 38 | 36.34 |
| D.R. Pringle | 7 | 1143 | 43 | 583 | 16 | 36.44 |
| N.A. Foster | 6 | 1051 | 22 | 617 | 16 | 38.56 |
| J.E. Emburey | 14 | 2637 | 123 | 1178 | 30 | 39.27 |

## West Indies

| | Tests | Balls | Mdns | Runs | Wkts | Average |
|---|---|---|---|---|---|---|
| W.K.M. Benjamin | 3 | 402 | 17 | 151 | 12 | 12.58 |
| C.E.L. Ambrose | 8 | 2011 | 88 | 752 | 42 | 17.90 |
| R.A. Harper | 10 | 1174 | 73 | 394 | 22 | 17.91 |
| J. Garner | 19 | 4428 | 211 | 1650 | 92 | 17.93 |
| M.D. Marshall | 21 | 4757 | 196 | 1994 | 107 | 18.64 |
| I.R. Bishop | 4 | 973 | 35 | 419 | 21 | 19.95 |
| K.D. Boyce | 7 | 1301 | 45 | 618 | 30 | 20.60 |
| M.A. Holding | 21 | 4486 | 188 | 2131 | 96 | 21.16 |
| E.A. Martindale | 10 | 1605 | 40 | 804 | 37 | 21.72 |
| C.C. Griffith | 15 | 2913 | 112 | 1291 | 57 | 22.65 |
| C.E.H. Croft | 7 | 1571 | 59 | 761 | 33 | 23.06 |
| A.M.E. Roberts | 14 | 2886 | 133 | 1174 | 50 | 23.48 |
| W.W. Daniel | 4 | 648 | 28 | 317 | 13 | 24.38 |
| L.G. Hylton | 6 | 965 | 32 | 418 | 16 | 26.12 |
| C.A. Walsh | 9 | 1702 | 60 | 758 | 29 | 26.14 |
| L.N. Constantine | 13 | 2788 | 110 | 1339 | 50 | 26.78 |
| S. Ramadhin | 18 | 7154 | 464 | 2201 | 80 | 27.51 |
| J.D.C. Goddard | 13 | 1695 | 96 | 537 | 19 | 28.26 |
| H.C. Griffith | 8 | 1860 | 69 | 850 | 30 | 28.33 |
| A.L. Valentine | 9 | 3836 | 282 | 1140 | 40 | 28.50 |
| L.R. Gibbs | 26 | 8844 | 497 | 2887 | 100 | 28.87 |
| V.A. Holder | 10 | 2573 | 136 | 981 | 33 | 29.73 |
| W. Ferguson | 5 | 1566 | 47 | 722 | 24 | 30.08 |
| R.S. Grant | 7 | 986 | 32 | 353 | 11 | 32.09 |
| B.D. Julien | 10 | 2220 | 105 | 812 | 25 | 32.48 |
| B.P. Patterson | 8 | 1284 | 35 | 781 | 24 | 32.54 |
| G.S. Sobers | 36 | 8753 | 410 | 3324 | 102 | 32.59 |
| W.W. Hall | 19 | 4271 | 139 | 2121 | 65 | 32.63 |
| G.N. Francis | 5 | 845 | 31 | 413 | 12 | 34.42 |
| C. Watson | 5 | 1194 | 39 | 593 | 16 | 37.06 |

## Best Innings Bowling Analysis

| | | | | |
|---|---|---|---|---|
| England in England | 8–103 | I.T. Botham | Lord's | 1984 |
| England in West Indies | 8–86 | A.W. Greig | Port-of-Spain | 1973–4 |
| West Indies in England | 8–92 | M.A. Holding | Oval | 1976 |
| West Indies in West Indies | 7–69 | W.W. Hall | Kingston | 1959–60 |

## Best Match Bowling Analysis

| | | | | |
|---|---|---|---|---|
| England in England | 12–119 | F.S. Trueman | Edgbaston | 1963 |
| England in West Indies | 13–156 | A.W. Greig | Port-of-Spain | 1973–4 |
| West Indies in England | 14–149 | M.A. Holding | Oval | 1976 |
| West Indies in England | 11–229 | W. Ferguson | Port-of-Spain | 1947–8 |

## Most Wickets in a Series

| | | | |
|---|---|---|---|
| England in England | 34 (ave 17.47) | F.S. Trueman | 1963 |
| England in West Indies | 27 (ave 18.66) | J.A. Snow | 1967–8 |
| West Indies in England | 35 (ave 12.65) | M.D. Marshall | 1988 |
| West Indies in West Indies | 27 (ave 16.14) | J. Garner | 1985–6 |
| | 27 (ave 17.85) | M.D. Marshall | 1985–6 |

## Best Bowling

### England

| | | | |
|---|---|---|---|
| A.W. Greig | 13–156 | Port-of-Spain | 1973–4 |
| F.S. Trueman | 12–119 | Edgbaston | 1963 |
| G.A.R. Lock | 11–48 | Oval | 1957 |
| C.S. Marriott | 11–96 | Oval | 1933 |
| T.E. Bailey | 11–98 | Lord's | 1957 |
| W. Voce | 11–149 | Port-of-Spain | 1929–30 |
| F.S. Trueman | 11–152 | Lord's | 1963 |
| A.P. Freeman | 10–93 | Old Trafford | 1928 |
| J.A. Snow | 10–142 | Georgetown | 1967–8 |
| G.T.S. Stevens | 10–195 | Bridgetown | 1929–30 |

### West Indies

| | | | |
|---|---|---|---|
| M.A. Holding | 14–149 | Oval | 1976 |
| K.D. Boyce | 11–147 | Oval | 1973 |
| S. Ramadhin | 11–152 | Lord's | 1950 |
| L.R. Gibbs | 11–157 | Old Trafford | 1963 |
| A.L. Valentine | 11–204 | Old Trafford | 1950 |
| W. Ferguson | 11–229 | Port-of-Spain | 1947–8 |
| M.D. Marshall | 10–92 | Lord's | 1988 |
| H.H.H. Johnson | 10–96 | Kingston | 1947–8 |
| L.R. Gibbs | 10–106 | Old Trafford | 1966 |
| A.M.E. Roberts | 10–123 | Lord's | 1976 |
| A.L. Valentine | 10–160 | Oval | 1950 |

## Hat-trick

P.J. Loader for England at Headingley in 1957. D. Shackleton at Lord's in 1963 and D.E. Malcolm at Port-of-Spain in 1989–90 both took three wickets in four balls for England.

## Wicket-keepers

| England | Tests | Dismissals |
|---|---|---|
| A.P.E. Knott | 22 | 43 |
| T.G. Evans | 16 | 35 |
| P.R. Downton | 16 | 33 |
| J.M. Parks | 12 | 31 |
| R.C. Russell | 4 | 14 |
| D.L. Bairstow | 2 | 7 |
| R. Swetman | 4 | 7 |
| A.J.W. McIntyre | 1 | 3 |
| J.T. Murray | 1 | 3 |
| C.J. Richards | 2 | 3 |
| K.V. Andrew | 1 | 1 |
| R.T. Spooner | 1 | 0 |

| West Indies | | |
|---|---|---|
| D.L. Murray | 28 | 94 |
| P.J.L. Dujon | 18 | 64 |
| F.C.M. Alexander | 7 | 27 |
| C.L. Walcott | 8 | 23 |
| D.A. Murray | 4 | 13 |
| T.M. Findlay | 2 | 9 |
| J.L. Hendriks | 4 | 8 |
| C.A. McWatt | 5 | 8 |
| D.W. Allan | 2 | 6 |
| T.R.O. Payne | 1 | 5 |
| R.B. Kanhai | 3 | 5 |

## All-rounders
Qualification: 10 wickets and a batting average of 20
The Index is calculated by dividing the batting average by the bowling average

| England | Tests | Runs | Average | Wkts | Average | Index |
|---|---|---|---|---|---|---|
| E.R. Dexter | 10 | 866 | 48.11 | 12 | 33.08 | 1.45 |
| T.E. Bailey | 11 | 343 | 31.18 | 29 | 29.55 | 1.06 |
| A.W. Greig | 13 | 795 | 36.16 | 36 | 35.58 | 1.02 |
| I.T. Botham | 19 | 757 | 21.03 | 58 | 35.84 | 0.59 |
| F.J. Titmus | 9 | 244 | 16.27 | 15 | 40.73 | 0.40 |
| West Indies | | | | | | |
| G.S. Sobers | 36 | 3214 | 60.64 | 102 | 32.59 | 1.86 |
| K.D. Boyce | 7 | 216 | 27.00 | 30 | 20.60 | 1.31 |
| F.M.M. Worrell | 25 | 1979 | 54.97 | 28 | 43.25 | 1.27 |
| W. Ferguson | 5 | 190 | 38.00 | 24 | 30.08 | 1.26 |
| M.A. Holding | 21 | 468 | 24.63 | 96 | 21.16 | 1.16 |
| B.D. Julien | 10 | 430 | 33.08 | 25 | 32.48 | 1.02 |
| J.D.C. Goddard | 13 | 430 | 26.88 | 19 | 28.26 | 0.95 |
| L.N. Constantine | 13 | 563 | 24.48 | 50 | 26.78 | 0.91 |
| R.S. Grant | 7 | 220 | 22.20 | 11 | 32.09 | 0.69 |

## Leading Catchers

| England | Tests | Catches |
|---|---|---|
| T.W. Graveney | 19 | 24 |
| W.R. Hammond | 13 | 22 |
| G.A. Gooch | 21 | 22 |
| M.C. Cowdrey | 21 | 21 |
| A.W. Greig | 13 | 17 |

| England | Tests | Catches |
|---|---|---|
| G.A.R. Lock | 13 | 17 |
| F.S. Trueman | 18 | 16 |
| I.T. Botham | 19 | 16 |
| P.J. Sharpe | 6 | 12 |
| A.J. Lamb | 18 | 12 |
| J.H. Edrich | 14 | 11 |
| D.L. Underwood | 17 | 11 |
| D.I. Gower | 19 | 11 |
| E.H. Hendren | 9 | 10 |
| D.B. Close | 11 | 9 |
| L. Hutton | 13 | 9 |
| M.W. Gatting | 9 | 7* |
| F.C. Hayes | 9 | 7 |
| R. Illingworth | 13 | 7 |
| R.G.D. Willis | 13 | 7 |
| J.E. Emburey | 14 | 7† |
| K.F. Barrington | 17 | 7 |
| G. Boycott | 29 | 7 |

* Plus two catches taken as substitute
† Plus one catch taken as substitute

| West Indies | Tests | Catches |
|---|---|---|
| G.S. Sobers | 36 | 40 |
| C.H. Lloyd | 34 | 31 |
| C.G. Greenidge | 32 | 29 |
| I.V.A. Richards | 31 | 25 |
| L.R. Gibbs | 26 | 21 |
| R.C. Fredericks | 16 | 20 |
| R.B. Kanhai | 30 | 20 |
| L.N. Constantine | 13 | 19 |
| E.D. Weekes | 17 | 19 |
| F.M.M. Worrell | 25 | 17 |
| R.A. Harper | 10 | 15 |
| R.B. Richardson | 12 | 14 |
| R.S. Grant | 7 | 13 |
| G.E. Gomez | 14 | 13 |
| G.A. Headley | 16 | 13 |
| A.I. Kallicharran | 16 | 13 |
| J. Garner | 19 | 13 |
| D.L. Haynes | 27 | 13 |
| J.D.C. Goddard | 13 | 10 |
| C.L. Walcott | 12 | 9 |
| M.D. Marshall | 21 | 9 |
| W. Ferguson | 5 | 8 |
| R.J. Christiani | 8 | 8 |
| S.M. Nurse | 11 | 8* |
| J.B. Stollmeyer | 14 | 8 |
| C.C. Griffith | 15 | 8 |
| C.C. Hunte | 15 | 8* |
| B.F. Butcher | 20 | 8 |
| C.A. Best | 6 | 7 |
| G.C. Grant | 7 | 7 |
| A.L. Logie | 8 | 7 |
| M.A. Holding | 21 | 7 |

* Plus one catch taken as substitute
The figures for Kanhai and Walcott do not include those catches taken while keeping wicket.

# Bibliography

Allen, David Rayvern, (ed.) *Arlott on Cricket* (Collins)

Arlott, John, *100 Greatest Batsmen* (Queen Anne Press)
   *Fred* (Eyre and Spottiswoode)

Bowen, Rowland, *Cricket: A History* (Eyre and Spottiswoode)

Constantine, Learie, *Cricket in the Sun* (Stanley Paul)
   *Cricket Crackers* (Stanley Paul)

Cowdrey, Colin, *MCC* (Hodder and Stoughton)

Cozier, Tony, *The West Indies: Fifty Years of Test Cricket* (Angus and Robertson)

Engel, Matthew (ed.), *The Guardian Book of Cricket* (Pavilion)

Frindall, Bill, *The Wisden Book of Test Cricket* (Queen Anne Press)
   *The Wisden Book of Cricket Records* (Queen Anne Press)

Hutton, Len, *Fifty Years in Cricket* (Stanley Paul)

Gibson, Alan, *The Cricket Captains of England* (Cassell)

Green, Benny, *The Wisden Book of Obituaries* (Queen Anne Press)

Greenidge, Gordon, *Gordon Greenidge* (David and Charles)

James, C.L.R., *Beyond a Boundary* (Hutchinson)
   *Cricket* (Allison and Busby)

*James Lillywhite's Cricketer's Annual*

McDonald, Trevor, *Clive Lloyd* (Grafton)

Manley, Michael, *A History of West Indies Cricket* (André Deutsch)

Martin-Jenkins, Christopher, *The Complete Who's Who of Test Cricketers* (Orbis)

Mosey, Don, *Botham* (Methuen)

Nicole, Christopher, *West Indian Cricket* (Phoenix House)

Robertson-Glasgow, R.C., *Cricket Prints* (Werner Laurie)

Ross, Alan, *The West Indies at Lord's* (Eyre and Spottiswoode)
   *Through the Caribbean* (Pavilion)

Snow, John, *Cricket Rebel* (Hamlyn)

Sobers, Sir Garfield, *Sobers: Twenty Years at the Top* (Macmillan)

Stollmeyer, Jeff, *Everything Under the Sun* (Stanley Paul)

Swanton, E.W. (ed.), *Barclays World of Cricket* (Collins)
   *As I said at the Time* (Collins Willow)
    *West Indian Adventure* (Museum Press)
Trueman, Fred, *My Most Memorable Matches* (Stanley Paul)
Williams, Marcus (ed.), *Double Century* (Collins Willow)
*Wisden Cricketers' Almanack*
Wynne-Thomas, Peter, *England on Tour* (Hamlyn)

## Periodicals

*Cricket*
*The Cricketer*
*Wisden Cricket Monthly*

# Index